THE AUTHORITY OF THE SECURITY COUNCIL UNDER CHAPTER VII OF THE UN CHARTER

Studies and Materials on the Settlement of International Disputes

Volume 8

The Authority of the Security Council under Chapter VII of the UN Charter

Legal Limits and the Role of the International Court of Justice

by

David Schweigman

KLUWER LAW INTERNATIONAL
THE HAGUE / LONDON / BOSTON

A C.I.P. Catalogue record for this book is available from the Library of Congress

ISBN 90-411-1641-9

Published by Kluwer Law International,
P.O. Box 85889, 2508 CN The Hague, The Netherlands.

Sold and distributed in North, Central and South America
by Kluwer Law International,
101 Philip Drive, Norwell, MA 02061, U.S.A.
kluwerlaw@wkap.com

In all other countries, sold and distributed
by Kluwer Law International, Distribution Centre,
P.O. Box 322, 3300 AH Dordrecht, The Netherlands.

Printed on acid-free paper

Kluwer Law International incorporates the publishing programmes of
Graham & Trotman Ltd, Kluwer Law and Taxation Publishers,
and Martinus Nijhoff Publishers.

Printed in the Netherlands.

Note by the Series Editor

The present series *Studies and Materials on the Settlement of International Disputes* (SMSID) started as a contribution to the United Nations Decade of International Law (the programme announced by the UN General Assembly for the period 1990-1999) which attached particular importance to the issue of dispute settlement. The series intends to address the issue of international dispute settlement and prevention from an interdisciplinary perspective - law, economics, history and politics - with the primary objective, however, to search for answers to the question of how to strengthen the rule of law in international relations. For practical purposes, this objective requires a broad perspective and must cover not only the analysis of the peaceful settlement of international disputes, but also the role of the use of force and its legitimacy. Furthermore, while the traditional focus of studies in this area has been limited to interaction between states, the series encourages the analysis also of international dispute settlement involving international organizations and non-state actors, including individuals, minorities, indigenous people, non-governmental organizations, and transnational companies. Finally, the series will also assist in exploring more in depth the linkages between dispute settlement in "public international law" and "international commercial arbitration" and their significance for enhancing the international rule of law.

The first volume of the series was published in 1996 by Dr. Mojtaba Kazazi on the topic *Burden of Proof and Related Issues*, an excellent study on evidence before international tribunals. The second volume, which also appeared in 1996, was written by Professor Karel Wellens and undertook a functional and well-researched analysis of the hitherto widely unknown field of *Economic Conflicts before the World Court (1922-1995)*. The third volume of the series, published in 1998, by Professor Juliane Kokott continued research into the area explored by Dr. Kazazi and addressed *The Burden of Proof in Comparative and International Human Rights Law* comparing civil law and common law approaches in an in-depth study with a focus on the American and German legal systems. The fourth volume *International Law in Post-Colonial Africa*, written by Professor Tiyanjana Maluwa, appeared in 1999 and contains an illuminating and scholarly written analysis, including a number of case studies, of the contribution of African States to the development of international law in a variety of areas, including dispute settlement. The fifth volume *Exclusion from Participation in International Organisations: The Law and Practice behind Member States' Expulsion and Suspension of Membership*, a thorough study on dispute settlement between member states and international organizations and their organs, was prepared by Professor Konstantinos D. Magliveras and also published in 1999. The sixth volume *Judicial Review, the International Court of Justice and Judicial Review: A Study of the Court's Powers with Respect to Judgements of the ILO and UN Administrative Tribunals*, written by Dr. Kaiyan Homi Kaikobad, was printed in 2000. The seventh volume *Liability of Multinational Corporations Under International Law*, co-edited by Menno Kamminga and Saman Zia-Zarifi and appearing in 2000, entered new and important ground in the general discussion on the role of multinational companies.

The present eighth volume *The Authority of the Security Council under Chapter VII of the UN Charter* is produced by David Schweigman, a younger Dutch scholar, who has worked as a researcher at the T.M.C. Asser Institute in The Hague. As its subtitle indicates, the book deals with the *Legal Limits and the Role of the International Court of Justice*. The – very readable and clear – text provides a comprehensive survey and lucid analysis of the legal problems arising from the activism of the UN Security Council that emerged since the end of the Cold War. The book is a significant contribution to the continuing discussion of the relevant issues, based on a fresh look at the practice of the Security Council, the jurisprudence of the International Court and the views in the literature.

Peter Malanczuk

Series Editor
Director of the GLODIS-Institute
Chair of International Law
Erasmus University Rotterdam
Honorary Professor, Peking University

The Hague, April 2001

Preface and Acknowledgments

This work was originally submitted as a doctoral thesis at the Erasmus University of Rotterdam. The research was made possible by funding from the T.M.C. Asser Institute in The Hague, The Netherlands, for which I am indebted to them. The author is grateful for additional aid provided by the Netherlands Organization for Scientific Research (NWO), the Amsterdamse Universiteits Vereniging and the Dutch Permanent Mission to the United Nations in New York.

I would like to gratefully acknowledge the assistance and support received from my colleagues at the Asser Institute. Olivier Ribbelink in particular has been most encouraging, although his thorough reading and comments sometimes made me wonder where and when the work would end. I also wish to thank Peter Malanczuk, whose suggestions always seemed to be on the mark and who kept me focused on the overall direction of the research. Peter Morris carefully edited the manuscript, for which I am much obliged.

Without the help of friends and family this work would probably never have been completed. My love goes out to A.S., B.S. and C.S. I hope I can match your continuous support.

The research for this work was completed by September 2000. Any shortcomings that may be found in this study are solely attributable to the author.

David Schweigman
Amsterdam, March 2001

Abbreviations

AFL	Armed Forces of Liberia
AJICL	African Journal of International and Comparative Law
AJPIL	Austrian Journal of Public International Law
AJIL	American Journal of International Law
ASICL	African Society of International and Comparative Law
BYIL	British Yearbook of International Law
CJTL	Columbia Journal of Transnational Law
CYIL	Canadian Yearbook of International Law
D&R	Demokratie und Recht
EC	European Community
ECOMOG	ECOWAS Cease-Fire Monitoring Group
ECOWAS	Economic Community of West African States
EJIL	European Journal of International Law
EPIL	R. Bernhardt (ed.), Encyclopedia of International Law
FRY	Federal Republic of Yugoslavia
GYIL	German Yearbook of International Law
HILJ	Harvard International Law Journal
ICJ	International Court of Justice
ICLQ	International and Comparative Law Quarterly
ICTR	International Criminal Tribunal for Rwanda
ICTY	International Criminal Tribunal for Yugoslavia
ILA	International Law Association
ILC	International Law Commission
ILJ	International Law Journal
ILM	International Legal Materials
ILR	International Law Review
IMCO	Inter-Governmental Maritime Consultative Organization
INPFL	Independent National Patriotic Front of Liberia
JIL	Journal of International

	Law
LJIL	Leiden Journal of International Law
LNTS	League of Nations Treaties Series
MJIL	Michigan Journal of International Law
MNF	Multinational Force
MONUA	United Nations Observer Mission in Angola
MPLA	Movimento Popular de Libertaçâo de Angola
NATO	North Atlantic Treaty Organization
NILR	Netherlands International Law Review
NJB	Nederlands Juristenblad
NJIL	Nordic Journal of International Law
NPFL	National Patriotic Front of Liberia
NYIL	Netherlands Yearbook of International Law
NYUJIL	New York University Journal of International Law
NYUJILP	New York University Journal of International Law and Policy
OAU	Organization of African Unity
OAS	Organization of American States
ONUC	Opération des Nations Unies au Congo
PCIJ	Permanent Court of International Justice
PYIL	Polish Yearbook of International Law
Recueil des Cours	Académie de droit international, The Hague, Recueil des Cours
RGDIP	Revue Générale de Droit International Public
RICJ	Review of the International Commission of Jurists
RPF	Rwandese Patriotic Front
RUF	Revolutionary United Front
SCOR	Security Council Official Records
SHIRBRIG	Multinational United Nations Stand-by Forces High Readiness Brigade
SJIR	Schweizerische Jahrbuch für Internationales Recht
SNM	Somali National Movement
SPM	Somali Patriotic Movement
SSDF	Somali Salvation Democratic Front
SZIER	Schweizerische Zeitschrift für internationales und europäisches Recht
ULIMO	United Liberation Movement for Liberia

UNAMIR	United Nations Assistance Mission for Rwanda
UNAMSIL	United Nations Mission in Sierra Leone
UNCC	United Nations Compensation Commission
UNCIO	United Nations Conference on International Organization
UNDPI	United Nations Department of Public Information
UNEF I	United Nations Emergency Force
UNIKOM	United Nations Iraq-Kuwait Observation Mission
UNITA	União Nacional para a Independência Total de Angola
UNITAF	Unified Task Force
UNMIH	United Nations Mission in Haiti
UNMOVIC	United Nations Monitoring, Verification and Inspection Commission
UNOMIL	United Nations Observer Mission in Liberia
UNOMSIL	United Nations Observer Mission in Sierra Leone
UNOMUR	United Nations Observer Mission Uganda-Rwanda
UNOSOM	United Nations Operation in Somalia
UNPA	United Nations Protected Area
UNPREDEP	United Nations Preventive Deployment Force
UNPROFOR	United Nations Protection Force
UNSCOM	United Nations Special Commission
UNTS	United Nations Treaties Series
USC	United Somali Congress
VJIL	Virginia Journal of International Law
VJTL	Vanderbilt Journal of Transnational Law
WEU	Western European Union
YBILC	Yearbook of the International Law Commission
YPA	Yugoslav People's Army
ZaöRV	Zeitschrift für ausländisches Recht und Völkerrecht

Contents

Introduction

Since the end of the Cold War the UN Security Council has displayed a hitherto unknown activism in using its enforcement powers to maintain international peace and security under the collective security system envisaged in Chapter VII of the UN Charter. The resolutions adopted by the Security Council since 1990 invoking Chapter VII are unprecedented both in number and in the scope of their content. This includes the authorizations for the use of force in the cases of Iraq, former Yugoslavia, Somalia, Haiti and Rwanda.[1] Moreover, the Security Council has creatively assumed new functions of various kinds under Chapter VII, *inter alia*, by curtailing the sovereignty of a defeated aggressor state by imposing the conditions of a termination of hostilities (Iraq), intervening with military force for humanitarian reasons into the anarchy of another state (Somalia), limiting the right of self-defence of a UN member state through maintaining an arms embargo (Bosnia Herzegovina), imposing sanctions for providing shelter to alleged terrorists (Sudan and Afghanistan), and ordering Libya to extradite two nationals allegedly responsible for acts of terrorism to the courts of two permanent members of the Security Council (the *Lockerbie* case). In addition, the Security Council has created a new administrative instrument for the settlement of claims for war damages and changed the rules of state responsibility with the establishment of the United Nations Compensation Commission for Claims Against Iraq in Geneva, denying the defendant state any meaningful standing in the sense of procedural justice.[2] The Security Council has also used its authority under Chapter VII

---

1 See, for example, H. Freudenschuß, *Between Unilateralism and Collective Security: Authorizations of the Use of Force by the UN Security Council*, 5 EJIL (1994) 492-531; P.M. Dupuy, *Sécurité Collective de la Paix dans la pratique contemporaine du Conseil de Sécurité*. In: U. Beyerlin, *et. al.* (eds.) Recht zwischen Umbruch und Bewahrung (1995) 41-56.

2 See P. Malanczuk, *International Business and New Rules of State Responsibility?: The Law Applied by the United Nations (Security Council) Compensation Commission for Claims Against Iraq*. In: K.H. Böckstiegel, Perspectives of Air Law, Space Law, and International Business Law for the Next Century (1996) 117-145; V. Gowlland-Debbas, *Security Council Enforcement Action and Issues of State Responsibility*, 43 ICLQ (1994) 55-98.

to establish International Criminal Tribunals for war crimes committed in Rwanda and former Yugoslavia.

Such developments have given rise to concern that the Security Council "is trying to do too much, too quickly"[3], that the Security Council is being made a tool of the great powers, notably the USA, and that, in view of its perceived antiquated composition and method of decision-making (vetopower of the five permanent members), it lacks "legitimacy" and needs to be reformed.[4] On the other hand, as in the case of the conflict in former Yugoslavia, the Security Council has been criticized for not venturing far enough in its activities. In this connection, the issue whether there are "constitutional" or legal limits to the authority of the Security Council to act under Chapter VII (and what the legal consequences of such limits may be) has become a central question in the recent literature.[5]

This discussion has been enhanced by two cases recently brought before the International Court of Justice.[6] The developments have necessarily put the question of the controlling role of the International Court of Justice *vis-à-vis* the Security Council as the "ultimate guardian of UN legality"[7] into a new perspective. In a broader sense, the question of controlling the legality of the Security Council's actions relates to the

---

3 S.D. Murphy, *The Security Council, Legitimacy, and the Concept of Collective Security After the Cold War*, 32 CJTL (1994) 201-288.

4 See, for example, D.D. Caron, *The Legitimacy of the Collective Authority of the Security Council*, 87 AJIL (1993) 552-588.

5 *E.g.* M.J. Herdegen, *The 'Constitutionalization' of the UN Security System*, 27 VJTL (1994) 135-159; E. McWhinney, *The International Court as Emerging Constitutional Court and the Co-ordinate UN Institutions (especially the Security Council): Implications of the Aerial Incident at Lockerbie*, 30 CYIL (1992) 261-272; T.D. Gill, *Legal and Some Political Limitations on the Power of the U.N. Security Council to Exercise its Enforcement Powers under Chapter VII of the Charter*, 26 NYIL (1995) 33-138; J.E. Alvarez, *Judging the Security Council*, 90 AJIL (1996) 1-39.

6 The *Questions of Interpretation and Application of the 1971 Montreal Convention Arising from the Aerial Incident at Lockerbie* cases (Libya v. resp. US and UK), and the *Case Concerning Application of the Convention on the Prevention and Punishment of the Crime of Genocide* (Bosnia and Herzegovina v. Yugoslavia (Serbia and Montenegro)).

7 *E.g.* T.M. Franck, *The 'Powers of Appreciation': Who is the Ultimate Guardian of UN Legality?*, 86 AJIL (1992) 519-523; S.I. Bortz, *Avoiding a Collision of Competence: The Relationship between the SC and the ICJ in Light of* Libya v. United States, 2 Florida State University Journal of Transnational Law & Policy (1993) 353-378; B. Graefrath, *Leave to the Court What Belongs to the Court: The Libyan Case*, 4 EJIL (1993) 184-205; W.M. Reisman, *The Constitutional Crisis in the United Nations*, 87 AJIL (1993) 83-100; C. Tomuschat, *The Lockerbie Case Before the International Court of Justice*, 48 RICJ (1992) 38-48; G. Watson, *Constitutionalism, Judicial Review, and the World Court*, 34 HILJ (1993) 1-25; M. Weller, *Premature End to the 'New World Order'?*, 4 AJICL (1992) 303-324; C. Scott, *et. al.*, *A Memorial for Bosnia, Framework of Legal Arguments Concerning the Lawfulness of the maintenance of the UN Security Council's Arms Embargo on Bosnia and Herzegovina*, 16 MJIL (1994) 1-140.

'rule of law' in international relations.[8] As will be seen below, the United Nations Charter confers considerable powers on the Security Council with regard to the maintenance of international peace and security. Decisions taken by the Council pursuant to that responsibility bind member states and can have far-reaching legal, military, economic and political effects on member states. Countries and their populations targeted by sanctions, for example, can experience severe economic and humanitarian difficulties, while member states implementing the sanctions may also incur substantial economic losses as a result. It goes without saying, moreover, that the decision to use force is one of the – if not the – most intrusive and disruptive actions states can engage in.

In exercising and interpreting its authority, the Council undoubtedly possesses a "margin of appreciation".[9] This leads to the question of whether the international rule of law requires that the Council adheres to the principle of legality in exercising its functions and powers,[10] and that consequently international law determines the extent of that margin. Or, in the alternative, whether the Council is free to do as it deems fit, restrained only by the political expediencies and opportunities of the moment.

Given the strong impact of the Council's decisions taken in pursuance of its responsibility for the maintenance of international peace and security, these questions are not merely of academic interest. The decisions can influence the day to day lives of people and change the rights and duties of states. The interest in the topic has proven to be cyclical. With a more active Council the need felt to control it has become stronger, as happened in the early 1990s. *Vice versa*, the general inability of the Council to take action during the Cold War made it a predominantly theoretical issue.[11] The activism exhibited by the Council at the beginning of the 1990s has gradually receded.[12] However, this does not mean that the issue should now go back to the exclusive realm of academia. The unprecedented number and scope of the

---

8 *Cf.* G. Arangio-Ruiz, *The 'Federal Analogy' and UN Charter Interpretation: A Crucial Issue*, 8 EJIL (1997) 1-28, 1-2.

9 G.D.S. Taylor, *The Content of the Rule Against Abuse of Rights in International Law*, 46 BYIL (1972-1973) 323-352, at 325.

10 See J. Delbrück, *Peacekeeping by the United Nations and the Rule of Law*. In: R.J Akkerman, P.J. van Krieken, C.O. Pannenborg (eds.), Declarations on Principles: A Quest for Universal Peace (1977) 73-99.

11 For older works see, *e.g.*, J.L. Kunz, *Legality of the Security Council Resolutions of June 25 and 27, 1950*, 45 AJIL (1951) 137-142; R. Higgins, *The Place of International Law in the Settlement of Disputes by the Security Council*, 64 AJIL (1970) 1-18; F. Morgenstern, *Legality in International Organizations*, 48 BYIL (1976-1977) 241-257.

12 See B. Fassbender, Quis judicabit? *The Security Council, Its Powers and Its Legal Control*, 11 EJIL (2000) 219-231.

Council's decisions during that period warrant further study as to the legal basis and limits to the Council's authority with regard to the maintenance of international peace and security. Not only are several decisions taken during that era still operative, the actions taken by the Council will certainly serve as precedents for future action by the Council.

The optimism about a rejuvenated Security Council exhibited in the early 1990s turned into scepticism about whose interests were served by the newborn, and concern arose with regard to the legal protection of the entities affected by the Council's decisions. Although this work focuses on the latter aspect of the Council's working, this does not mean to say that the optimism was ill-founded.[13] Nor does it mean that efforts should be made to constrain an international Leviathan, the metaphor that easily springs to mind. Within the current community of states, the Security Council is the only universal organ with the legal authority to enforce its will in pursuance of that high goal mentioned in the preamble to the United Nations Charter: to "live together in peace with one another as good neighbours". The achievement of this formidable goal requires great powers, but at the same time it is believed that with great powers come great responsibilities. In the long run, moreover, it is to be expected that a Council whose decisions are perceived to be legitimate will be more effective in pursuing its aims. For any exercise of legal authority depends on the willingness of those responsible for its execution. Within the legal community of states, this is probably more true than anywhere else.

The Problems Addressed in this Work

There are several ways one could approach the question of the Council's legitimacy. From a political viewpoint, for example, one could look at the way Council decisions are made. This would include an analysis of the factors influencing the Council's actions, of the pressure exerted by certain members on and outside the Council, and of the interest served by the decisions made. This book, however, relates to the legal aspects of the Council's legitimacy. The central issue in this legal approach is whether international law provides for rules defining and limiting the Council's powers under Chapter VII of the UN Charter. The first operative question examined in the following

---

13 *Cf.* Greenwood, according to whom the "increased activity and effectiveness of the Security Council in addressing peace and security is one of the most positive developments to have occurred in international law." C. Greenwood, *The Impact of Decisions of the Security Council on the International Court of Justice*. In: W.P. Heere (ed.), International Law and The Hague's 750th Anniversary (1999) 81-86, at 81.

chapters, therefore, is: *What are the legal limits to the Council's authority under Chapter VII of the Charter of the United Nations?*[14] An important aspect of this question is the role the International Court of Justice can fulfil in determining these limits. The second operative question of the book therefore runs as follows: *To what extent can the International Court of Justice determine the legal limits of the Security Council's authority under Chapter VII of the Charter of the United Nations, and judicially review decisions taken under that Chapter?* The work is limited to decisions of the Council taken under Chapter VII of the Charter because it is primarily under this chapter that the Council can take decisions that are binding on member states.[15] Although a substantial amount of literature has been published on the issue of the Council's legitimacy, particularly in the last decade, this volume adopts a new approach in that it purports to provide a comprehensive overview of the legal questions and complexities involved.

The Structure of the Work

The operative questions formulated above will be dealt with in six chapters. Chapter 1 relates to methodology, more specifically the interpretation of treaties under international law. Since a substantial part of the work involves the interpretation of the Charter and resolutions of the Security Council, it is necessary to first look at the various ways such an interpretation can be approached. The chapter will establish a framework within which interpretation will take place in this work. The second chapter is concerned with the authority of the Council under the Charter. It provides an overview of the Council's functions and powers under the Charter, in particular Chapter VII, and the main interpretative problems associated with the provisions of the Charter relevant to the Council. Chapter 3 deals with the way the Council has employed these powers in practice. It chronologically describes the Council's practice under Chapter VII in order to determine the evolution of those powers and to establish the kind of problems that can be raised by their application. The chapter is concluded with a classification of the new functions assumed by the Council. The fourth chapter relates to the first operative question. Herein the problems with the Council's practice that were identified in chapter 3 will be addressed in detail. It looks at the legal limits that could provide for the parameters of lawful Security Council action under Chapter VII of the Charter. These limits could be based on the law of the Charter as well as

14 Phrased in this way the assumption is that such limits do exist, although the outcome of the work could be otherwise, *i.e.* that such limits do not exist.

15 For a discussion of other Charter provisions that might confer a power to take binding decisions on the Council see *infra*, paragraph 2.3.1.

non-Charter sources of international law. The assessment of these limits is based on an analysis of the Charter and extra-Charter sources, on international jurisprudence and on the scholarly literature. Chapter 5 is concerned with the consequences of illegal Security Council decisions and remedies available to affected states. This relates to the second operative question posed in this book, the role the International Court of Justice can play in remedying illegal Council decisions, including a possible power of judicial review by the Court. Thereto the main problems associated with such a role (the principle of litispendence and the political question doctrine) are first described, followed by an assessment of the *de lege lata* role the Court can play. The Charter, the Statute and Rules of the Court, the jurisprudence of the Court, and legal literature are the main tools for answering the second question. The sixth chapter deals with the Council's legitimacy in a broader context, and discusses the ways by which its legitimacy could be enhanced. This includes proposals to change the Council's composition, the distribution and usage of the veto and ways to enhance the transparency of its decision-making. The conclusions will answer the two operative questions posed in this book. It provides an overview of the legal limits to the Council's authority under Chapter VII of the Charter, and of the role of the International Court of Justice in determining these limits and testing Security Council decisions under Chapter VII against these limits.

1.

The Interpretation of Treaties

In order to answer the question of the legal limits to the Council's authority under Chapter VII of the Charter, the second chapter of this volume will provide an overview of that authority. Such an overview will necessarily involve an interpretation of the provisions of the Charter. Therefore this chapter will first examine the various ways in which such an interpretation can be approached.

Due to its complex nature, and the many issues involved, the interpretation of treaties is one of the most debated topics in international law.[16] The following will provide an overview of the main schools of thought on the topic, the approach followed by the 1969 Vienna Convention on the Law of Treaties[17] and the particular issues arising from the interpretation of constituent instruments of international organizations. The chapter will be concluded with a statement of the author's approach to interpretation.

---

[16] See, *e.g.*, the *Third Report on the Law of Treaties* by H. Waldock, Special Rapporteur to the ILC, 2 YBILC (1964) 5-65, 53; I. Sinclair, *The Vienna Convention on the Law of Treaties* (1984), 114; M.N. Shaw, *International Law* (1997), 655. In a comment to its Draft Convention on the Law of Treaties, the Harvard Law School states that: "The question as to the existence or utility of rules of international law governing the interpretation of treaties is one which has given rise to a vast amount of discussion by, and to disagreement among, jurists." Harvard Law School, *Research in International Law, Comment on Article 19 of the Draft Convention on the Law of Treaties*, 29 AJIL (1935), Suppl., at 939.

[17] 1155 UNTS 331 ff.; 8 ILM (1969), 679 ff.

1.1 The Need for and Purpose of Interpretation

Organs of international organizations, states (in their capacity as members of organs of international organizations or as parties to treaties), international courts and tribunals, and scholars of international law are regularly faced with the question of how treaty provisions or other legal texts, including resolutions of the Security Council,[18] should be interpreted.[19] This is in large part due to the indeterminacy of language.[20] Indeed, on a closer look almost every term may be interpreted in various ways. In the words of Judge Spender: "what makes sense to one may not make sense to another. Ambiguity may lie hidden in the plainest and most simple of words even in their natural and ordinary meaning."[21]

A legal text may also be unclear, incomplete or contradictory because political differences between the negotiating parties necessitated a compromise formulation,[22] or simply because the ambiguity was overlooked by the drafters.[23] This may be illustrated by the *IMCO* case,[24] in which the International Court of Justice had to interpret the term "largest ship-owning nations" employed in the constitution of the Inter-Governmental Maritime Consultative Organization (IMCO). The choice it faced was whether this referred to nations having the largest registered tonnage of beneficially owned ships, or of nations with the largest registered tonnage, irrespective of beneficial ownership.[25]

In addition to the inherent ambiguity of language, a legal text may also *become* unclear, incomplete or contradictory due to – often unforeseen – changes in the social,

---

[18] *Cf.* M.C. Wood, *The Interpretation of Security Council Resolutions*, 2 Max Planck Yearbook of United Nations Law (1998) 73-95.

[19] Generally see, *e.g.*, R. de Lange, *Publieke Rechtsvinding* (1991); C. Baldus, *Regelhafte Vertragsauslegung nach Parteirollen im klassischen römischen Recht und in der modernen Völkerrechtswissenschaft* (1998).

[20] Generally see B. Bix, Law, *Language, and Legal Determinacy* (1993).

[21] *Certain Expenses of the United Nations (Art. 17, Para. 2, of the Charter)*, Adv. Op., Sep. Op. Spender, ICJ Rep. (1962), at 184.

[22] *Cf.* Judge Alvarez, according to whom: "Multilateral treaties are not drafted with the help of a dictionary, and their wording is often the result of a compromise which influences the terms used in the text." *Competence of the General Assembly for the Admission of a State to the United Nations*, Adv. Op., Diss. Op. Alvarez, ICJ Rep. (1950), at 17.

[23] See E. Gordon, *The World Court and the Interpretation of Constitutive Treaties: Some Observations on the Development of an International Constitutional Law*, 59 AJIL (1965) 794-833, 803-805.

[24] The *Constitution of the Maritime Safety Committee of the Inter-Governmental Maritime Consultative Organization* case, ICJ Rep. (1960), 150 ff.

[25] On the *IMCO* case see also *infra*, the text accompanying notes 872-875.

political or technological operating sphere of a treaty. As an example of unforeseen circumstances one may refer to the situation that occurred at the International Court of Justice in 1981. In that year a judge had passed away a few weeks before his term of office, and the terms of four other judges had ended. Article 14 of the Statute of the International Court of Justice holds that in the event of a vacancy the Secretary-General will issue invitations "within one month of the occurrence of the vacancy" for the nomination of candidates, whilst the time-limit for issuing invitations for regular elections was three months (Article 5(1) of the Statute). A literal interpretation of Article 14 would lead to a situation in which a judge is elected for a few weeks, after which the seat would become eligible again during regular elections. This unpractical result was avoided by leaving the seat open until the next elections.[26]

Thus, legal texts have frequently to be interpreted so as to establish a less ambiguous or contradictory meaning.[27] Historically, this process is associated with establishing the original intention of the parties to the treaty.[28] This appears to be self-evident, because by signing a treaty the parties voluntarily establish a legal regime that contains mutual rights and duties in pursuance of a common goal. Whenever uncertainties arise with regard to the meaning of a particular provision, it seems appropriate to ascertain what the intentions of the parties were when they signed the treaty. In this view, the correct interpretation of a provision is that which coincides with what the parties wanted to achieve with the treaty. However, there have always been differences of opinion on the question of where to find evidence of these intentions. The various schools of thought on treaty interpretation, which will be considered below, provide different answers to this question.

---

[26] On the election see S. Rosenne, *The Election of Five Members of the International Court of Justice in 1981*, 76 AJIL (1982) 364-370.

[27] According to one definition, the object of interpretation in the field of public international law "is to establish with some degree of persuasiveness and if possible agreement the objective rights and duties of two or more States or international organizations parties to a given treaty, in relation to a concrete situation said to come within the reach of the treaty." S. Rosenne, *Developments in the Law of Treaties 1945-1986* (1989), at 224.

[28] Thus, Jennings and Watts, for example, submit that "the purpose of interpreting a treaty is to establish the meaning of the text which the parties must be taken to have intended it to bear in relation to the circumstances with reference to which the question of interpretation has arisen." R.Y. Jennings, A. Watts, *Oppenheim's International Law* (1996), at 1267. According to Reuter: "the purpose of interpretation is to ascertain the intention of the parties from a text." P. Reuter, *Introduction to the Law of Treaties* (1989), at 74. Similarly, Lauterpacht concludes that the "function of interpretation" is "ascertaining what was the intention of the parties". H. Lauterpacht, *The Development of International Law by the International Court* (1958), at 27. Fitzmaurice notes that "no one seriously denies that the *aim* of treaty interpretation is to give effect to the intention of the parties." G. Fitzmaurice, *The Law and Procedure of the International Court of Justice* (1986), at 338.

In addition to the issue 'how to determine the intention of the parties', or 'where to look for evidence of these intentions', the evolution of international treaty law has posed different, more fundamental issues. As will be seen below, these developments warrant the question whether it is still feasible to state that the primary aim and goal of treaty interpretation is the determination of the original intentions of the parties.[29] It will also become apparent that the answer to this preliminary question is dependent on the theoretical outlook of the interpreter.

1.2 Doctrinal Approaches to Interpretation

The main theories on treaty interpretation are represented by the teleological, the subjective, and the textual schools. The teleological school emphasizes the importance of the object and purpose of a treaty. In this approach, the preferred interpretation of a provision is the one that best serves the object and purpose of the treaty. Such interpretations may even set aside the original intentions of the parties, for in the teleological view, the general aim of the treaty prevails over the intentions held at the time of the conclusion of a treaty.[30] This theory allows for gaps to be filled and texts to be interpreted liberally along the lines of the object and purpose of the treaty. As regards international institutional law, in case of gaps or ambiguities in a constituent instrument, this school emphasizes the need for the effective functioning of an organization rather than the sovereignty of its members.[31] This is an application of the principle of "maximum effectiveness", expressed in the rule *ut res magis valeat quam pereat*, – it is better for a thing to have effect than to be made void.[32] The principle, also known as *la règle de l'effet utile*, assumes every provision to be included for a reason, and that it should not be rendered redundant. The second assumption is that a provision should be interpreted in accordance with the aim of the instrument as a whole, which is known in French as *la règle de l'efficacité*. The teleological approach

---

29 See Sinclair, *op. cit. supra* n.16, 114-115.

30 A variant of the teleological approach is the New Haven school's approach, which attempts to give effect to the "genuine shared expectations of the parties, subject to overriding community policies". See for such an approach M.S. McDougal, H.D. Lasswell, J.C. Miller, *The Interpretation of Agreements and World Public Order: Principles of Content and Procedure* (1967), 40-41.

31 See P. Malanczuk, *Akehurst's Modern Introduction to International Law* (1997), at 336.

32 Fitzmaurice, *op. cit. supra* n.28, at 49. According to Waldock, however, this principle does not "necessarily lead to an extensive rather than a restrictive view of the effects of a treaty." Waldock, *op. cit. supra* n.16, at 60.

is commonly associated with multilateral conventions of a general nature, such as the UN Charter.[33]

In contrast to the teleological approach, those adhering to the subjective school postulate that an interpreter must first and foremost try to ascertain the intention of the parties to a treaty. An important representative of this school is H. Lauterpacht, according to whom:

> the intention of the parties – express or implied – is the law. Any considerations – of effectiveness or otherwise – which tend to transform the ascertainable intention of the parties into a factor of secondary importance are inimical to the true purpose of interpretation.[34]

A succinct expression of the position and assumptions of the subjective school may be found in the following proposal of the Harvard Law School Draft Convention on the Law of Treaties:

> A treaty is to be interpreted in the light of the general purpose which it is intended to serve. The historical background of the treaty, *travaux préparatoires*, the circumstances of the parties at the time the treaty was entered into, the change in these circumstances sought to be effected, the subsequent conduct of the parties in applying the provisions of the treaty and the conditions prevailing at the time interpretation is being made, are to be considered in connection with the general purpose which the treaty is intended to serve.[35]

The subjective school thus adopts the classical view on interpretation, according to which 'the intention of the parties is the law'. In establishing the correct meaning of a provision in a text, one must therefore in the first place look at what the parties intended to achieve in drafting and signing the treaty. The interpreter would hence have to take into account the historical background and the circumstances in which the treaty was signed. Accordingly, a major aid in the interpretative process is recourse to the *travaux préparatoires* of a treaty.

The textual or literal meaning school presumes that the intention of the parties is adequately expressed in the text of a treaty.[36] The primary means of determining the

---

[33] In the words of Fitzmaurice "the general multilateral convention of the 'normative', and, particularly, of the sociological or humanitarian type." Fitzmaurice, *op. cit. supra* n.28, at 341.

[34] H. Lauterpacht, *Restrictive Interpretation and the Principle of Effectiveness in the Interpretation of Treaties*, 16 BYIL (1949) 48-85, at 73.

[35] Harvard Law School, *Research in International Law, Article 19 of the Draft Convention on the Law of Treaties*, 29 AJIL (1935), Suppl., at 937.

[36] Waldock has described the textual approach as follows: "it takes as the basic rule of treaty interpretation the primacy of the text as evidence of the intentions of the parties. It accepts the view that the text must be presumed to be the authentic expression of the intentions of the parties; and that, in consequence, the starting point and purpose of interpretation is to elucidate the meaning of the text, not to investigate *ab initio* the intentions of the parties." Waldock, *op. cit. supra* n.16, at 56.

content of a provision is therefore an analysis of its text, in accordance with the ordinary meaning of the words employed. Vattel was an early proponent of this approach, as he argued that "when a deed is worded in clear and precise terms, when its meaning is evident and leads to no absurdity, there is no ground for refusing to accept the meaning which the deed naturally presents."[37]

1.3 The Vienna Convention on the Law of Treaties

After a long drafting history in the International Law Commission,[38] the Vienna Convention of the Law of Treaties was opened for signature in 1969.[39] This important instrument is "a compound of codification and of progressive development of customary international law."[40] The International Court of Justice, moreover, has ruled on more than one occasion that the rules on interpretation contained in the Convention amount to customary international law.[41]

The Vienna Convention of the Law of Treaties primarily adopts the textual approach to treaty interpretation. Thus, in the first paragraph of Article 31 it is stipulated that, as a 'general rule of interpretation', a treaty "shall be interpreted in good faith in accordance with the ordinary meaning to be given to the terms of the treaty in their context and in the light of its object and purpose."

As regards the context, the second paragraph of the same Article holds that:

> The context for the purpose of the interpretation of a treaty shall comprise, in addition to the text, including its preamble and annexes:
> (a) any agreement relating to the treaty which was made between all the parties in connexion with the conclusion of the treaty;
> (b) any instrument which was made by one or more parties in connexion with the conclusion of the treaty and accepted by the other parties as an instrument related to the treaty.

---

[37] E. von Vattel, quoted in P.K. Menon, *The Law of Treaties between States and International Organizations* (1992), at 74.

[38] On which see, *e.g.*, S. Rosenne, *The Law of Treaties: A Guide to the Legislative History of the Vienna Convention* (1970).

[39] Adopted on 23 May 1969; it entered into force on 27 Jan. 1980.

[40] D.J. Harris, *Cases and Materials on International Law* (1991), at 729. *Cf.* Sinclair, *op. cit. supra* n.16, chapter 1; M. Dixon, *Textbook on International Law* (1996), 54.

[41] See, *e.g.*, the *Case concerning Oil Platforms* (Prel. Obj.), Iran v. US, ICJ Rep. (1996), para. 23 at 812; the *Case concerning the Arbitral Award of 13 July 1989* (Judgment), Guinea-Bissau v. Senegal, ICJ Rep. (1991), para. 48 at 20-21; the *Case Concerning the Gabcíkovo-Nagymaros Project* (Judgment), Hungary v. Slovakia, 25 Sept 1997, ICJ Rep. (1997), para. 46; and the Advisory Opinion on the *Legality of the Use by a State of Nuclear Weapons in Armed Conflict*, 8 July 1996, ICJ Rep. (1996), para. 19.

The parties to a treaty may, furthermore, either expressly or implicitly engage in interpretative acts, as indicated by paragraph 3 of Article 31:

There shall be taken into account, together with the context:
(a) any subsequent agreement between the parties regarding the interpretation of the treaty or the application of its provisions;
(b) any subsequent practice in the application of the treaty which establishes the agreement of the parties regarding its interpretation.

Thus, the general rule of interpretation embodied in the Vienna Convention is that one must first look at the ordinary meaning of the terms of the treaty in their context and in the light of its object and purpose. This context is provided by the relation to other articles, the preamble to the treaty and its annexes, agreements between parties made in connection with the conclusion of the treaty, and the instrument as a whole (the object and purpose of the treaty). Furthermore, agreements made with regard to the interpretation of the treaty or the application of its provisions – such as the rules of procedure of an organ – and the subsequent practice of the parties establishing agreement regarding the interpretation, are primary sources for determining the 'correct' meaning of a term.

Article 32 of the Convention stipulates that recourse may be had to the "supplementary means of interpretation" in order to provide for additional evidence for an interpretation based on Article 31, or when such an interpretation leads to an ambiguous or unreasonable result:

Recourse may be had to supplementary means of interpretation, including the preparatory work of the treaty and the circumstances of its conclusion, in order to confirm the meaning resulting from the application of article 31, or to determine the meaning when the interpretation according to article 31:
(a) leaves the meaning ambiguous or obscure; or
(b) leads to a result which is manifestly absurd or unreasonable.

The Convention thus provides for a mixture of all methods of interpretation.[42] Indeed it has been justifiably concluded that "international law does not in itself seem to answer the question as to the exclusive availability of one method over another."[43] Similarly the Special Rapporteur on the law of treaties to the International Law Commission, Waldock, observed that:

the jurisprudence of international tribunals furnishes examples of all the different approaches to interpretation

---

[42] *Cf.* Koskenniemi, according to whom Art. 31 of the Convention "refers to virtually all thinkable interpretative methods." M. Koskenniemi, *From Apology to Utopia: The Structure of International Legal Argument* (1989), n.89 at 292.

[43] R.St.J. MacDonald, *The United Nations Charter: Constitution or Contract?*. In: R.St.J. MacDonald, D.M. Johnston (eds.), The Structure and Process of International Law (1991) 63-86, at 65.

– textual, subjective and teleological ... it also shows that, if the textual method of interpretation predominates, none of these approaches is exclusively the correct one, and that their use in any particular case is to some extent a matter of choice and appreciation.[44]

In conclusion, there are several doctrinal approaches to treaty interpretation, and both customary and treaty law provide for a mixture of these approaches toward the matter. The following will address the interpretation of a specific instrument, the United Nations Charter. Attention will be given to the constituent nature of the Charter and the consequences thereof for its interpretation. Among these consequences to be considered are the use of the *travaux préparatoires* and of the subsequent practice of the organization as interpretative aids.

1.4 The United Nations Charter as a Constitution

The United Nations Charter has certain features distinguishing it from an 'ordinary' treaty.[45] The Charter has, *inter alia*, been characterized as a constitution for the world community,[46] containing elements of both a *traité-contrat* and a *traité-loi*.[47]

The Charter is a constitution in that it establishes the United Nations, provides for the functions and powers the organization may exercise, and distributes them among the organs of the organization.[48] As such, it is the 'supreme law' of the organization.[49] In the more than half a century in which the Charter has existed, amendments to it have been rare.[50] The circumstances surrounding the adoption of the Charter have,

---

44 Waldock, *op. cit. supra* n.16, at 54.

45 For a discussion see, *e.g.*, Rosenne, *op. cit. supra* n.27, chapter 4.

46 G. Ress, *The Interpretation of the Charter*. In: B. Simma (ed.), The Charter of the United Nations (1994) 25-44, 27. *Cf.* P.M. Dupuy, *The Constitutional Dimension of the Charter of the United Nations Revisited*, 1 Max Planck Yearbook of United Nations Law (1991) 1-33; B. Fassbender, *UN Security Council Reform and the Right of Veto: A Constitutional Perspective* (1998), Part I.

47 The former referring to the contractual nature of a contract, containing (concrete) reciprocal rights and duties, and the latter to the normative or law-making capacity of a treaty, setting standards and creating rights and duties which are not necessarily reciprocal or confined to the signing parties. See Rosenne, *op. cit. supra* n.27, 182-184.

48 See, *e.g.*, L.M. Goodrich, E. Hambro, A.S. Simons, *Charter of the United Nations* (1969), 13; K. Skubiszewski, *Remarks on the Interpretation of the United Nations Charter*. In: R. Bernhardt, *et. al.* (eds.), Völkerrecht als Rechtsordnung, International Gerichtsbarkeit, Menschenrechte, Festschrift für Hermann Mosler (1983) 891-902, 890-894.

49 Skubiszewski, *op. cit. supra* n.48, 892.

50 In fact the Charter has been amended on one occasion only (see GA Res. 1991 A and B (XVIII), 17 Dec. 1963). This related to the composition of United Nations organs, *i.e.* the Security Council (Arts. 23 and 27) and the Economic and Social Council (Art. 61).

however, changed significantly. In view of this, various scholars have argued that the Charter should be interpreted in a dynamic and teleological manner. Shaw, for example, submits that:

there is ... the special nature of the constituent instruments as forming not only multilateral agreements but also constitutional documents subject to constant practice, and thus interpretation, both of the institution itself and of member-states and others in relation to it. This of necessity argues for a more flexible or purpose-orientated method of interpretation.[51]

Judge Weeramantry also submits that:

In the interpretation of a multilateral convention ... which sets before itself certain sociological or humanitarian goals, the task of interpretation should be guided by the object and purpose which the Convention sets before itself. A literal interpretation, using strict methods of anchoring interpretation to the

---

[51] M.N. Shaw, *International Law* (1995), at 778. Similarly, Ress holds that "because the Charter has formally remained almost unchanged as a legal basis for the acts of its organs ... and its member states ... the need arises for adapting the Charter to the changing tasks by way of an evolutionary dynamic interpretation." Ress, *op. cit. supra* n.46, at 28. Sohn observes that: "The Charter of the United Nations, like the Constitution of the United States, is almost immutable as far as its text is concerned, but over less than fifty years its interpretations changed as much as those of the Constitution of the United States in two hundred years." L.B. Sohn, *The UN System as Authoritative Interpreter of its Law*. In: O. Schachter, C.C. Joyner (eds.), United Nations Legal Order (1995) 169-229, at 227. Alvarez, moreover, states that "an institution, once established, acquires a life of its own, independent of the elements which have given birth to it, and it must develop, not in accordance with the views of those who created it, but in accordance with the requirements of international life." *Conditions of Admission of a State to Membership of the United Nations (Article 4 of the Charter)*, Ind. Op. Alvarez, ICJ Rep. (1948), at 68. In a similar vein Goodrich, Hambro and Simons submit that: "The Charter as a constitution, and even as a treaty, is not a static thing. It and the Organization that it creates must be adapted to new and changing circumstances and to the desires and expectations of members. ... It can be generally be said of treaties and of constitutions that substantive changes and adaptations are more commonly achieved by a process of interpretation and application to situations as they arise than by formal amendment." Goodrich, *et. al.*, *op. cit. supra* n.48, at 13. According to Waldock "there is a need to provide for flexibility and to allow for the development of the Charter ... in order to adapt it to new conditions". H. Waldock, *General Course on Public International Law*, 106 Recueil des Cours (1962), at 34. *Cf.* Jennings and Watts, according to whom: "Especially with a treaty of a constitutional character, it will often be appropriate to lay particular emphasis on the object and purpose of the treaty when interpreting its provisions." Jennings, Watts, *op. cit. supra* n.28, n.13 at 1273; Bailey and Daws, who note that: "The challenge, then, is to use whatever flexibility the Charter allows so as to adapt the Organization to a world which differs greatly from that of 1942-1945". S.D. Bailey, S. Daws, *The Procedure of the UN Security Council* (1998), at 7. See also G. Schermers, N.M. Blokker, *International Institutional Law: Unity within Diversity* (1995), 719; and R. Higgins, *The Development of International Law through the Political Organs of the United Nations* (1969), at 309. More generally, Kelsen observes that "The fact that the legal norms as formulated in words having frequently more than one meaning is the reason why every legal instrument has its own life, more or less independent of the wishes and expectations of its begetters." H. Kelsen, *The Law of the United Nations* (1964), xiv.

letter rather than the spirit of the convention, would be inappropriate.[52]

The argument is supported by the change in membership of the organization. As the total number of states grew, so did the membership of the United Nations.[53] This is in accordance with the universal character of the organization, which – in the terminology of the Charter – is open to all peace-loving states that accept the obligations contained in the Charter and that are able and willing to carry out those obligations.[54] As a matter of principle and equity it would seem that the intention of the present members should prevail over the intention of the original members, which at this time form a minority.[55]

Consequently the principle of contemporaneity, according to which "a treaty is to be interpreted in the light of the general rules of international law in force at the time of its conclusion"[56] has been significantly reduced as a principle accompanying the interpretation of the Charter. This reduces the role the *travaux préparatoires* may play in the Charter interpretation.[57] It can certainly be submitted that by joining the organization new members become bound by the legal regime of the organization, including the preparatory works of the constituent instrument. Today, however, such a contention appears to be too legalistic. For "the intention of the present majority cannot be explained on the basis of what was said at San Francisco."[58] Moreover, usage of the *travaux préparatoires* as a means of determining the intentions of the original parties to a multilateral treaty such as the United Nations Charter is a difficult task. As

---

52 *Legality Of The Use By A State Of Nuclear Weapons In Armed Conflict*, Adv. Op., Diss. Op. Weeramantry, ICJ Rep. (1996), at 148.

53 Whilst there were 51 original members in 1945, on 1 July 2000 the United Nations had 188 member states.

54 Art. 4(1) of the Charter.

55 In the words of Malanczuk, "the fact that the majority of the members of the United Nations joined the United Nations after 1945 and were not represented at the San Francisco Conference makes it politically awkward to rely on the *travaux préparatoires* of the Charter." Malanczuk, *op. cit. supra* n.31, at 366.

56 Jennings, Watts, *op. cit. supra* n.28, at 1281.

57 According to Bernhardt "practice subsequent to the conclusion of a treaty is now a widely recognized means of interpretation which can hardly be reconciled with a doctrine according a prominent place to preparatory work." R. Bernhardt, *Interpretation in International Law*, 2 EPIL (1995) 1416-1426, at 1421. Similarly, Azevado submits: "it is well known that (according to those who are in favour of using them) the value of *travaux préparatoires* is based, for purposes of interpretation, on the *voluntas legislatoris*, to which no great importance is attached today." *Competence of the General Assembly for the Admission of a State to the United Nations*, Adv. Op., Diss. Op. Azevado, ICJ Rep. (1950), at 23.

58 Skubiszewski, *op. cit. supra* n.48, at 895.

observed by Kelsen:

> it is more than doubtful whether there exists at all such a thing as the 'will of the legislator', especially where the law is the result of a complex procedure in which many individuals participate, such as the procedure ... through which a multilateral treaty is negotiated and signed by many plenipotentiaries and ratified by many governments.[59]

In the context of treaty interpretation, the intentions of the original parties may therefore be said to have lessened in weight, in favour of the views, opinions and intentions, of the present members. The subsequent practice of the member states and of the organs of the organization has accordingly become more important.[60] Note that subsequent practice has two elements. In the first sense it may be an aid to determine the original intentions of the parties; subsequent practice then refers to the application of the parties' intentions and conversely the intentions can be deduced from this application. The subsequent practice may also form an autonomous factor as an expression of consensus between the parties to a treaty.[61] Practice in the latter sense has become all the more important since the United Nations Charter itself is silent on interpretation.

Notwithstanding the absence of Charter provisions on the interpretation of the Charter, the organs of the United Nations interpret the provisions relating to their particular functions on a day to day basis. During the San Francisco conference on the establishment of the United Nations, the issue arose as to the status of such interpretations. Belgium had submitted proposals to the effect that the International Court of Justice was to be the interpretative organ of the United Nations. In response thereto, Committee IV/2 referred the matter to a subcommittee, which issued a report that was approved by the Committee. An often-quoted passage in this report states that:

> in the course of the operations from day to day of the various organs of the Organization, it is inevitable that each organ will interpret such parts of the Charter that are applicable to its particular functions. The process is inherent in the functioning of any body which operates under an instrument defining its functions and

---

[59] Kelsen, *op. cit. supra* n.51, at xiv. In a more literary fashion, Sinclair points out that "in the case of multilateral conventions, a search for the common intentions of the parties can be likened to a search for the pot of gold at the end of the rainbow." Sinclair, *op. cit. supra* n.16, at 130. See also Higgins, *op. cit. supra* n.51, 308-309; and Judge Alvarez in his dissenting opinion in the *Competence of the General Assembly for the Admission of a State to the United Nations*, Advisory Opinion, ICJ Rep. (1950), at 18.

[60] Generally see W. Karl, *Vertrag und spätere Praxis im Völkerrecht* (1983). See also Kunz, *op. cit. supra* n.11, 138; and S. Engel, *'Living' International Constitutions and the World Court (The Subsequent Practice of International Organs Under their Constituent Instruments)*, 16 ICLQ (1967) 865-910.

[61] C.F. Amerasinghe, *Interpretation of Texts in Open International Organizations*, 65 BYIL (1994) 175-209, at 200; Malanczuk, *op. cit. supra* n.31, 367; Ress, *op. cit. supra* n.46, 39-42.

powers.[62]

The subcommittee later went on to state that: "it is to be understood, of course, that if an interpretation made by any organ of the Organization or by a committee of jurists is not generally acceptable it will be without binding force."[63]

The notion of a "generally acceptable"[64] interpretation, however, poses various problems. In the decision-making process, an interpretative decision of an organ may be supported unanimously by its members, by a large majority or by a simple majority. In the first situation there does not seem to be a question concerning the general acceptability of the decision.[65] Dependent on the size of the minority and the degree of consistent repetition of the practice, decisions supported by a large majority are probably also generally acceptable.[66] A simple majority, on the other hand, would not suffice. Incidentally, the dissenting minority of states would remain under an obligation not to obstruct the functioning of the organization since, by joining the organization, the members consented to its methods of decision-making.[67] The ensuing practice would, however, not be considered legally relevant with regard to the interpretation of the instrument upon which the organ based its actions.

From the above it follows that a determination of the degree of acceptability of an interpretation made by an organ of an international organization depends on the amount of support it has received from the members of the organ concerned, and of the members of the organization not represented in the organ. An example of a generally acceptable dynamic interpretation of the Charter is the practice of the Security Council with regard to its voting procedures. According to Article 27(3) of the Charter, decisions of the Security Council on non-procedural matters "shall be made by an affirmative vote of nine members including the concurring votes of the permanent members". During the course of its operations, however, the Council consistently treated an abstention from voting by a permanent member as being

---

62 13 UNCIO Docs, at 709.

63 *Ibid.*, at 710.

64 The correct meaning probably being 'accepted' rather than 'acceptable'. See Skubiszewski, *op. cit. supra* n.48, n.35 at 898.

65 Although, theoretically speaking, a problem could arise if an organ not composed of all members of the organization, such as the Security Council, unanimously takes a decision which is opposed by a majority or a large minority of member states not represented at the organ. According to Ress, "if the organ's competence to interpret is binding, the practice in application does not necessarily reflect a consensus among member states." Ress, *op. cit. supra* n.46, at 40.

66 See C.F. Amerasinghe, *Principles of the Institutional Law of International Organizations* (1996), 51; Ress, *op. cit. supra* n.46, 41.

67 See *infra*, paragraph 5.2.

equivalent to a concurring vote. At fist sight this does not appear to be in conformity with the ordinary meaning of the term "including the concurring votes" employed in Article 27(3). Nevertheless, the practice reflects a consensus within the United Nations as to the effective functioning of the Council, and was declared to be "generally accepted" by the International Court of Justice in 1971.[68]

1.5 The Approach towards Interpretation Adopted in this Work

The conclusion to be drawn from the foregoing paragraphs is that, in interpreting the United Nations Charter, emphasis should be placed on the object and purpose of the organization. This choice to adopt the teleological approach is governed by the constituent nature of the Charter,[69] and by the need to adapt to the changes occurring within international relations, an important aspect thereof being the increase in the membership of the United Nations. The general consequence of this decision is that the relevance of the preparatory work of the Charter is reduced as an interpretative aid, in favour of the subsequent practice of the organization. The above position must, however, be qualified. The interpretation of treaties in general, and that of constituent instruments in particular, is a complex issue that does not easily warrant absolute statements. Distinctive features of the United Nations Charter, moreover, require special attention as to its interpretation.

In the first place, the Charter was deliberately loosely formulated. Drafted mainly by politicians, its provisions are often formulated in general and broad terms.[70] Consequently, the *travaux préparatoires* of the Charter can and will provide a useful starting point for interpreting its provisions. It may be noted that the open-texture of the Charter is one of the reasons that its interpretation is open to permanent debate. Indeed it has been observed that: "it is no exaggeration to say that the whole history of the United Nations has been a series of disputes about the correct interpretation of

---

68 See *infra*, the text accompanying notes 201-203.

69 The ICJ has recently described the special characteristics of constitutive treaties as follows: "the constituent instruments of international organizations are ... treaties of a particular type; their object is to create new subjects of law endowed with a certain autonomy, to which the parties entrust the task of realizing common goals. Such treaties can raise specific problems of interpretation owing, *inter alia*, to their character which is conventional and at the same time institutional; the very nature of the organization created, the objectives which have been assigned to it by its founders, the imperatives associated with the effective performance of its functions, as well as its own practice, are all elements which may deserve special attention when the time comes to interpret these constituent treaties." *Legality of the Use by a State of Nuclear Weapons in Armed Conflict*, Adv. Op., ICJ Rep. (1996), para. 19 at 75.

70 See for example Art. 1 of the Charter, describing the purposes of the organization.

the Charter."[71]

Secondly, the United Nations is a highly politicized organization. Interpretative decisions will therefore usually be based on policy rather than legal considerations. In this way Rosenne, for example, refers to "the deliberate political input into the interpretative processes through the procedures of decision-making by voting or by consensus", which makes the "legal problem ... not simply how to interpret and apply any particular provision of the constituent instrument".[72] In a similar vein, Goodrich, Hambro and Simons observe that:

> since the responsibility for interpretation is vested in organs and members alike, the process is more likely to be political than judicial. This means that the view taken of the meaning of the Charter in any particular situation is more often than not the result of a bargaining process or an exercise of power than an attempt to apply Charter provisions by a process of reasoning based on accepted principles of interpretation.[73]

As a side effect of the political bias within the United Nations, there is a tendency amongst its organs not to mention the particular provisions upon which they have acted. It is correspondingly more difficult to ascertain how a particular provision of the Charter has been interpreted in practice; such an ascertainment requires a preliminary determination of what Article(s) are being invoked.

Thirdly, an inherent problem with the teleological approach to treaty interpretation is that it tends to weaken the constitutional character of the Charter, in favour of what the majority favours at a given moment.[74] As Ress correctly observes, "the legal relevance of subsequent practice reduces the possibility of *ultra vires* action of the UN."[75] Therefore, albeit emphasis should be placed on the object and purpose of the organization in the interpretation of the Charter, it has been observed that: "one must be careful not to take this too far and ascribe extensive powers to international organisations upon ambiguous grounds of, for example, effectiveness, since this will

---

71 Malanczuk, *op. cit. supra* n.31, at 364.

72 Rosenne, *op. cit. supra* n.27, at 192.

73 Goodrich, *et. al.*, *op. cit. supra* n.48, at 15. In a similar fashion Kelsen states that "he is aware that the international community established at the San Francisco Conference is by its very nature a political phenomenon and that a merely juristic interpretation cannot do justice to it." Kelsen, *op. cit. supra* n.51, at xvii.

74 Rosenne rather sharply states that "the overall picture of interpretation of the Charter of the United Nations ... is an unhappy one. Provisions of the Charter itself, let alone the rules of procedure, are 'established' or 'destablished' at the behest of the majority of the day or at the whim of a politically determined President confident that a challenge to any ruling of his will be rebuffed." Rosenne, *op. cit. supra* n.27, at 244.

75 Ress, *op. cit. supra* n.46, at 39. So also Fassbender, who submits that "to license informal amendments is to generate a gray area in which the border between law and no-more-law, and law and not-yet-law becomes blurred." Fassbender, *op. cit. supra* n.16, at 139.

inevitably lead to conflict with member-states and third parties."[76]

In this context one might refer to Gordon, who has observed that the interpreter adhering to the teleological principle is "usually confronted not with a choice of either giving no effect or unlimited effect to a treaty, but rather with the problem of deciding *how* effective the treaty should be made."[77] The point to be made is that if one includes subsequent organizational practice as a source of treaty interpretation, this does not mean that every interpretation proposed or acted upon by that organization must be deemed *intra vires*, simply because a majority in the organ supported it. It is true that the International Court of Justice has concluded that "when the Organization takes action which warrants the assertion that it was appropriate for the fulfilment of one of the stated purposes of the United Nations, the presumption is that such action is not *ultra vires* the Organization."[78]

But in situations where such practice would run counter to the natural or ordinary meaning of the Charter provisions, the burden of proof would lie with the party proposing the alternative interpretation. In other words, that party would have to establish that its interpretation is generally acceptable. This corresponds with Article 31(3)b of the Vienna Convention, which lists the subsequent practice of the parties to a treaty as a primary source of treaty interpretation to the extent that the practice "establishes the agreement of the parties regarding its interpretation." Thus, practice alone does not suffice, it should be accompanied by an "*opinio iuris* ... [in] the sense that the practice is lawful or not lawful under the governing provisions of the constitution."[79]

The fourth point to be made, is that "interpretation is a process ... it cannot be reduced to a few propositions capable of purely automatic application in all circumstances."[80] The rules will therefore serve as a guideline, not a strict set of rules.[81]

---

76 Shaw, *op. cit. supra* n.16, at 778. So also Waldock, who remarks that "there is also a need to protect members against the creation, by changing majorities, of new obligations not dreamed of by the 'begetters'." Waldock, *op. cit. supra* n.51, at 35. Similarly, Skubiszewski states: "obviously, the perception of the Charter as a constitution does not entail the power to extend, alter or disregard its provisions under the guise of interpretation." Skubiszewski, *op. cit. supra* n.48, at 893.

77 Gordon, *op. cit. supra* n.23, at 797 (emphasis added).

78 *Certain Expenses of the United Nations (Art. 17, Para. 2, of the Charter)*, Adv. Op., ICJ Rep. (1962), at 168. See also *infra*, the text accompanying note 1210.

79 Amerasinghe, *op. cit. supra* n.66, 50.

80 Sinclair, *op. cit. supra* n.16, at 153. See also Dixon, *op. cit. supra* n.40, 63.

81 As observed by Waldock, "in a sense, all 'rules' of interpretation have the character of 'guidelines' since their application in a particular case depends so much on the appreciation of the context and the circumstances of the point to be interpreted." H. Waldock, *Sixth Report on the Law of Treaties*, 2 YBILC (1966) 51-103, at 94.

This is confirmed by an analysis of the case-law of the International Court of Justice, that does not reveal a particularly consistent attitude towards the method of treaty interpretation.[82] Although by and large the Court employs the ordinary meaning reasoning,[83] it has on several occasions used intentional[84] and teleological[85] methods of interpretation in order to provide a solution for the legal problems at stake.

Finally, it must be mentioned that rules of interpretation are sometimes contradictory in themselves. Consider, for example, the aforementioned *règle de la effet utile*, according to which the very provision is included for a reason, and should therefore be made effective. Simultaneously, the *règle de l'efficacité* holds that a provision should be interpreted in accordance with the object and purpose of the organization. In certain situations these two assumptions of the teleological method may conflict. As an example one may refer to the controversy that evolved with regard to the interpretation of Article 43 of the Charter.[86] It can, and has, been argued that the provision was included for a reason, and that in the absence of special agreements provided for by Article 43, the Security Council cannot be engaged in forcible measures under Article 42 of the Charter. On the other hand, such an interpretation would clearly defeat the object and purpose of the organization, *i.e.* the maintenance

---

[82] See T. Sato, *Evolving Constitutions of International Organizations* (1996). His analysis of the Court's methods of interpretation between 1948-1982 reveals that "the Court, under the guiding principle of promoting the effectiveness of international organizations, applied *either the teleological approach* or *the textual approach* whenever the occasion requires." *Loc. cit.*, at 154.

[83] The predominant cases in this respect are the *First and Second Admission* cases (ICJ Rep. (1948), 57 ff. and ICJ Rep. (1950), 4 ff.); and the *Constitution of the Maritime Safety Committee of the Inter-Governmental Maritime Consultative Organization* case, ICJ Rep. (1960), 150 ff. For more recent applications of the textual method by the International Court of Justice see, *e.g.*, the *Arbitral Award of 31 July 1989* (Merits), Guinea Bissau v. Senegal, ICJ Rep. (1991), para. 48 at 69-70; *Land, Island and Maritime Frontier Dispute* (Merits), El Salvador v. Honduras, Nicaragua intervening, ICJ Rep. (1992), paras. 373-380 at 582-586; *Territorial Dispute* (Merits), Libya v. Chad, ICJ Rep. (1994), para. 43 at 21-22; *Maritime Delimitation and Territorial Questions between Qatar and Bahrain* (Jur.), Qatar v. Bahrain, ICJ Rep. (1995), 18.

[84] See, *e.g.*, the *Anglo-Iranian Oil Company* case (Prel. Obj.), UK v. Iran, ICJ Rep. (1952), 105-106.

[85] The *Certain Expenses* case, ICJ Rep. (1962), 151 ff.; the *Reparation for Injuries* case, ICJ Rep. (1949), 171 ff.; and the *Ambatielos* case(Prel. Obj.), Greece v. UK, ICJ Rep. (1952), 28 ff.

[86] Art. 43(1) holds that "all Members of the United Nations, in order to contribute to the maintenance of international peace and security, undertake to make available to the Security Council, on its call and in accordance with a special agreement or agreements, armed forces, assistance, and facilities, including rights of passage, necessary for the purpose of maintaining international peace and security."

of international peace and security. In this case the teleological assumptions lead to contradictory results, casting doubts as to their applicability in all cases.

Bearing in mind the qualifications mentioned above, this work will emphasize the object and purpose of the United Nations in interpreting the Charter. The next chapter will provide an overview of the functions and powers of the Security Council under that instrument.

2.

The Authority of the Security Council under the UN Charter

2.1 Introduction

The following will provide an overview of the functions and powers ascribed to the Security Council by the United Nations Charter, as well as its composition and procedures. Thereto the relevant provisions of the Charter will be analyzed, as well as the main problems encountered in their application by the Organization. The latter reference to the practice will not be exhaustive, since the application by the Council of its Chapter VII powers is described in detail in chapter three. However, as has been established in the preceding chapter, an exposition of the Charter scheme regarding the Security Council based solely on what was intended by the founding states would provide the reader with a rather incomplete picture of the authority of the Council under the United Nations Charter.

2.2 The Establishment of the United Nations

The failure to prevent the outbreak of World War II, and the ensuing demise of the League of Nations,[87] did not mean that the notion of collective security through international organization was altogether abandoned during, and after, the Second World War.[88] In as early as 1941, Prime Minister Churchill and President Roosevelt

---

[87] For an overview see F.P. Walters, *A History of the League of Nations* (1965).

[88] Indeed, according to Grewe "the genesis of the UN began in the very moment in which the

issued the Atlantic Charter, in which they declared that they "hope to see established a peace which will afford to all nations the means of dwelling on safety within their own boundaries." In the "Declaration of United Nations", of 1 January 1942, 26 signatory states adhered to the principles contained in the Atlantic Charter. These general expressions were developed into the "Proposals for the Establishment of a General International Organization" during the two Dumbarton Oaks Conferences in 1944.[89] It was on the basis of these proposals that the United Nations Conference on International Organization (UNCIO) was convened,[90] during which the United Nations Charter was drafted. The Charter was adopted by the Conference on 25 June 1945 and entered into force on 24 October of that year. As can be read in the preamble, the primary objective of the founders of the UN was to "save succeeding generations from the scourge of war". Therefore, the first paragraph of the first article of the Charter states that the purpose of the United Nations is, *inter alia*:

> To maintain international peace and security, and to that end: to take effective collective measures for the prevention and removal of threats to the peace, and for the suppression of acts of aggression or other breaches of the peace, and to bring about by peaceful means, and in conformity with the principles of justice and international law, adjustment or settlement of international disputes or situations which might lead to a breach of the peace.

It is hence safe to say that, at the time of its establishment, the maintenance of international peace and security was the main *raison d 'être* of the Organization.[91]

2.3 Functions and Powers of the Security Council

The Security Council is a principal organ of the United Nations, established together with the General Assembly, the Economic and Social Council, the Trusteeship Council, the International Court of Justice, and the Secretariat, by Article 7. The main

---

collapse of the League became evident." W.G. Grewe, *History*. In: B. Simma, *et. al.* (eds.), The Charter of the United Nations (1994) 1-23, at 2.

89 Attended by France, the UK, and the US; and respectively the Soviet Union (21 Aug. to 28 Sept.) and China (29 Sept. to 7 Oct.). An instructive work on the Conferences is provided by R.C. Hilderbrand, *Dumbarton Oaks: The Origins of the United Nations and the Search for Postwar Security* (1990). The Dumbarton Oaks proposals are reproduced in Doc. 1 G/1, 3 UNCIO Docs. 1-23.

90 The invitation to the conference, the text of which was agreed upon during the Yalta Summit, read that its purpose was to "prepare the Charter of ... an Organization along the lines proposed in the informal conversation of Dumbarton Oaks."

91 See K. Herndl, *Reflections on the Role, Functions and Procedures of the Security Council of the United Nations*, 206 Recueil des Cours (1987) 289-395, 301; Goodrich, *et. al.*, *op. cit. supra* n.48, 25-26.

Charter provisions defining its functions and powers will be presented in numerical order below.

2.3.1 Articles 24 and 25 of the Charter

Firstly, paragraph 1 of Article 24 of the Charter states that:

> In order to ensure prompt and effective action by the United Nations, its Members confer on the Security Council primary responsibility for the maintenance of international peace and security, and agree that in carrying out its duties under this responsibility the Security Council acts on their behalf.

The primary responsibility for the maintenance of international peace and security is thus conferred upon the Security Council under Article 24(1). During the UNCIO, various proposals were put forward which provided for a larger role of the General Assembly in the preservation of international peace.[92] For several reasons, however, these proposals were not adopted. Decisive was that there existed "general agreement as to the paramount importance of the Security Council being placed in a position to act quickly and effectively."[93] Participation of the General Assembly in matters relating to the maintenance of international peace and security would hamper this objective:

> it is impossible to conceive of swift and effective action if the decision of the Council must be submitted to ratification by the Assembly, or if the measures adopted by the Council are susceptible of revision by the Assembly.[94]

It was further noted that the Council included a majority of members elected by the General Assembly. Hence it was optimistically concluded that the Council "must be granted full confidence since, aside from the question of the unanimity of the permanent members, it expresses, in the final analysis, only the opinions of the Assembly."[95]

In the practice of the United Nations, the term "primary" has been interpreted so as not to mean "exclusive". Thus in 1950 the General Assembly, in response to the deadlock that existed in the Security Council, adopted the *Uniting for Peace* resolution,[96] in which it asserted a secondary or subsidiary competence with regard to

---

92 For an overview of the proposed amendments see, *e.g.*, Doc. 360 III/1/16, 11 UNCIO Docs., 767-769.

93 Statement of Mr. Morgenstierne, the Norwegian President of Commission III. Doc. 943 III/5, 11 UNCIO Docs., at 13.

94 Report of Paul-Boncour, 11 UNCIO Docs., at 14.

95 *Ibid.*

96 GA Res. 377(V), 3 Nov. 1950. Adopted by 52 votes to 2, with 2 abstentions.

the maintenance of international peace and security.[97] In pursuance of this secondary competence, the General Assembly established a United Nations Emergency Force (UNEF I) during the 1956 Suez crisis.[98] The legality of the *Uniting for Peace* resolution and the subsequent establishment of UNEF I were strongly opposed by the Soviet Union and its allies. This prompted the General Assembly to request the International Court of Justice for an advisory opinion on the question whether the expenditures of UNEF I and of the Opération des Nations Unies au Congo (ONUC)[99] were expenses of the Organization within the meaning of Article 17(2) of the Charter.[100] In its opinion the Court examined the respective functions of the Security Council and the General Assembly, concluding that "the responsibility conferred [under Article 24(1)] is "primary", not "exclusive."[101] Such Council exclusivity is solely reserved for coercive or enforcement action under Chapter VII of the Charter.[102] According to the Court, however, the peacekeeping operations at stake were *not* enforcement actions. Consequently, the Assembly was competent "to organize peace-keeping operations, at the request or with the consent, of the States concerned" under the first sentence of Article 11(2).[103]

The second paragraph of Article 24 holds:

In discharging these duties the Security Council shall act in accordance with the Purposes and Principles of

---

97 On the resolution see, *e.g.*, B. Nolte, *Uniting for Peace*. In: R. Wolfrum (ed.), United Nations: Law, Policies and Practice (1995) 1341-1348.

98 By GA Res. 1000 (ES-I), adopted – by 57 votes to nil, with two abstentions – at the first emergency session under the mechanism prescribed by the *Uniting for Peace* resolution. For documentation on UNEF I see, *e.g.*, R.C.R. Siekmann, *Basic Documents on United Nations and Related Peace-Keeping Forces* (1989), 3-71.

99 Established by the 'enabling' Security Council resolution 143 (1960), which "authorized" the Secretary-General to take the necessary steps to provide the Republic of Congo with "such military assistance as may be necessary".

100 GA Res. 1731 (XVI), adopted on 20 Dec. 1961.

101 *Certain Expenses of the United Nations (Art. 17, Para. 2, of the Charter)*, Adv. Op., ICJ Rep. (1962), at 163.

102 *Ibid.*

103 *Ibid.*, at 164. This conclusion rests on a specific interpretation of Art. 11(2), which reads: "The General Assembly may discuss any questions relating to the maintenance of international peace and security brought before it by any Member of the United Nations, or by the Security Council, or by a state which is not a Member of the United Nations in accordance with Article 35, paragraph 2, and, except as provided in Article 12, may make recommendations with regard to any such questions to the state or states concerned or to the Security Council or to both. Any such question on which action is necessary shall be referred to the Security Council by the General Assembly either before or after discussion." The Court considered that "the kind of action referred to in Article11(2) is coercive or enforcement action." *Ibid.*

the United Nations. The specific powers granted to the Security Council for the discharge of these duties are laid down in Chapters VI, VII, VIII, and XII.

The first sentence of paragraph 2 indicates that in the discharge of its responsibility, the Council has to act in accordance with the purposes and principles of the organization, which are laid down in Articles 1 and 2 of the Charter. It may be recalled that the first paragraph of Article 1 stipulates that the Council shall act in conformity with the "principles of justice and international law" in settling a dispute. Commentators have noted that the first sentence of Article 24(2) does not automatically warrant the conclusion that the Council is bound by the "principles of justice and international law" in exercising its functions.[104] This holds true because Article 1 distinguishes between collective measures in order to maintain and restore peace, and the peaceful settlement of disputes. The obligation to act in conformity with international law is only prescribed for the latter category, and the negotiating history of the Charter reveals that this was done deliberately. An amendment that would have extended the obligation to act in conformity with the principles of justice and international law to measures taken by the Council pursuant to its responsibility for the maintenance of international peace and security, was rejected by the major powers as curtailing the Council's freedom of (swift) action. The significance of this omission is, however, a matter of debate.[105] Thus, during the discussions at the UNCIO itself, the US delegate argued that "the Charter had to be considered in its entirety and if the Security Council violated its principles and purposes it would be acting *ultra vires*".[106] This interpretation seems to conform to the current understanding that the Council has to observe "at least the limits of the law of the Charter"[107] in exercising its functions.

There is some difficulty with the second sentence of paragraph 2 of Article 24, which refers to the specific powers of the Council for the discharge of the duties mentioned in 24(1). This could be read as an affirmation of the principle that (organs) of international organizations are "competent to act only as far as powers have been attributed to them by the member states."[108] In this restrictive interpretation it is merely

[104] Kelsen, *op. cit. supra* n.51, 294-295; D. Akande, *The International Court of Justice and the Security Council: Is there Room for Judicial Control of Decisions of the Political Organs of the United Nations?*, 46 ICLQ (1997) 318-319.

[105] See Goodrich, *et. al.*, *op. cit. supra* n.48, 27-28; Kelsen, *op. cit. supra* n.51, 291-292; Akande, *op cit supra* n.104, 317-321.

[106] Doc. 555.III/1/27, 11 UNCIO, at 379.

[107] J. Delbrück, *Article 24*. In: B. Simma, *et. al.* (eds.), The Charter of the United Nations (1994) 397-407, at 401.

[108] Schermers, Blokker, *op. cit. supra* n.51, at 141.

declaratory of the "governance of limited enumerated powers".[109] It is, however, generally accepted that the insertion of "specific" powers in paragraph 2 does not imply that the Council is *only* granted the powers mentioned here.[110] Firstly, the Council has additional powers defined in other chapters of the Charter than enumerated in 24(2), notably Chapters IV, V and XIV. Secondly, in the Court's Advisory Opinion on *Namibia* it held that the "reference in paragraph 2 of this Article [24] to specific powers of the Security Council under certain chapters of the Charter does not exclude the existence of general powers to discharge the responsibilities conferred in paragraph 1."[111]

This amounts to a general power of the Council on the basis of Article 24(1), in addition to the specific powers mentioned in Article 24(2). Thirdly, it follows from the Court's dictum in the *Reparation for Injuries* case,[112] that the Council possesses further competences not expressly enumerated in the Charter but necessary for the exercise of its responsibility.[113] The doctrine of implied powers was restated by the International Court of Justice in the *Legality of The Use by a State of Nuclear Weapons in Armed Conflict* advisory opinion as follows:

> international organizations are subjects of international law which do not, unlike States, possess a general competence. International organizations are governed by the "principle of speciality", that is to say, they are invested by the States which create them with powers, the limits of which are a function of the common interests whose promotion those States entrust to them. ... The powers conferred on international organizations are normally the subject of an express statement in their constituent instruments. Nevertheless, the necessities of international life may point to the need for organizations, in order to achieve their objectives, to possess

---

[109] T. Franck, *Fairness in International Law and Institutions* (1995), at 219.

[110] See, *e.g.*, Goodrich, *et. al.*, *op. cit. supra* n.48, 204; Delbrück, *op. cit. supra* n.107, 403; Kelsen, *op. cit. supra* n.51, 283-285; R. Sonnenfeld, *The Obligation of UN Member-States 'to Accept and Carry out the Decisions of the Security Council'*, 8 PYIL (1976) 129-154, 136-137; Herndl, *op. cit. supra* n.91, 326-331. According to the last-mentioned Chapter VI has even "more or less fallen into disuse", in favour of an exercise of the general competence granted to the Council under Art. 24. *Ibid.*, at 331.

[111] *Legal Consequences for States of the Continued Presence of South Africa in Namibia (South West Africa) Notwithstanding Security Council Resolution 276 (1970)*, Adv. Op., ICJ Rep. (1971), para. 110 at 52. Certainly Kelsen would not have agreed with this interpretation, for he submitted that "it is impossible to interpret Article 24 to mean that it confers upon the Council powers not conferred upon it in other Articles of the Charter." Kelsen, *op. cit. supra* n.51, at 284.

[112] The often-quoted passage relating to the implied powers of the organization, holds that: "under international law, the Organization must be deemed to have those powers which, though not expressly provided in the Charter, are conferred upon it by necessary implication as being essential to the performance of its duties." ICJ Rep. (1949), at 182.

[113] See Gill, *op. cit. supra* n.5, 68-72.

subsidiary powers which are not expressly provided for in the basic instruments which govern their activities. It is generally accepted that international organizations can exercise such powers, known as "implied" powers.[114]

The drafters of the Charter were cautious to avoid charging another toothless organ, as the League Council had been, with the supervision of international peace and security. Therefore Article 25 holds that: "The Members of the United Nations agree to accept and carry out the decisions of the Security Council in accordance with the present Charter."

Decisions made by the Council are binding on member states, that much is clear. Several problems, however, arise out of this seemingly unambiguous provision.[115] The first relates to the following question: what exactly amounts to a decision? The second problem is related to the relevance and interpretation of the phrase "in accordance with the present Charter." The Charter itself does not settle the first question, because its terminology in this respect is not very consistent.[116] It is generally acknowledged, for example, that the powers of the Council relating to the pacific settlement of disputes (Chapter VI of the Charter) are recommendatory,[117] and therefore necessarily non-binding. Goodrich, Hambro and Simons, however, refer to the controversy that arose within the Council in relation to Article 34 when it considered the Greek frontier incidents in 1947.[118] The Soviet Union then took the position that "all decisions taken under Chapter VI ... are in the nature of recommendations"[119] and therefore not legally binding. The US, *per contra*, argued that decisions to investigate, taken under Article 34, bind member states.[120]

---

[114] *Legality of The Use by a State of Nuclear Weapons in Armed Conflict*, Adv. Op., ICJ Rep. (1996), para. 25 at 78.

[115] Generally see R. Lagoni, *Resolution, Declaration, Decision*. In: R. Wolfrum (ed.), United Nations: Law, Policies and Practice (1995) 1081-1091; J. Delbrück, *Article 25*. In: B. Simma, *et. al.* (eds.), The Charter of the United Nations (1994) 407-418, 410-413.

[116] Thus, for example, Arts. 15(1), 25, 27(2), 27(3), 37(2), 39, 40, 41, 44, 48, 49, 94(1) of the Charter refer to decisions in one form or another. Arts. 4(2), 5, 6, 36(1), 36(3), 37(2), 38, 39, 93(2), 94(2) and 97 relate to recommendations of the Council. Other phrases include 'acting' or the 'taking of action' (Arts. 24(2) and 42); 'calling upon' (Arts. 33(2) and 40); and 'utilizing' (Art. 53).

[117] See, *e.g.*, Bailey, Daws, *op. cit. supra* n.51, 269-271; C. Eagleton, *The Jurisdiction of the Security Council over Disputes*, 40 AJIL (1946) 513-533, 514; Malanczuk, *op. cit. supra* n.31, 386-387; R. Higgins, *Peace and Security. Achievements and Failures*, 6 EJIL (1995) 445-460, 445-446.

[118] See Goodrich, *et. al.*, *op. cit. supra* n.48, 209.

[119] Statement made during the 167th meeting of the Security Council, 25 July 1947, SCOR., 2nd Yr., at 1541.

[120] *Ibid.* This position corresponds with that of Lagoni, according to whom the "prevailing view" is that the Council may also take binding decisions "with respect to the investigation of disputes

Certainly measures taken by the Council under Chapter VII of the Charter fall into the category of binding decisions. The position, taken by some,[121] that these are the only provisions does not live up to scrutiny, however. A Belgian proposal to specifically limit the undertaking of members to decisions under Chapter VII was rejected during the UNCIO.[122] Moreover, the International Court of Justice has held that "it is not possible to find in the Charter any support" for the contention that "Article 25 of the Charter applies only to enforcement measures adopted under Chapter VII of the Charter."[123] The Court noted that Article 25 is placed immediately after Article 24, and not in Chapter VII. Hence the Court concluded that an interpretation that limits the domain of binding decisions to those decisions taken under Chapter VII would render Article 25 "superfluous, since this [binding] effect is secured by Articles 48 and 49 of the Charter."[124]

The conclusion, therefore, is that one must look at the wording and context of a resolution in order to determine whether the Council intended to issue a decision or a recommendation. In the words of the International Court of Justice:

> the language of a resolution of the Security Council should be carefully analyzed before a conclusion can be made as to its binding effect. In view of the nature of the powers under Article 25, the question whether they have in fact been exercised is to be determined in each case, having regard to the terms of the resolution to be interpreted, the discussions leading to it, the Charter provisions invoked and, in general, all circumstances that might assist in determining the legal consequences of the resolution of the Security Council.[125]

The second issue related to Article 25 is whether the insertion "in accordance with the present Charter" refers to the decisions of the Council, or to the obligations of the

---

(Article 34) and the enforcement of judgments of the ICJ (Article 94 para. 2)." Lagoni, *op. cit. supra* n.115, at 1087.

[121] This was argued by the counsel for South Africa during the proceedings in the 1970 *Namibia* advisory opinion.

[122] See Doc. 597 III/1/30, 11 UNCIO Docs., 393-395. The proposed amendment did receive a majority of 14 to 13 in Committee 1 of Commission III, but thus lacked the necessary two-thirds majority. In view of this, Sonnenfeld correctly observes that "the preparatory work offers no conclusive evidence" as to what Council decisions are to be considered binding. Sonnenfeld, *op. cit. supra* n.110, at 135.

[123] *Legal Consequences for States of the Continued Presence of South Africa in Namibia (South West Africa) Notwithstanding Security Council Resolution 276 (1970)*, Adv. Op., ICJ Rep. (1971), para. 113 at 53.

[124] *Ibid.* On Articles 48 and 49 see *infra*, paragraph 2.3.3. On the *Namibia* Adv. Op. see, *e.g.*, J.A. Frowein, *Article 39*. In: B. Simma, *et. al.* (eds.), The Charter of the United Nations (1994) 605-616, 613-614; and J.A. Frowein, *Collective Enforcement of International Obligations*, 47 ZaöRV (1987) 67-79, 69-70; and R. Higgins, *The Advisory Opinion on Namibia: Which UN Resolutions are Binding Under Article 25 of the Charter?*, 32 ICLQ (1972) 269-286, 286.

[125] *Ibid.*, para. 114 at 53.

member states to accept and carry out these decisions. The wording is ambiguous, and recourse to the *travaux préparatoires* does not resolve this ambiguity.[126] It is generally assumed, however, that it refers to the decisions of the Council, in the sense that they must be decisions which, according to the Charter, are binding.[127]

2.3.2 Chapter VI: 'Pacific Settlement of Disputes'

The responsibility of the Council with regard to international peace and security is specified in Chapters VI and VII. Chapter VI, entitled "Pacific Settlement of Disputes", provides for action by the Council in case of international disputes or situations which do not (yet) pose a threat to international peace and security. Herein its powers are generally confined to making recommendations, the Council can generally not issue binding decisions under Chapter VI.[128] The major competences of the Council under Chapter VI (Articles 33-38) are as follows:

- The making of recommendations on the procedures or methods of adjustment of a dispute (Articles 33(2) and 36(1)).
- The power to investigate a dispute (fact-finding) (Article 34).
- The making of recommendations on the settlement of disputes (Article 37(2) and 38).

2.3.3 Chapter VII: 'International Peace and Security'

The most extensive powers of the Council in pursuance of its responsibility for the maintenance of international peace and security are laid down in Chapter VII, entitled "Action with Respect to Threats to the Peace, Breaches of the Peace, and Acts of Aggression". The system laid down in this Chapter is, in itself, quite simple. According to that system the Council shall first decide whether a particular situation calls for action (Article 39). If such a situation has arisen, it may either make recommendations (Article 39), take provisional measures (Article 40), or decide on enforcement measures not involving the use of force (Article 41), in order to remedy

[126] During discussions on the matter the Australian delegate submitted that the phrasing was unsatisfactory, but the Committee dealing with the structure and procedures of the Council did not come up with an alternative. See Doc. 597 III/1/30, 11 UNCIO Docs., 393-395.

[127] See Goodrich, *et. al.*, *op. cit. supra* n.48, 208. They maintain that members are "obligated to carry out only those decisions that were legally mandatory." See also Kelsen, *op. cit. supra* n.51, 95-96.

[128] Art. 34 being a possible exception. See *supra*, the text accompanying notes 118-120.

the situation. And if the Council considers these non-belligerent measures to be ineffective, it may authorize the use of measures involving the use of force, to put an end to a threat or breach of the peace (Article 42).

A closer look reveals some difficulties with this scheme. Consider (the introductory) Article 39 of Chapter VII, which holds that:

> The Security Council shall determine the existence of any threat to the peace, breach of the peace, or act of aggression and shall make recommendations, or decide what measures shall be taken in accordance with Articles 41 and 42, to maintain or restore international peace and security.

It follows from Article 39 that in order for the Council to make recommendations under it, or to take enforcement measures under Articles 41 and 42, it has first to determine that a threat or breach of the peace, or act of aggression, has occurred.[129] One may ask, however, how international peace – and subsequent threats to and breaches of it – is to be defined.[130] The Charter itself is silent on the term, and the *travaux préparatoires* indicate that this was done deliberately. During the UNCIO, the wide discretion afforded to the Council in the Dumbarton Oaks proposals as regards the determination of which situations pose a threat to international peace and security, was a matter of serious debate. After consideration, however, it was decided "to leave to the Council the entire decision, and also the entire responsibility for that decision, as to what constitutes a threat to the peace, a breach of the peace, or an act of aggression."[131]

Hence a first reading of Article 39 and the *travaux préparatoires* suggests that "it is completely within the discretion of the Security Council to decide what constitutes a 'threat to the peace.'"[132] Or in the words of Malanczuk: "a threat to the peace seems to be whatever the Security Council says is a threat to the peace".[133]

---

129 See F.L. Kirgis, *The Security Council's First Fifty Years*, 89 AJIL (1995) 506-539, 512; Gowlland-Debbas, *op. cit. supra* n.2, 61.

130 Generally see H. Neuhold, *Threat to the Peace*, 3 EPIL (1997) 935-938.

131 Doc. 943 III/5, 11 UNCIO Docs., at 17.

132 Kelsen, *op. cit. supra* n.51, at 727.

133 Malanczuk, *op. cit. supra* n.31, at 426. Similarly, Reisman notes that the: "United Nations system was essentially designed to enable the Permanent Five, if all agree, to use Charter obligations and the symbolic authority of the organization as they think appropriate to maintain or restore international peace, as they define it." W.M. Reisman, *Peacemaking*, 18 Yale JIL (1993) 415-423, at 418. Kooijmans similarly refers to "the complete discretion the Security Council has with regard to the interpretation of the three concepts 'threat to the peace', 'breach of the peace' and 'act of aggression'." P.H. Kooijmans, *The Enlargement of the Concept 'Threat to the Peace'*. In: J.R. Dupuy, The Development of the Role of the Security Council (1993) 111-121, at 111. See also *infra*, paragraph 5.3.5, in which the definition of international peace is assessed in greater detail.

On a minimum level the term peace includes the absence of inter-state use of force,[134] which may be called the negative definition of peace.[135] It is questionable, however, whether the understanding of the term according to this minimum content suffices.[136] The practice of the Council certainly indicates that it adopts a more positive approach to peace.[137]

Similar semantic difficulties arise with "an act of aggression", the latter being, according to one commentator, "without doubt ... the most controversial word in modern international law".[138] During the UNCIO it was decided against the inclusion of a definition of aggression, the inclusion of which was proposed by some states in order to ensure that the Council would take appropriate action in such cases, and in order to deter states from engaging in aggressive acts. The majority view, however, was that such a listing would be "necessarily incomplete", so that the Council "would have a tendency to consider of less importance the acts not mentioned therein." Furthermore, it was felt that the inclusion of definitions was risky: "automatic action by the Council might bring about a premature application of enforcement measures."[139]

The current understanding of an "act of aggression" involves the (first)[140] use of

---

134 *Cf.* Art. 2(4) of the Charter, which holds that: "All Members shall refrain in their international relations from the threat or use of force against the territorial integrity or political independence of any state, or in any other manner inconsistent with the Purposes of the United Nations."

135 Which is the most common usage. Thus the Shorter Oxford English Dictionary (1993) describes peace as "freedom from, or cessation of, war or hostilities; the or a state of a nation or community in which it is not at war with another." According to Jennings, "the United Nations Charter was drafted in the belief that the danger to be dealt with was the orthodox war between clear sovereign states." R.Y. Jennings, *Broader Perspectives in International Law*. In: A. Anghie, G. Sturgess (eds.), Legal Visions of the 21st Century: Essays in Honour of Judge Christopher Weeramantry (1998) 497-507, at 501.

136 Certainly the resolutions of the GA in which it has (partially) defined peace, go beyond this minimal content. See, *e.g.*, "Essentials for Peace", Res. 290 (IV), 1 Dec. 1949; "Peace through deeds", Res. 380 (V), 17 Nov. 1950; "Peaceful and Neighborly relations among states", Res. 1236 (XII), 14 Dec. 1957.

137 See K. Skubiszewski, *Peace and War*, 4 EPIL (1982) 74-78, 74-75; D. Blumenwitz, *Maintenance of International Peace and Security*. In: R. Wolfrum (ed.), United Nations: Law, Policies and Practice (1995) 865-870. The entry for peace in J.R. Fox, Dictionary of International and Comparative Law (1992) states: "more than the absence of war, peace includes cooperation and respect among states and the amicable settlement of disagreements." The practice of the Council will be considered in detail *infra*, in chapter 3.

138 T.W. Bennet, *A Linguistic Perspective of the Definition of Aggression*, 31 GYIL (1988) 48-69, at 48.

139 Doc. 943 III/5, 11 UNCIO Docs., at 17.

140 *Cf.* Bennet, *op. cit. supra* n.138, at 61: "Aggressive acts are unilateral in the sense that they do not follow as consequences of external causes." See also Art. 2 of the "Definition of Aggression", annexed to GA Res. 3314 XXIX, 14 Dec. 1974, which holds that: "The first use of armed force by a State in

armed force and the designation of a guilty party. In its practice, however, the Council has seldom designated a guilty party under these terms.[141]

As observed by Kelsen, the inclusion of the power to make recommendations in Article 39, in addition to its powers already mentioned in Articles 37(2) and 38, is somewhat oblique. Recommendations made under Article 39 would therefore only seem "justifiable in case of a threat of the peace if the Security Council had no opportunity of making recommendations in earlier stage of affairs."[142] Whether or not the wording "shall" means that it was intended that the Council is obliged to make a determination in every situation that may be considered a threat to, or a breach of, the international peace, or an act of aggression, seems to have been settled negatively by the Council's practice. The paralysis of the organ prior to 1989 generally precluded the organ from making determinations under Article 39.[143]

Prior, and supplementary, to the measures contemplated in Articles 41 and 42, the Council may take preventive provisional measures under Article 40:

> In order to prevent an aggravation of the situation, the Security Council may, before making the recommendations or deciding upon the measures provided for in Article 39, call upon the parties concerned to comply with such provisional measures as it deems necessary or desirable. Such provisional measures shall be without prejudice to the rights, claims, or position of the parties concerned. The Security Council shall duly take account of failure to comply with such provisional measures.

Given its incorporation in Chapter VII, the application of Article 40 seems to require a prior determination of the Council pursuant to Article 39.[144] Doubts have been cast as to the binding character of measures taken under Article 40. The general opinion is that this depends on the intention of the Council, and that the Council may both make recommendations and take binding decisions under Article 40.[145]

---

contravention of the Charter shall constitute *prima facie* evidence of an act of aggression". For an analysis of the resolution see, *e.g.*, B.B. Ferencz, *Defining Aggression: Where it Stands and Where it's Going*, 66 AJIL (1972) 491-508; J. Stone, *Hopes and Loopholes in the 1974 Definition of Aggression*, 71 AJIL (1977) 221-246; and T. Bruha, *Die Definition der Aggression* (1980).

141 An example is S/Res. 507 (1982), on which see *infra*, note 210.

142 Kelsen, *op. cit. supra* n.51, at 734.

143 According to Kelsen, one can only speak of a legal obligation if a sanction is provided for the non-performance of that obligation. Since the Charter does not provide for any sanctions against organs, "it makes no legal difference whether the Charter stipulates that an organ 'may' or that an organ 'shall' perform a definite function. In both cases the organ is legally authorised, not obliged ... to act as determined by the Charter." *Ibid.*, at 154.

144 See J.A. Frowein, *Article 40*. In: B. Simma, *et. al.* (eds.), The Charter of the United Nations (1994) 617-621, 618. See also Kelsen, *op. cit. supra* n.51, 739; Goodrich, *et. al.*, *op. cit. supra* n.48, 303; and R. Sonnenfeld, *Resolutions of the United Nations Security Council* (1988), 92.

145 See Kelsen, *op. cit. supra* n.51, 740-744; Frowein, *op. cit. supra* n.144, 620; Goodrich, *et. al.*, *op. cit.*

Article 41 of the Charter reads:

> The Security Council may decide what measures not involving the use of armed force are to be employed to give effect to its decisions, and it may call upon the Members of the United Nations to apply such measures. These may include complete or partial interruption of economic relations and of rail, sea, air, postal, telegraphic, radio, and other means of communication, and the severance of diplomatic relations.

This is a departure from the League system, in which it was left to the individual members to apply non-forcible sanctions.[146] The provision is somewhat awkwardly phrased, for a literal interpretation implies that the measures under Article 41 are taken in order to 'give effect to' decisions taken under different provisions of the Charter. This is not the case: Article 41 itself provides the basis for making such decisions and the taking of measures to ensure their implementation.[147] It is clear from the permissive language ("may include") that the specific examples of non-forcible measures mentioned here are not to be seen as exhaustive.[148] The drafting history suggests that the application of measures by virtue of Article 41 is not dependent on a prior application of provisional measures under Article 40.[149]

The crux of Chapter VII is Article 42, which reads as follows:

> Should the Security Council consider that measures provided for in Article 41 would be inadequate or have proved to be inadequate, it may take such action by air, sea, or land forces as may be necessary to maintain or restore international peace and security. Such action may include demonstrations, blockade, and other operations by air, sea, or land forces of Members of the United Nations.

A preliminary question is whether the recourse to forcible measures is conditional on the prior application of measures under Article 41, and a subsequent finding of the Council that these measures have been inadequate or ineffective. The text (the phrase "would be inadequate") and the drafting history[150] indicate that this is not necessary, meaning that the Council may utilize Article 42 if it foresees that non-violent measures will be inadequate.[151] An Article 39 determination, however, is a necessary condition

---

supra n.48, 306-308.

146 See Art. 16(1) of the League Covenant.

147 J.A. Frowein, *Article 41*. In: B. Simma, *et. al.* (eds.), The Charter of the United Nations (1994) 621-628, at 624; Kelsen, *op. cit. supra* n.51, 744.

148 J.P. Cot, A. Pellet, *La Charte des Nations Unies* (1985), 695.

149 The UNCIO Drafting Committee 3 on 'Enforcement Arrangements' was "unanimous in the belief that ... in the case of flagrant aggression imperiling the existence of a member of the organization, enforcement measures should be taken without delay, and to the full extent required by the circumstances." Report of Paul-Boncour, Doc. 881/III/3/46, 12 UNCIO Docs. 502 ff., at 507.

150 See the 'Statement of the Rapporteur', Doc. 134/III/3/3, 12 UNCIO Docs., 572 ff., at 573.

151 In the words of Frowein: "it is sufficient that the SC opts immediately for Art. 42 on the basis

for measures taken under both Articles 41 and 42.[152]

Article 42 seems to refer to action taken by the organization itself. Strictly speaking, this is not true. Goodrich, Hambro and Simons have noted that the architects of the Charter generally had three alternatives on how to supply the Council with the armed forces necessary for carrying out its decisions.[153] The first was an international standing force under the control of the United Nations organization. This did not prove to be acceptable as it was too strong an encroachment on national sovereignty.[154] The second alternative was to establish *ad hoc* coalitions of national forces under some form of international control. This closely resembled the League of Nations system, which had been discredited by its failure to prevent World War II, and was therefore rejected. The third option was that of national forces supplied to the Council by the United Nations members by advance agreement. The latter formula was adopted, and therefore Article 43 of the Charter provides for the conclusion of special agreements between member states and the Security Council,[155] by which the members make troops available to the Council.[156] In addition, Article 47(1) establishes a Military Staff Committee, that was to be responsible for assisting the Council in planning the application of armed force;[157] the strategic direction of the armed forces placed under the authority of the Council;[158] and generally to advise and assist the Council on all questions relating to the Council's military requirements for the maintenance of international peace and security.[159] The absence of agreement on the specific modalities of the use of force during the UNCIO is reflected by the second sentence of Article 47(3), according to which questions relating to the command of armed forces placed at the disposal of the Security Council "shall be worked out subsequently."

---

of a prognosis of the possible ineffectiveness of measures under Art. 41." J.A. Frowein, *Article 42*. In: B. Simma, *et. al.* (eds.), The Charter of the United Nations (1994) 628-636, at 631.

152 See *infra*, text accompanying notes 682 and 813.

153 Goodrich, *et. al.*, *op. cit. supra* n.48, 317-319. See also the 'Summary Report' of the 2nd meeting of Committee III/3, Doc. 140/III/3/4, 12 UNCIO Docs., 278 ff., at 278-279. For a discussion of the negotiations on these matters during the Dumbarton Oaks Conference see Hilderbrand, *op. cit. supra* n.89, 141-158.

154 For recent discussions of such standing forces see *infra*, the text accompanying notes 713-716.

155 On Art. 43 generally, see J.W. Houck, *The Commander in Chief and United Nations Charter Article 43: A Case of Irreconcilable Differences?*, 12 Dickinson JIL (1993) 1-28.

156 See Art. 45, according to which the Members of the Organization "shall hold immediately available national air-force contingents for combined international enforcement action".

157 Art. 46.

158 Art. 47(3).

159 Art. 47(1). See also Art. 25, second sentence.

The system regarding the use of force by the Council established under Chapter VII has effectively fallen into desuetude. To begin with, the special agreements mentioned in Article 43 have never been concluded, whilst the Military Staff Committee has effectively remained dormant since the submission of its report on the questions mentioned in Article 47(3) in 1947.[160] The drafters of the Charter seem to have taken into account that agreements under Article 43 would be not be concluded, or only with substantial delays, for Article 106, placed in Chapter XVII (entitled "Transitional Security Arrangements"), provides that:

> Pending the coming into force of such special agreements referred to in Article 43 as in the opinion of the Security Council enable it to begin the exercise of its responsibilities under Article 42, the parties to the Four-Nation Declaration, signed at Moscow October 30, 1943, and France, shall, in accordance with the provisions of paragraph 5 of that Declaration, consult with one another and as occasion requires with other Members of the United Nations with a view to such joint action on behalf of the Organization as may be necessary for the purpose of maintaining international peace and security.

In practice, the application of force pursuant to Article 42 is not coordinated by the Council, but applied by the members directly,[161] in accordance with the decisions of the Council.[162] Indeed, in the *Certain Expenses* case the International Court of Justice held that the taking of enforcement action by the Council is not dependent on agreements concluded *ex* Article 43:

> an argument which insists that all measures taken for the maintenance of international peace and security must be financed through agreements concluded under Article 43, would seem to exclude the possibility that the Security Council might act under some other Article of the Charter. The Court cannot accept so limited a view of the powers of the Security Council under the Charter. It cannot be said that the Charter has left the Security Council impotent in the face of an emergency situation when agreements under Article 43 have not been concluded.[163]

---

[160] SCOR (2), Special Suppl. 1, 424 ff. On the functioning of the Committee see Bailey, Daws, *op. cit. supra* n.51, 274-281.

[161] *Cf.* Art. 48:
"1. The action required to carry out the decisions of the Security Council for the maintenance of international peace and security shall be taken by all the Members of the United Nations or by some of them, as the Security Council may determine.
2. Such decisions shall be carried out by the Members of the United Nations directly and through their action in the appropriate international agencies of which they are members."

[162] Schachter notes on Art. 43 agreements that "during the early years, and even recently, it was thought that such agreements were a condition precedent to collective military measures undertaken by the Security Council." O. Schachter, *Authorized Uses of Force by the United Nations and Regional Organizations*. In: L.F. Damrosch, D.J. Scheffer (eds.), Law and Force in the New International Order (1991), at 68.

[163] *Certain Expenses of the United Nations* case, ICJ Rep. (1962), at 167.

Despite the non-use of Article 43, its inclusion does provide for an important limitation on the Council's power to apply force under Article 42. Such application depends on the consent of member states: "operations can only be carried out with *ad hoc* troops provided voluntarily".[164] This is inferred from paragraph 3 of Article 43, which holds that the special agreements between the Council and members "shall be subject to ratification by the signatory states in accordance with their respective constitutional processes." Since member states cannot be obliged to provide troops under Article 43 without their consent (the ratification requirement), the same holds true *mutatis mutandis* for providing troops pursuant to a request made by the Council under Article 42.[165]

Article 48(1) reaffirms the obligation of the member states to carry out the decisions of the Council already mentioned in Article 25,[166] whilst the second paragraph provides that these decisions "shall be carried out by the Members of the United Nations directly and through their action in the appropriate international agencies of which they are members."[167] In the latter case Chapter VIII applies, which regulates the relationship between the Security Council and regional arrangements or agencies.[168]

---

[164] J.A. Frowein, *Article 43*. In: B. Simma, *et. al.* (eds.), The Charter of the United Nations (1994) 636-639, at 639. *Cf.* the Report of Paul-Boncour, Doc. 881/III/3/46, 12 UNCIO Docs. 502 ff., at 508; L.M. Goodrich, E. Hambro, *Charter of the United Nations* (1949), 279-280; Higgins, *op. cit. supra* n.117, 447; J.J. Paust, *Peace-making and Security Council Powers: Bosnia-Herzegovina Raises International and Constitutional Questions*, 19 Southern Illinois University Law Journal (1994) 131-151, 143.

[165] See Schachter, *op. cit. supra* n.162, 69-71. The requirement of consent by the troop-providing state becomes all the more apparent when Article 43 is read in conjunction with Article 44. The latter holds that: "When the Security Council has decided to use force it shall, before calling upon a Member not represented on it to provide armed forces in fulfilment of the obligations assumed under Article 43, invite that Member, if the Member so desires, to participate in the decisions of the Security Council concerning the employment of contingents of that Member's armed forces."

[166] See also Art. 49, according to which "the Members of the United Nations shall join in affording mutual assistance in carrying out the measures decided upon by the Security Council."

[167] According to Bryde, Art. 48 "aims at flexibility in the execution of enforcement measures." B.O. Bryde, *Article 48*. In: B. Simma, *et. al.* (eds.), The Charter of the United Nations (1994) 651-655, at 653.

[168] According to Hummer and Schweitzer, military pacts such as NATO do not fall into this category. See W. Hummer, M. Schweitzer, *Article 52*. In: B. Simma, *et. al.* (eds.), The Charter of the United Nations (1994) 679-722, 690-691. According to them, a regional agency or arrangement may be defined as "a union of states or an international organization based upon a collective treaty or a constitution and consistent with the Purposes and Principles of the UN, whose primary task is the maintenance of peace and security under the control and within the framework of the UN." *Ibid.*, at 699. Applying this definition they conclude that only three international organizations, the OAS, the OAU and the League of Arab States fall within the terms of Art. 52. Similarly, Bothe submits that "NATO or WEU are not regional arrangements within the meaning of Article 53 of the United Nations Charter." M. Bothe, *The Legitimacy of the Use of Force to Protect Peoples and*

Article 52(1), placed in Chapter VIII, holds that:

> Nothing in the present Charter precludes the existence of regional arrangements or agencies for dealing with such matters relating to the maintenance of international peace and security as are appropriate for regional action, provided that such arrangements or agencies and their activities are consistent with the Purposes and Principles of the United Nations.

Indeed, the Charter seems to prefer 'local' dispute settlement, since Article 52(2) stipulates that members of the UN shall first attempt to settle local disputes through such regional arrangements before referring them to the Security Council.[169] In addition, enforcement measures taken under Articles 41 and 42, may be implemented by regional arrangements or agencies.[170] Conversely, regional agencies may not take enforcement action without due authorization by the Council.[171] The latter provision exemplifies the changes in the *jus ad bellum* established by the Charter: with the exception of self-defence, states may not unilaterally or collectively resort to force failing an authorization or call thereto by the Security Council.[172]

Minorities. In: C. Brölmann, *et. al.* (eds.), Peoples and Minorities in International Law (1993) 289-299, at 298. Simma also contends that "NATO is not a regional organization in the sense of Chapter VIII of the Charter." B. Simma, *NATO, the UN and the Use of Force: Legal Aspects*, 10 EJIL (1999) 1-22, at 10. *Cf.* also J. Wolf, *Regional Arrangements and the UN Charter*, 6 EPIL (1983) 289-295. In its recent practice, however, the Security Council has mandated NATO to carry out decisions of the Council. See *infra*, paragraph 3.6.2.5. Indeed, according to Wolfrum, Security Council resolution 787 (1992) has broadened the concept so as to include NATO. See R. Wolfrum, *Der Beitrag regionaler Abmachungen zur Friedenssicherung: Möglichkeiten und Grenzen*, 53 ZäöRV (1993) 576-602. See to the same effect D.A. Leurdijk, *Before and After Dayton: The UN and NATO in the Former Yugoslavia*. In: T.G. Weiss (ed.), Beyond UN Subcontracting: Task-Sharing with Regional Security Arrangements and Service-Providing NGOs (1998) 49-66, 51-52.

169 For recent examples see *infra*, paragraphs 3.5, 3.6 and 3.12.

170 Art. 53(1). For a discussion of the relationship between the Security Council and regional arrangements see, *e.g.*, Z. Deen-Racsmány, *A Redistribution of Authority Between the UN and Regional Organizations in the Field of the Maintenance of Peace and Security*, 13 LJIL (2000) 297-331; C. Gray, *Regional Arrangements and the United Nations Collective Security System*. In: H. Fox (ed.), The Changing Constitution of the United Nations (1997) 91-116.

171 In the case of Kosovo, NATO used armed force absent a clear authorization by the Security Council, which has led to doubts as to its legality. Similar doubts have been raised in the case of unilateral and bilateral strikes against Iraq in order to enforce compliance with United Nations sanctions. See *infra*, the text accompanying notes 467-469, respectively 326-331.

172 *Cf.* Gardam, who submits that "the only current source of *ius ad bellum* is the Charter itself. Under the UN Charter, the use of force is restricted to self-defence under Article 51 and collective enforcement action under Chapter VII." J.G. Gardam, *Legal Restraints on Security Council Military Enforcement Action*, 17 MJIL (1996) 285-322, at 295. In addition, it is sometimes maintained that customary international law recognizes a right of humanitarian intervention, that is a right of armed intervention on humanitarian grounds. The literature on this alleged right is extensive. See, *e.g.*, R.B. Lillich (ed.), *Humanitarian Intervention and the United Nations* (1973); F.R. Téson,

2.4 The Exception: Self-Defence

The United Nations Charter aims to establish a Security Council monopoly on the power to take decisions to use force in international relations.[173] Thus Article 2(4) contains a general obligation for states not to use force in their relations. The exception is provided by Article 51, according to which:

> Nothing in the present Charter shall impair the inherent right of individual or collective self-defence if an armed attack occurs against a Member of the United Nations, until the Security Council has taken measures necessary to maintain international peace and security. Measures taken by Members in the exercise of this right of self-defence shall be immediately reported to the Security Council and shall not in any way affect the authority and responsibility of the Security Council under the present Charter to take at any time such action as it deems necessary in order to maintain or restore international peace and security.

Thus, albeit the 'inherent right to self-defence'[174] in case of an armed attack is not impaired by the Charter, in principle the right is subsumed by the Security Council once the Council has taken the measures necessary for the restoration of international

---

Humanitarian Intervention: An Inquiry into Law and Morality (1997); P. Malanczuk, *Humanitarian Intervention and the Legitimacy of the Use of Force* (1993); G. Ezejiofor, E.K. Quashigah, *The United Nations and Humanitarian Intervention in the Contemporary World Situation*, ASICL, 5th Annual Congress (1993) 36-63; S.D. Murphy, *Humanitarian Intervention: The United Nations in an Evolving World Order* (1996).

[173] See H. Kelsen, *Collective Security and Collective Self-Defense under the Charter of the United Nations*, 42 AJIL (1948) 783-796, 784.

[174] Art. 51, and in particular the term "inherent", has given rise to much debate. A great deal of the confusion is due to the fact that the term 'inherent', in the words of Kelsen, "presupposes the existence of the right of self-defence as established, not by positive international law, but by natural law". Kelsen, *op. cit. supra* n.51, at 791. Aside from this terminological confusion, at least two interpretations of the right of self-defence under Article 51 are possible. According to the restrictive interpretation, which prevails, individual or collective self-defence is only justified when an armed attack has occurred. In this view Article 51 refers to the right of non-United Nations members to defend themselves against an armed attack. The extensive interpretation maintains that Art. 51 does not intend to interfere with the customary right of self-defence, a right that is sometimes said to include the right to protect the lives and property of a state's nationals abroad, and thus is not restricted to instances in which armed attacks against a state have occurred. See A. Randelzhofer, *Article 51*. In: B. Simma, *et. al.* (eds.), The Charter of the United Nations (1994) 661-678, 666-667; K.C. Kenny, *Self-Defence*. In: R. Wolfrum (ed.), United Nations: Law, Policies and Practice (1995) 1162-1170, 1163-1164; J. Combacau, *The Exception of Self-Defence in U.N. Practice*. In: A. Cassese (ed.), The Current Legal Regulation of the Use of Force (1986) 9-38, 11-12. It may be noted that in the *Nicaragua* case the International Court of Justice confirmed that the customary right of self-defence existed alongside Art. 51, but stated that its scope and content corresponds almost exactly to Art. 51. *I.e.* it is limited to a reaction to an armed attack. *Case Concerning Military and Paramilitary Activities in and Against Nicaragua* (Merits), Nic. v. US, ICJ Rep. (1986), para. 188. For a discussion of the judgment see, *e.g.*, H.G. Maier (ed.), *Appraisals of the ICJ's Decision: Nicaragua v. United States (Merits)*, 81 AJIL (1987) 77-183.

peace and security.[175] The wording also seems to imply that a state exercising its right of (collective) self-defence is obliged to report its measures to the Council.[176]

These far-reaching provisions notwithstanding, the Council's inability to act during the first 45 years of its existence have made them, in the words of one observer, "almost devoid of practical significance."[177] It was not until the 1990s that the correct interpretation of Article 51 regained its importance.[178]

2.5 Relationship with other Organs

As seen above, Article 24 confers primary responsibility for the maintenance of international peace and security on the Security Council. Other principal organs, however, also have responsibilities in this field, notably the International Court of Justice and the General Assembly.

The International Court of Justice, the principal judicial organ of the United Nations, is the only organ other than the Security Council that has the power to issue externally binding decisions. That is to say, provided that states have expressed their consent to have their disputes adjudicated by the Court, its decisions bind those states. Moreover, the Court can also clarify the legal underpinnings of certain actions of the organization in an advisory opinion. Although these opinions are strictly speaking recommendatory, they can (de)legitimize these actions, and the organs of the United Nations would be obliged to take the opinions of the Court into account. It can occur, and indeed it has happened, that the Court and Council are simultaneously seized of

---

[175] Randelzhofer, *op. cit. supra* n.174, 676. Similarly, Greig submits that "implicit in the formulation of Article 51 ... is the notion that the reporting of measures would normally be a prelude to action of some sort by the Security Council that would bring to an end the need for the State, which has been the victim of an armed attack, to continue to exercise its right of self-defense." D.W. Greig, *Self-defense and the Security Council: What does Article 51 Require?*, 40 ICLQ (1991) 366-403, at 366-367.

[176] See, *e.g.*, O. Schachter, *Self-Defense and the Rule of Law*, 83 AJIL (1989) 259-277, 263 and para. 44 of the Advisory Opinion of the International Court of Justice on the *Legality of the Threat or Use Of Nuclear Weapons*, 8 July 1996. Therein the Court stated that "Article 51 specifically requires that measures taken by States in the exercise of the right of self-defence shall be immediately reported to the Security Council." In the *Nicaragua* case, however, the International Court of Justice held that the lawfulness of the use of force in self-defence under customary law is not dependent on compliance with this requirement. *Case Concerning Military and Paramilitary Activities in and Against Nicaragua* (Merits), Nic. v. US, ICJ Rep. (1986), para. 200.

[177] Randelzhofer, *op. cit. supra* n.174, at 677.

[178] In particular by virtue of *Operation Desert Storm* in Iraq, on which see *infra*, paragraphs 3.4.2.2 and 3.4.4.

a matter. This has created complex jurisdictional issues, which will be taken up later.[179]

Although Article 10 stipulates that the General Assembly "may discuss any questions or any matters within the scope of the present Charter or relating to the powers and functions of any organs provided for in the present Charter", Article 12(1) regulates potential jurisdictional conflicts between the Council and Assembly. It provides that:

> while the Security Council is exercising in respect of any dispute or situation the functions assigned to it in the present Charter, the General Assembly shall not make any recommendation with regard to that dispute or situation unless the Security Council so requests.

This provision has not precluded the Assembly from asserting a larger competence with regard to the maintenance of international peace and security. An example hereof is the *Uniting for Peace* resolution mentioned in the beginning of this chapter, by which the General Assembly assumed additional responsibilities for the maintenance of international peace and security in the light of the voting-paralysis in the Security Council during the Cold War.[180] In view of Article 24(1), which confers primary responsibility for the maintenance of international peace and security on the Security Council, the legality of this resolution and the ensuing actions were challenged by several member states of the United Nations. These challenges eventually led to a request for an advisory opinion of the International Court of Justice on the question whether the expenses of certain operations, pursuant to the *Uniting for Peace* resolution, were regular expenses of the organization to be borne by its members according to the apportionment by the General Assembly.[181] Commenting on the Assembly, one author has concluded that there is a "practice that has developed since 1960 under which the Assembly considers itself free to adopt recommendations on matters that are actively dealt with by the Council and simultaneously with the Council's exercise of functions in respect of those matters."[182]

Thus, issues of respective competences may also arise in the relationship between the Security Council and the General Assembly. Resolutions of the Assembly are legally non-binding, however.[183] The problem of both organs issuing contradictory binding

---

179 See *infra*, paragraphs 5.3.2.1-5.3.4.5.

180 On the voting-paralysis in the Council see *infra*, the text accompanying notes 1253-1254.

181 The 1962 *Certain Expenses* case, ICJ Rep. (1962). Herein the Court held that these expenses were indeed regular expenses of the Organization.

182 Y.Z. Blum, *Eroding the United Nations Charter* (1993), at 130.

183 Except for decisions related to the internal law of the United Nations, such as decisions on the budget of the organization.

decisions is therefore non-existent. Suffice it here to mention that "a general duty to co-operate exists", which has been called the principle of organ loyalty.[184]

2.6 Composition and Procedure of the Council

The Security Council is currently composed of fifteen members,[185] five of which have a permanent seat: China, France, Russia,[186] the UK and the US. The non-permanent members are elected by the GA for a two-year period.[187] In line with the requirement of an "equitable geographical distribution", mentioned in the third sentence of Article 23(1), the ten non-permanent members are composed of 5 African and Asian states, 2 Latin American and Caribbean, 2 Western, and 1 Eastern European state.[188]

Article 28(2) stipulates that the Council "shall be so organized as to be able to function continuously." It is therefore provided that each member shall be represented at all times at the seat of the organization, and that the Council holds meetings with intervals not exceeding fourteen days.[189] They can be convened after a request by any state (member or non-member of the United Nations);[190] the General Assembly;[191] the Secretary-General[192]; or at the discretion of the President of the Council.[193]

During the negotiations on the establishment of the United Nations, one of the most complicated matters proved to be the voting procedure. The Dumbarton Oaks proposals provided for a permanent seat for the five major powers.[194] In addition, the

---

[184] M. Hilf, *Article 29*. In: B. Simma, *et. al.* (eds.), The Charter of the United Nations (1994) 480-486, at 485.

[185] Art. 23(1). An amendment to this article entered into force on 31 Aug. 1965, by which the membership of the Council was increased from eleven to fifteen members.

[186] The Russian Federation took over the seat of the Soviet Union in 1991 without any formal amendment of the Charter. For an assessment see Y.Z. Blum, *Russia Takes Over the Soviet Union's Seat at the United Nations*, 3 EJIL (1992) 345-361.

[187] Art. 27(1).

[188] See *nfra*, note 1269.

[189] Rule 1 of the Provisional Rules of Procedure, adopted by the Council pursuant to Art. 30 of the Charter. If there is no item that warrants consideration by the Council, this fourteen-day requirement may be waived. Bailey, Daws, *op. cit. supra* n.51, 23.

[190] Arts. 35(1), 35(2), 94(2), and Rule 3 of the Provisional Rules of Procedure.

[191] Arts. 11(2), 11(3) and Rule 3 of the Provisional Rules of Procedure.

[192] Art. 99 and Rule 3 of the Provisional Rules of Procedure.

[193] Rule 1 of the Provisional Rules of Procedure.

[194] A US proposal that Brazil be granted a permanent seat as the representative of Latin America was not adopted due to the opposition of the Soviet Union. See Hilderbrand, *op. cit. supra* n.89, 123-127.

proposals included a right of veto for the permanent members on substantive matters. During the Dumbarton Oaks Conference, however, agreement could not be reached on the question whether a permanent member was to be allowed to exercise its veto when that member was involved in a dispute under consideration by the Security Council. The UK favoured abstention in these matters, whilst the Soviet Union insisted on the applicability of the veto in all cases. In the end a compromise was formulated during the Yalta summit, according to which members of the Council involved in a dispute under consideration by the Council, were to abstain from voting (only) in the event of the Council exercising its powers under Chapter VI. The Yalta formula was opposed by the smaller and medium-sized states, but on various occasions the major powers made it clear that there could be no deviation from it.[195]

The text governing the voting procedure of the Council is incorporated in Article 27 of the Charter, which provides that:

1. Each member of the Security Council shall have one vote.
2. Decisions of the Security Council on procedural matters shall be made by an affirmative vote of nine members.
3. Decisions of the Security Council on all other matters shall be made by an affirmative vote of nine members including the concurring votes of the permanent members; provided that, in decisions under Chapter VI, and under paragraph 3 of Article 52, a party to a dispute shall abstain from voting.

Problems similar to the question of what constitutes a binding decision under Article 25 arise from paragraph 3 of this provision, for the Charter does not provide for a clear distinction between procedural (or substantive) and non-procedural matters. Furthermore, as observed by Kelsen, things are complicated by the fact that such distinctions have "no fixed meaning, but change their significance according to the standpoint from which they are viewed. The same matter may be 'procedural' from one point of view and 'substantive' from another."[196]

In general, however, there has been agreement between the members of the Council that the following categories of matters are non-procedural in the sense of Article 27(3):[197]

---

[195] Indeed, "the sponsoring governments made it clear that complete acceptance of the Yalta Formula without any changes was a *conditio sine qua non* for the adoption of the Charter." B. Simma, S. Brunner, *Article 27*. In: B. Simma, *et. al.* (eds.), The Charter of the United Nations (1994) 430-469, at 436. See also Fassbender, *op. cit. supra* n.46, 163-170; D.E. Lee, *The Genesis of the Veto*, 1 International Organization (1947) 33-42.

[196] Kelsen, *op. cit. supra* n.51, at 246-247.

[197] Simma, Brunner, *op. cit. supra* n.195, 438-439; Goodrich, *et. al.*, *op. cit. supra* n.48, 223. For an extensive overview of the matters treated as non-procedural by the Council see Fassbender, *op. cit. supra* n.46, 333-334.

- Matters relating to the Council's discharge of its responsibility for the maintenance of international peace and security under Chapters VI and VII.
- Matters relating to the admission, expulsion of members, and the suspension of their membership rights (Articles 4, 5 and 6).
- Matters relating to the execution of judgments by the International Court of Justice (Article 94) and the request for an advisory opinion of the International Court of Justice (Article 96).
- Recommendations for the appointment of the Secretary-General (Article 97).

Procedural matters, then, are matters relating to the internal procedure of the Council, such as the inclusion of items on the agenda; adjournment and suspension of meetings; and matters designated as procedural by the Charter in Articles 28-32.[198]

Note that in case of disagreement between the members concerning the preliminary question whether a matter is procedural or not, the question is treated as a substantive matter by the Council, necessitating the concurrent votes of permanent members. This is the so-called double veto.[199] In addition, enforcement measures taken under Chapter VII by the Council can only be terminated by the Council, a decision subject to the veto. This has been referred to as the "reverse" veto.[200]

In the early years of the UN, differences of opinion arose with regard to the requirement that a decision on non-procedural matters is to be adopted with the "concurring votes" of the permanent members. Particularly controversial has been the Security Council action concerning Korea in 1950, when the Soviet Union was absent from the Council meetings as a protest against the representation of China by Taiwan in the United Nations.[201] A uniform practice has, however, evolved, according to

---

198 According to Bruha, this list is even shorter. He asserts that "the only decisions which clearly cannot be vetoed by the permanent members are those concerning the election of judges of the ICJ ... the summoning of revisionary conferences (Article 109 para. 1) and the recommendations of the Security Council mentioned in Article 17 para. 3, which are made on the basis of Chapter VI and Article 52 para. 3, in so far as a permanent member is a party to the conflict concerned." T. Bruha, *Security Council*. In: R. Wolfrum, United Nations: Law, Policies and Practice (1995) 1147-1161, at 1152.

199 See L. Gross, *The Question of Laos and the Double Veto in the Security Council*, 54 AJIL (1960) 118-131; Bailey, Daws, *op. cit. supra* n.51, 240-249.

200 See Caron, *op. cit. supra* n.4, 577-588.

201 See Y.L. Liang, *Abstention and Absence of a Permanent Member in Relation to Voting Procedure in the Security Council*, 44 AJIL (1950) 694-708; C.A. Stavropoulos, *The Practice of Voluntary Abstentions by Permanent Members of the Security Council under Article 27, Paragraph 3, of the Charter of the United Nations*, 61 AJIL (1967) 737-752; Kunz, *op. cit. supra* n.11; L. Gross, *Voting in the Security Council: Abstention from Voting and Absence from Meetings*, 60 Yale Law Journal (1951) 209-257. Gross argues that the resolutions of the Security Council were invalid due to the absence of the Soviet Union. For the

which the voluntary absence of a meeting or the abstention from voting does not preclude the adoption of a decision under Article 27(3).[202] The validity of this interpretation was confirmed by the International Court of Justice in 1971.[203]

Article 29 stipulates that the Council "may establish such subsidiary organs as it deems necessary for the performance of its functions." This is a broad formulation (as the Council "deems necessary") that seems to provide for a large discretion on the part of the Council.[204] Indeed, in its extensive practice the Council has established subsidiary organs in various forms and for different purposes.[205] Between 1946 and 1984, 83 subsidiary organs were established; between 1989 and 1997 another 34, including peacekeeping forces and sanctions committees.[206] The most recent examples include the establishment of International Tribunals for Crimes committed in Rwanda and former Yugoslavia. The open-texture of Article 29 and the innovative use made of it by the Council recently, have led to the question of the exact scope of the Council's powers under the Article.[207]

---

opposite view see M.S. McDougal, N. Gardner, *The Veto and the Charter: An Interpretation for Survival*, 60 Yale Law Journal (1951) 258-292.

202 See Simma, Brunner, *op. cit. supra* n.195, 447-455.

203 In the Advisory Opinion on the *Legal Consequences of the Continued Presence of South Africa in Namibia (South West Africa) Notwithstanding Security Council Resolution 276 (1970)*, the Court pronounced itself on South Africa's contention that the resolution by which the Council requested the opinion, resolution 284 (1970), was invalid due to the abstention of two permanent members. The Court held that: "the proceedings of the Security Council extending over a long period supply abundant evidence that presidential rulings and the positions taken by members of the Council, in particular its permanent members, have consistently and uniformly interpreted the practice of voluntary abstention by a permanent member as not constituting a bar to the adoption of resolutions ... This procedure followed by the Security Council, which has continued unchanged after the amendment in 1965 of Article 27 of the Charter, has been generally accepted by the Members of the United Nations and evidences a general practice of the Organization." ICJ Rep. (1971), at 22.

204 Thus Hilf, commenting on the Article and the related Rules of Procedure, maintains that "the SC wished to retain as much room for manoeuvre as possible for the sake of effectiveness and to avoid formalization in order to most flexibly utilize the machinery for establishing subsidiary organs." Hilf, *op. cit. supra* n.184, at 481-482.

205 *Cf.* Bailey and Daws, according to whom: "A subsidiary organ may be one person or a committee, a peace-keeping force or a tribunal; it can be established either by the Security Council or by the President of the Council and/or the Secretary-General pursuant to a decision of the Council; it can conduct its operations at the UN Headquarters or in the field; it can be given an *ad hoc* assignment or a continuing responsibility." Bailey, Daws, *op. cit. supra* n.51, at 333.

206 See Hilf, *op. cit. supra* n.184, 482; Bailey, Daws, *op. cit. supra* n.51, 333-334. For an overview of the main subsidiary organs established by the Council under Article 29 see *ibid.*, 334-378.

207 See *infra*, paragraphs 3.6.2.7 and 3.9.2.3, and the text accompanying note 902.

2.7 Summary

The United Nations Charter confers primary responsibility on the Security Council for the maintenance of international peace and security (Article 24). As a corollary the members have bound themselves to accept and carry out the decisions of the Council (Article 25). This far-reaching provision was inspired by the failure of the League system, which was based on the voluntary application of sanctions by its members. The decisions referred to in Article 25 are predominantly those taken under Chapter VII of the Charter, for the powers of the Council with regard to the pacific settlement of disputes (Chapter VI) are generally recommendatory, whilst it remains controversial whether other provisions (*e.g.* Article 24) afford a sufficient basis for the Council to take legally binding decisions. In taking decisions under Chapter VII the permanent members of the Council may cast a veto (Article 27(3)), whilst it is by now generally accepted that abstention from voting by a permanent member on a non-procedural issue amounts to a concurring vote. Chapter VII of the Charter provides that the Council may take enforcement measures, after it has determined that a situation poses a threat to, or breach of, international peace and security, or an act of aggression (Article 39). Neither international peace nor aggression is defined in the Charter, which gives the Council a considerable margin of appreciation under Article 39. Enforcement measures include, in the first place, non-forcible measures under Article 41. The measures listed non-exhaustively in Article 41 include economic and diplomatic sanctions. If the Council deems such measures to be, or have been, inadequate in restoring international peace and security, it may have recourse to forcible action (Article 42). The Charter originally provided for agreements between the Council and member states of the United Nations, by which the members would make troops available to the Council (Article 43). These agreements have never been concluded, so that the Council depends on *ad hoc* contributions of forces by member states in order to carry out Article 42 measures.

Such is the system established by the United Nations Charter. The way in which this system has been brought into practice will be considered in the next chapter.

3.

Subsequent Practice: The Council's Application of its Powers

Following the overview of the Security Council's authority as ascribed to it by Chapter VII of the Charter, this chapter will examine the various ways in which the Council has applied the provisions of Chapter VII. Such an examination is necessary in order to determine what problems are encountered by the Council and states with the provisions of Chapter VII of the Charter. This determination will provide the framework wherein the legal limits to the Council's authority will be assessed.

The twelve case studies below are ordered chronologically, and the criterion for their inclusion has been the application of enforcement measures under Chapter VII by the Council.[208] This means that the measures taken were binding and taken against the will of the state concerned.[209] Cases in which a determination was made under Article 39 but in which no subsequent action was taken,[210] fall outside the purview of this work and are therefore not included.[211] All case studies begin with a statement of

[208] See the *Certain Expenses* case, ICJ Rep. (1962), 151 ff. In this case the Court ruled that enforcement action means action taken against a state and authorized by the Council under Chapter VII of the Charter. *Ibid.*, 164-165 and 177.

[209] See Frowein, *op. cit. supra* n.151, 632.

[210] *E.g.* S/Res. 502 (1982), 3 April 1982, in which the Council determined that a breach of the peace had occurred because of the Argentinian invasion of the Falklands, and in which the Council "demanded" an immediate withdrawal of Argentinian troops and a cessation of hostilities; or S/Res. 496 (1981), 15 Dec. 1981 and S/Res. 507 (1982), 28 May 1982, in which the Council condemned "the mercenary aggression" against the Seychelles, aggression that was "prepared in and executed from South Africa."

[211] Similarly, borderline cases such as Korea and the Congo are excluded. Although in resolution

the relevant background, a survey of the Council's actions in the case and are concluded with a summary and an analysis of the relevant articles on which the Council based its actions. In the concluding paragraph, paragraph 3.15, the studies will be ordered systemically, meaning that the various actions taken by the Council will be categorized according to their cause of action and their form and content.

3.1 South Africa 1960-1994

The first time the Council took enforcement measures under Chapter VII of the Charter against a member state of the United Nations was in the case of South Africa.

3.1.1 Factual Background

From the inception of the United Nations onwards, the discriminatory policies of South Africa[212] had been on the agenda of the Security Council and the General Assembly. Thus, in as early as 1946, the Assembly, in response to an application made by the Indian government, stated that the treatment of Indians by the Union of South Africa impaired friendly relations between the states and that the Indians should be accorded a treatment in conformity with international (including United Nations Charter) standards.[213] In response, South Africa consistently maintained that its policies were a matter of domestic concern and that the United Nations was hence not competent to deal with them.[214] The Assembly, however, was of a different opinion. According to the Assembly, the apartheid issue was subject to its jurisdiction in view of the legally binding commitment of the United Nations to the international protection of human rights.[215] Moreover, the Assembly repeatedly characterized the

---

83 (1950) the Council determined that the "armed attack on the Republic of Korea ... constitutes a breach of the peace", the Council merely 'recommended' that UN members "furnish such assistance to the Republic of Korea as may be necessary to repel the armed attack and to restore international peace and security in the area." See Malanczuk, *op. cit. supra* n.31, 392. Similarly, the UN involvement in the Congo did not amount to enforcement action. See Kirgis, *op. cit. supra* n.129, 512.

212 For a concise overview of the apartheid system see, *e.g.*, J. Delbrück, *Apartheid*. In: R. Wolfrum (ed.), United Nations: Law, Policies and Practice (1995) 27-38.

213 A/Res. 44 (I), 8 December 1946. For an overview of the UN actions on South Africa between 1948-1960 see, *e.g.*, UNDPI, *The United Nations and Apartheid, 1948-1994* (1994), 8-28.

214 See, *e.g.*, UN Yearbook, Special Edition, UN Fiftieth Anniversary, 1945-1995, 52, 53, 57, and 58.

215 *E.g.* A/Res 616 B (VII), 5 Dec. 1952; A/Res. 820 (IX), 14 Dec. 1954; A/Res. 917 (X), 6 Dec. 1955; A/Res. 1598 (XV), 13 April 1961.

apartheid system as a crime against humanity.[216] A turning point in the treatment of South Africa proved to be the 1960 Sharpeville killings, which provoked international condemnation of the apartheid policies and an even more active stance by the Assembly, which hinted that the situation in South Africa had repercussions on the maintenance of international peace and security. This varied from noting "with grave concern" that "these policies have led to international friction and that their continuance endangers international peace and security",[217] to calling for a severance of diplomatic and economic relations[218] and recommending that the Security Council consider "the question of apartheid with a view to adopting, under Chapter VII of the Charter of the United Nations, effective measures to ensure the full implementation of comprehensive mandatory sanctions against South Africa."[219] As part of a controversial move, South Africa was additionally effectively excluded from participating in the Assembly and most of the specialized agencies, resulting from the Assembly's declaration that "the South African regime has no right to represent the people of South Africa".[220]

3.1.2 Security Council Action concerning South Africa

The Council repeatedly determined that (the consequences of) the apartheid policy might threaten international peace and security, at first without actually making a determination under Article 39. Various terms were used to this effect. Thus, in resolution 134 (1960), for example, the Council considered the "situation arising out of the large-scale killings of unarmed and peaceful demonstrators against racial discrimination and segregation in the Union of South Africa", on which occasion it recognized "that the situation in ... South Africa is one that has led to international friction and if continued might endanger international peace and security."[221] South

---

[216] A/Res. 2202 (XXI), 16 Dec. 1966; A/Res. 3324 E (XXIX), 16 Dec. 1974.

[217] A/Res. 1598 (XV), 13 April 1961.

[218] A/Res. 1761 (XVII), 6 Nov. 1962.

[219] A/Res. 2396 (XXIII), 2 Dec. 1968.

[220] A/Res. 3151 G (XXVIII), 14 Dec. 1973. In the doctrine the majority view is that the Assembly was acting beyond its powers by excluding South Africa. See, *e.g.*, Blum, *op. cit. supra* n.182, 43-55; P.T. Stoll, *Conflicts, South Africa*. In: R. Wolfrum (ed.), United Nations: Law, Policies and Practice (1995) 317-329, 320-321. Stoll notes that a proposal put before the Security Council to expel South Africa from the United Nations was vetoed by France, the UK and the US on 30 October 1974. *Loc. cit.*, 320.

[221] S/Res. 134 (1960), 1 April 1960, adopted by nine votes in favour, with two abstentions (France and the UK). The meeting had been requested by 29 African and Asian member states on March

Africa had been invited to participate in the debate, which it did, at the same time asserting that the United Nations was not competent to interfere by virtue of Article 2(7) of the Charter. In resolution 181 (1963), moreover, the Council expressed its conviction "that the situation in South Africa is seriously disturbing international peace and security",[222] whilst in resolution 282 (1970) it held that the "policies of apartheid and the constant build-up of the South African military and police forces" constitute "a potential threat to international peace and security."[223] Furthermore, in response to the Soweto killings which occurred on 16 June 1976 the Council adopted resolution 392 (1976), in which it reaffirmed that the "policy of apartheid is a crime against the conscience and dignity of mankind and seriously disturbs international peace and security."[224] The aforementioned resolutions, moreover, affirmed the right of self-determination by the South African people and recognized their legitimate struggle against apartheid and racial discrimination. Alongside the treatment of its population by the South African regime, the relations between South Africa and other states in the region (the so-called 'frontline' states) were also placed on the Council's agenda. Thus in a resolution which was adopted as a reaction to the violation of "the sovereignty, air space and territorial integrity of the Republic of Zambia", the Council expressed its conviction that "the deteriorating situation in southern Africa could constitute a threat to international peace and security."[225]

As regards the imposition of sanctions, the Council, absent a determination under Article 39, initially limited itself to 'calling upon' the international community to establish an arms embargo against South Africa.[226] The Council did establish an expert committee which was to "undertake a technical and practical study and report to the Council as to the feasibility, effectiveness and implications of measures which could, as appropriate, be taken by the Council under the Charter of the United Nations."[227] However, the committee's recommendation that the Council consider a comprehensive

---

25 of that year (see S/4279 and Add.1) in response to the Sharpeville killings on 21 March.

[222] S/Res. 181 (1963), 7 Aug. 1963.

[223] S/Res. 282 (1970), 23 July 1970.

[224] S/Res. 392 (1976), 19 June 1976.

[225] S/Res. 393 (1976), 30 July 1976.

[226] *E.g.* S/Res. 181 (1963), in which the Council "*solemnly calls upon* all States to cease forthwith the sale and shipment of arms, ammunition of all types and military vehicles to South Africa"; S/Res. 182 (1963), 4 Dec. 1963; S/Res. 191 (1964), 18 June 1964; S/Res. 282 (1970), 23 July 1970; S/Res. 311 (1972), 4 Feb. 1972.

[227] S/Res. 191 (1964), 18 June 1964.

embargo on *inter alia* trade, the supply of arms and petroleum,[228] was not followed by the Council.

The position changed when the Council unanimously adopted resolution 418 (1977) on 4 November 1977. Herein it: "*determines*, having regard to the policies and acts of the South African Government, that the acquisition by South Africa of arms and related *matériel* constitutes a threat to the maintenance of international peace and security."

In the same resolution the Council, for the first time in its history, applied sanctions under Chapter VII against a member state of the United Nations by deciding, amongst other things, that:

> all States shall cease forthwith any provision to South Africa of arms and related material of all types, including the sale or transfer of weapons and ammunition, military vehicles and equipment, para-military police equipment, and spare parts for the aforementioned, and shall cease as well the provision of all types of equipment and supplies and grants of licensing arrangements for the manufacture or maintenance of the aforementioned.

Similar to the Rhodesian case, the Council decided to establish, under rule 28 of its provisional rules of procedure, a committee which was to oversee the implementation of the sanctions and "to study ways and means by which the mandatory arms embargo could be made more effective against South Africa and to make recommendations to the Council."[229] The Council could not agree on enlarging the scope of the sanctions and confined itself to recommend further extensions to the embargo during the 1980s, that is on a non-mandatory basis.[230] In view of the non-compliance by some states, influenced by their – at times considerable – economic interests in South Africa,[231] the Council reaffirmed the continuing validity of the sanctions on several occasions.[232] In

---

[228] See 'Report of the Expert Committee established in pursuance of Security Council resolution 191 (1964)', S/6210, 2 March 1965.

[229] S/Res. 421 (1977), 9 Dec. 1977.

[230] S/Res. 558 (1984), 13 Dec. 1984 (requesting all states to refrain from importing arms, ammunition of all types and military vehicles produced in South Africa); S/Res. 569 (1985), 26 July 1985 (urging member states to, *inter alia*, suspend all new investment in South Africa, to prohibit the sale of coins minted in South Africa, to restrict cultural and sports relations, and to prohibit new contracts in the nuclear field); S/Res. 591 (1986), 28 Nov. 1986 (requesting all states to, amongst other things, refrain from any cooperation in the nuclear field).

[231] See N.D. White, *The United Nations and the Maintenance of International Peace and Security* (1990), 82.

[232] *E.g.* S/Res. 558 (1984), in which the Council "*reaffirms* its resolution 418 (1977) and stresses the continuing need for the strict application of all its provisions."

resolution 556 (1984), moreover, the Council characterized 'apartheid' as a "crime against humanity".[233]

In an effort to support the changes occurring in South Africa at the beginning of the 1990s, the Council decided to establish a United Nations Observer Mission in South Africa (UNOMSA),[234] whose mandate included the monitoring of the first democratic elections held in 1994. With the abolishment of the apartheid system and the establishment of a multi-party democracy, the sanctions against South Africa were no longer necessary. In 1994 the Council, therefore, "*decides*, acting under Chapter VII of the Charter of the United Nations, to terminate forthwith the mandatory arms embargo and other restrictions related to South Africa imposed by resolution 418 (1977) of 4 November 1977."[235] In resolution 930 (1994), adopted on 27 June 1994, the Council terminated UNOMSA and removed the question of South Africa from the list of matters of which the Council is seized.

3.1.3 Summary

The Council repeatedly expressed its concern regarding the situation posed by the apartheid system in South Africa and hinted that the system constituted a breach of international peace and security. Although these statements were made as early as 1960, it was not until 1977 that the Council decided to take enforcement measures in the form of an arms embargo. Attempts to enhance the sanctions were warded off and with the abolishment of apartheid in the early 1990s, the Council terminated the embargo in 1994.

3.1.4 Analysis: The Application of Chapter VII by the Council

Influenced by the new member states of the United Nations and the wave of decolonization, the Assembly consistently took the lead in condemning the apartheid policies and calling for further action. According to one observer, prior to the adoption of resolution 418 (1977) the "General Assembly ... pre-empted the Security Council's prerogative of making a finding under Article 39. The majority ignored the division of powers."[236] Indeed, the Council adopted a more cautious approach to the

---

[233] S/Res. 556 (1984), 23 Oct. 1984, para. 1.

[234] S/Res. 894 (1994), 14 Jan. 1994. See also S/Res. 772 (1992), 17 Aug. 1992.

[235] S/Res. 919 (1994), 25 May 1994.

[236] White, *op. cit. supra* n.231, at 120.

situation in South Africa. For a long period of time it referred to a 'potential threat to international peace' but was reluctant to actually make a determination under Article 39. The Council's actions were accordingly confined to recommendations. The situation changed with the adoption of resolution 418 (1977), which imposed an arms embargo under Article 41 of the Charter. Attempts to enhance the sanctions were unsuccessful in view of the lack of consensus within the Council, with some of its members fearing for their substantial economic interests in South Africa. The release of Nelson Mandela and the holding of free elections in the early 1990s, made it possible for the Council to terminate the sanctions in 1994.

3.2 Southern Rhodesia 1963-1979

The first instance in which the Security Council utilized the sanctions provisions under Chapter VII of the Charter occurred in the context of Southern Rhodesia's decolonization. This case will be considered below.

3.2.1 Factual Background

Southern Rhodesia, which is now known as Zimbabwe, was annexed by the UK in 1923. Together with Northern Rhodesia and Nyasiland, it joined the Federation of Nyasiland in 1953, which stood under UK control. After the dissolution of the Federation in 1963, the white minority of European settlers in Southern Rhodesia sought independence from the UK. The settlers had installed an essentially racist regime which ensured their dominance over the black majority of the population,[237] and their leader Ian Smith made it quite clear that this policy would remain in force after independence.[238] Britain, however, made the granting of independence subject to certain conditions which were to ensure some form of majority rule in Rhodesia. These conditions laid down by the UK were not accepted and on 11 November 1965 the settlers unilaterally declared their independence.[239]

---

[237] The 1961 constitution, which included voting eligibility provisions connected to property and education, assured the 6% white population "dominance in every aspect of internal public order." M.S. McDougal, W.M. Reisman, *Rhodesia and the United Nations: The Lawfulness of International Concern*, 62 AJIL (1968) 1-19, at 2. See also P.T. Stoll, *Conflicts, Rhodesia/Zimbabwe*. In: R. Wolfrum (ed.), United Nations: Law, Policies and Practice (1995) 311-316, 311.

[238] See McDougal, Reisman, *op. cit. supra* n.237, n.9 at 2.

[239] For the text of the declaration see 35 ILM (1966), 230 ff. In 1964 Northern Rhodesia and Nyasiland had already become the independent states of Zambia and Malawi. For an appraisal of the lawfulness of the declaration of independence see, *e.g.*, J. Nkala, *The United Nations, International*

The situation in Southern Rhodesia had earlier drawn the attention of the United Nations, with the General Assembly adopting various resolutions on the matter. In 1962, the Assembly asked its 'Special Committee on the Situation with regard to the Implementation of the Declaration on the Granting of Independence to Colonial Countries and Peoples' to establish whether or not Southern Rhodesia was to be considered a self-governing-territory.[240] Pursuant to the Committee's advice, the Assembly declared Southern Rhodesia a non-self governing territory under Article 73 of the Charter,[241] thereby overriding Britain's claim that the situation in its colony was a matter falling within its domestic jurisdiction.[242] In 1965 two resolutions were devoted to the possibility of a unilateral declaration of independence by Southern Rhodesia. In resolution 2012 (XX), adopted on 12 October 1965, the General Assembly "condemns any attempt on the part of the Rhodesian authorities to seize independence by illegal means in order to perpetuate minority rule in Southern Rhodesia." This was affirmed by resolution 2022 (XX), in which the Assembly also decided to refer the matter to the Security Council as it "threatens international peace and security".[243] Finally, when the declaration of independence was issued on 11 November 1965,[244] it was "condemned" by the General Assembly on the same day.[245] The main force behind the condemnation of the declaration of independence was the Organization of African Unity (OAU), which established an economic blockade of Southern Rhodesia on 5 December 1965.[246]

Law, and the Rhodesian Crisis (1985), 43-52.

240 A/Res. 1745 (XVI), 23 Feb. 1962.

241 A/Res. 1747 (XVI), 28 June 1962. Article 73 is part of Chapter XI, entitled "Declaration Regarding Non-self-governing Territories". It holds, *inter alia*, that "members of the United Nations which have or assume responsibilities for the administration of territories whose peoples have not yet attained a full measure of self-government recognize the principle that the interests of the inhabitants of these territories are paramount, and accept as a sacred trust the obligation to promote to the utmost, within the system of international peace and security established by the present Charter, the well-being of the inhabitants of these territories."

242 See V. Gowlland-Debbas, *Collective Responses to Illegal Acts in International Law* (1990), 95-132.

243 A/Res. 2022 (XX), 5 Nov. 1965.

244 Text in 5 ILM (1966), 230-231.

245 A/Res. 2024 (XX), 11 Nov. 1965.

246 On the OAU actions regarding Rhodesia see Gowlland-Debbas, *op. cit. supra* n.242, 551-555.

3.2.2 Security Council Action concerning Southern Rhodesia

Similar to the Assembly, the Council did not recognize Britain's claim that the Rhodesian situation fell within its domestic jurisdiction.[247] Thus, resolution 202 (1965), amongst other things, recalled General Assembly resolution 1747 (XVI), and requested the UK "to take all necessary action to prevent a unilateral declaration of independence".[248] When independence was indeed proclaimed the Council, in an emergency session, decided "to condemn the unilateral declaration of independence made by the racist minority in Southern Rhodesia."[249] On this occasion, it also called upon all states "to refrain from rendering any assistance to this illegal régime." In its next resolution on the situation, the Council opened the door to Chapter VII of the Charter by determining that the "situation arising from the proclamation of independence by the illegal régime is extremely grave ... and that its continuance in time constitutes a threat to international peace and security."[250]

This was accompanied by a call upon the UK to "take immediate measures in order to allow the people of Southern Rhodesia to determine their own future" and upon "all States to refrain from any action which would assist and encourage the illegal régime".[251]

The cautious approach with regard to Article 39 was abandoned by the Council through its adoption of resolution 221 (1966).[252] During the preceding meeting, which had been requested by the UK, the Council considered the situation arising from oil shipments from Portugal to Mozambique, which were subsequently transported to Southern Rhodesia through pipelines. The Council determined that these shipments resulted in a situation which "constitutes a threat to the peace". In paragraph 5 of resolution 221 (1966) the Council then:

---

247 See Stoll, *op. cit. supra* n.237, 131. Stoll observes that "later the United Kingdom limited itself to registering its reservations about pursuing the theme." For an assessment of the involvement of the United Nations with Southern Rhodesia and domestic jurisdiction see, *e.g.*, Nkala, *op. cit. supra* n.239, 31-42.

248 S/Res. 202 (1965), 6 May 1965.

249 S/Res. 216 (1965), 12 Nov. 1965.

250 S/Res. 217 (1965), 20 Nov. 1965, para. 1. A draft resolution submitted by the Ivory Coast on behalf of the African states but which was not adopted, envisaged more radical measures, including a determination that "the situation resulting from the declaration of independence constituted a threat to international peace and security", and the application of enforcement measures under Articles 41, 42 and 43. See S/6929, paras. 1 and 8-9.

251 *Ibid.*, paras. 7-8.

252 S/Res. 221 (1966), 9 April 1966. Adopted by 10 votes to none, with France abstaining.

calls upon the Government of the United Kingdom of Great Britain and Northern Ireland to prevent, by the use of force if necessary, the arrival at Beira of vessels reasonably believed to be carrying oil destined for Southern Rhodesia, and empowers the United Kingdom to arrest and detain the tanker known as the *Joanna V* upon her departure from Beira in the event her oil cargo is discharged there.

Pursuant to this resolution, a British armed vessel stopped and diverted the tanker *Manuela* on the high seas. The British vessel informed its captain that the "tanker could not be allowed to proceed to Beira" in view of resolution 221 (1966), and that "the British Government had authority if necessary to use force to prevent this."[253]

On 16 December 1966, resolution 232 (1966) was adopted. In this resolution the Council, after expressing its concern as to the fact that its "efforts so far and the measures taken by the administering Power have failed to bring the rebellion in Southern Rhodesia to an end", for the first time in its history imposed mandatory sanctions under Article 41 of the Charter. Explicitly "acting in accordance with Articles 39 and 41 of the United Nations Charter" the Council first *determined* that "the present situation in Southern Rhodesia constitutes a threat to international peace and security", and, secondly, *decided* to impose an economic embargo against it. This included an import ban on commodities such as iron and copper, and a prohibition on selling military equipment to Rhodesia.[254] The Rhodesian government was not invited to participate in the debate, notwithstanding its request to do so made as early as 18 May 1966.[255] In 1968 the Council, in view of the fact that the domestic situation had not changed, and "acting under Chapter VII of the Charter", further tightened the economic sanctions.[256] It simultaneously decided "to establish, in accordance with rule 28 of the provisional rules of procedure" a Committee which was to oversee the implementation of the sanctions.[257] The non-compliance by several states

[253] Quoted in J.E.S. Fawcett, *Security Council Resolutions on Rhodesia*, 41 BYIL (1965-1966) 103-121, at 118. In the end the *Joanna V* left Beira without discharging oil, so no action was taken against her.

[254] See S/Res. 232 (1966), 16 Dec. 1996 (adopted by 11 votes to none, with 4 abstentions), para. 2.

[255] On 18 May 1966, the Secretary-General of the United Nations reported to the Council that he had received a telegram from the Rhodesian government requesting an invitation to participate in the Council's debate on Rhodesia by virtue of Article 32 of the Charter, according to which "any Member of the United Nations which is not a member of the Security Council ... if it is a party to a dispute under consideration by the Security Council, shall be invited to participate, without vote, in the discussion relating to the dispute". The Secretary-General contended that since the GA had determined that Rhodesia was a non-self-governing territory in resolution 1747 (XVI) it could no longer invoke Article 32, thereby suggesting that Rhodesia did not meet the requirement of statehood implicit in Article 32. He furthermore stated that it was the policy of the secretariat not to deal with illegal régimes, a characterization of the Rhodesian régime made by the Council. This argumentation was endorsed by the Council. See SCOR, 1208th meeting, 18 May 1966, paras. 3-9.

[256] S/Res. 253 (1968), 29 May 1968, adopted unanimously, paras. 3-6.

[257] See para. 20 of Res. 253 (1968). The Committee was later known as the 'Watchdog Committee',

notwithstanding,[258] the sanctions were gradually intensified during the 1970s,[259] whilst ongoing attempts to settle the conflict 'internally' were not recognized by the Security Council. Thus, in resolution 423 (1978) of 14 March 1978 the Council declared "illegal and unacceptable any internal settlement concluded under the auspices of the illegal régime". This referred to the "Rhodesian Constitutional Agreement" between the government of Rhodesia and several nationalist movements,[260] signed on 3 March 1978 in Salisbury.[261] Similarly, elections held in April 1979 subsequent to the Salisbury agreement were branded as being "designed to perpetuate white racist minority rule."[262] It was not until the Lancaster House Conference agreement was concluded on 21 December 1979[263] by the Governments of the UK, Southern Rhodesia and the Patriotic Front that the sanctions were lifted. By resolution 460 (1979) the Council terminated the measures "taken against Southern Rhodesia under Chapter VII of the Charter pursuant to resolutions 232 (1966), 253 (1968) and subsequent related resolutions" on the same day. After free elections were held in February 1980, Southern Rhodesia became the independent State of Zimbabwe on 18 April 1980 and was admitted to the United Nations on 25 August 1980.

3.2.3 Summary

Despite the UK's invocation of the domestic jurisdiction principle, the Security Council seized and acted upon the situation in Southern Rhodesia. The Council initially confined itself to 'calls upon' the international community not to assist the white settlers in their aspirations towards independence. The declaration of independence was condemned by the Council, but it was not until a year later that the Council took enforcement measures. One of these was a call upon the UK to prevent vessels from discharging oil destined for Rhodesia. In addition, the Council

---

on which see P.J. Kuyper, *The Limits of Supervision: The Security Council Watchdog Committee on Rhodesian Sanctions*, 25 NILR (1978) 159-194.

258 Notably South-Africa, Portugal, the US and the UK. See, *e.g.*, resolutions 318 (1972), 28 July 1972; 320 (1972), 29 Sept. 1972; and 333 (1973), 22 May 1973.

259 *E.g.* S/Res. 277 (1970), 18 March 1970; S/Res. 333 (1972), 22 May 1972; S/Res. 388 (1976), 6 April 1976; and S/Res. 409 (1977), 27 May 1977.

260 As observed by Hargreaves, "though this new constitution seemed revolutionary to most white Rhodesians, it entrenched control of the security forces, judiciary, and civil service in firm white hands". J.D. Hargreaves, *Decolonization in Africa* (1988), at 225.

261 The Salisbury agreement is reproduced in 17 ILM (1978) 261-264.

262 S/Res. 448 (1979), 30 April 1979. See also S/Res. 445 (1979), 8 March 1979.

263 Reproduced in 19 ILM (1980) 387-408.

established an economic embargo in 1996, an embargo that was gradually tightened until democratic elections enabled the Council to lift the sanctions in 1980.

3.2.4 Analysis: The Application of Chapter VII by the Council

The Southern Rhodesia case is the first in which the Council applied mandatory sanctions under Chapter VII of the Charter. By and large the measures taken by the Council coincided with the gradual increase of pressure envisaged in Chapter VII. The Council first condemned the Unilateral Declaration of Independence in resolution 216 (1965) and in resolution 217 (1965) it (cautiously) determined that the continuance of the situation in Rhodesia would lead to a threat to the peace. Indeed, the Council specifically decided that the oil shipments to Rhodesia led to a situation which constituted such a threat in resolution 221 (1966), followed by a determination that the overall situation in Rhodesia represented a threat to the peace in resolution 232 (1966). The discretion left to states in taking measures against Rhodesia was decreased accordingly. Whilst resolutions 216 (1965) and 217 (1965) still "called upon" the international community to refrain from lending assistance to the Rhodesian government, resolution 232 (1966) and subsequent resolutions imposed mandatory sanctions. These measures were explicitly taken under Articles 39 and 41 of the Charter. The actions taken by the Council thus follow the procedure prescribed by the Charter quite neatly, with the exception of paragraph 5 of resolution 221 (1966). Herein the Council *called upon* the UK "to prevent, by the use of force if necessary" the arrival of oil shipments to a neighbouring country of Rhodesia. The Security Council even went further, specifically "empowering" the UK to use force in detaining a tanker. Such authority could probably only have been given under Article 42,[264] to which reference was not made. This, however, remains a matter of debate. Thus Gowlland-Debbas asserts that:

> all that can be said with any degree of certainty with respect to the legal basis of SC Resolution 221 is that it was adopted within the framework of Chapter VII and that it could not be said to constitute a decision under either Articles 41 or 42.[265]

---

[264] See U. Beyerlin, *Sanctions*, In: R. Wolfrum (ed.), United Nations: Law, Policies and Practice (1995) 1111-1128, 1117.

[265] Gowlland-Debbas, *op. cit. supra* n.242, at 418-419. In a similar vein Fawcett concludes that para. 5 of S/Res. 221 (1966) was not adopted under Art. 42, since the Council did not have "plain" grounds for believing that measures under Art. 41 would be inadequate." See Fawcett, *op. cit. supra* n.253, at 119-120. On the legal basis of resolution 221 (1966) see also J.F. Murphy, *Force and Arms*. In: C.C. Joyner (ed.), The United Nations and International Law (1997) 97-130, 109-110.

She alternatively suggests that Article 39 may have provided the legal basis for paragraph 5 of resolution 221 (1966), but from a legal perspective it seems quite doubtful that a state can be 'empowered' to use force through a recommendation. Indeed, Article 42 appears to be the only appropriate basis for resolution 221, paragraph 5, notwithstanding the latter's ambiguous formulation.[266] The broad competence assigned to the Council by virtue of Article 42, moreover, does not preclude it from *authorizing* the use of force by an individual state for a limited purpose.[267]

3.3 Libya and the Lockerbie Incident 1988-2000

3.3.1 Factual Background

On 21 December 1988, Pan Am Flight 103 exploded over Lockerbie, Scotland, killing all 259 passengers and 11 local residents. Nearly three years later, on 14 November 1991, a Grand Jury in the District of Columbia, United States, indicted two Libyan nationals,[268] *inter alia* for placing the bomb which had caused the plane to crash.[269] Following the charges against Libya, the United Kingdom and the United States issued a joint declaration on 27 November 1991.[270] In this declaration the two governments insisted that Libya surrender the accused for trial; accept responsibility for the actions of its officials; disclose all its knowledge of the crime; and pay appropriate compensation. In response, on 18 January 1992, Libya denied the allegations,[271] expressed its willingness to settle the dispute in accordance with Article 33(1) of the Charter,[272] and requested arbitration under Article 14(1) of the 1971

---

[266] Frowein, *op. cit. supra* n.151, 633-634

[267] *Ibid.*, 634. This runs contrary to Gowlland-Debbas, according to whom "collective action under Articles 41 and 42 is usually associated with mandatory action, [whilst] SC Res. 221 clearly places no such obligation on Member States." Gowlland-Debbas, *op. cit. supra* n.242, at 417. On the issue of 'authorizations' to use force by the Council see also *infra*, paragraph 3.15.2.3.

[268] On the same day the Lord Advocate of Scotland announced that two Libyan nationals, allegedly officers of the Libyan Intelligence Services, had been charged with, amongst other things, conspiracy and murder. This announcement is reproduced in 31 ILM (1992), 718.

[269] The indictment is annexed to UN Doc. S/23317. For a brief overview of the evidence leading to the accusations, see C.C. Joyner, W.P. Rothbaum, *Libya and the Aerial Incident at Lockerbie: What Lessons for International Extradition Law?*, 14 MJIL (1993) 222-261, 225-227.

[270] UN Doc. S/23308, reproduced in 31 ILM (1992), 722.

[271] See the Libyan letter to the SC, dated 29 Nov. 1991, in UN Doc. S/23417.

[272] See the Libyan letter to the SC, dated 20 Nov. 1991, in UN Doc. S/23226, Annex.

Montreal Convention.[273] It declared that the Libyan constitution did not allow for extradition of its nationals, but that criminal proceedings would be instituted against the suspects. In that context, Libya invited the United Kingdom and the United States to nominate lawyers who could ensure the fairness and propriety of the enquiry,[274] but these invitations were not accepted.[275]

3.3.2 Security Council Action concerning Libya

The United Kingdom, the US and in addition France,[276] presented their cases to the Security Council, which considered them on 21 January 1992. Resolution 731 (1992) was adopted on the same day. In the preamble to this resolution the Council expressed its 'deep concern' over "the results of investigations, which implicate officials of the Libyan Government." Moreover, in paragraph 2, the Council 'strongly deplored' that fact that: Libya had "not yet responded effectively to the ... requests to cooperate fully in establishing responsibility for the terrorist acts referred to above against Pan Am Flight 103 and UTA Flight 772."[277] Accordingly, the Council 'strongly urged' the Libyan government "immediately to provide a full and effective response to those requests so as to contribute to the elimination of international terrorism."[278]

Alternatively, on 3 March 1992, Libya instituted parallel proceedings at the International Court of Justice against the United Kingdom and the United States.[279] In its application the Libyan government submitted that it had taken all necessary

---

[273] The 1971 Montreal Convention for the Suppression of Unlawful Acts Against the Safety of Civil Aviation. Reproduced in 10 ILM (1971), 1151 ff. The Libyan request is reproduced in UN Doc. S/23441.

[274] See the letter of the Libyan representative to the Security Council, dated 29 Nov. 1991, contained in UN Doc. S/23417.

[275] Thus Pickering, the US representative to the United Nations, submitted in a statement following the adoption of resolution 731 (1992) that: "The Council has been confronted with the extraordinary situation of a State and its officials which are implicated in two ghastly bombings of civilian airliners..This is a situation to which standard procedures are clearly inapplicable." S/PV.3033, at 78. He furthermore contended that "the issue at hand is not some difference of opinion or approach that can be mediated or negotiated." *Ibid.*, at 79.

[276] The French claim is related to the bombing in the airspace of Niger of UTA Flight 772, which was heading from N'Djamena (Niger) to Paris and exploded over Niger's Ténéré desert on 19 Sept. 1989. 171 people were killed in this incident, and France holds Libyan nationals responsible for the bombing.

[277] S/Res. 731 (1992), 21 Jan. 1992, para. 2.

[278] *Ibid.*, para. 3.

[279] The *Lockerbie* case will be considered in detail *infra*, paragraph 5.3.4.4.

steps to try its own nationals in accordance with the 1971 Montreal Convention. In addition to the filing of the application instituting proceedings against the United States and the United Kingdom, Libya requested the indication of interim measures of protection. The measures requested aimed to prevent the defendant states from "taking any action against Libya calculated to coerce or compel Libya to surrender the accused individuals to any jurisdiction outside of Libya."[280]

Three days after the oral hearings on the request had closed, however, the Security Council adopted resolution 748 (1992).[281] In the preamble thereof, the Council expressed its conviction that "the suppression of acts of international terrorism, including those in which States are directly or indirectly involved, is essential for the maintenance of international peace and security."

The Council subsequently 'reaffirmed' that:

> in accordance with the principle in Article 2, paragraph 4, of the Charter of the United Nations, every State has the duty to refrain from organizing, instigating, assisting or participating in terrorist acts in another State or acquiescing in organized activities within its territory directed towards the commission of such acts, when such acts involve a threat or use of force.

Accordingly the Council determined:

> in this context that the failure by the Libyan Government to demonstrate by concrete actions its renunciation of terrorism and in particular, its continued failure to respond fully and effectively to the requests in Resolution 731 (1992), constitute a threat to international peace and security.

Explicitly acting under Chapter VII of the Charter, the Council decided that Libya must comply with resolution 731, including the surrender of the suspects.[282] If Libya failed to do so, all states were to adopt coercive measures against Libya by 15 April 1992. These measures included an aerial and arms embargo and diplomatic sanctions.[283]

Since the Libyan government refused to comply with resolution 748 (1992), the embargo came into effect on 15 April 1992. In November 1993 the Council reviewed

---

[280] *Ibid.*, para. 11.

[281] On 31 March 1992. Adopted by ten votes in favour, with five abstentions (China, Cape Verde, India, Morocco and Zimbabwe).

[282] The operative part reads in full that Libya "must now comply without any further delay with paragraph 3 of Resolution 731 (1992) regarding the requests contained in documents S/23306, S/23308 and S/23309." Commenting on this, Tomuschat notes that "the reader remains somewhat puzzled by the fact that, through multiple reference, it appears to try to hide what specific demands are addressed to Libya." Tomuschat, *op. cit. supra* n.7, at 48.

[283] S/Res. 748 (1992), 31 March 1992, paras. 4-6.

the situation, on which occasion it enlarged the scope of the sanctions. In the preamble of resolution 883 (1993) the Council once again determined that Libya's non-compliance with resolutions 731 (1992) and 748 (1992) constituted a "threat to international peace and security."[284] Amongst other things, while deciding that all states were to freeze Libyan funds and resources abroad,[285] the Council imposed additional economic sanctions and tightened the existing aerial embargo.[286]

After years of negotiations, a compromise was reached between Libya, the US and the UK. Under this compromise the suspects were extradited to the Netherlands on 5 April 1999, where they are currently being tried under Scottish criminal law.[287] The sanctions were consequently suspended under the provisions of paragraph 8 of resolution 1192 (1998).[288]

3.3.3 Summary

Three years after the explosion of Pan Am Flight 103 the Council, through resolution 731 (1992), urged the Libyan government to extradite its nationals allegedly responsible for placing a bomb on the flight. This request was denied by Libya, which instead presented the case to the International Court of Justice based on the 1971 Montreal Convention. During the proceedings Libya asked the Court to indicate

284 S/Res. 883 (1993), 11 Nov. 1993.

285 *Ibid.*, para. 3. The only exception is made for "funds or other financial resources derived from the sale or supply of any petroleum or petroleum products, including natural gas and natural gas products, or agricultural products or commodities, originating in Libya ... provided that any such funds are paid into separate bank accounts exclusively for these funds." *Ibid.*, para. 4.

286 *Ibid.*, paras. 5-6.

287 The trial commenced on 3 May 2000, with the defendants, *inter alia*, being charged with murder and conspiracy to commit murder. Both defendants deny the charges and during the proceedings the defence has suggested that the Palestinian Popular Front might be responsible for the attacks. See M. Asser, 'The Palestinian Connection', 4 May 2000. Accessed at http://news.bbc.co.uk on 20 July 2000.

288 S/Res. 1192 (1998), 27 Aug. 1998. Para. 8 determines that the sanctions imposed by resolutions 748 (1992) and 883 (1993) "shall be suspended immediately if the Secretary-General reports to the Council that the two accused have arrived in the Netherlands for the purpose of trial before the court described in paragraph 2 or have appeared for trial before an appropriate court in the United Kingdom or the United States, and that the Libyan Government has satisfied the French judicial authorities with regard to the bombing of UTA 772." In a statement issued on 8 April 1999 the President of the Security Council announced that: "The Security Council notes that ... the conditions set forth in paragraph 8 of resolution 1192 (1998) for the immediate suspension of the measures set forth in resolutions 748 (1992) and 883 (1993) have been fulfilled." S/PRST/1999/10, 8 April 1999.

interim measures of protection so as to ensure that the US and the UK would not take any action against Libya with regard to the extradition of its nationals. With the case still pending before the Court, the Council determined by resolution 748 (1992) that the non-extradition of the Libyan nationals constituted a threat to international peace and security, and demanded that Libya extradite the suspects. Failure to do so would result in the imposition of sanctions. As Libya remained defiant in the face of the Council's demands, the sanctions became operative in April 1992, were tightened in 1993, only to be suspended in 1998 subsequent to the agreement to try the suspects in the Netherlands.

3.3.4 Analysis: The Application of Chapter VII by the Council

After investigations had indicated that Libyan officials were responsible for the Lockerbie explosion, the Council adopted resolution 731 (1992) under Chapter VI of the Charter. Herein Libya was 'strongly urged' to comply with the extradition requests made by the US and the UK, language reminiscent of Chapter VI of the Charter.[289] Libya did not comply with this legally non-binding appeal, and instead took the extradition issue to the World Court. These actions prompted the Council to adopt resolution 748 (1992), in which it invoked Article 39 by determining that the non-compliance by Libya with the requests contained in resolution 731 (1992) constituted a threat to the international peace and security. Moreover, the Council decided that a failure by Libya to comply with resolution 731 (1992) would lead to sanctions being taken against it. As Libya turned down the Council's demands, the sanctions, imposed under Article 41 of the Charter, became operative in April 1992. In November 1993 the Council adopted resolution 883 (1993), by which it reaffirmed its earlier Article 39 determination that the non-extradition of its nationals by Libya constituted a threat to international peace and imposed additional sanctions under Article 41.

3.4 Iraq 1990-2000

In the Iraq-Kuwait conflict the Council, freed from the historical antagonism between East and West which had effectively paralyzed it for 45 years, for the first time

289 The resolution was adopted with the concurring votes of France, the UK and US, which has led some to doubt its procedural validity, since Art. 27(3) of the Charter provides that "in decisions under Chapter VI ... a party to a dispute shall abstain from voting." See on this, *e.g.*, Graefrath, *op. cit. supra* n.7, 187-188; M. Mohr, *Der Lockerbie-Fall vor UN-Sicherheitsrat und Internationalen Gerichtshof*, 20 D&R (1992) 305-314; and Weller, *op. cit. supra* n.7, 313.

performed its functions in a way that resembles the collective security system envisaged by the Charter. Indeed in this case, the Council took a wide array of measures under Chapter VII of the Charter. As such, the case is important as regards the development of the Council's powers under Chapter VII of the United Nations Charter.

3.4.1 Factual Background: The Invasion of Kuwait

Following a period of strong tension between the neighbouring countries, Iraqi forces invaded Kuwait on 2 August 1990.[290] The tensions related to the exact location of the Iraq-Kuwait border,[291] the rights to the Rumeila oil field situated on that border, and the amount of oil produced by Kuwait, a production which according to Iraq exceeded the quotas agreed upon with the OPEC.[292] Iraq initially tried to justify its action as an intervention upon the request of a friendly state,[293] a claim which was clearly unfounded.[294] After the invasion Iraq first installed a government in Kuwait, then declared its annexation of Kuwait on 8 August 1990, and claimed that the country was a province of Iraq on 28 August.

3.4.2.1 Condemnation and Sanctions

The invasion by Iraq was condemned by the Security Council on the same day it occurred. Indeed, in resolution 660 (1990) the Council determined "that there exists

---

290 Generally see C. Warbrick, *The Invasion of Kuwait by Iraq – Part I*, 40 ICLQ (1991) 482-492.

291 Although Kuwait and Iraq reached an agreement on the independence of Kuwait in 1963 (reproduced in 485 UNTS. 321 ff.), on that occasion both states did not decide on the exact location of their boundary. See M.H. Mendelson, S.C. Hulton, *The Iraq-Kuwait Boundary*, 64 BYIL (1993) 135-195, 135-139.

292 See T. Eitel, *The Escape and Parole of the Imprisoned God of War: An Overview of the Second Gulf War from the Perspective of International Law*, 35 GYIL (1992) 170-189, 171-174.

293 The Iraqi representative asserted that "the Free Provisional Government of Kuwait requested my Government to assist it to establish security and order so that the Kuwaitis would not have to suffer. My Government decided to provide such assistance solely on that basis." He furthermore stated that "Iraq is pursuing no goal or objective in Kuwait and desires ... good-neighbourly relations with Kuwait". S/PV.2932, 2 Aug. 1990.

294 Indeed, according to Eitel "this claim, which if serious surely merits scrutiny, was in the case of Kuwait, however, so threadbare that no effort was ever made to present even an autochthonous (puppet) government." Eitel, *op. cit. supra* n.292, at 174. On the legal justifications of the invasion by Iraq see also, *e.g.*, N.D. White, H. McCoubrey, *International Law and the Use of Force in the Gulf*, 10 International Relations (1991) 347-373, 347-349. They conclude at 349 that the invasion "was a clear breach of the principle on the non-use of force contained in article 2(4) of the Charter."

a breach of international peace and security" and explicitly "acting under Articles 39 and 40 of the Charter" demanded "that Iraq withdraw immediately and unconditionally all its forces to the positions in which they were located on 1 August 1990."[295] This prompt action was followed by the adoption of resolution 661 (1990) a few days later.[296] Herein the Council expressed its deep concern on the non-implementation of resolution 660 (1990) by Iraq and its determination to "bring the invasion and occupation of Kuwait by Iraq to an end and to restore the sovereignty, independence and territorial integrity of Kuwait." To that end the Council first affirmed "the inherent right of individual or collective self-defence in response to the armed attack by Iraq against Kuwait, in accordance with Article 51 of the Charter." Secondly the Council, "acting under Chapter VII of the Charter of the United Nations," imposed sanctions against Iraq. These included a complete ban on the import of products originating in Iraq or Kuwait and a ban on the export of products or commodities to those countries.[297] In line with its earlier practice, the Council also decided to establish a Committee "consisting of all the members of the Council" which was to oversee the implementation of the sanctions.

Meanwhile, in response to a request by Saudi Arabia and other Gulf states, various Western powers formed a defensive alliance, allegedly in order to prevent Iraq from attacking other countries in the region, in particular Saudi Arabia.[298] Under the name "Desert Shield" this alliance deployed soldiers and *matériel* in the region, in the end consisting of several hundred thousand troops.

The Council's condemnation of the invasion and its demand that Iraq must unconditionally withdraw its troops were reiterated in a series of resolutions in the following weeks. Herein the Council, *inter alia*, decided that "annexation of Kuwait by Iraq under any form and whatever pretext has no legal validity, and is considered null and void."[299]

---

[295] S/Res. 660 (1990), 2 Aug. 1990. Adopted by a vote of 14 in favour with 1 abstention.

[296] S/Res. 661 (1990), 6 Aug. 1990. Adopted by a vote of 13 in favour and 2 abstentions.

[297] *Ibid.*, para. 3. Furthermore the Council decided, in para. 4, that "all States shall not make available to the Government of Iraq or to any commercial, industrial or public utility undertaking in Iraq or Kuwait, any funds or any other financial or economic resources and shall prevent their nationals and any persons within their territories from removing from their territories or otherwise making available to that Government or to any such undertaking any such funds or resources and from remitting any other funds to persons or bodies within Iraq or Kuwait, except payments exclusively for strictly medical or humanitarian purposes and, in humanitarian circumstances, foodstuffs".

[298] D. Gilman, *The Gulf War and the United Nations Charter: Did the Security Council Fulfill its Original Mission?*, 24 Connecticut Law Review (1992) 1131-1157, 1149; Eitel, *op. cit. supra* n.292, 178-179.

[299] S/Res. 662 (1990), 9 Aug. 1990. Adopted unanimously.

In the meantime Iraq ordered the closure of foreign embassies in Kuwait, took a small British military mission in Kuwait hostage and placed Western citizens in the vicinity of military locations as a human shield. This prompted a reaction by the Council, which, "acting under Chapter VII", demanded that Iraq safeguard the lives of nationals from third countries in Iraq and Kuwait.[300]

On 12 August 1990, the US announced that it had ordered its navy to block Iraqi oil exports and all but humanitarian imports. According to the US, this blockade was justified as being taken "on behalf of the Government of Kuwait, and in accordance with Article 51 ... to ensure that the U.N.-mandated economic sanctions against Iraq and Kuwait are immediately and effectively implemented."[301]

Pressure exerted by the US eventually led to the adoption of resolution 665 (1990) on 25 August, by which the Security Council mandated such maritime blockades. Herein the Council:

> calls upon those Member States co-operating with the Government of Kuwait which are deploying maritime forces to the area to use such measures commensurate to the specific circumstances as may be necessary under the authority of the Security Council to halt all inward and outward maritime shipping in order to inspect and verify their cargoes and destinations and to ensure strict implementation of the provisions related to such shipping laid down in resolution 661 (1990).[302]

In its next resolution, the Council reasserted its authority with regard to the implementation of the sanctions established under resolution 661 (1990). Herein it recognized that, in the context of the exception clauses mentioned in paragraphs 3(c) and 4 of resolution 661 (1990), "circumstances may arise in which it will be necessary for foodstuffs to be supplied to the civilian population in Iraq or Kuwait in order to relieve human suffering."[303] However, the Council *emphasized* that "it is for the Security Council, alone or acting through the Committee, to determine whether humanitarian circumstances have arisen." Hence, "acting under Chapter VII of the Charter", it:

> decides that in order to make the necessary determination whether or not for the purposes of paragraph 3 (c) and paragraph 4 of resolution 661 (1990) humanitarian circumstances have arisen, the Committee shall keep the situation regarding foodstuffs in Iraq and Kuwait under constant review.[304]

In addition to the determination that the annexation of Kuwait is to be considered

---

[300] S/Res. 664 (1990), 18 Aug. 1990. Adopted unanimously. See also S/Res. 674 (1990), 29 Oct. 1990.

[301] Transcript of US Statements About Measures Against Iraq, N.Y. Times, 13 Aug. 1990, at A11. Quoted in Gilman, *op. cit. supra* n.298, at 1150. See also White, McCoubrey, *op. cit. supra* n.294, 350.

[302] S/Res. 665 (1990), 25 Aug. 1990, para. 1. Adopted by 13 votes to none, with 2 abstentions.

[303] S/Res. 666 (1990), 13 Sept. 1990, preamble. Adopted with 13 votes in favour, 2 against.

[304] *Ibid.*, para. 1.

"null and void" as declared by the Council in resolution 662(1990), in resolution 674 (1990) the Council "reminds Iraq that under international law it is liable for any loss, damage or injury arising in regard to Kuwait and third States, and their nationals and corporations, as a result of the invasion and illegal occupation of Kuwait by Iraq."[305]

3.4.2.2 The Authorization to Use Force to Liberate Kuwait

In resolution 670 (1990) the Council repeated its demand that Iraq must withdraw its troops unconditionally, warning Iraq that failure to do so "could lead to further serious action by the Council under the Charter of the United Nations, including under Chapter VII."[306] Again Iraq did not respond effectively, which prompted the Council to impose an ultimatum on Iraq. In resolution 678 (1990), adopted on 29 November 1990, the Council:

Acting under Chapter VII of the Charter,

1. Demands that Iraq comply fully with resolution 660 (1990) and all subsequent relevant resolutions, and decides, while maintaining all its decisions, to allow Iraq one final opportunity, as a pause of goodwill, to do so;

2. Authorizes Member States co-operating with the Government of Kuwait, unless Iraq on or before 15 January 1991 fully implements, as set forth in paragraph 1 above, the foregoing resolutions, to use all necessary means to uphold and implement resolution 660 (1990) and all subsequent relevant resolutions and to restore international peace and security in the area.

When Iraq failed to meet the deadline, a coalition of more than 20 states which were aiding Kuwait commenced with *Operation Desert Storm* on 17 January 1991, with a view to liberating Kuwait. Despite the quite unorthodox methods of warfare that Iraq resorted to, such as the use of prisoners of war as protective shields and the torching of several Kuwaiti oil fields, the technical superiority of the coalition forces enabled the campaign to rapidly drive the Iraqi forces out of Kuwait and subsequently to occupy part of Iraqi territory. The commanders of the Iraqi and coalition forces then agreed on a "provisional suspension of offensive action" on 3 March 1991.

---

[305] S/Res. 674 (1990), 29 Oct. 1990, para. 8. Adopted by 13 votes to none, with 2 abstentions. *Cf.* the preamble to resolution 667 (1990), adopted on 16 Sept. 1990, in which the Council 'recalls' the "Vienna Conventions of 18 April 1961 on diplomatic relations and of 24 April 1963 on consular relations, to both of which Iraq is a party" and 'considers' that "the decision of Iraq to order the closure of diplomatic and consular missions in Kuwait and to withdraw the immunity and privileges of these missions and their personnel is contrary to the decisions of the Security Council, the international Conventions mentioned above and international law."

[306] S/Res. 670 (1990), 25 Sept. 1990. Adopted by 14 votes to none.

The military success of the operation prompted Iraq to notify the allies and the Council that it was willing to meet its demands.[307] The Council took note of this in resolution 686 (1991), simultaneously imposing additional criteria for a cease-fire. In paragraph 2 of resolution 686 (1991) the Council:

Demands that Iraq implement its acceptance of all [relevant resolutions] and in particular that Iraq:

(a) Rescind immediately its actions purporting to annex Kuwait;
(b) Accept in principle its liability for any loss, damage, or injury arising in regard to Kuwait and third States, and their nationals and corporations, as a result of the invasion and illegal occupation of Kuwait by Iraq.[308]

Iraq was, furthermore, not to engage in hostilities or "provocative actions" against "all Member States", and was to release all prisoners of war.[309] In paragraph 4, moreover, the Council explicitly 'recognized' that "the provisions of paragraph 2 of resolution 678 (1990) remain valid" until Iraq complied with the Council's demands.

3.4.2.3 The Cease-Fire and Resolution 687 (1991)

The cease-fire was sealed by resolution 687 (1991),[310] which has become known as the "mother of all resolutions", largely as a response to President Saddam Hussein's claims that the coalition forces would face a "mother of all battles" in Kuwait. In this voluminous resolution the Security Council imposed an additional set of conditions to be accepted by Iraq in order for the cease-fire to be implemented,[311] conditions which Iraq reluctantly agreed to on 6 April 1991.[312] The measures taken by the

---

[307] See S/22275.

[308] S/Res. 686 (1991), 2 March 1991. Adopted by 11 votes to one, with 3 abstentions.

[309] *Ibid.*, para. 3.

[310] S/Res. 687 (1991), 3 April 1991, adopted by 12 votes to 1 (Cuba), with 2 abstentions. In the preamble the Council, *inter alia*, welcomed "the restoration to Kuwait of its sovereignty, independence and territorial integrity and the return of its legitimate Government" and reaffirmed "the need to be assured of Iraq's peaceful intentions in the light of its unlawful invasion and occupation of Kuwait."

[311] In para. 33 of S/Res. 687 (1991) the Council: "Declares that, upon official notification by Iraq to the Secretary-General and to the Security Council of its acceptance of the provisions above, a formal cease-fire is effective between Iraq and Kuwait and the Member States cooperating with Kuwait in accordance with resolution 678 (1990)."

[312] By the 'Letter dated 6 April 1991 from the Permanent Representative of Iraq to the UN to the Secretary-General', S/22456, 6 April 1991, in which Iraq protested against various features of resolution 687 (1991) but nevertheless indicated that it "had no choice but to accept this resolution". Subsequently a formal cease-fire came into effect on 11 April 1991. See 'Letter dated 11 April 1991 from the President of the Security Council to the Permanent Representative of Iraq to the UN',

Council, once again explicitly under Chapter VII of the Charter, can be considered under several main headings according to their subject matter. The first measures relate to the demarcation and recognition of the boundary between Iraq and Kuwait, the second to the disarmament of Iraq, the third to the liability of Iraq for the invasion of Kuwait and ensuing damages, and the fourth to the sanctions established under resolution 661 (1990).

3.4.2.3.1 The Iraq-Kuwait Boundary

As regards the boundary between Iraq and Kuwait, in paragraph 2 the Council:

> Demands that Iraq and Kuwait respect the inviolability of the international boundary and the allocation of islands set out in the 1963 "Agreed Minutes Between the State of Kuwait and the Republic of Iraq Regarding the Restoration of Friendly Relations, Recognition and Related Matters", signed by them in the exercise of their sovereignty at Baghdad on 4 October 1963 and registered with the United Nations and published by the United Nations in document 7063, United Nations, Treaty Series, 1964.

Indeed, in paragraph 4 the Council "decides to guarantee the inviolability of the above-mentioned international boundary and to take as appropriate all necessary measures to that end in accordance with the Charter of the United Nations." These measures included a request to the Secretary-General to make plans for the deployment of a United Nations observer unit that was to "monitor the Khor Abdullah and a demilitarized zone, which is hereby established, extending ten kilometers into Iraq and five kilometers into Kuwait from the boundary referred to in the [1963 Agreed Minutes]."

The Secretary-General's report[313] was approved by the Council in resolution 689 (1991), on which occasion it determined that the United Nations Iraq-Kuwait Observation Mission (UNIKOM) "can only be terminated by a decision of the Council. The Council shall therefore review the question of termination or continuation every six months."[314]

Another measure related to the exact demarcation of the Iraqi-Kuwait border, a task which was entrusted to the United Nations Iraq-Kuwait Boundary Demarcation Commission pursuant to the report submitted to the Council by the Secretary-

---

S/22485, 11 April 1991.

313 S/22454, 5 April 1991.

314 S/Res. 689 (1991), adopted unanimously on 9 April 1991. In 1993 the mandate of UNIKOM was extended in view of border incidents involving Iraqi troops so as to include the capacity to use force in self-defence if necessary. S/Res. 806 (1993), 5 Feb. 1993.

General.[315] The Demarcation Commission consisted of five members: a representative of Kuwait, a representative of Iraq and three independent experts. Its mandate was to "demarcate in geographical coordinates of latitude and longitude the international boundary set out in the Agreed Minutes." Decisions were adopted by majority, whilst these decisions were to be final and binding. The decisions of the Demarcation Commission[316] were approved by the Council by resolution 833 (1993).[317] Herein the Council was cautious to note in the preamble that "through the demarcation process the Commission was not reallocating territory between Kuwait and Iraq, but it was simply carrying out the technical task necessary to demarcate for the first time the precise coordinates of the boundary set out in the [1963 Agreed Minutes]". The Council then, "acting under Chapter VII of the Charter of the United Nations":

> 5. Demands that Iraq and Kuwait in accordance with international law and relevant Security Council resolutions respect the inviolability of the international boundary, as demarcated by the Commission, and the right to navigational access.[318]

When Iraq deployed troops in the direction of the border of Kuwait in October 1994, the Council deemed this to be a violation of Iraq's obligation to "respect the inviolability of the international boundary." Therefore it adopted resolution 949, the preamble of which recognized that "any hostile or provocative action directed against its neighbours by the Government of Iraq constitutes a threat to peace and security in the region." Accordingly the Council, "acting under Chapter VII of the Charter", demanded that Iraq "immediately complete the withdrawal of all military units recently deployed to southern Iraq to their original positions."[319]

---

315 S/22558, 2 May 1991, submitted in accordance with para. 3 of resolution 687 (1991), which called "upon the Secretary-General to lend his assistance to make arrangements with Iraq and Kuwait to demarcate the boundary between Iraq and Kuwait."

316 The final report of the Demarcation Commission is annexed to the 'Letter dated 21 May 1993 from the Secretary-General addressed to the President of the Security Council', S/25811, and is reproduced in 32 ILM (1993) 1427-1462. For an analysis of the Commission's work see, *e.g.*, Mendelson, Hulton, *op. cit. supra* n.291. See also H.H.G. Post, *Adjudication as a Mode of Acquisition of Territory?: Some Observations on the Iraq-Kuwait Boundary Demarcation in Light of the Jurisprudence of the International Court of Justice*. In: V. Lowe, M. Fitzmaurice (eds.), Fifty Years of the International Court of Justice (1996) 237-263; J. Klabbers, *No More Shifting Lines?: The Report of the Iraq-Kuwait Boundary Demarcation Commission*, 43 ICLQ (1994) 904-913.

317 S/Res. 833 (1993), 27 May 1993. See also S/Res. 773 (1992), 26 Aug. 1992.

318 As correctly observed by Klabbers, this is a "gratuitous act, of a symbolic rather than substantive nature" since the decisions of the Demarcation Commission were deemed binding and final in the first place. Klabbers, *op. cit. supra* n.316, n.48 at 912.

319 S/Res. 949 (1994), 15 Oct. 1994, para. 2.

3.4.2.3.2 Disarmament[320]

As regards the disarmament of Iraq, in paragraph 8 of resolution 687 (1991) the Council:

> Decides that Iraq shall unconditionally accept the destruction, removal, or rendering harmless, under international supervision, of:
> (a) All chemical and biological weapons and all stocks of agents and all related subsystems and components and all research, development, support and manufacturing facilities;
> (b) All ballistic missiles with a range greater than 150 kilometers and related major parts, and repair and production facilities.

In paragraph 12, moreover, it was decided that Iraq "shall unconditionally agree not to acquire or develop nuclear weapons or nuclear-weapons-usable material or any subsystems or components or any research, development, support or manufacturing facilities related to the above".

A strict monitoring system was devised to oversee the implementation of the above provisions, which included the International Atomic Energy Agency (IAEA) and a newly established subsidiary organ of the Security Council, the United Nations Special Commission (UNSCOM) on Iraq.[321] In resolution 707 (1991) the Security Council mandated them to *inter alia* inspect Iraqi military locations as deemed appropriate, by demanding that Iraq:

> (i) provide full, final and complete disclosure, as required by resolution 687 (1991), of all aspects of its programmes to develop weapons of mass destruction and ballistic missiles with a range greater than 150 kilometers, and of all holdings of such weapons, their components and production facilities and locations, as well as all other nuclear programmes, including any which it claims are for purposes not related to nuclear-weapons-usable material, without further delay,
> (ii) allow the Special Commission, the IAEA and their Inspection Teams immediate, unconditional and unrestricted access to any and all areas, facilities, equipment, records and means of transportation which they wish to inspect."[322]

The programme thus devised is rather unprecedented and has been described as "the most comprehensive international monitoring system ever established in the sphere of arms control."[323] To put it mildly, Iraq has not fully cooperated with the Council's

---

[320] Generally see T. Marauhn, *The Implementation of Disarmament and Arms Control Obligations Imposed upon Iraq by the Security Council*, 52 ZäöRV (1992) 781-803.

[321] See S/Res. 687 (1991), paras. 9 (b)(i), (ii), and (iii); 12 and 13.

[322] S/Res. 707 (1991), 15 Aug. 1991, para. 3. Adopted unanimously.

[323] S/1994/11138, 7 Oct. 1994. According to others: "the disarmament regime imposed upon Iraq is draconian in the extreme ... constitut[ing] a movement from a full exercise of sovereignty to a diminished exercise of sovereignty." A.J.R. Groom, E. Newman, P. Taylor, *Burdensome Victory: The*

disarmament regime: it has repeatedly refused access to inspection teams and withheld information on its military capacity.[324] In response, the Security Council has adopted several resolutions demanding strict compliance by Iraq with its obligations under resolution 687 (1991).[325] Moreover, in controversial moves, the UK and the US bombed missile sites throughout the 1990s.[326] This scenario occurred in 1998, for example. Although the Secretary-General of the United Nations had reached an agreement with Iraq on 23 February 1998[327] on cooperation by Iraq with UNSCOM, Iraq decided on 5 August 1998 to "suspend" its cooperation with UNSCOM and the IAEA "on all disarmament activities and restrict ongoing monitoring and verification activities at declared sites."[328] On 31 October 1998, moreover, Iraq announced that it would stop cooperating with UNSCOM altogether.[329] This prompted the US and UK to bomb Iraq in December 1998 (*Operation Desert Fox*), strikes that continued throughout 1999. The operation was arguably based on Iraq's continued refusal to comply with the disarmament regime and both states referred to resolution 1154 (1998) as providing a legal basis for the use of force.[330] In paragraph 3 of resolution 1154 (1998) the Council:

United Nations and Iraq. In: D. Bourantonis, M. Evriviades (eds.), A United Nations for the Twenty-First Century: Peace, Security and Development (1996) 149-167, at 155.

[324] *Cf.* "the actual process of verification and inspection has been a cat and mouse affair, with the minimum of co-operation from Iraq to ensure that the Coalition does not take drastic action of a military nature." A.J.R. Groom, E. Newman, P. Taylor, *Burdensome Victory: The United Nations and Iraq*. In: D. Bourantonis, M. Evriviades (eds.), A United Nations for the Twenty-First Century: Peace, Security and Development (1996) 149-167, at 156.

[325] *E.g.* S/Res. 1115 (1997), 21 June 1997; S/Res. 1134 (1997), 23 Oct. 1997.

[326] See C. Gray, *After the Ceasefire: Iraq, the Security Council and the Use of Force*, 65 BYIL (1994) 135-174, 154-156 and 161-174; L. Condorelli, *A Propos de L'attaque Américaine Contre L'irak du 26 Juin 1993: Lettre D'un Professeur Désemparé aux Lecteurs du Jedi*, 5 EJIL 5 (1994) 134-144; D. Kritsiotis, *The Legality of the 1993 US Missile Strike on Iraq and the Right of Self-Defence in International Law*, 45 ICLQ (1996) 162-177; W.M. Reisman, *The Raid on Baghdad: Some Reflections on its Lawfulness and Implications*, 5 EJIL (1994) 120-133; and J. Lobel, M. Ratner, *Bypassing the Security Council: Ambiguous Authorizations to Use Force, Cease-fires and the Iraqi Inspection Regime*, 93 AJIL (1999) 124-154.

[327] 'Memorandum of Understanding signed by the Deputy Prime Minister of Iraq and the Secretary-General on 23 February 1998', S/1998/166.

[328] See S/Res. 1194 (1998), 9 Sept. 1998, preamble.

[329] See S/Res. 1205 (1998), 5 Nov. 1998, in which the Council notes "with alarm the decision of Iraq on 31 October 1998 to cease cooperation with the United Nations Special Commission, and its continued restrictions on the work of the International Atomic Energy Agency (IAEA)."

[330] For an analysis of the possible legal justifications for *Operation Desert Fox*, see S.M. Condron, *Justification for Unilateral Action in Response to the Iraqi Threat: A Critical Analysis of Operation Desert Fox*, 161 Military Law Review (1999) 115-180.

Stresses that compliance by the Government of Iraq with its obligations, repeated again in the memorandum of understanding, to accord immediate, unconditional and unrestricted access to the Special Commission and the IAEA in conformity with the relevant resolutions is necessary for the implementation of resolution 687 (1991), but that any violation would have severest consequences for Iraq.

The US and UK contended that the phrase "severest consequences" included the use of force. Other (permanent) members did not agree, however, arguing that the strikes are illegal without a Security Council resolution explicitly authorizing states to use force against Iraq.[331]

Prior to *Operation Desert Fox* UNSCOM had left Iraq. Disagreement in the Council as to how long the sanctions against Iraq should remain in force and the conditions under which they are to be lifted, resulted in uncertainty regarding the future of UNSCOM.[332] In December 1999 the Council decided to replace UNSCOM with the United Nations Monitoring, Verification and Inspection Commission (UNMOVIC).[333] The resolution establishing UNMOVIC provides that the Council will suspend several sanctions in force against Iraq if the latter cooperates with the inspection regime.[334] Iraq, however, denounced the resolution because it does not "address Iraq's legitimate right to secure a lifting of the embargo having met its commitments under UN accords."[335]

---

331 *Cf.* the statement made by a spokesman of the Chinese Foreign Ministry on 17 Dec. 1998: "We are shocked. The United States has not received permission from the UN Security Council and took unilateral action in using force against Iraq, violating the UN Charter and international principles." In a similar vein, the President of the Russian Federation, Boris Yeltsin, stated that: "The United States and Britain have crudely violated the UN charter and generally accepted principles of international law and the norms and rules of responsible behaviour of states", and that the strikes "should be considered a blow to the whole system of international security, the central link of which is the United Nations and its Security Council." Quoted in: 'Russia and China condemn air action against Saddam', Daily Telegraph, 18 Dec. 1998. Accessed at http://www.telegraph.co.uk on 10 Jan. 2000.

332 See, *e.g.*, C. Lockwood, 'UN votes to send arms inspectors back to Iraq', 18 Dec. 1999. Accessed at http://www.telegraph.co.uk on 15 July 2000.

333 S/Res. 1284 (1999), 17 Dec. 1999 (11 in favour with China, France, Russia and Malaysia abstaining). In para. 1 the Council: "Decides to establish, as a subsidiary body of the Council, the United Nations Monitoring, Verification and Inspection Commission (UNMOVIC) which replaces the Special Commission established pursuant to paragraph 9 (b) of resolution 687 (1991)." After it proved difficult to achieve consensus within the Council as to who was to fill the post, Hans Blix became Chairman of UNMOVIC on 1 March 2000.

334 See S/Res. 1284 (1999), para. 33.

335 Statement by the Iraqi Deputy Prime Minister, Tariq Aziz. Quoted in 'Iraq Condemns UN Resolution', 20 Feb. 2000. Accessed at http://news.bbc.co.uk on 15 July 2000.

3.4.2.3.3 Iraqi Reparations[336]

As regards the liability of Iraq for damages the Council, in paragraph 16 of resolution 687 (1991), reaffirmed that Iraq "is liable under international law for any direct loss, damage, including environmental damage and the depletion of natural resources, or injury to foreign Governments, nationals and corporations, as a result of Iraq's unlawful invasion and occupation of Kuwait." In paragraph 18 the Council, then, "decides also to create a fund to pay compensation for claims that fall within paragraph 16 above and to establish a Commission that will administer the fund." The United Nations Compensation Fund was to be paid for by Iraq "based on a percentage of the value of the exports of petroleum and petroleum products", whilst the Secretary-General was *directed* to develop a "programme to implement the decisions in paragraphs 16, 17 and 18", including recommendations as to the procedure of the Commission and the administration of the Fund.

Pursuant to this directive, the Secretary-General submitted a report to the Council,[337] part I of which relates to the institutional framework of the Commission and part II to its procedure. Subsequently the Council, explicitly "acting under Chapter VII of the Charter of the United Nations," decided to "establish the Fund and Commission referred to in paragraph 18 of resolution 687 (1991) in accordance with Part I of the Secretary-General's report."[338] This means that the United Nations Compensation Commission (UNCC) "will function under the authority of the Security Council and be a subsidiary organ thereof."[339] The UNCC is headed by a 15-member Governing Council, which is "composed of the representatives of the current members of the Security Council at any given time"[340] and which is assisted by legal and financial experts called Commissioners and also includes a secretariat headed by an Executive Secretary.[341]

---

336 Generally see B. Graefrath, *Iraqi Reparations and the Security Council*, 54 ZaöRV (1994) 1-68.

337 'Report of the Secretary-General Pursuant to Paragraph 19 of Security Council Resolution 687', S/22559.

338 S/Res. 692 (1991), 20 May 1991 (adopted by 14 votes to none, with 1 abstention), para. 3.

339 S/22559, para. 4.

340 *Ibid.*, para. 5.

341 On the UNCC see, *e.g.*, C. Alzamora, *Reflections on the UN Compensation Commission*, 9 Arbitration International (1993) 349-358; D.J. Bederman, *The United Nations Compensation Commission and the Tradition of International Claims Settlement*, 27 NYUJILP (1994) 1-42; C.N. Brower, *The Lessons of the Iran-U.S. Claims Tribunal Applied to Claims Against Iraq*. In: R.B. Lillich (ed.), The United Nations Compensation Commission (1995) 15-27; D.D. Caron, *The UNCC and the Search for Practical Justice*. In: R.B. Lillich (ed.), The United Nations Compensation Commission (1995) 367-377; P. Conlon,

The Security Council did not embrace part II of the Secretary-General's report relating to the procedure of the UNCC. In paragraph 5 of resolution 692 (1991), it merely "directs the Governing Council to proceed in an expeditious manner to implement the provisions of Section E of resolution 687 (1991), *taking into account* the recommendations in section II of the Secretary-General's report."[342]

The report's recommendations thus serve as guidelines, and are not binding on the Governing Council. It may be noted that section II of the report stated that:

> The Commission is not a court or an arbitral tribunal before which the parties appear; it is a political organ that performs an essentially fact-finding function of examining claims, verifying their validity, evaluating losses, assessing payments and resolving disputed claims. It is only in this last respect that a quasi-judicial function may be involved. Given the nature of the Commission, it is all the more important that some element of due process be built into the procedure. It will be the function of the commissioners to provide this element.[343]

As a specific measure that would provide for "some element of due process" the report suggested that: "Iraq will be informed of all claims and will have the right to present its comments to the commissioners within the time-delays fixed by the Governing Council or the Panel dealing with the individual claim."[344] This recommendation was not followed by the Governing Council. Instead, the provisional rules for the claims procedure stipulate that Iraq is entitled to receive the periodic reports of the Executive Secretary on the claims submitted, and to comment thereon.[345]

The procedure of the Commission differentiates between six categories of claims,[346]

Legal Problems at the Centre of United Nations Sanctions, 65 NJIL (1996) 73-90; J.R. Crook, *The UNCC and its Critics: Is Iraq Entitled to Due Process?*. In: R.B. Lillich (ed.), The United Nations Compensation Commission (1995) 77-101; F.L. Kirgis, *Claims Settlement and the United Nations Legal Structure*. In: R.B. Lillich (ed.), The United Nations Compensation Commission (1995) 103-116; B.G. Affaki, *The United Nations Compensation Commission: A New Era in Claims Settlements?*, 10 Journal of International Arbitration (1993) 21-57; F.E. McGovern, *The Intellectual Heritage of Claims Processing at the United Nations Compensation Commission*. In: Lillich, R.B. (ed.), The United Nations Compensation Commission (1995) 187-203; H. Wassgren, *The UN Compensation Commission: Lessons of Legitimacy, State Responsibility, and War Reparations*, 11 LJIL (1998) 473-492.

342 Emphasis added.

343 S/22559, para. 20.

344 *Ibid.*, para. 26.

345 See 'Provisional Rules for Claims Procedure', Art. 16. The rules are annexed to Decision 10 of the Governing Council, S/AC.26/1991/10, 26 June 1992. Reproduced in 31 ILM (1992), 1009.

346 The differentiation was established by the Governing Council in its first (S/AC.26/1991/1, 2 Aug. 1991) and seventh (S/AC.26/1991/7/Rev.1, 17 March 1992) decisions. They relate to individuals with claims of less than $100,000 (category A-C), individuals with claims over $100,000 (category D), corporations and other entities (E) and governments and international organizations (F).

of which the first three have been given priority in their processing.[347] The claims are submitted to the Secretariat by the governments of the claimants by means of standard forms.[348] A panel of Commissioners then evaluates the claims and prepares a recommendation for the Governing Council.[349] The Governing Council decides on these recommendations by means of majority voting,[350] decisions which are final.[351] Once the extent of the reparation is thus established, it is paid for by the United Nations Compensation Fund, of which Iraq is the sole contributor.[352]

3.4.2.3.4 Continuing Sanctions

As regards the sanctions, in paragraph 22 the Council decided not to lift them until the UNCC was established and working and "upon Council agreement that Iraq has

---

[347] For an overview of the Commission's work see, *e.g.*, Malanczuk, *op. cit. supra* n.2; N. Wühler, *Causation and Directness of Loss as Elements of Compensability before the United Nations Compensation Commission*. In: R.B. Lillich (ed.), The United Nations Compensation Commission (1995) 207-234; and R.J. Bettauer, *The United Nations Compensation Commission-Developments since October 1992*, 89 AJIL (1995) 416-423.

[348] The standard forms are devised and distributed by the Commission's secretariat in accordance with Art. 6(1) of the Provisional Rules for Claims Procedure.

[349] As of 15 June 2000, the Panel of Commissioners had issued 18 recommendations on claims falling under Category A-C; 5 on Category D; 29 on Category E; and 5 on Category F. The recommendations may be accessed at http://www.unog.ch/uncc.

[350] The only exception being the vote on the extent of Iraq's contribution to the Fund, which requires unanimity.

[351] Article 40 (4) of the Provisional Rules for Claims Procedure holds that: "Decisions of the Governing Council will be final and are not subject to appeal or review on procedural, substantive or other grounds." The Commission received nearly 2.6 million claims, which request compensation of 322 billion US dollars. As of 16 June 2000, the Commission had awarded $15 billion in a total of 2,588,728 claims, claims that sought $54 billion in compensation. At that time 13,086 claims remained to be resolved, seeking $267 billion in compensation. See 'Status of Claims Processing', 16 June 2000. Accessed at http://www.unog.ch/uncc on 15 July 2000.

[352] By S/Res. 705 (1991), 15 Aug. 1991, the Council decided that the amount of compensation to be paid by Iraq will not exceed 30% of the annual value of its petroleum and petroleum-related exports. See also S/Res. 706 (1991), 15 Aug. 1991 and S/Res. 712 (1991), 15 Sept. 1991, which authorized the import of Iraqi petroleum of 1.6 billion dollars under certain conditions. When Iraq did not meet these conditions the Security Council adopted resolution 778 (1991) on 2 Oct. 1991, which established that States were to seize frozen Iraqi assets and redirect 30% thereof to the Compensation Fund. Under the "oil-for-food" scheme established by resolution 986 (1995), moreover, Iraq was allowed to export oil, the revenues of which were to be used for humanitarian purposes (see S/Res. 986 (1995), 14 April 1995, paras. 1, 6-10). In para. 8(c) of that resolution it was decided that 30% of these revenues would be transferred to the UNCC. The "oil-for-food" scheme was renewed throughout 1995-2000 (see, *e.g.*, resolutions 1143 (1997), 4 Dec. 1997; 1210 (1998), 24 Nov. 1998; 1281 (1999), 10 Dec. 1999; 1302 (2000), 8 June 2000).

completed all actions contemplated in paragraphs 8, 9, 10, 11, 12 and 13". In paragraph 28 the Council agrees to review the sanctions regime against Iraq "on a regular basis". It may not come as a surprise that Iraq has only partially and reluctantly complied with the Council's demands contained in resolution 687 (1991). In response, the Council decided not to lift the sanctions against Iraq.

3.4.2.4 The Kurds in Iraq

When *Operation Desert Storm* was inflicting severe damage on Iraqi forces, the Kurdish population in Northern Iraq followed the Shi'ite example in the South by beginning widespread uprisings against the regime of Saddam Hussein in March 1991.[353] The uprising proved successful until Iraqi reinforcements, no longer engaged in combat against coalition forces, crushed the rebellious factions. This caused an exodus of Kurdish refugees into Iranian and Turkish territories, an exodus which was televised daily. In response, the Council adopted resolution 688 (1991).[354] In the preamble to this resolution the Council first stated that it was "mindful of its duties and its responsibilities under the Charter of the United Nations for the maintenance of international peace and security", and 'recalled' Article 2 (7) of the Charter. Then, however, the Council determined that:

> the repression of the Iraqi civilian population in many parts of Iraq, including most recently in Kurdish populated areas, which led to a massive flow of refugees towards and across international frontiers and to cross-border incursions, which threaten international peace and security in the region.

Accordingly, the Council insisted that Iraq "allow immediate access by international humanitarian organizations to all those in need of assistance in all parts of Iraq and to make available all necessary facilities for their operations."[355] In paragraph 6, moreover, the Council "appeals to all Member States and to all humanitarian organizations to contribute to these humanitarian relief efforts." Subsequently, armed forces from, *inter alia*, France, the UK, the US and the Netherlands launched

---

[353] See P. Malanczuk, *The Kurdish Crisis and Allied Intervention in the Aftermath of the Second Gulf War*, 2 EJIL (1991) 114-132; P. Akhavan, *Lessons from Iraqi Kurdistan: Self-Determination and Humanitarian Intervention Against Genocide*, 11 Netherlands Quarterly of Human Rights (1993) 41-62, 42-43; I. Österdahl, *By All Means Intervene! The Security Council and the Use of Force under Chapter VII of the UN Charter in Iraq (to Protect the Kurds), in Bosnia, Somalia, Rwanda and Haiti*, 66 NJIL (1997) 241-271, 242-248.

[354] S/Res. 688 (1991), 5 April 1991. Adopted by 10 votes to 3, with 2 abstentions.

[355] *Ibid.*, para. 3. See also para. 2, in which the Council: "Demands that Iraq, as a contribution to remove the threat to international peace and security in the region, immediately end th[e] repression".

Operation Provide Comfort on 17 April 1991. The forces established a triangle zone in Northern Iraq of almost 10,000 square km. which was declared inaccessible to Iraqi forces.

3.4.3 Summary

The invasion of Kuwait by Iraq on 2 August 1990 was promptly condemned by the Council as constituting a breach of international peace and security in resolution 660 (1990). This determination under Article 39 of the Charter is certainly beyond dispute.[356] The Council moreover demanded that Iraq withdraw its troops as a measure under Article 40. The Council thereafter gradually tightened its grip on Iraq. It established extensive sanctions against Iraq by means of resolution 661 (1990), while simultaneously affirming the right of self-defence under Article 51. In resolution 665 (1990), furthermore, member states aiding Kuwait were 'called upon' to use naval force if necessary to enforce the sanctions. And in resolution 678 (1990) the Council authorized states to use all necessary means to liberate Kuwait if Iraq did not withdraw its troops before or on 15 January 1991. When Iraq did not respond adequately, coalition forces indeed succeeded in driving out the Iraqi forces from Kuwait. A defeated Iraq was then obliged to accept additional and sometimes far-reaching demands under resolutions 686 (1991) and 687 (1991) before a formal cease-fire could enter into force in April 1991. As a result of the extensive demands and the non-cooperative attitude of Iraq the sanctions remained in force.

3.4.4 Analysis: The Application of Chapter VII by the Council

With the exception of the above-mentioned resolution 660 (1990) and the affirmation of the inherent right of self-defence under Article 51 in resolutions 661 (1990) and 678 (1990), the Council refrained from specifying the exact legal basis for its actions. In most cases the Council merely stated that it "is acting under Chapter VII of the Charter." The absence of such specifications does not usually represent an observer with problems. Thus the sanctions imposed under resolution 661 (1990), for instance, can only be seen as being based on Article 41 of the Charter.

---

356 As observed by Schachter, the invasion represented the first forcible invasion and purported annexation of the territory of a member state since the United Nations was founded. He furthermore notes that the Council could have pronounced it an act of aggression, a label which it withheld in order not to prejudice possible negotiations with Iraq. O. Schachter, *United Nations Law in the Gulf Conflict*, 85 AJIL (1991) 452-473, 452-453.

Other measures, however, raise more complex interpretative issues. Resolution 665 (1990), for example, did not directly refer to any Charter provisions, nor even to Chapter VII in general. What it did do was recall resolutions 660 (1990) and 661 (1990), determine that Iraq had violated its obligations thereunder, and subsequently 'call upon' members to take such measures as were necessary to ensure the implementation of the sanctions imposed under resolution 661 (1990). Despite this somewhat ambiguous formulation, the measures were understood to include the use of (naval) force.[357] Therefore, one has to conclude that paragraph 1 of resolution 665 (1990) was based on Article 42 of the Charter,[358] a precedent for which can be found in the Rhodesian case, when the Council adopted resolution 221 (1966) authorizing the arrest and detainment of the tanker *Joanna V* upon her departure from Beira.[359]

In resolution 688 (1991) the Council determined that the consequences of the repression of the Iraqi civilian population threatened "international peace and security in the region." Although the Council 'insisted' that Iraq allow immediate access by humanitarian organizations in Iraq, and 'appealed' to all member states to "contribute to humanitarian relief efforts", taken as a whole, the resolution does not seem to authorize the use of force.[360] The establishment of safety zones in Iraq through *Operation Provide Comfort* can therefore not be said to have been mandated by resolution 688 (1991) of the Security Council.

The characterization and identification of the legal authority on which *Operation Desert Storm* was based led to an intense debate among legal scholars.[361] It may be recalled that resolution 678 (1990): "authorizes Member States co operating with the Government of Kuwait ... to use all necessary means to uphold and implement resolution 660 (1990) and all subsequent relevant resolutions and to restore international peace and security in the area." This phrasing, and in particular the term 'authorizes', has given rise to controversy as to whether *Operation Desert Storm* is to be considered an enforcement action on the part of the Security Council under Articles

---

[357] See Schachter, *op. cit. supra* n.356, 454; B. Graefrath, M. Mohr, *Legal Consequences of an Act of Aggression: The Case of the Iraqi Invasion and Occupation of Kuwait*, 43 Österreichische Zeitschrift für öffentliches Recht und Völkerrecht (1992) 109-138, 114-115; Freudenschuß, *op. cit. supra* n.1, 493-496. Conforti somewhat euphemistically refers to 'police actions' under resolution 665 (1990). B. Conforti, *Non-Coercive Sanctions in the United Nations Charter: Some Lessons from the Gulf War*, 2 EJIL (1991) 110-113, 113.

[358] See Frowein, *op. cit. supra* n.151, 634.

[359] See *supra*, note 252.

[360] See Malanczuk, *op. cit. supra* n.353, 127-130; Schachter, *op. cit. supra* n.356, 468-469.

[361] Generally see Frowein, *op. cit. supra* n.151, 634-635; Freudenschuß, *op. cit. supra* n.1, 523-527.

39-42 of the Charter; an act of collective self-defence by the coalition headed by the US; a mixture of both; or neither.

Those adhering to the view that it was an enforcement action maintain, for example, that the "the Security Council did not authorize a liberation campaign as directed in Article 51, but rather it delegated its own mission to the coalition, namely the enforcement of resolutions and the maintenance of the peace."[362] In a similar vein, White and Ülgen ask themselves: "If the military action in the Gulf was in collective self-defence, why was there a need for an enabling resolution?"[363] They contend that "UN-authorised actions are collective enforcement actions with a sound constitutional basis in the UN Charter."[364] Raič, moreover, maintains that:

> This resolution [678 (1990)] goes further in the authorization of the member states than the United States and United Kingdom could have reached under Article 51. It gives the member states the mandate not only to liberate Kuwait but also to restore international peace and security in the area.[365]

In a similar fashion Farer submits that:

> Self-defence seems a slender justification for wiping out Iraq's capacity to produce or deploy in the foreseeable future nuclear, chemical, and bacteriological weapons systems and for carving a Kurdish haven out of Iraqi territory. These measures are far more easily justified as prophylactic measures to eliminate a threat to international peace and security. Hence the broad support these measures have enjoyed does evidence

---

[362] Eitel, *op. cit. supra* n.292, at 183 (it may be noted that Eitel interprets Article 51 quite broadly here, for Article 51 reaffirms the 'inherent right of self-defence' rather than 'directs a liberation campaign'). At the same time he rhetorically asks how an alliance for self-defence could go "beyond liberating Kuwait, restore peace and security to the region?" *Cf.* K.H. Kaikobad, *Self-defence, Enforcement Action and the Gulf Wars, 1980-88 and 1990-91*, 63 BYIL (1992) 299-366, 353-363, who similarly concludes that the legal basis of Resolution 678 "can more convincingly be found in the scheme set out in Articles 39 to 42" than Article 51. See to the same effect Frowein, *op. cit. supra* n.151, 635.

[363] N.D. White, Ö. Ülgen, *The Security Council and the Decentralized Military Option: Constitutionality and Function*, 44 NILR (1997) 378-413, at 392.

[364] *Ibid.*, at 379. They qualify this by stating that: "In general terms ... it is true to say that the military responses authorised by the UN to date are best categorised as somewhere between 'multilateral' and 'collective'. Truly collective responses would involve a collective military operation under the original Charter scheme as well as a collective authorisation by the Council. 'Multilateral' responses are simply those undertaken by a group of States outside the UN security system. The current system as developed by the Council involves collective authorisation by that body, but lacks true collectivity in the command, control and composition of the force. Although this is a recognition that the current system falls short of the Charter ideal, it does not make it unconstitutional." *Ibid.*, at 381.

[365] D. Raič, *The Gulf Crisis and the United Nations*, 4 LJIL (1991) 119-134, at 131. *Cf.* R. Higgins, *The UN Security Council and the Individual State*. In: H. Fox (ed.), The Changing Constitution of the United Nations (1997) 43-51, 46.

consensus about the Council's authority to legitimate action which would not be justifiable as self-defence under Article 51.[366]

The majority view is that resolution 678 (1990) symbolically legitimized the pursuance of the right of collective self-defence, a political act without which the international community could also have acted.[367] Proponents of this view contend that the Council not only consistently and explicitly affirmed this right during the conflict, but also that the United Nations did not play a role of any significance in the conduct of the hostilities.[368] Thus Bothe, for example, submits that:

> the Council must at least retain some kind of control over military action if it is to be justified under Article 42 et seq. ... Peace-keeping by the Council is meant to be a real alternative to unilateral use of force. It is thus not the role of the Security Council just to give its blessing to a unilateral use of force.[369]

This position was also taken by Secretary-General Pérez de Cuéllar, according to whom the Gulf War "was not a United Nations war. General Schwarzkopf was not wearing a blue helmet. The success ... is the result of a multilateral action authorized, and therefore, legitimized by the United Nations."[370]

According to others, resolution 678 (1990) is unprecedented and cannot be traced to a specific provision of the Charter. Thus, Weston contends that the Security Council, with the adoption of the resolution, "created an entirely new precedent, seemingly on the basis of some assumed penumbra of powers available to the Council

---

366 T. Farer, *The Future of International Law Enforcement under Chapter VII: Is There Room for 'New Scenarios'?*. In: J. Delbrück, The Future of International Law Enforcement: New Scenarios - New Law? (1993) 39-56, at 41.

367 *E.g.* Groom, *et. al.*, submit that "the Gulf crisis was ... not an example of the use of the enforcement procedures of the UN; it was a coalition sanctioned to act with the authority of the organisation." Groom, *et. al.*, *op. cit. supra* n.323, at 153. *Cf.* E.V. Rostow, *Until What? Enforcement Action or Collective Self-Defense?*, 85 AJIL (1991) 506-516, 506-510; R. Lavalle, *The Law of the United Nations and the Use of Force, under the Relevant Security Council Resolutions of 1990 and 1991, to Resolve the Persian Gulf Crisis*, 23 NYIL (1992) 3-65, 53; Schachter, *op. cit. supra* n.356, 459-461; Conforti, *op. cit. supra* n.357, 111; S. Sucharitkul, *The Process of Peace-Making following Operation 'Desert Storm'*, 43 AJPIL (1992) 1-30, 4-12.

368 According to Gilman, amongst others, the Council cannot take enforcement measures under Art. 42 because this requires "a sufficient number of special agreements" to be concluded under Art. 43. Therefore, "if the Security Council was acting under Article 42, it was attempting to exercise powers which, in the absence of the special agreements, it did not yet possess." Gilman, *op. cit. supra* n.298, at 1151. Such a limited view of the Council's powers, however, is not sustainable. See *supra*, page 39; and Schachter, *op. cit. supra* n.356, 463-465; T. Franck, F. Patel, *UN Police Action in Lieu of War: The Old Order Changeth*, 85 AJIL (1991) 63-74, 66-70.

369 Bothe, *op. cit. supra* n.168, at 296.

370 Quoted in Eitel, *op. cit. supra* n.292, at 182.

under chapter VII – an Article 42½ – authorization, as some UN watchers have called it."[371]

The more convincing argument seems to be that the actions of the Council prior to and in pursuance of resolution 678 (1990) present a mixed form of action. In the words of Gill:

> The effect of resolution 678 in legal terms was to subsume or incorporate the right of self-defence into the right of the Council to authorize the use of military enforcement measures under Articles 39 and 42 of the Charter. As such, the military operations launched by the coalition had a dual legal basis; they were both a form of collective authorized military enforcement action and a lawful exercise of collective self-defence.[372]

Operation Desert Storm certainly was an act of collective self-defence on behalf of Kuwait, a right explicitly recognized by the Council. At the same time, however, the use of the term "authorize" implies that such authorization could also be withdrawn. The states conducting the operation were therefore not entirely free in choosing when and how to apply force against Iraq.[373] This became all the more apparent with the adoption of resolutions 686 (1991) and 687 (1991) in the aftermath of the war, when the Council changed the objectives of the actions against Iraq by imposing additional demands on Iraq before a cease-fire would be effective. The Council's demands thus transformed the action from an act of self-defence into an enforcement action.[374]

During and after the Second Gulf War, the Council certainly employed a flexible interpretation of a threat to the peace under Article 39. Its actions were taken in response to a clearly unlawful invasion of Kuwait by Iraq, and initially consisted of measures aimed at restoring the territorial integrity and independence of Kuwait. When the non-forcible sanctions were not successful the Council resorted to forcible action, which succeeded in liberating Kuwait. After the Iraqi forces were driven out, however, the Council was apparently not convinced that international peace and security in the region had been restored, and it imposed a severe sanctions regime on Iraq.

---

371 B.H. Weston, *Security Council Resolution 678 and Persian Gulf Decision Making: Precarious Legitimacy*, 85 AJIL (1991) 518-522, at 522. See also Schachter, *op. cit. supra* n.356 (submitting at 461 that under a doctrine of implied powers Chapter VII alone could provide an adequate basis for the adoption of resolution 678 by the Council); and Freudenschuß, *op. cit. supra* n.1, 526-527.

372 Gill, *op. cit. supra* n.5, at 100. *Cf.* B. Simma, *Does the UN Charter provide an Adequate Legal Basis for Individual or Collective Responses to Violations of Obligations Erga Omnes?*. In: J. Delbrück (ed.), The Future of International Law Enforcement: New Scenarios - New Law? (1993) 125-146, 138-139.

373 See Schachter, *op. cit. supra* n.356, 460; Franck, Patel, *op. cit. supra* n.368, 63-64.

374 *Cf.* N. Rostow, *The International Use of Force after the Cold War*, 32 HILJ (1991) 411-421, who submits at 420 that: "The U.N. defence of Kuwait was in fact an example of collective security in action – the exercise of the right of collective self-defence."

3.5 Liberia 1990-1997

3.5.1 Factual Background[375]

The dictatorial military regime headed by Master-Sergeant Samuel Doe, which had assumed control of the country in 1980, was threatened by an insurgency movement in 1989, a movement called the National Patriotic Front of Liberia (NPFL) and which was led by a former government official, Charles Taylor. The insurgency movement itself, however, became divided as a former Taylor commander, Prince Johnson, formed the Independent National Patriotic Front of Liberia (INPFL) which wanted to prevent an all-out victory by the NPFL. Thereafter a civil war erupted between the two parties and Doe's Armed Forces of Liberia (AFL).[376] According to one observer the ensuing conflict is best described as "une lutte armée pour la conquête du pouvoir politique sur un fond de tensions ethniques."[377] Indeed, during the period under consideration various factions[378] were engaged in hostilities against each other and the civilian population, costing an estimated 150,000 civilian lives.[379] In response to the deteriorating situation in Liberia, the Economic Community of West African States (ECOWAS)[380] sent in a Cease-Fire Monitoring Group (ECOMOG) on 25 August 1990.[381] ECOMOG, which initially comprised about 4,000 troops,[382] was welcomed by

---

[375] Generally see F. Meledje Djedjro, *La Guerre Civile du Libéria et la Question de L'ingérence dans les Affaires Intérieures des États*, 26 Revue Belge de Droit International (1993) 393-436; G. Nolte, *Restoring Peace by Regional Action: International Legal Aspects of the Liberian Conflict*, 53 ZaöRV (1993) 601-637; R. Kramer, 'Special Report: Liberia: A Casualty of the Cold War's End', 1995. Accessed at http://www.africanews.org/usaf/liberia.html on 19 Feb. 1998.

[376] Doe was killed on 10 Sept. 1990 by Johnson's INPFL forces. Doe loyalists later formed a new group, the United Liberation Movement of Democracy for Liberia (ULIMO).

[377] Meledje *op. cit. supra* n.375, at 395. G. Nolte quotes the ECOWAS Secretary-General describing the situation in Liberia in 1990 as a "slaughterhouse". Nolte, *op. cit. supra* n.375, at 607.

[378] See M.A. Vogt, *The Involvement of ECOWAS in Liberia's Peacekeeping*. In: E.J. Keller, D. Rothschild (eds.), Africa in the New International Order: Rethinking State Sovereignty and Regional Security (1996) 165-183, 174-176 on the proliferation of factions within Liberia.

[379] 'Final Report of the Secretary-General on The United Nations Observer Mission in Liberia', S/1997/712, 12 Sept. 1997, para. 22.

[380] ECOWAS was established by a treaty signed on 28 May 1975 (reproduced in 14 ILM (1975), 1200-1209), a treaty which was revised on 24 July 1993. The current sixteen member states are: Benin, Burkina Faso, Cape Verde, Côte d'Ivoire, Gambia, Ghana, Guinea, Guinea Bissau, Liberia, Mali, Mauritania, Niger, Nigeria, Senegal, Sierra Leone, and Togo.

[381] On which generally see R.A. Mortimer, *ECOMOG, Liberia, and Regional Security in West Africa*. In: E.J. Keller, D. Rothschild (eds.), Africa in the New International Order: Rethinking State Sovereignty and Regional Security (1996) 149-164; Vogt, *op. cit. supra* n.378; C.E. Adibe, *The Liberian*

Doe and Johnson, but not by Taylor, who by then controlled the largest part of the country. ECOMOG and the NPFL engaged in hostilities in September and October 1990 in and around the capital Monrovia. Relative stability recurred when a cease-fire was signed between the NPFL and ECOWAS in November 1990, and an agreement known as the Yamoussoukro IV Accord was reached between the major warring parties on 30 October 1991.[383] A year later, however, on 15 October 1992, ECOMOG and the NPFL again commenced fighting each other. At the end of 1995, moreover, heavy fighting broke out between ECOMOG and the United Liberation Movement for Liberia (ULIMO), a new group formed by Doe loyalists.

3.5.2.1 Establishment of a Weapons Embargo

In the preamble to resolution 788 (1992) the Council unanimously determined that "the deterioration of the situation in Liberia constitutes a threat to international peace and security, particularly in West Africa as a whole."[384] The Council, moreover, recognized "the need for increased humanitarian assistance" and the importance of "a peaceful resolution of the Liberian conflict by creating the necessary conditions for free and fair elections in Liberia". Subsequently, the Council decided, in paragraph 8 of resolution 788 (1992):

> under Chapter VII of the Charter of the United Nations, that all States shall, for the purposes of establishing peace and stability in Liberia, immediately implement a general and complete embargo on all deliveries of weapons and military equipment to Liberia until the Security Council decides otherwise.

Conflict and the ECOWAS-UN Partnership. In: T.G. Weiss (ed.), Beyond UN Subcontracting: Task-Sharing with Regional Security Arrangements and Service-Providing NGOs (1998) 67-90.

[382] Nigeria was the largest troop-contributing country to ECOMOG, which led to fears of regional domination by other ECOWAS countries. As of 24 Feb. 1995, the troop-contributing countries to ECOMOG included Nigeria (4,908); Ghana (1,028); Guinea (609); Sierra Leone (359); Gambia (10) and Mali (10). These figures exclude Tanzania and Uganda who joined ECOMOG in January 1994.

[383] The Accord provided for a Transitional Government with three branches: legislative, executive and judicial, as well as general and Presidential elections to be held within 7 months of the signing of the Accord.

[384] S/Res. 788 (1992), 19 Nov. 1992.

Despite this decision weapons continued to flow into the country,[385] to which the Council responded by reaffirming States' obligations to comply with the embargo[386] and establishing a Sanctions Committee.[387]

3.5.2.2 Action through Regional Arrangements

Strictly speaking, peacekeeping operations fall outside the scope of the present work, since they require the prior consent of the parties as to their establishment and are therefore not to be considered as enforcement actions by the Council under Chapter VII.[388] The peacekeeping mission sent to Liberia by the ECOWAS, however, gradually assumed enforcement characteristics. As one observer on ECOMOG has noted: "the peacekeeping operation [turned] into an enforcement operation without losing general international backing."[389] Since the operation was endorsed by the Security Council, the enforcement characteristics of ECOMOG warrant its inclusion below.

---

[385] See, *e.g.*, Mortimer, *op. cit. supra* n.381, 159.

[386] *Cf.* the following statement by the Council, in which it: "Calls upon all States strictly to abide by and comply with the general and complete embargo on all deliveries of weapons and military equipment to Liberia imposed by resolution 788 (1992) under Chapter VII of the United Nations Charter." (S/Res. 813 (1993), 26 March 1993, para. 9). For similar statements see, *e.g.*, S/Res. 950 (1994), 21 Oct. 1994, para. 6; S/Res. 972 (1995), 13 Jan. 1995, para. 6; and S/Res. 1071 (1996), 30 Aug. 1996, para. 12.

[387] In S/Res. 985 (1995), 13 April 1995, para. 4, the Council: "Urges all States, and in particular all neighbouring States, to comply fully with the embargo on all deliveries of weapons and military equipment to Liberia imposed by resolution 788 (1992), and to that end decides to establish, in accordance with rule 28 of its provisional rules of procedure, a Committee of the Security Council, consisting of all the members of the Council".

[388] See the *Certain Expenses* case, in which the Court held that peacekeeping forces are not enforcement actions, actions which can only be authorized by the Security Council under Chapter VII of the Charter (ICJ Rep. (1962), 166). The exact Charter basis of peacekeeping forces, however, remains unclear. Rudolph summarizes this legal indeterminancy as follows: "Although there is no doubt that the establishment of peacekeeping forces is covered by the mandate of the United Nations to preserve and re-establish international peace and security, there is uncertainty as exactly how to classify peace-keeping forces under the Charter." K. Rudolph, *Peace-Keeping Forces*. In: R. Wolfrum (ed.), United Nations: Law, Policies and Practice (1995) 957-969, at 961. *Cf.* Shaw, *op. cit. supra* n.16, 846. For an analysis of the possible legal bases see, *e.g.*, D. Ciobanu, *The Power of the Security Council to Organize Peace-Keeping Operations*. In: A. Cassese (ed.), United Nations Peace-Keeping (1978) 15-53; J.W. Halderman, *Legal Basis for United Nations Armed Forces*, 56 AJIL (1962) 971-996. For a historical overview of peacekeeping see A. James, *Peacekeeping in International Politics* (1990); and for an overview of United Nations peacekeeping operations see M. Bothe, *Peace-Keeping*. In: B. Simma, *et. al.* (eds.), The Charter of the United Nations (1994) 565- 603; and UNDPI, *The Blue Helmets: A Review of United Nations Peace-keeping* (1996).

[389] Mortimer, *op. cit. supra* n.381, at 161.

The initiatives undertaken by ECOWAS were repeatedly approved by the Council in its resolutions on Liberia.[390] This approval was operationalized when the three major warring factions[391] signed an agreement in Cotonou on 25 July 1993, which called upon the United Nations and ECOMOG to assist in the implementation of the Agreement. The Security Council subsequently adopted resolution 866 (1993), wherein it emphasized that "the Peace Agreement assigns ECOMOG the primary responsibility of supervising the implementation of the military provisions of the Agreement and envisages that the United Nations role shall be to monitor and verify this process."

On the same occasion, the Council noted that this would be the first time the United Nations would cooperate "with a peace-keeping mission already set up by another organization, in this case ECOWAS." According to the Council the "United Nations involvement would contribute significantly to the effective implementation of the Peace Agreement".

Therefore, the Council decided to establish the United Nations Observer Mission in Liberia (UNOMIL) "under its authority and under the direction of the Secretary-General through his Special Representative".[392] UNOMIL was, *inter alia*, mandated "Without participation in enforcement operations, to coordinate with ECOMOG in the discharge of ECOMOG's separate responsibilities both formally, through the Violations Committee, and informally."[393] In addition, UNOMIL was to "assist in the monitoring of compliance with the embargo on delivery of arms and military equipment to Liberia and the cantonment, disarmament and demobilization of combatants."[394]

The Council stressed more than once that close cooperation between ECOMOG

---

[390] See, *e.g.*, the preamble to resolution 788 (1992), adopted on 19 Nov. 1992, in which the Council, after "recalling the provisions of Chapter VIII of the Charter of the United Nations", welcomed "the continued commitment of the Economic Community of West African States (ECOWAS) to and the efforts towards a peaceful resolution of the Liberian conflict." In paragraph 9, moreover, the Council: "Decides within the same framework that the embargo imposed by paragraph 8 shall not apply to weapons and military equipment destined for the sole use of the peacekeeping forces of ECOWAS in Liberia".

[391] The NPFL, ULIMO and the political component of the AFL, the Interim Government of National Unity (IGNU).

[392] S/Res. 866 (1993), 22 Sept. 1993, para. 2. The participating countries were Bangladesh, China, the Czech Republic, Egypt, Guinea-Bissau, India, Jordan, Kenya, Malaysia, Pakistan, and Uruguay.

[393] *Ibid.*, para. 3(h). The Violations Committee was established pursuant to the Cotonou Agreement and was comprised of representatives of the United Nations, ECOMOG and the three Liberian factions.

[394] *Ibid.*, para. 3(b).

and the relatively small UNOMIL[395] was necessary. Thus in resolution 1083 (1996), for example, the Council 'emphasized' that "the continued presence of UNOMIL is predicated on the presence of ECOMOG and its commitment to ensure the safety of UNOMIL."[396] Prior to this resolution, the Council had already 'welcomed':

> the steps taken by the Secretary-General to establish a Trust Fund, which would facilitate the sending of reinforcements by African States to ECOMOG, assist in supporting troops of participating ECOMOG countries and also assist in mine-clearing, humanitarian and development activities, as well as the electoral process, and calls on Member States to support the peace process in Liberia by contributing to the Trust Fund.[397]

The mandate of UNOMIL was extended on various occasions,[398] in an environment which remained volatile. Indeed, hostilities between and the harassment of UNOMIL, ECOMOG troops and humanitarian aid workers on the one hand, and faction members on the other, occurred repeatedly, whilst ECOMOG was engaged in heavy fighting with ULIMO in 1995-1996. The Council continuously condemned these actions. Thus, in Resolution 950 (1994), the Council:

> Condemns the widespread killings of civilians and other violations of international humanitarian law by the factions in Liberia, and the detention and maltreatment of UNOMIL observers, ECOMOG soldiers, humanitarian relief workers and other international personnel and demands that all the factions strictly abide by applicable rules of international humanitarian law.[399]

In resolution 1001 (1995) the Council expressed its impatience with the situation. After "emphasizing that the people of Liberia bear the ultimate responsibility for achieving peace and national reconciliation," the Council made further extensions of UNOMIL's

---

395 The maximum strength of UNOMIL was 303 military observers, 20 military medical personnel, and 45 military engineers.

396 S/Res. 1083 (1996), 27 Nov. 1996, preamble.

397 S/Res. 866 (1993), 22 Sept. 1993, para. 6. This appeal was repeated on various occasions. Thus in para. 9 of S/Res. 911 (1994), adopted on 21 April 1994, the Council: "Encourages Member States to provide support for the peace process in Liberia by contributing to the Trust Fund or by providing other assistance to facilitate the sending of reinforcements by African States to ECOMOG, assist in supporting troops of participating ECOMOG countries and also assist in humanitarian and development activities, as well as the electoral process." So also in S/Res. 1083 (1996), 27 Nov. 1996, para. 11, the Council: "Reiterates strongly its appeal to all States to provide financial, logistical and other assistance in support of ECOMOG to assist it in carrying out its mission and to contribute to the United Nations Trust Fund for Liberia in order to help implement the peace process, including demobilization and reintegration."

398 Resolutions 911 (1994), 21 April 1994; 950 (1994), 21 Oct. 1994; 972 (1995), 13 Jan. 1995; 985 (1995), 13 April 1995; 1001 (1995), 30 June 1995; 1014 (1995), 15 Sept. 1995; 1020 (1995), 10 Nov. 1995; 1041 (1996), 29 Jan. 1996; 1059 (1996), 31 May 1996; 1071 (1996), 30 Aug. 1996; 1083 (1996), 27 Nov. 1996; 1100 (1997), 27 March 1997; 1116 (1997), 27 June 1997.

399 S/Res. 950 (1994), 21 Oct. 1994, para. 7.

presence contingent upon substantial progress in arriving at national unity.[400] Herein the Council also:

Demands once more, that all factions in Liberia strictly respect the status of ECOMOG and UNOMIL personnel, as well as organizations and agencies delivering humanitarian assistance throughout Liberia, and further demands that these factions facilitate such deliveries and that they strictly abide by applicable rules of international humanitarian law.[401]

In resolution 1020 (1995), UNOMIL's mandate was extended, so as to include the investigation and reporting to the Secretary-General on violations of human rights.[402] This specific extension was included in response to the numerous violations of civilians' human rights by the warring factions.[403]

Despite the impatience expressed by the Council in resolution 1001 (1995), it was not until 30 September 1997 that UNOMIL was dismantled in accordance with resolution 1116 (1997).[404] Elections had been held by then,[405] while a new government was installed on 2 August 1997.

3.5.3 Summary

The Council's involvement with the situation in Liberia has been twofold. It first established a weapons embargo under resolution 788 (1992). This embargo did not produce the desired effects, which prompted the Council to 'call upon' and 'remind'

---

400 In para. 2 of S/Res. 1001 (1995), adopted on 30 June 1995, the Council: "Stresses that continued international community support for the peace process in Liberia, including the continued presence of UNOMIL, is contingent on immediate actions by the Liberian parties to peacefully resolve their differences and achieve national reconciliation."

401 S/Res. 1001 (1995), para. 13.

402 S/Res. 1020 (1995), 10 Nov. 1995, para. 2(f). See also para. 10 of resolution 1059 (1996), 31 May 1996, in which the Council: "Stresses the importance of respect for human rights in Liberia."

403 *Cf.* the 'Final Report of the Secretary-General on The United Nations Observer Mission in Liberia', S/1997/712, 12 Sept. 1997, para. 23: "The conflict in Liberia was essentially a power struggle with some ethnic elements, but the command and control exercised by faction leaders over their commanders and troops in the field was often loose. The central government, law and order, and physical infrastructure of Liberia had been either seriously degraded or had disappeared altogether. As a result, the fighting was characterized by widespread lawlessness, the easy availability of small arms and gross violations of human rights by all factions against innocent civilians."

404 In S/Res. 1116 (1997), 27 June 1997, para. 1, the Council: "Decides to extend the mandate of UNOMIL until 30 September 1997, in the expectation that it will terminate on that date." ECOMOG's mandate formally ended on 2 Feb. 1998, but the complete withdrawal did not take place until Oct. 1999.

405 On 19 July 1997, which were supervised by UNOMIL in accordance with resolution 1020 (1995).

States of their obligation to comply with its decisions and establish a Sanctions Committee. Specific additional measures against a violating state were, however, not taken.

The second form of action was the Council's decision to endorse and cooperate with the regional peacekeeping mission present in Liberia since 1990, the ECOMOG. Whilst in previous resolutions on Liberia the Council had consistently commended the efforts of ECOMOG, a formal cooperation between the United Nations and ECOMOG was established by resolution 866 (1993). Through this resolution UNOMIL was established, a small unit which maintained close ties with the ECOMOG, and indeed depended on the latter for its presence in Liberia.

3.5.4 Analysis: The Application of Chapter VII by the Council

The weapons embargo established pursuant to resolution 778 (1992) was a measure taken under Article 41 of the Charter. In the same resolution the Council decided under Article 39 that "the deterioration of the situation in Liberia constitutes a threat to international peace and security, particularly in West Africa as a whole."

UNOMIL was established 'under the authority' of the Security Council (resolution 866 (1993)), and is thus to be seen as a measure taken under Article 29 of the Charter. In other words, UNOMIL was a subsidiary organ of the Security Council. The decision to include cooperation with ECOMOG in UNOMIL's mandate must be seen in the light of Chapter VII and Chapter VIII (Articles 52 and 53) of the Charter. The Council acknowledged this by recalling the provisions of Chapter VIII in resolution 788 (1992). The regional peacekeeping mission was thus utilized as a mechanism for pursuing and enforcing the Council's mandate under Chapter VII of the Charter.

3.6 Former Yugoslavia 1991-2000

The break up of the Socialist Federal People's Republic of Yugoslavia (SFPRY) into several sovereign states has been a long, complex and violent process. Several international initiatives have been taken in order to contain the process,[406] with different levels of success. Amongst these initiatives are actions taken by the Security Council, which devoted a long series of resolutions on the matter, several of which were taken under Chapter VII.

---

[406] On which see, *e.g.*, B. de Rossanet, *Peacemaking and Peacekeeping in Yugoslavia* (1996).

3.6.1 Factual Background: The Break up of Yugoslavia[407]

The SFPRY was formed in 1946 under communist rule headed by President Tito. The state consisted of six republics and two provinces: Bosnia and Herzegovina; Croatia; Macedonia; Montenegro; Serbia (which included the autonomous provinces of Kosovo and Vojvodina); and Slovenia. With the death of President Tito in 1980 internal stability was threatened, and in the late 1980s nationalist sentiments came to play an increasing role in Yugoslav politics. These sentiments culminated in calls for secession, which in the period considered here led to five wars. The first two were the struggles for independence by Slovenia and Croatia; the third was formed by the aspiration of the Croatian Serbs in Krajina to join Serbia; the fourth and most protracted war was related to the establishment of the Republic of Bosnia and Herzegovina; and the fifth resulted from the calls for independence from the Albanians in the Serb province Kosovo. The background to these conflicts will be considered below, followed by an overview of the actions taken by the Council.

Slovenia

Slovenia announced its independence on 25 June 1991, subsequent to a plebiscite held on 23 December 1990, in which a majority voted in favour of secession. In response, the federal Yugoslav People's Army (YPA)[408] sent troops into the republic, which resulted in a ten-day war. This conflict ended with the signing of the Brioni Agreement, which was brokered by the European Community (EC) on 7 July 1991.[409] Subsequently, the Republic of Slovenia was recognized by the EEC on 15 January 1992[410] and admitted to the United Nations on 22 May 1992.[411]

---

[407] Generally see R.H. Ullman, *Introduction: The World and Yugoslavia's Wars*. In: R.H. Ullman (ed.), The World and Yugoslavia's Wars (1996) 1-8; T.G. Weiss, *Collective Spinelessness: U.N. Actions in the Former Yugoslavia*. In: R.H. Ullman (ed.), The World and Yugoslavia's Wars (1996) 59-96; M. Weller, *The International Response to the Dissolution of the Socialist Federal Republic of Yugoslavia*, 86 AJIL (1992) 569-607; C.J. Garris, *Bosnia and the Limitations of International Law*, 34 Santa Clara Law Review (1994) 1039-1087.

[408] Also known as the Yugoslav National Army (JNA).

[409] The agreement between Federal, Croatian and Slovenian authorities provided for the withdrawal of Federal troops from Slovenia; demobilisation of Slovenian troops; talks on the future of the State; and the dispatch of EC observers to Slovenia and Croatia. The YPA eventually withdrew its troops in Oct. 1991.

[410] On 16 Dec. 1991 the Foreign Ministers of the EC declared in Brussels that Slovenia would be recognized as an independent state by 15 Jan. 1992.

[411] A/Res. 46/236, 22 May 1992.

Croatia

Croatia's struggle for independence was of greater concern to the Serbian leadership. Similar to Slovenia, Croatia declared its independence on 25 June 1991. Here too a plebiscite, held on 19 May 1991, had resulted in a majority voting in favour of secession. The YPA responded by sending in troops, and by July 1991 the situation had escalated into a full-scale war between Croatians and the Serbian minority in Krajina backed by the YPA. Despite several cease-fire agreements, hostilities continued from 1991 until 1996. The EC recognized Croatia on the same day as Slovenia, that is 15 January 1992,[412] and Croatia was admitted to the United Nations on 22 May 1992.[413]

Bosnia-Herzegovina

Following the elections in 1990 in which his party took the most seats, A. Izetbegovic was appointed as President of the Republic of Bosnia and Herzegovina. In practice, a collective Presidency was installed consisting of two Muslims, two Serbs, two Croats and one person of another ethnic background. On 29 February and 1 March 1992 a referendum was held in which the majority of Bosnian Muslims and Croats voted in favour of independence, with most of the Bosnian Serbs boycotting the vote. Subsequently, Bosnia-Herzegovina declared its independence in April 1992. In response the Bosnian Serbs, headed by Radovan Karadzic and assisted by the YPA, launched attacks against the Muslim and Croat population, with the goal of joining Serb-populated regions with Serbia. On 19 May 1992 the YPA's withdrawal from Bosnia and Herzegovina was announced, but in reality 85% of the troops were demobilized and all the army's equipment was left behind.[414] Practically, therefore, the YPA remained assisting the Serbian population in Bosnia-Herzegovina. This led to a complex war between Bosnian Muslims, Croats and Serbs,[415] in which the parties shifted their alliances more than once. The fighting in Bosnia was particularly

---

[412] Following a strong German lobby in favour of recognition. See R.H. Ullman, *The Wars in Yugoslavia and the International System after the Cold War*. In: R.H. Ullman (ed.), World and Yugoslavia's Wars (1996) 16-20.

[413] A/Res. 46/238, 22 May 1992.

[414] See V. Morris, M.P. Scharf, *An Insider's Guide to the International Criminal Tribunal for the former Yugoslavia* (1995), 20.

[415] Who respectively accounted for 44, 17 and 31 percent of the total population of Bosnia-Herzegovina.

gruesome[416] and included acts which have come to be known as "ethnic cleansing".[417] Similar to Croatia and Slovenia, Bosnia and Herzegovina was admitted to the United Nations on 22 May 1992.[418]

Serbia and Montenegro

Slobodan Milosovic became the Serbian Communist Party Chief in 1986. His efforts to create a centralized Yugoslavia under Serbian dominance were opposed by Croatia and Slovenia, which at first preferred a loose confederation of states, but eventually declared their independence. Serbia and Montenegro proclaimed the establishment of the Federal Republic of Yugoslavia (FRY) on 27 April 1992. International recognition has, however, been withheld. Within the United Nations, for example, the FRY has not been regarded as the automatic successor to Yugoslavia. Thus in the preamble to resolution 757 (1992), adopted on 30 May 1992, the Council noted that "the claim by the Federal Republic of Yugoslavia (Serbia and Montenegro) to continue automatically the membership of the former Socialist Federal Republic of Yugoslavia in the United Nations has not been generally accepted."[419]

Kosovo

Tensions between ethnic Albanians and Serbs in the Serb province of Kosovo intensified during the 1990s. The autonomous status of the province was revoked by

---

416 According to Ullman, "for sheer horror, especially for the savagery of crimes against noncombatants, the only apt comparison with the Yugoslav conflict is World War II itself." Ullman, *op. cit. supra* n.407, at 1.

417 See, *e.g.*, N. Lerner, *Ethnic Cleansing*. In: Y. Dinstein, M. Tabori (eds.), War Crimes in International Law (1996) 107-122; D. Petrovic, *Ethnic Cleansing – An Attempt at Methodology*, 5 EJIL (1994) 342-359.

418 A/Res. 46/237, 22 May 1992.

419 In para. 1 of S/Res. 777 (1992), adopted on 19 Sept. 1992, the Council accordingly "considers that the Federal Republic of Yugoslavia (Serbia and Montenegro) cannot continue automatically the membership of the former Socialist Federal Republic of Yugoslavia in the United Nations; and therefore recommends to the General Assembly that it decide that the Federal Republic of Yugoslavia (Serbia and Montenegro) should apply for membership in the United Nations and that it shall not participate in the work of the General Assembly." The FRY has yet to apply for membership. On the membership and admission of Yugoslavia to the United Nations see, *e.g.*, Y.Z. Blum, *UN Membership of the 'New' Yugoslavia: Continuity or Break*, 86 AJIL (1992) 831-833; V.D. Degan, O.E. Bring, M.K. Malone, *Correspondents' Agora: UN Membership of the former Yugoslavia*, 87 AJIL (1993) 240-248; Weller, *op. cit. supra* n.407. See also paras. 3-4 of the Sep. Op. of Judge Oda in the *Case Concerning Legality of Use of Force* (Provisional Measures), Yugoslavia v. Netherlands, Order of 2 June 1999, ICJ Rep. (1999).

Milosovic in 1989, and since then both groups have lived in what has been described as a "system of apartheid."[420] In 1998 the Kosovo Liberation Army started an armed struggle for independence from the FRY.

3.6.2 Security Council Action concerning former Yugoslavia

The Security Council took action in various fields in response to the crisis in former Yugoslavia. These actions extend to the establishment of sanctions, the establishment of peacekeeping operations, and cooperation with regional arrangements.

3.6.2.1 The Establishment of Embargoes

The Council's involvement in the Yugoslav crisis began with the unanimous adoption of resolution 713 (1991) on 25 September 1991. Herein the Council expressed its concern that "the continuation of this situation constitutes a threat to international peace and security" and recalled "its primary responsibility under the Charter of the United Nations for the maintenance of international peace and security", as well as "the provisions of Chapter VIII of the Charter of the United Nations". The latter reference to the 'Regional Arrangements' chapter was included in the context of the efforts of the European Community to resolve the crisis, efforts which were "commended". In paragraph 6 of resolution 713 (1991), the Council imposed a weapons embargo on Yugoslavia by deciding:

> under Chapter VII of the Charter of the United Nations, that all States shall, for the purposes of establishing peace and stability in Yugoslavia, immediately implement a general and complete embargo on all deliveries of weapons and military equipment to Yugoslavia until the Security Council decides otherwise following consultation between the Secretary-General and the Government of Yugoslavia.[421]

In accordance with its earlier practice, a Sanctions Committee was established to oversee the implementation of the measures.[422] By resolution 727 (1992), adopted on 8 January 1992, moreover, the Council reaffirmed resolution 713 (1991) and referred to the applicability of the embargo in "in all areas that have been part of Yugoslavia."

The weapons embargo established by resolution 713 (1991) was later complemented

---

[420] J. Perlez, 'Ethnic Conflict in Kosovo has Centuries Old Roots', NY Times, 5 May 1999. Accessed at http://www.nytimes.com on 10 July 2000.

[421] According to Stremlau "these sanctions locked in a huge military advantage for the Serbs". J. Stremlau, *Sharpening International Sanctions*, Report of the Carnegie Commission on Preventing Deadly Conflict (1996), at 26.

[422] S/Res. 724 (1991), para. 5.

by sanctions specifically aimed at the FRY. In resolution 757 (1992), an embargo was established against the FRY in response to its ongoing interference in Bosnia and Herzegovina.[423] The embargo, established as a measure under Chapter VII of the Charter, encompassed economic, diplomatic, scientific and cultural measures.[424] Following an initial tightening of the sanctions,[425] the embargo has gradually and partially been lifted in view of the FRY's increased cooperation with the United Nations, particularly by sealing off its boundary with Bosnia and Herzegovina.[426] Following the signing of the Dayton Peace Agreement,[427] moreover, the sanctions were formally lifted by the Council on 1 October 1996.[428] In 1998, however, the Council decided to reimpose an arms embargo against the FRY in response to the situation in Kosovo.[429]

3.6.2.2 The Establishment of Peacekeeping Operations

Peacekeeping operations fall outside the scope of the present work.[430] As happened in Liberia, however, the United Nations peacekeeping operations in Yugoslavia gradually assumed enforcement characteristics.[431] As one commentator observes, the "typically peace-keeping character of UNPROFOR was gradually more and more mixed with

423 See also S/Res. 752 (1992), 15 May 1992, in which the Council, *inter alia,* "demands that all forms of interference from outside Bosnia-Herzegovina, including by units of the Yugoslav People's Army (JNA) as well as elements of the Croatian Army, cease immediately."

424 See S/Res. 757 (1992), 30 May 1992, paras. 4-11.

425 S/Res. 787 (1992), 16 Nov. 1992, paras. 9-10; S/Res. 820 (1993), 17 April 1993, paras. 12-29.

426 See S/Res. 1015 (1995), 15 Sept. 1995; S/Res. 1003 (1995), 5 July 1995; S/Res. 988 (1995), 21 April 1995; S/Res. 970 (1995), 12 Jan. 1995.

427 The 'General Framework Agreement for Peace in Bosnia and Herzegovina' between Bosnia and Herzegovina, Croatia, and the FRY, signed on 21 Nov. 1995. Reproduced in 35 ILM (1996) 172-183.

428 S/Res. 1074 (1996), 1 Oct. 1996, para. 2.

429 See *infra,* the text accompanying note 464.

430 See *supra,* page 89.

431 For the United Nations peacekeeping involvement in Liberia see *supra,* paragraph 3.5.2.2.

peace-enforcement."[432] This characteristic warrants the inclusion of the operations in this chapter.

With the fighting in (the territory of former) Yugoslavia continuing, the Council contemplated the establishment of a peacekeeping operation. Thereto the Council, in resolution 721 (1990),[433] invited the Secretary-General to negotiate with the parties concerned and submit recommendations for the establishment of such a force. The report,[434] which, *inter alia*, called for the establishment of a United Nations Protection Force (UNPROFOR), was approved by the Council and UNPROFOR was subsequently established by resolution 743 (1992).[435] Its mandate was originally confined to certain Croatian areas in which the Serbs constituted a majority or substantial minority of the population, but was later extended to include Bosnia and Herzegovina and the former Yugoslav Republic of Macedonia.[436] UNPROFOR was deployed in Croatia within United Nations Protected Areas (UNPAs) which were to be demilitarized and in which all persons were to be protected from military attacks.[437] After its mandate was extended several times,[438] UNPROFOR was divided into three separate missions in March 1995.[439]

---

[432] D.A. Leurdijk, *The United Nations and NATO in Former Yugoslavia, 1991-1996: Limits to Diplomacy and Force* (1996), at 22. He notes at 5 that: "Contrary to its own basics, the Security Council sent UNPROFOR to Bosnia in a hostile environment. This decision would ultimately lead to an incredible confusion about the powers – or better, the limits – of a peace-keeping operation, a situation which was further complicated, at a later stage, by adding other concepts and instruments, including peace-enforcement." The situation has been described by Kooijmans in the following terms: "For the first time in history we have a situation where peace is simultaneously *enforced* through comprehensive non-military sanctions and *kept* by impartial peace-keeping forces and all this under the heading of a 'threat to the peace'." Kooijmans, *op. cit. supra* n.133, at 117. See also Weiss, *op. cit. supra* n.407, 61; Stremlau, *op. cit. supra* n.421, 28.

[433] S/Res. 721 (1991), 27 Nov. 1991. Adopted unanimously.

[434] S/23280, 11 Dec. 1991.

[435] S/Res. 743 (1992), 21 Feb. 1992, adopted unanimously. See also S/Res. 749 (1992), 7 April 1992, which authorizes "the earliest possible full deployment of the UNPROFOR." On UNPROFOR generally see UNDPI, *op. cit. supra* n.388, 513-541.

[436] S/Res. 795 (1992), adopted on 11 Dec. 1992.

[437] By S/Res. 762 (1992), 30 June 1992, UNPROFOR's mandate was extended to the so-called "pink zones", areas within Croatia but outside the agreed UNPA boundaries. Additional extensions were made by S/Res. 769 (1992), 7 Aug. 1992; and S/Res. 779 (1992), 6 Oct. 1992.

[438] See S/Res. 807 (1993), 19 Feb. 1993; S/Res. 815 (1993), 30 March 1993; S/Res. 847 (1993), 30 June 1993; S/Res. 871 (1993), 4 Oct. 1993; S/Res. 908 (1994), 31 March 1994; S/Res. 947 (1994), 30 Sept. 1994.

[439] S/Res. 981 (1995), 31 March 1995, created the 'United Nations Confidence Restoration Operation in Croatia' (UNCRO) under Chapter VII (which was terminated by S/Res. 1026 (1995), 30 Nov. 1995). S/Res. 982 (1995), 31 March 1995, adopted under Chapter VII of the Charter,

Notwithstanding its earlier consent to the deployment of UNPROFOR, the Croatian government launched an offensive in a number of locations controlled by UNPROFOR on 22 January 1993. This action and the forcible response by the Serbs, who *inter alia* seized heavy weapons from a UNPROFOR-controlled storage, were condemned by the Council in resolution 802 (1993). On this occasion the Council also, without referring to any Charter provisions, demanded "the immediate cessation of hostile activities by Croatian armed forces ... and the withdrawal of the Croatian armed forces from these areas"; and that the Serbs return the seized heavy weapons.[440]

This was not the only setback which the peacekeeping force encountered. The Croatian army, for example, overran the Serb-controlled and United Nations Protected Area (UNPA) of Krajina at the beginning of August 1995.[441]

3.6.2.3 Humanitarian Assistance and the Embargo on Military Flights

One of UNPROFOR's primary tasks was to ensure the provision of humanitarian assistance. Thereto in paragraph 8 of resolution 758 (1992) the Council:

> Demands that all parties and others concerned create immediately the necessary conditions for unimpeded delivery of humanitarian supplies to Sarajevo and other destinations in Bosnia and Herzegovina, including the establishment of a security zone encompassing Sarajevo and its airport and respecting the agreements signed in Geneva on 22 May 1992.[442]

When the parties did not abide by this warning, the Council adopted resolution 770 (1992). Herein the Council, explicitly acting under Chapter VII of the United Nations Charter:

> Calls upon States to take nationally or through regional agencies or arrangements all measures necessary to facilitate in coordination with the United Nations the delivery by relevant United Nations humanitarian

---

limited UNPROFOR's mandate to Bosnia-Herzegovina. Furthermore, S/Res. 983 (1995), 31 March 1995, without referring to Chapter VII, created the 'United Nations Preventive Deployment Force' (UNPREDEP).

[440] S/Res. 802 (1993), 25 Jan. 1993. Croatia and local Serb authorities ultimately signed an agreement regarding the implementation of resolution 802 (1993) on 6 April 1993.

[441] On which occasion one peacekeeper was killed and several others were injured after Croat troops opened fire on UN forces. See T. Butcher, 'Croats Launch Huge Attack to Recapture Rebel Region', Daily Telegraph, 7 Aug. 1995. Accessed at http://www.telegraph.co.uk on 14 Jan. 1998.

[442] S/Res. 758 (1992), 8 June 1992.

organizations and others of humanitarian assistance to Sarajevo and wherever needed in other parts of Bosnia and Herzegovina.[443]

This was followed by resolution 781 (1992), in which the Council:

Acting pursuant to the provisions of resolution 770 (1992) aimed at ensuring the safety of the delivery of humanitarian assistance in Bosnia and Herzegovina,

1. Decides to establish a ban on military flights in the airspace of Bosnia and Herzegovina, this ban not to apply to United Nations Protection Force flights or to other flights in support of United Nations operations, including humanitarian assistance.[444]

3.6.2.4 The Establishment of 'Safe Areas'

On 16 April 1993 the Council adopted the first in a series of resolutions by which it introduced so-called safe areas. In resolution 819 (1993) it expressed its "concern" with regard to the "pattern of hostilities by Bosnian Serb paramilitary units against towns and villages in eastern Bosnia", and reaffirmed that "any taking or acquisition of territory by the threat or use of force, including through the practice of 'ethnic cleansing', is unlawful and unacceptable." After noting that the paramilitary units had interdicted humanitarian convoys, the Council:

acting under Chapter VII of the Charter of the United Nations,

1. Demands that all parties and others concerned treat Srebrenica and its surroundings as a safe area which should be free from any armed attack or any other hostile act.

The number of safe areas was extended with the adoption of resolution 824 (1993), wherein the Council:

acting under Chapter VII of the Charter,

Declares that the capital city of the Republic of Bosnia and Herzegovina, Sarajevo, and other such threatened areas, in particular the towns of Tuzla, Zepa, Gorazde, Bihac, as well as Srebrenica, and their surroundings

---

[443] Para. 2 of S/Res. 770 (1992), 13 Aug. 1992. Adopted by 12 votes in favour with 3 abstentions. Leurdijk observes that this "was the first time that, acting under Chapter VII, the Security Council gave the authorisation to use of force for humanitarian purposes." Leurdijk, *op. cit. supra* n.432, at 23. See also S/Res. 761 (1992), 29 June 1992; and S/Res. 776 (1992), 14 Sept. 1992. In para. 4 of resolution 761 (1992) the Council had demanded "that all parties and others concerned cooperate fully with UNPROFOR and international humanitarian agencies and organizations and take all necessary steps to ensure the safety of their personnel; in the absence of such cooperation, the Security Council *does not exclude other measures to deliver humanitarian assistance to Sarajevo and its environs*" (emphasis added).

[444] S/Res. 781 (1992), adopted on 9 Oct. 1992.

should be treated as safe areas by all the parties concerned and should be free from armed attacks and from any other hostile act.[445]

A month later the Council "acting under Chapter VII of the Charter of the United Nations", decided "to ensure full respect for the safe areas referred to in resolution 824 (1993)."[446] Thereto the mandate of UNPROFOR was extended,[447] including an authorization to use force in "self-defence" if necessary in order to reply to "bombardments against the safe areas by any of the parties or to armed incursion into them or in the event of any deliberate obstruction in or around those areas to the freedom of movement of UNPROFOR or of protected humanitarian convoys."[448]

These provisions notwithstanding, the safe areas have repeatedly been violated by the conflicting parties. Thus Bihac was attacked by Bosnian Serbs in November 1994, whilst Srebrenica was overrun on 11 July 1995[449] and Zepa on 20 July.[450] Indeed,

---

[445] S/Res. 824 (1993), 6 May 1993, para. 3. In para. 4 the Council: "Further declares that in these safe areas the following should be observed: (a) The immediate cessation of armed attacks or any hostile act against these safe areas, and the withdrawal of all Bosnian Serb military or paramilitary units from these towns to a distance wherefrom they cease to constitute a menace to their security and that of their inhabitants to be monitored by United Nations military observers; (b) Full respect by all parties of the rights of the United Nations Protection Force (UNPROFOR) and the international humanitarian agencies to free and unimpeded access to all safe-areas in the Republic of Bosnia and Herzegovina and full respect for the safety of the personnel engaged in these operations."

[446] S/Res. 836 (1993), adopted on 4 June 1993, para. 4.

[447] In para. 5 of S/Res. 836 (1993) the Council: "Decides to extend to that end the mandate of UNPROFOR in order to enable it, in the safe areas referred to in resolution 824 (1993), to deter attacks against the safe areas, to monitor the cease-fire, to promote the withdrawal of military or paramilitary units other than those of the Government of the Republic of Bosnia and Herzegovina and to occupy some key points on the ground, in addition to participating in the delivery of humanitarian relief to the population as provided for in resolution 776 (1992) of 14 September 1992."

[448] *Ibid.*, para. 9.

[449] The next day the Daily Telegraph reported that: "Nato planes twice attacked Bosnian Serb tanks around Srebrenica, destroying two. But further strikes were called off when the Serbs threatened to kill the Dutch peacekeepers they are holding, the Dutch defence minister, Joris Voorhoeve, said in The Hague." R. Fox, 'Serbs Capture UN Safe Haven: Troops and Refugees Flee for their Lives.' Accessed at http://www.telegraph.co.uk on 8 Jan. 1998.

[450] On 19 July 1995, the Daily Telegraph reported that "the defenders of the Muslim enclave of Zepa yesterday surrounded the 79 United Nations Ukrainian soldiers in the town, saying they would use them as human shields against a Bosnian Serb assault." T. Butcher, P. Bishop, 'Muslims use UN Men as Shields'. Accessed at http://www.telegraph.co.uk on 15 Jan. 1998. Without success, however, for by the 20th of July the enclave had been seized by the Serbs.

according to one observer "among the most unsafe locations in the Balkans, indeed in the world, were the so-called safe areas."[451]

3.6.2.5 Cooperation with Regional Arrangements

In its efforts to contain the conflicts in former Yugoslavia, the United Nations cooperated with other organizations and regional arrangements, particularly the European Community and NATO. The cooperation with the latter in the enforcement of Security Council decisions will be considered below. NATO contributed to the Council's efforts with four operations: *Operation Maritime Monitor, Operation Sharp Guard* and operations *Deny Flight* and *Close Air Support*.

In December 1992, NATO announced its willingness to support peacekeeping operations and to oversee the implementation of Security Council resolutions on the former Yugoslavia.[452] Indeed, under *Operation Maritime Monitor*, NATO ships had entered the Adriatic Sea as early as July 1991 to monitor compliance with the sanctions regime established by resolution 713 (1991), and later resolution 757 (1992).[453]

In paragraph 12 of resolution 787 (1992) the Council:

> Acting under Chapters VII and VIII of the Charter of the United Nations, calls upon States, acting nationally or through regional agencies or arrangements, to use such measures commensurate with the specific circumstances as may be necessary under the authority of the Security Council to halt all inward and outward maritime shipping in order to inspect and verify their cargoes and destinations and to ensure strict implementation of the provisions of resolutions 713 (1991) and 757 (1992).[454]

According to NATO this resolution authorized it to board and search ships in the Adriatic Sea, as in fact it was already doing. NATO interpreted its mandate even more widely when the Council enlarged the scope of the sanctions against Serbia and Montenegro by deciding to "prohibit all commercial maritime traffic from entering the

---

[451] Weiss, *op. cit. supra* n.407, at 64. So P. Bishop, reporting for the Daily Telegraph on 12 July 1995, submitted that "the term 'safe area' has become one of the most notorious examples of Orwellian 'newspeak' of our time." P. Bishop, 'Safe areas' are havens only in name. Accessed at http://www.telegraph.co.uk on 8 Jan. 1998.

[452] NATO Basic Fact Sheet No. 4, March 1997. Accessed on 1 Dec. 1997, as http://www.nato.int/docu/facts/bpfy.htm.

[453] Similarly the Western European Union (WEU) was also involved in monitoring compliance with the UN sanctions, under *Operation Sharp Fence*. See Leurdijk, *op. cit. supra* n.432, 24-26.

[454] S/Res. 787 (1992), 16 Nov. 1992.

territorial sea of the Federal Republic of Yugoslavia (Serbia and Montenegro)".[455] In doing so the Council reaffirmed:

> the authority of States acting under paragraph 12 of resolution 787 (1992) to use such measures commensurate with the specific circumstances as may be necessary under the authority of the Security Council to enforce the present resolution and its other relevant resolutions, including in the territorial sea of the Federal Republic of Yugoslavia (Serbia and Montenegro).[456]

This resolution prompted the establishment of *Operation Sharp Guard* on 8 June 1993, a combined NATO and Western European Union (WEU) operation which was to "monitor and enforce compliance with UN sanctions in accordance with United Nations Security Council resolutions 713, 757, 787 and 820." As announced by NATO, the combined Task Force "will, in particular, aim at preventing all unauthorized shipping from entering the territorial waters of the Federal Republic of Yugoslavia (Serbia and Montenegro)."[457] Under this operation NATO and WEU ships entered FRY' territorial waters in order to stop, board and search suspicious ships, in the end without actually employing force.[458] The operation was suspended after the signing of the Dayton Agreement and the adoption of resolutions 1021 (1995)[459] and 1022 (1995).[460]

In resolution 781 (1993) the Council had established a no-fly zone over Bosnia and Herzegovina. When it became apparent that the parties were not complying with this decision, the Council:

> authorizes Member States, seven days after the adoption of this resolution, acting nationally or through regional organizations or arrangements, to take, under the authority of the Security Council and subject to close coordination with the Secretary-General and UNPROFOR, all necessary measures in the airspace of the Republic of Bosnia and Herzegovina, in the event of further violations to ensure compliance with the ban on flights referred to in paragraph 1 above, and proportionate to the specific circumstances and the nature of the flights.[461]

---

455 S/Res. 820 (1993), 17 April 1993, para. 28. The citation continues with: "except when authorized on a case-by-case basis by the Committee established by resolution 724 (1991) or in case of force majeure".

456 S/Res. 820 (1993), 17 April 1993, para. 29.

457 NATO Press Release (93) 41, issued on 8 June 1993. Accessed at gopher://gopher.nato.int on 18 Dec. 1997.

458 See Leurdijk, *op. cit. supra* n.432, 25-27.

459 S/Res. 1021 (1995), 22 Nov. 1995.

460 S/Res. 1022 (1995), 22 Nov. 1995, para. 1. But according to para. 2, *Operation Sharp Guard* may be resumed if "the Federal Republic of Yugoslavia or the Bosnian Serb authorities are failing significantly to meet their obligations under the Peace Agreement."

461 S/Res. 816 (1993), 31 March 1993, para. 4.

Pursuant to this resolution NATO established *Operation Deny Flight*, under which the first military engagement ever was undertaken by NATO by shooting down four warplanes on 28 February 1994. In order to protect UNPROFOR, moreover, *Operation Close Air Support* was initiated, which purported to provide aerial protection for the United Nations peacekeepers.[462]

In paragraph 10 of resolution 836 (1993) the Council decided that:

> Member States, acting nationally or through regional organizations or arrangements, may take, under the authority of the Security Council and subject to close coordination with the Secretary-General and UNPROFOR, all necessary measures, through the use of air power, in and around the safe areas in the Republic of Bosnia and Herzegovina, to support UNPROFOR in the performance of its mandate set out in paragraph 5 and 9 above.

In response to the attack on Bihac by Krajina Serbs, the Council adopted resolution 958 (1994) on 19 November 1994. Herein the Council extended the authorization given in paragraph 10 of resolution 836 (1993) to Croatia. Pursuant to this resolution NATO aircraft *inter alia* bombed a Serb airbase at Ubdina and missile sites in the area surrounding Ubdina.[463]

In 1998 the FRY engaged in hostilities with the Kosovo Liberation Army in Kosovo. In response, the Security Council adopted resolution 1160 (1998). Herein the Council condemned the use of force by both parties and, "acting under Chapter VII of the Charter", decided to reimpose an arms embargo on the FRY.[464] Furthermore, the Council stated that failure to achieve a peaceful resolution to the situation in Kosovo could "lead to the consideration of additional measures."[465] In resolution 1199 (1998) the Council 'affirmed' that the situation in Kosovo "constitutes a threat to peace and security in the region", and stated that "further action and additional measures to maintain or restore peace and stability in the region" would be considered if the situation did not improve.[466] When this did not happen, NATO decided to intervene. In a controversial operation (*Operation Allied Force*) NATO planes struck targets in Serbia between 23 March and 10 June 1999. The operation was, amongst other things, based on the non-compliance by Serbia with Security Council resolutions 1160 (1998)

---

[462] Which was successful when strikes were carried out in order to assist United Nations personnel in Gorazde on 10 and 11 April 1994, but was unsuccessful in protecting United Nations troops in Srebrenica in July 1995.

[463] See R. Fox, J. Muir, 'RAF Bombers Knock Out Serb Airbase', 22 Nov. 1994. Accessed at http://www.telegraph.co.uk on 15 Jan. 1998.

[464] See S/Res. 1160 (1998), 31 March 1998, para. 8. The arms embargo had earlier been lifted, on which see *infra*, note 472.

[465] *Ibid.*, para. 19.

[466] S/Res. 1199 (1998), 23 Sept. 1998, para. 16.

and 1199 (1998),[467] although the resolutions themselves do not seem to authorize the use of force.[468] Furthermore, allegations were made that NATO did not respect humanitarian law in the course of the operation, but a Committee established by the Prosecutor of the International Tribunal for the former Yugoslavia concluded that there seemed to be insufficient evidence that "particularly heinous offences" had been committed.[469]

3.6.2.6 The Termination of Hostilities[470]

After three weeks of negotiations which were initiated by the US, a peace treaty was initialed by the Presidents of Croatia, Bosnia-Herzegovina and Serbia on 21 November

---

[467] According to para. 2 of a Statement issued by the NATO Council at the Ministerial Meeting in Brussels on 12 April 1999, the: "Federal Republic of Yugoslavia (FRY) has repeatedly violated United Nations Security Council resolutions. The unrestrained assault by Yugoslav military, police and paramilitary forces, under the direction of President Milosevic, on Kosovar civilians has created a massive humanitarian catastrophe which also threatens to destabilise the surrounding region. Hundreds of thousands of people have been expelled ruthlessly from Kosovo by the FRY authorities. We condemn these appalling violations of human rights and the indiscriminate use of force by the Yugoslav government. These extreme and criminally irresponsible policies, which cannot be defended on any grounds, have made necessary and justify the military action by NATO."

[468] On the legal basis of the operation see, *e.g.*, J.I. Charney, *Anticipatory Humanitarian Intervention in Kosovo*, 93 AJIL (1999) 834-841; C.M. Chinkin, *Kosovo: A 'Good' or 'Bad' War?*, 93 AJIL (1999) 841-847; R.A. Falk, *Kosovo, World Order, and the Future of International Law*, 93 AJIL (1999) 847-857; T.M. Franck, *Lessons of Kosovo*, 93 AJIL (1999) 857-860; L. Henkin, *Kosovo and the Law of 'Humanitarian Intervention'*, 93 AJIL (1999) 824-828; W.M. Reisman, *Kosovo's Antinomies*, 93 AJIL (1999) 860-862; K.W. Alexander, *NATO's Intervention in Kosovo: The Legal Case for Violating Yugoslavia's National Sovereignty in the Absence of Security Council Approval*, 22 Houston JIL (2000) 403-449; D. Kritsiotis, *The Kosovo Crisis and NATO's Application of Armed Force Against the Federal Republic of Yugoslavia*, 49 ICLQ (2000) 330-359; J. Currie, *NATO's Humanitarian Intervention in Kosovo: Making or Breaking International Law?*, 36 CYIL (1998) 303-331; Simma, *op. cit. supra* n.168; and A. Cassese, *Ex iniuria ius oritu: Are We Moving Towards International Legitimation of Humanitarian Countermeasures in the World Community?*, 10 EJIL (1999) 23-30. The latter two authors conclude that the use of force is "contrary to the United Nations Charter" and was not authorized by the Security Council. Indeed, on 29 April 1999 the FRY instituted proceedings at the International Court of Justice against Belgium, Canada, France, Germany, Italy, the Netherlands, Portugal, Spain, the UK and the US, alleging that the states had violated their obligation not to use force against another state.

[469] See the 'Final Report to the Prosecutor by the Committee Established to Review the NATO Bombing Campaign Against the Federal Republic of Yugoslavia', June 2000, para. 90. Accessed at http://www.un.org/icty/pressreal/ (as 'nato061300.htm') on 15 June 2000. The Committee was established under Art. 18 of the Tribunal's Statute on 14 May 1999. On the Yugoslavia Tribunal see *infra*, paragraph 3.6.2.7.

[470] See J.R.W.D. Jones, *The Implications of the Peace Agreement for the International Criminal Tribunal for the former Yugoslavia*, 7 EJIL (1996) 226-244.

1996 at the US Air Force base at Dayton, US.[471] According to the agreement, which was signed in Paris on 1 December, Bosnia is to remain one state, called the Union of Bosnia-Herzegovina. The union is formed by two parts: the Muslim-Croat Federation and the Bosnian Serb Republic. The territory of the former comprises 51% of the territory of Bosnia-Herzegovina, the latter 49%. The agreement furthermore stipulates that the Presidency of the Union will rotate between the Muslim, Croat and Serb communities.

The Council subsequently terminated the arms embargo imposed upon the territory of the former Yugoslavia.[472] Moreover, as part of the agreement the Security Council "immediately and effectively" suspended the sanctions against the FRY.[473]

In accordance with paragraph 1 (a) of Article I of the Agreement on the Military Aspects of the Peace Settlement (Annex 1-A to the Peace Agreement), the Council also transferred the authority of UNPROFOR to a multinational implementation force (IFOR).[474] The involvement of the Council did not end at this stage, however. Thus, for example, the Basic Agreement on the Region of Eastern Slavonia, Baranja, and Western Sirmium, signed on 12 November 1995 by the Government of the Republic of Croatia and the local Serb community,[475] requested the Security Council to establish a Transitional Administration to govern the Region during the transitional period. In response the Council adopted resolution 1037 (1996) on 15 January 1996. Herein the Council:

Determining that the situation in Croatia continues to constitute a threat to international peace and security,

1. Decides to establish for an initial period of 12 months a United Nations peace-keeping operation for the Region referred to in the Basic Agreement, with both military and civilian components, under the name 'United Nations Transitional Administration for Eastern Slavonia, Baranja and Western Sirmium' (UNTAES).[476]

---

[471] Reproduced in 35 ILM (1996), 172-183.

[472] See S/Res. 1021 (1995), 22 Nov. 1995, para. 1.

[473] S/Res. 1022 (1995), 22 Nov. 1995. The sanctions were later terminated (S/Res. 1074 (1996), 1 Oct. 1996, para. 2.).

[474] S/Res. 1031 (1995), 15 Dec. 1995, paras. 12-38.

[475] Reproduced as UN Doc. S/1995/951.

[476] "Acting under Chapter VII of the Charter" the mandate was extended until 15 July 1997 by S/Res. 1079 (1996) on 15 Nov. 1996; and until 15 Jan. 1998 by S/Res. 1120 (1997), 14 July 1997.

3.6.2.7 The International Criminal Tribunal for former Yugoslavia[477]

On several occasions the Council addressed the issue of violations of humanitarian law by the parties to the Yugoslav conflict. Thus in paragraph 10 of resolution 764 (1992) the Council:

> reaffirms that all parties are bound to comply with the obligations under international humanitarian law and in particular the Geneva Conventions of 12 August 1949, and that persons who commit or order the commission of grave breaches of the Conventions are individually responsible in respect of such breaches.[478]

In the preamble to resolution 808 (1993) the Security Council again expressed "its grave alarm at the violations of international humanitarian law occurring within the territory of the former Yugoslavia, including reports of mass killings and the continuance of the practice of 'ethnic cleansing'."[479]

Herein the Council also determined "that this situation constitutes a threat to international peace and security." Subsequently, the Council decided in paragraph 1, that "an international tribunal shall be established for the prosecution of persons responsible for serious violations of international humanitarian law committed in the territory of the former Yugoslavia since 1991."

In pursuance thereof, the Secretary-General was requested to submit a report "on all aspects of this matter, including specific proposals and where appropriate options

---

[477] The literature on the Yugoslavia Tribunal is quite extensive. See, *e.g.*, V. Morris, M.P. Scharf, *An Insider's Guide to the International Criminal Tribunal for the Former Yugoslavia* (1994); H. Ascensio, *The Rules of Procedure and Evidence of the ICTY*, 9 LJIL (1996) 467-478; O.Q. Swaak-Goldman, *The ICTY and the Right to a Fair Trial: A Critique of the Critics*, 10 LJIL (1997) 215-222; S.D. Murphy, *Progress and Jurisprudence of the International Criminal Tribunal for the Former Yugoslavia*, 93 AJIL (1999) 57-97; A. Bodley, *Weakening the Principle of Sovereignty in International Law: The International Criminal Tribunal for the Former Yugoslavia*, 31 NYUJIL (1999) 417-471; R.C. Pruitt, *Guilt by Majority in the International Criminal Tribunal for the Former Yugoslavia: Does This Meet the Standard of Proof 'Beyond Reasonable Doubt'?*, 10 LJIL (1997) 557-578; M. Scharf, V. Epps, *The International Trial of the Century? A 'Cross-Fire' Exchange on the First Case Before the Yugoslavia War Crimes Tribunal*, 29 Cornell ILJ (1996) 635-664; M. Cherif Bassiouni, *Former Yugoslavia: Investigating Violations of International Humanitarian Law and Establishing an International Criminal Tribunal*, 18 Fordham ILJ (1995) 1191-1211; R. Dixon, *New Developments in the International Criminal Tribunal for the Former Yugoslavia: Prominent Leaders Indicted and Jurisdiction Established*, 8 LJIL(1995) 449-462.

[478] S/Res. 764 (1992), adopted on 13 July 1992. So also in para. 3 of S/Res. 771 (1992), adopted on 13 Aug. 1992, the Council "demands that all parties and others concerned in the former Yugoslavia, and all military forces in Bosnia and Herzegovina, immediately cease and desist from all breaches of international humanitarian law." And in the preamble to S/Res. 780 (1992), it expressed "its grave alarm at continuing reports of widespread violations of international humanitarian law occurring within the territory of the former Yugoslavia and especially in Bosnia and Herzegovina, including reports of mass killings and the continuance of the practice of 'ethnic cleansing'."

[479] S/Res. 808 (1993), 22 Feb. 1993.

for the effective and expeditious implementation of the decision contained in paragraph 1 above" within 60 days. The report issued by the Secretary-General[480] contained an elaboration on the Tribunal and a draft Statute, which was approved by the Council on 25 May 1993. On that day it adopted resolution 827 (1993) in which the Council:

Acting under Chapter VII of the Charter of the United Nations,

1. Approves the report of the Secretary-General;

2. Decides hereby to establish an international tribunal for the sole purpose of prosecuting persons responsible for serious violations of international humanitarian law committed in the territory of the former Yugoslavia between 1 January 1991 and a date to be determined by the Security Council upon the restoration of peace and to this end to adopt the Statute of the International Tribunal annexed to the above-mentioned report.

The International Criminal Tribunal for the former Yugoslavia (ICTY)[481] was thus established as a measure under Article 41 of the Charter within the terms of Article 29.[482] The personal jurisdiction of the ICTY covers persons "responsible for serious violations of international humanitarian law committed in the territory of the former Yugoslavia since 1991".[483] These serious crimes include grave breaches of the 1949

---

480 S/25704, 3 May 1993.

481 In addition to the works cited *supra*, note 477, see on the ICTY also C. Meindersma, *Violations of Common Article 3 of the Geneva Conventions as Violations of the Laws or Customs of War under Article 3 of the Statute of the International Criminal Tribunal for the Former Yugoslavia*, 42 LJIL (1995), 375-398; C.C. Joyner, *Enforcing Human Rights Standards in the Former Yugoslavia: The Case for an International War Crimes Tribunal*, 22 Denver JIL and Policy (1994), 235-274; R. Wedgwood, *War Crimes in the Former Yugoslavia: Comments on the International War Crimes Tribunal*, 34 VJIL (1994), 267-276; D. Shraga, R. Zacklin, *The International Criminal Tribunal for the Former Yugoslavia*, 5 EJIL (1994), 360-380; J.C. O'Brien, *The International Tribunal for Violations of International Humanitarian Law in the Former Yugoslavia*, 87 AJIL (1993) 639-658; B.N. Patel, *Do the Rules of Evidence and Procedure of the International Criminal Tribunal for ex-Yugoslavia ensure a Fair Trial?*, 39 Indian JIL (1999), 464-469; M. Karagiannakis, *The Definition of Rape and its Characterization as an Act of Genocide - A Review of the Jurisprudence of the International Criminal Tribunals for Rwanda and the Former Yugoslavia*, 12 LJIL (1999), 479-490; P. Gaeta, *Is NATO Authorized or Obliged to Arrest Persons Indicted by the International Criminal Tribunal for the Former Yugoslavia?*, 9 EJIL (1998), 174-181.

482 *Cf.* S/25704, para. 28: "In this particular case, the Security Council would be establishing, as an enforcement measure under Chapter VII, a subsidiary organ within the terms of Article 29 of the Charter, but one of a judicial nature. This organ would, of course, have to perform its functions independently of political considerations; it would not be subject to the authority or control of the Security Council with regard to the performance of its judicial functions. As an enforcement measure under Chapter VII, however, the life span of the international tribunal would be linked to the restoration and maintenance of international peace and security in the territory of the former Yugoslavia, and Security Council decisions related thereto."

483 Art. 1 of the Tribunal's Statute. The Statute is annexed to the Secretary-General's report

Geneva Conventions; violations of the laws or customs of war; the committing of genocide; and crimes against humanity.[484] The Statute moreover holds that the tribunal and national courts have concurrent jurisdiction, with the provision that the tribunal "shall have primacy."[485] The Statute furthermore provides that the judges of the tribunal shall adopt their own rules of procedure.[486] The rights of the accused include the *non-bis-in-idem* principle.[487]

As regards the duty of states to assist the tribunal, Article 29, entitled "cooperation and judicial assistance", provides that:

1. States shall cooperate with the International Tribunal in the investigation and prosecution of persons accused of committing serious violations of international humanitarian law.
2. States shall comply without undue delay with any request for assistance or an order issued by a Trial Chamber, including, but not limited to:
(a) the identification and location of persons;
(b) the taking of testimony and the production of evidence;
(c) the service of documents;
(d) the arrest or detention of persons;
(e) the surrender or the transfer of the accused to the International Tribunal.

3.6.3 Summary

The Council's involvement with the crisis in the former Yugoslavia has been multidimensional. It established a weapons embargo on the territory of the former Yugoslavia in order to avoid a further escalation of the conflicts. The containment efforts by the Council had limited success. Although the economic embargo imposed against the FRY did succeed in seriously damaging its economy, it did not change the FRY's policies. The Council furthermore deployed peacekeeping troops, and declared several areas to be 'safe' or 'United Nations protected' with the purported aim being to protect the inhabitants and to prevent further escalation of the conflicts. These aspirations did not prove to be successful. After the end of the war it took the unique decision to establish an international criminal tribunal in order to prosecute individuals responsible for international crimes, a course of action later to be repeated in the case of Rwanda.[488]

(S/25704, Add. 1) and was approved by the Council in resolution 827 (1993). The Statute was amended by S/Res. 1166 (1998), 13 May 1998.

484 Arts. 2-5 of the Statute.

485 Art. 9(1) and (2) of the Statute.

486 Art. 15 of the Statute.

487 Art. 10 of the Statute.

488 On the Rwanda tribunal see *infra*, paragraph 3.9.2.3.

3.6.4 Analysis: The Application of Chapter VII by the Council

The Council generally refrained from specifying the exact legal basis for its actions. In most cases the Council merely stated that it "is acting under Chapter VII of the Charter", after a prior determination that a threat to peace and security existed. The imposition of the sanctions, the establishment of the ICTY and the declaration of UNPAs and safe areas must be seen as being based on Articles 41 and 29 of the Charter. The deployment of UNPROFOR against the will of the states concerned, however, raises the interpretative issue as to the legal basis of UNPROFOR's continued presence in Yugoslavia. For it went beyond the traditional requirement associated with peacekeeping operations that host-states consent to a peacekeeping force. In this sense, the deployment of UNPROFOR may be seen as an enforcement measure under both Articles 41 and 42 of the Charter. Similar to the Iraqi case, the cooperation with regional arrangements leads to the question whether the enforcement actions taken, for example in enforcing the no-fly zones, are to be considered United Nations actions or merely actions authorized by the Council.[489]

3.7 Angola 1991-2000

3.7.1 Factual Background

From 1975 onwards the former Portuguese colony of Angola became the victim of a civil war between its two main national liberation movements, the Movimento Popular de Libertaçâo de Angola (MPLA) and the União Nacional para a Independência Total de Angola (UNITA). The MPLA was actively supported by the Soviet Union and Cuba, the former supplying extensive military aid and the latter sending in troops in November 1975.[490] The Cuban backup enabled the Marxist-oriented MPLA to assume governmental control. UNITA, on the other hand, received aid from the US and South Africa. South Africa, moreover, repeatedly invaded Angola during the 1970s

[489] See Freudenschuß, *op. cit. supra* n.1, 504-511. See on the categorization of the actions in Iraq *supra*, paragraph 3.4.4.

[490] See J.A. Lefebvre, *Moscow's Cold War and Post-Cold War Policies in Africa*. In: E.J. Keller, D. Rothschild (eds.), Africa in the New International Order: Rethinking State Sovereignty and Regional Security (1996) 206-226.

and 1980s, in the context of the struggle for independence in Namibia[491] and of destabilizing the region.[492]

By a series of treaties Angola, South Africa and Cuba agreed to the withdrawal of South African and Cuban troops, to be completed in 1991.[493] Thereafter the civil war continued, with only a temporary suspension after the President of Angola and the President of UNITA had signed the Peace Accords for Angola ("Acordos de Paz para Angola") on 1 May 1991. After free elections had been held in 1992, the situation remained volatile, particularly since UNITA failed to acknowledge the results of the elections. On 20 November 1994 a new agreement was signed between the Angolan government and UNITA, the Lusaka Protocol. Despite these commitments progress towards national peace has been slow, with fighting repeatedly erupting between UNITA and government troops.

3.7.2 The Imposition of Sanctions

Between 1976 and 1991 the Security Council adopted a series of resolutions on the situation in Angola and Namibia.[494] According to South Africa, the situation in both countries was closely linked, and although this linkage was rejected by the Council[495] it did recur in the Council's handling of the situation in Angola and Namibia. The Council mainly focused on the repeated invasions of Angolan territory by South Africa, which were consistently "condemned" and which were held to threaten international

---

491 A struggle supported by Cuba and opposed by South Africa. See P.T. Stoll, *Namibia*. In: R. Wolfrum (ed.), United Nations: Law, Policies and Practice (1995) 904-912, 909.

492 See Stoll, *op. cit. supra* n.220, 325.

493 The Protocol of Geneva, signed by Angola, Cuba and South Africa on 5 Aug. 1988, provided in Article 4 that: "The complete withdrawal of South African forces from Angola shall ... be completed not later than 1 September 1988." The Protocol is annexed to S/20566, 4 April 1989 and reproduced in 28 ILM (1989) 952-954. In pursuance of Article 4 of the subsequent 'Agreement among the People's Republic of Angola, the Republic of Cuba, and the Republic of South Africa', 22 Dec. 1988 (reproduced in 28 ILM (1989) 957-958), Cuba and Angola signed an agreement for the "Conclusions of the Internationalist Mission of the Cuban Military Contingent" on the same day. The timetable appended thereto provided that the 50,000 Cuban troops would be completely withdrawn by 1 July 1991. The text is reprinted in 28 ILM (1989) 959-961.

494 For an overview see K.C. Wellens (ed.), *Resolutions and Statements of the United Nations Security Council (1946-1992): A Thematic Guide* (1993), 180-195, 240-282, and 285-191.

495 *Cf.* S/Res. 566 (1985), 19 June 1985, para. 7, in which the Council: "Rejects once again South Africa's insistence on linking the independence of Namibia to irrelevant and extraneous issues as incompatible with resolution 435 (1978), other decisions of the Security Council and the resolutions of the General Assembly on Namibia, including General Assembly resolution 1514 (XV) of 14 December 1960."

peace and security. Thus in 1979, for example, resolution 447 (1979) was adopted. Therein the Council:

> Condemns strongly the racist regime of South Africa for its premeditated, persistent and sustained armed invasions of the People's Republic of Angola, which constitute a flagrant violation of the sovereignty and territorial integrity of that country as well as a serious threat to international peace and security.[496]

Alongside these determinations that the South African actions posed a threat to international peace, the Council warned South Africa that it was contemplating "more effective" measures under Chapter VII of the Charter.[497] Despite these references to stronger measures, for a long period of time no sanctions were imposed against any party to the conflict in Angola because of their actions. The Council did consider that Angola was "entitled to appropriate redress for any material damage it has suffered" from the armed invasions,[498] but usually confined itself to calls for international support for the frontline states in pursuance of their right of self-defence under Article 51,[499] and calls for compliance with the arms embargo already in force against South Africa.[500]

The Council's approach changed in 1993. In that year the Council branded UNITA as the main wrongdoing party in the civil conflict. In resolution 864 (1993), the Council:

> condemns UNITA's repeated attempts to seize additional territory and its failure to withdraw its troops from the locations which it has occupied since the resumption of the hostilities, and demands once again that it

---

[496] S/Res. 447 (1979), 28 March 1979, para. 1. In the preamble to S/Res. 602 (1987), the Council also stated that it is "gravely concerned at racist South Africa's persistent violation of the sovereignty, airspace and territorial integrity of the People's Republic of Angola", and that "the pursuance of these acts of aggression against Angola constitutes a serious threat to international peace and security."

[497] In para. 8 of S/Res. 428 (1978), 6 May 1978, for example, the Council: "Decides to meet again in the event of further acts of violation of the sovereignty and territorial integrity of the People's Republic of Angola by the South African racist regime in order to consider the adoption of more effective measures, in accordance with the appropriate provisions of the Charter of the United Nations, including Chapter VII thereof." See also S/Res. 447 (1979), 28 March 1979, preamble.

[498] S/Res. 545 (1983), 20 Dec. 1983, para. 4. Similar statements were made by the Council in S/Res. 567 (1985), 20 June 1985, para. 4; S/Res. 475 (1980), 27 June 1980, para. 6; S/Res. 546 (1984), 6 Jan. 1984, para. 13; S/Res. 571 (1985), 20 Sept. 1985, para. 6. By para. 7 of S/Res. 571 (1985) the Council established a commission to assess the damage suffered by Angola, the report of which (S/17648) was endorsed in para. 1 of S/Res. 577 (1985), 6 Dec. 1985.

[499] See S/Res. 546 (1984), 6 Jan. 1984, paras. 5 and 6; S/Res. 574 (1985), 7 Oct. 1985, paras. 4 and 6.

[500] S/Res. 475 (1980), 27 June 1980, para. 4; S/Res. 546 (1984), 6 Jan. 1984, para. 4; S/Res. 571 (1985), 20 Sept. 1985, para. 4; S/Res. 574 (1985), 7 Oct. 1985, para. 5. On the sanctions against South Africa see *supra*, paragraph 3.1.2.

immediately do so and agree without delay to return its troops to United Nations-monitored areas as a transitional measure pending full implementation of the Acordos de Paz.[501]

In the preamble to section B of the resolution the Council then determined "that, as a result of UNITA's military actions, the situation in Angola constitutes a threat to international peace and security."

Subsequently the Council decided to impose sanctions against UNITA. In paragraph 19 of resolution 864 (1993) the Council, whilst "acting under Chapter VII of the Charter of the United Nations", decided:

with a view to prohibiting all sale or supply to UNITA of arms and related matériel and military assistance, as well as petroleum and petroleum products, that all States shall prevent the sale or supply, by their nationals or from their territories or using their flag vessels or aircraft, of arms and related materiel of all types, including weapons and ammunition, military vehicles and equipment and spare parts for the aforementioned, as well as of petroleum and petroleum products, whether or not originating in their territory, to the territory of Angola other than through named points of entry on a list to be supplied by the Government of Angola to the Secretary-General, who shall promptly notify the Member States of the United Nations.[502]

A few years later, when internal peace had still not been achieved,[503] the Council extended the scope of the sanctions against UNITA. After first "strongly deploring"

---

[501] S/Res. 864 (1993), 15 Sept. 1993, para. 8. In para. 10 the Council also: "Stresses once again the fundamental need to reinitiate without delay the peace talks under United Nations auspices with a view to the immediate establishment of a cease-fire throughout the country and the full implementation of the Acordos de Paz and resolutions of the Security Council." *Cf.* para. 13, in which the Council: "Strongly condemns the repeated attacks carried out by UNITA against United Nations personnel working to provide humanitarian assistance and reaffirms that such attacks are clear violations of international humanitarian law." See also the preamble to section B, in which the UNITA leadership is held " responsible for not having taken the necessary measures to comply with the demands made by the Council in its previous resolutions."

[502] In the following paragraph the Council then: "Calls upon all States, and all international organizations, to act strictly in accordance with the provisions of the present resolution, notwithstanding the existence of any rights or obligations conferred or imposed by any international agreement or any contract entered into or any licence or permit granted prior to the date of adoption of this resolution." Hereafter, however, the Council had to repeatedly call for compliance with the measures taken under para. 19 of resolution 864 (1993). See S/Res. 922 (1994), 31 May 1994, para. 8; S/Res. 932 (1994), 30 June 1994, preamble and para. 8; S/Res. 945 (1994), 29 Sept. 1994, para. 13; S/Res. 966 (1994), 8 Dec. 1994, preamble; S/Res. 1045 (1996), 8 Feb. 1996, para. 19; S/Res. 1055 (1996), 8 May 1996, para. 19; S/Res. 1064 (1996), 11 July 1996, para. 18; S/Res. 1075 (1996), 11 Oct. 1996, para. 17; S/Res. 1087 (1996), 11 Dec. 1996, para. 15.

[503] In a report submitted to the Council in August 1997, the Secretary-General submitted that the "military situation is currently characterized by persistent tensions affecting almost the entire country". 'Progress Report of the Secretary-General on the United Nations Observer Mission in Angola (MONUA)', S/1997/640, 13 Aug. 1997, para. 12. In addition, he observed that: "Both parties, but especially UNITA, have continued to impose restrictions on MONUA verification activities." *Ibid.*, para. 14.

UNITA's failure to "comply with its obligations under the 'Acordos de Paz' ... the Lusaka Protocol and with relevant Security Council resolutions", the Council determined that the "resulting situation in Angola constitutes a threat to international peace and security in the region."[504] Accordingly the Council, whilst "acting under Chapter VII of the Charter of the United Nations", took additional measures against UNITA. These measures include the denial of "entry into or transit through [states'] territories of all senior officials of UNITA and of adult members of their immediate families"; the suspension and cancellation of "all travel documents, visas or residence permits issued to senior UNITA officials and adult members of their immediate families"; and an aerial embargo.[505]

These sanctions were expanded in 1998. In that year the Council decided to freeze the funds and resources of senior officials of UNITA or "adult members of their immediate families",[506] and to prohibit the import or export of non-certified diamonds.[507] All sanctions remained in force in the period under consideration, although compliance with them has not been strict.[508] Termination of the sanctions depends on UNITA's cooperation towards peace in Angola.[509]

---

504 S/Res. 1127 (1997), 28 Aug. 1997, preamble to Section B.

505 See S/Res. 1127 (1997), 28 Aug. 1997, para. 4.

506 In para. 11 of S/Res. 1173 (1998), adopted on 12 June 1998, the Council, acting under Chapter VII of the Charter: "Decides that all States, except Angola, in which there are funds and financial resources, including any funds derived or generated from property of UNITA as an organization or of senior officials of UNITA or adult members of their immediate families ... shall require all persons and entities within their own territories holding such funds and financial resources to freeze them and ensure that they are not made available directly or indirectly to or for the benefit of UNITA as an organization or of senior officials of UNITA or adult members of their immediate families".

507 *Ibid.*, para. 12(b).

508 In this context see the 'Letter Dated 10 March 2000 from the Chairman of the Security Council Committee Established Pursuant to Resolution 864 (1993) Concerning the Situation in Angola Addressed to the President of the Security Council', S/2000/203, 10 March 2000. This letter contains a 'Report of the Panel of Experts on Violations of Security Council Sanctions Against UNITA', a Panel that was established by resolution 1237 (1999), 7 May 1999. The Report addresses, and gives concrete examples of, "Sanctions Busting on Arms and Military Equipment" (paras. 13-58); on "Petroleum and Petroleum Products" (paras. 59-74); on "Diamonds" (paras. 75-114); on "UNITA Finances and Assets" (paras. 115-128); and on "UNITA Representation and Travel Abroad" (paras. 129-162).

509 See S/Res. 1127 (1997), paras. 1 and 2. The situation in Angola was described by the Secretary-General in Dec. 1997 as follows: "The peace process continues to be slow, with intermittent surges of UNITA cooperation and long periods of stagnation following one another." 'Report of the Secretary-General on the United Nations Observer Mission in Angola (MONUA)', S/1997/959, 4 Dec. 1997, para. 22. In addition, he submitted that: "Both parties, but in particular UNITA, are responsible for this unsatisfactory state of affairs. Despite the repeated appeals by the international

3.7.3 Summary

The Council's actions concerning Angola focused on assisting the parties in achieving national peace and reconciliation. Thereto four peacekeeping missions were established, which were mainly to serve as an intermediary between the warring parties. But as genuine cooperation between the parties was absent, the situation in Angola remained volatile. This induced the Council to impose sanctions against what it regarded to be the main wrongdoer, UNITA. The sanctions initially covered arms and oil supplies, and were later expanded so as to include an aerial embargo and travel restrictions for UNITA members and the freezing of their funds.

3.7.4 Analysis: The Application of Chapter VII by the Council

Prior to 1991 the Council, on several occasions, invoked Article 39 of the Charter by determining that the South African interference in Angola constituted a threat to international peace and security. No follow-up actions were taken under either Article 41 or 42, however, probably because South Africa was already suffering from an arms embargo. When the outside interference in Angola had remitted by 1991, the Council focused on the national factions competing for control. Impatient with the progress being made, the Council took the unique action of imposing sanctions against UNITA in 1993. Thereto the Council first determined under Article 39 that "the situation in Angola constitutes a threat to international peace and security", and then imposed an arms and oil embargo under Article 41. As observed by Schrijver, this was the first time that the Council "imposed sanctions against a rebellious faction controlling part of the territory of a State."[510] The scope of the sanctions was extended in 1997 and 1998, so as to prohibit UNITA from having offices other than in Angola, to prohibit its officials from travelling abroad, and to freeze their funds and resources as well as those of their immediate family.

---

community, UNITA has continued to fail to comply with relevant Security Council resolutions demanding its unconditional cooperation in the fulfilment of its obligations under the Lusaka Protocol." *Ibid.*, para. 23.

[510] N. Schrijver, *The Use of Economic Sanctions by the UN Security Council: An International Law Perspective*. In: H.H.G. Post (ed.), International Economic Law and Armed Conflict (1994) 123-161, at 143. *Cf.* P.H. Kooijmans, *The Security Council and Non-state Entities as Parties to Conflicts*. In: K.C. Wellens (ed.), International Law: Theory and Practice (1998) 333-346.

3.8 Somalia 1992-1995

3.8.1 Factual Background[511]

The Somali Republic was formed in 1960 as a merger of the former British and Italian Somalilands. After a period of parliamentary democracy, which ended violently in 1969 with a *coup d 'état*, a single-party system headed by M.S. Barre was introduced in the mid 1970s. An abortive coup which was staged in 1978 led to the formation of the Somali Salvation Democratic Front (SSDF) in the North-East and the Somali National Movement (SNM) in the North-West. In addition, the United Somali Congress (USC) and the Somali Patriotic Movement (SPM) were formed during the late 1980s. These movements were predominantly based on clan loyalties. In December 1990 the USC established its *de facto* authority in Mogadishu, forcing M.S. Barre to flee. The USC itself was divided into several factions, however, including the Somali National Alliance headed by General Aidid, and these factions competed for control of Mogadishu. In addition, the SSDF took control of North-East Somalia and the SNM proclaimed the independent state of 'Somaliland' in the North-West. Thus by 1991 the country was being ravaged by battles among several militia with a complete absence of 'law and order'.[512] Somalia has henceforth often been described as a 'failed state'.[513]

In a report submitted to the Security Council in 1992, the Secretary-General described the overall situation in Somalia in the following terms:

The situation in Somalia continues to be of great concern to the international community. There is hardly any

---

[511] Generally see UNDPI, *The United Nations and Somalia, 1992-1996* (1996), 9-16; A. Simons, *Somalia: A Regional Security Dilemma*. In: E.J. Keller, D. Rothschild (eds.), Africa in the New International Order: Rethinking State Sovereignty and Regional Security (1996) 71-84; M. Mwagiru, *International Law, Politics, and the Re-invention of the Humanitarian Intervention: The Lesson of Somalia*, 34 Indian JIL (1994) 33-44.

[512] S.M. Makinda, for example, observes that "in Somalia ... law and order had completely broken down, the civil war had led to thousands of deaths, all state institutions had been destroyed, and there was no functioning government." S.M. Makinda, *Sovereignty and International Security: Challenges for the United Nations*, 2 Global Governance (1996) 149-168, at 162.

[513] On 'failed states' see G.B. Helman, S.R. Ratner, *Saving Failed States*, 89 Foreign Policy (1992-1993) 3-20; D. Thürer, *The 'Failed State' and International Law*, 81 International Review of the Red Cross (1999) 731-761; S.L. Woodward, *Failed States: Warlordism and 'Tribal' Warfare*, LII Naval War College Review (1999) 55-68. *Cf.* the reference to "collapsed structures of State authority" by Higgins, *op. cit. supra* n.117, at 460. For a critical analysis of the concept of (failed) statehood in Africa see R.C. Ezetah, *Legitimate Governance and Statehood in Africa: Beyond the Failed State and Colonial Self-Determination*. In: E.K. Quashigah, O.C. Okafor (eds.), Legitimate Governance in Africa: International and Domestic Legal Perspectives (1999) 419-459.

> governmental infrastructure in the country that could be relied upon. Physical infrastructure, such as transport, water, electricity, telephone communications, is also largely non-existent. Banditry is widespread and there is wide proliferation of weapons. The crisis in Somalia has regional consequences, as is already evidenced by the flow of Somali refugees to neighbouring countries, and there are grave concerns about the destabilizing effects it could have on the Horn of Africa.[514]

Throughout 1992 and 1993, moreover, a famine occurred within Somalia, particularly in the South, due to the ongoing violence which led to a massive displacement of people from their homes.

3.8.2 Security Council Action concerning Somalia

On 23 January 1992, the Security Council adopted resolution 733 (1992). In the preamble the Council noted that the situation had been put on the agenda pursuant to a request by Somalia. The Council then stated that it was "gravely alarmed at the rapid deterioration of the situation in Somalia and the heavy loss of human life and widespread material damage resulting from the conflict in the country and aware of its consequences on the stability and peace in the region."[515]

The Council then expressed its concern "that the continuation of this situation constitutes ... a threat to international peace and security." In paragraph 2 of resolution 933 (1992), it furthermore requested the Secretary-General to take action necessary to ensure that Somalia receives humanitarian assistance. This was accompanied by a 'strong urge' on "all parties to the conflict immediately to cease hostilities and agree to a cease-fire and to promote the process of reconciliation and of political settlement in Somalia".

In addition, the Council established an arms embargo on Somalia. Thereto in paragraph 5 the Council:

> decides, under Chapter VII of the Charter of the United Nations, that all States shall, for the purposes of establishing peace and stability in Somalia, immediately implement a general and complete embargo on all deliveries of weapons and military equipment to Somalia until the Security Council decides otherwise.

Similar to its earlier practice, the Council also established a Committee consisting of the members of the Council, which was to oversee the implementation of the sanctions.[516]

Thereafter the efforts of the United Nations initially concentrated on the capital

---

514 'Report of the Secretary-General on the situation in Somalia, recommending the establishment of the United Nations Operation in Somalia (UNOSOM)', S/23829, 21 April 1992, para. 56.

515 S/Res. 733 (1992), 23 Jan. 1992, preamble.

516 S/Res. 751 (1992), 24 April 1992, para. 11.

of Somalia, Mogadishu. After the Secretary-General mediated between the two main parties competing for control of Mogadishu, a cease-fire agreement was reached between the USC and Aidid on 3 March 1992. The agreement *inter alia* provided for "the implementation of measures aimed at stabilizing the cease-fire by means of a United Nations monitoring mechanism."[517] As a follow up a technical team was sent to Somalia in accordance with resolution 746 (1992),[518] which managed to negotiate additional commitments by the conflicting parties. Thus in letters dated 27 March 1992, General Aidid and President Mohamed agreed to the deployment of observers in Mogadishu in order to monitor the cease-fire agreement and consented to "the deployment of adequate United Nations security personnel to protect its personnel and safeguard its activities".[519]

In accordance with this agreement, the Secretary-General recommended the establishment of a peacekeeping force called the 'United Nations Operation in Somalia' (UNOSOM), a recommendation approved by the Council in resolution 751 (1992).[520] In paragraph 2 of the resolution, the Council "decides to establish under its authority ... a United Nations Operation in Somalia (UNOSOM)."

UNOSOM's mandate was extended with the adoption of resolution 767 (1992),[521] so as to include four operational zones in the North-West, North-East, Central and South Somalia.[522] The troops to be deployed within these zones,[523] however, never reached their destination, as the conflicting parties withdrew their earlier consent to the establishment of a peacekeeping force.[524] Moreover, international aid provided by the United Nations had become a target of armed attacks.[525]

---

[517] 'Agreement on the implementation of the cease-fire signed by Interim President Ali Mahdi Mohamed', reproduced in the 'Report of the Secretary-General on the situation in Somalia, proposing to dispatch a technical team to prepare an operational plan for the monitoring of the cease fire in Mogadishu and to explore ways of ensuring the unimpeded delivery of humanitarian assistance', S/23693, 11 March 1992, Annex III. In fact, the agreement consists of two identical declarations by, respectively, President Mohamed and General Aidid.

[518] S/Res. 746 (1992), 17 March 1992.

[519] The letters are annexed to the 'Report of the Secretary-General on the situation in Somalia, recommending the establishment of the United Nations Operation in Somalia (UNOSOM)', S/238929/Add.1, 21 April 1992. The "activities" mentioned in the quote mainly refer to the delivery of humanitarian assistance.

[520] S/Res. 751 (1992), 24 April 1992.

[521] S/Res. 767 (1992), 24 July 1992.

[522] See S/24343, 22 July 1992, paras. 57-60.

[523] Provided for by S/Res. 775 (1992), 28 Aug. 1992.

[524] See UNDPI, *op. cit. supra* n.511, at 27-29.

[525] The reasons for these attacks have been described as follows: "In the absence of a government

The ongoing warfare and the interference with the deliverance of humanitarian aid led to a different approach by the United Nations. In response to a letter from the Secretary-General[526] the Security Council determined in resolution 794 (1992) that "the magnitude of the human tragedy caused by the conflict in Somalia, further exacerbated by the obstacles being created to the distribution of humanitarian assistance, constitutes a threat to international peace and security."[527]

In paragraph 3, moreover, the Council demanded that "all parties, movements and factions in Somalia take all measures necessary to ensure the safety of United Nations and all other personnel engaged in the delivery of humanitarian assistance". Then the Council, whilst "acting under Chapter VII of the Charter of the United Nations", authorized the Secretary-General and member states "to use all necessary means to establish as soon as possible a secure environment for humanitarian relief operations in Somalia".[528]

In addition the Council, in paragraph 16 of resolution 794 (1992), while "acting under Chapters VII and VIII of the Charter", called "upon States, nationally or through regional agencies or arrangements, to use such measures as may be necessary to ensure strict implementation of paragraph 5 of the resolution 733 (1992)." At the same time, the Council made it clear that action under this resolution was to be of a temporary nature. Thus, in paragraph 18 a request was made to:

---

or governing authorities capable of maintaining law and order, Somali authorities at all levels were competing for anything of value. International aid had become a major (and in some areas the only) source of income and was the target of all the authorities, sometimes no more than two or three bandits with guns. In essence, humanitarian supplies became the basis of an otherwise non-existent Somali economy." United Nations Department of Public Information, *The Blue Helmets: A Review of United Nations Peace-keeping* (1996), at 293.

526 S/24868, 30 Nov. 1992. In this letter the Secretary-General offered five options to the Council with regard to further United Nations action in Somalia: i) the continuation and intensification of UNOSOM I as a traditional peacekeeping operation; ii) a withdrawal of the military components of UNOSOM I, leaving it to "the humanitarian agencies to negotiate the best arrangements they can with the various faction and clan leaders"; iii) a "show of force" by UNOSOM in Mogadishu "in order to create conditions there for the safe delivery of humanitarian relief"; iv) "a country-wide enforcement operation undertaken by a group of Member States authorized by the Security Council to do so"; v) "a country-wide enforcement operation to be carried out under United Nations command and control." The latter option was described by the Secretary-General as "consistent with the recent expansion of the Organization's role in the maintenance of international peace and security".

527 S/Res. 794 (1992), 3 Dec. 1992 (adopted unanimously), preamble.

528 *Ibid.*, para. 10. In para. 12, moreover, the Council: "Authorizes the Secretary-General and the Member States concerned to make the necessary arrangements for the unified command and control of the forces involved."

the Secretary-General and, as appropriate, the States concerned to report to the Council on a regular basis, the first such report to be made no later than fifteen days after the adoption of this resolution, on the implementation of this resolution and the attainment of the objective of establishing a secure environment so as to enable the Council to make the necessary decision for a prompt transition to continued peace-keeping operations.

Pursuant to resolution 794 (1992) a Unified Task Force (UNITAF) started *Operation Restore Hope*, with the first US marines landing in Mogadishu on 9 December 1992. The operation was commanded by the US, which also provided the largest contingent of the approximately 35,000 troops. The UNITAF quickly took control of large parts of the country and secured the delivery of humanitarian assistance in those parts.[529]

It had been decided that the UNITAF would be a temporary measure to be succeeded by a United Nations peacekeeping mission, which was to become UNOSOM II. By March 1993 the UNITAF commander declared "all areas stable or reasonably stable",[530] although the Secretary-General concluded that "the effort undertaken by UNITAF to establish a secure environment in Somalia is far from complete and in any case has not attempted to address the situation throughout all of Somalia".[531] Nonetheless, the Secretary-General submitted his proposals on UNOSOM II. According to the Secretary-General, UNOSOM II would not be able to implement its mandate "unless it is endowed with enforcement powers under Chapter VII of the Charter."[532] This course of action was followed by the Security Council, which decided in resolution 814 (1993), as a measure taken under Chapter VII of the Charter, to expand the size of UNOSOM and "its mandate in accordance with the recommendations contained in ... the report of the Secretary-General of 3 March 1993 and the provisions of this resolution."[533] The provisions mentioned in paragraph 5 above include paragraphs 10 and 12, wherein the Council:

Requests the Secretary-General to support from within Somalia the implementation of the arms embargo established by resolution 733 (1992), utilizing as available and appropriate the UNOSOM II forces authorized by this resolution, and to report on this subject, with any recommendations regarding more effective measures if necessary, to the Security Council;

Requests the Secretary-General to provide security, as appropriate, to assist in the repatriation of refugees and the assisted resettlement of displaced persons, utilizing UNOSOM II forces, paying particular attention to those areas where major instability continues to threaten peace and security in the region.

---

529 For an account of *Operation Restore Hope* see, *e.g.*, UNDPI, *op. cit. supra* n.388, 295.

530 Quoted in 'Report of the Secretary-General submitted in pursuance of paragraphs 18 and 19 of resolution 794 (1992)', S/25354, 3 March 1993, para. 6.

531 *Ibid.*, para. 58.

532 *Ibid.*

533 S/Res. 814 (1993), 26 March 1993, para. 5.

More generally, in paragraph 14 the Secretary-General is requested:

> through his Special Representative, to direct the Force Commander of UNOSOM II to assume responsibility for the consolidation, expansion and maintenance of a secure environment throughout Somalia, taking account of the particular circumstances in each locality, on an expedited basis in accordance with the recommendations contained in his report of 3 March 1993, and in this regard to organize a prompt, smooth and phased transition from UNITAF to UNOSOM II.[534]

Aside from this military task, the Secretary-General was also requested to "provide humanitarian and other assistance to the people of Somalia in rehabilitating their political institutions and economy and promoting political settlement and national reconciliation."[535] This 'peace-building' effort was to be a follow-up to earlier initiatives at national reconciliation and nation-building.[536]

Both the military and peace-building tasks, however, were soon challenged by an attack on UNOSOM II forces on 5 June 1993, in which 25 Pakistani peacekeepers were killed. In response the Council adopted resolution 837 (1993).[537] In paragraph 5 of that resolution the Council, acting under Chapter VII of the Charter:

> Reaffirms that the Secretary-General is authorized under resolution 814 (1993) to take all necessary measures against all those responsible for the armed attacks ... including against those responsible for publicly inciting such attacks, to establish the effective authority of UNOSOM II throughout Somalia, including to secure the investigation of their actions and their arrest and detention for prosecution, trial and punishment.[538]

As the SNA was held responsible for the attack,[539] an arrest warrant for General Aidid

---

[534] This would, *inter alia*, include maintaining security required for the delivery of humanitarian assistance, the disarming of local militia and control of heavy weapons. See S/25354, para. 57.

[535] S/Res. 814 (1993), para. 4. *Cf.* the preamble, in which the Council recognizes "that the re-establishment of local and regional administrative institutions is essential to the restoration of domestic tranquillity".

[536] On 11-13 March 1993, a United Nations Conference on Humanitarian Assistance to Somalia was held in Addis Ababa. The conference adopted a programme that included the re-establishment of local administrative capacity and police forces. On 27 March 1993, moreover, agreement was reached between 15 Somalian political movements on the establishment of governmental structures, a process that was to be assisted by the United Nations Secretary-General. See UNDPI, *op. cit. supra* n.388, 298-299.

[537] S/Res. 837 (1993), 6 June 1993, adopted unanimously.

[538] Freudenschuß notes that "this formulation is somewhat misleading because Resolution 814 ... did not contain such a specific authorization of the Secretary-General." Freudenschuß, *op. cit. supra* n.1, at 516.

[539] A responsibility that was confirmed by an investigation into the incident conducted by T. Farer. The Executive Summary of his Report of the Investigation, S/26351, 24 Aug. 1993, determines that "the claim that General ... Aidid authorized the 5 June attack ... and that the attack was executed by elements of the political faction known as SNA is supported by clear and convincing evidence."

was issued and UNOSOM II troops engaged in hostilities with the SNA in the surroundings of Mogadishu in June 1993. Additional forces were supplied by the US, moreover, in support of UNOSOM II's mandate to achieve a secure environment, forces that were not under United Nations command.[540] In October 1993 further fighting erupted between the SNA and US troops, and in an incident occurring on 3 October, 18 US soldiers were killed. Although progress was made outside the capital, these events – which were graphically televised throughout the world – proved decisive for the future of UNOSOM II. On 7 October 1993 the US announced that it would withdraw its troops by 31 March 1994, which prompted other nations to follow. Consequently, the Security Council gradually reduced the United Nations involvement in Somalia.[541] After the size of UNOSOM II was reduced by the Council in resolution 897 (1994),[542] and hostilities continued between United Nations forces and the SNA, a decision to withdraw from Somalia was taken on 4 November 1994. In the preamble to resolution 954 (1994) of that day the Council 'recognized' that:

> the lack of progress in the Somali peace process and in national reconciliation, in particular the lack of sufficient cooperation from the Somali parties over security issues, has fundamentally undermined the United Nations objectives in Somalia and, in these circumstances, continuation of UNOSOM II beyond March 1995 cannot be justified.

The Council then, acting under Chapter VII of the Charter, extended the mandate of UNOSOM II "for a final period until 31 March 1995." It was furthermore decided in paragraph 5 that:

> every effort should be made to withdraw all UNOSOM II military forces and assets from Somalia in a secure and orderly manner as soon as possible ... before the expiry date of the current mandate of UNOSOM II and without compromising on the paramount need of ensuring the safety of UNOSOM II personnel.

And in doing so the Council, in paragraph 6, authorized:

> UNOSOM II military forces to take those actions necessary to protect the UNOSOM II mission and the withdrawal of UNOSOM II personnel and assets, and, to the extent that the Force Commander deems it practicable and consistent, in the context of withdrawal, to protect personnel of relief organizations.

---

540 See UNDPI, *op. cit. supra* n.388, 301.

541 Thus in resolution 885 (1993), adopted on 16 Nov. 1993, for example, the Council "suspended" arrest actions against persons involved in actions against UNOSOM II troops, and called for "appropriate provision" to be made for persons already detained. Consequently, 42 detainees were released.

542 S/Res. 897 (1994), 4 Feb. 1994.

3.8.3 Summary

The Council first decided to establish a weapons and arms embargo on the territory of Somalia, followed by the sending of troops on a traditional peacekeeping mission (UNOSOM). When these measures proved ineffective in ensuring the delivery of humanitarian assistance in response to the famine, a more ambitious form of action was pursued. The UNITAF was sent in (*Operation Restore Hope*) as a peace-enforcement mechanism, which partially succeeded. The successor to UNITAF, UNOSOM II, was given a wide mandate, including enforcement powers. Thus similar to the Liberian and Yugoslav cases,[543] the involvement of the United Nations in Somalia evolved from traditional peacekeeping to peace-enforcement, with a limited level of success.[544] UNOSOM II soon became engaged in a struggle with one of the major factions in Somalia, the SNA. The ensuing violence and casualties led the contributing nations, notably the US, to withdraw their contingents from Somalia. The intervention therefore did not restore law and order in Somalia, in part because the United Nations forces had to operate in a hostile environment. As Aristodemou observes, the United Nations troops "once welcomed to feed the hungry were denounced as neo-colonialist oppressors."[545]

3.8.4 Analysis: The Application of Chapter VII by the Council

The Council's actions began with the adoption of resolution 733 (1992), in which it expressed its concern that the "continuation of this situation constitutes ... a threat to international peace and security." Although some contend otherwise,[546] it is hard to see how this could be qualified other than as a determination under Article 39 triggering further action under Chapter VII. Especially when one considers that in the same resolution the Council "decides, under Chapter VII of the Charter of the United

---

543 See *supra*, paragraphs 3.5.2.2 and 3.6.2.2.

544 For an account of the intervention in Somalia see, *e.g.*, A.S. Natsios, *Humanitarian Relief Interventions in Somalia: The Economics of Chaos*, 3 International Peacekeeping (1996) 68-91.

545 M. Aristodemou, *Choice and Evasion in Judicial Recognition of Governments: Lessons from Somalia*, 5 EJIL (1994) 532-555, at 550.

546 M.E. Tzartzouras maintains that "even though Chapter VII machinery was used for its [resolution 733 (1992)] enforcement, its legal basis was the *request* by the Somali government (whether legitimate or not), and not a 'threat to international peace' under Article 39 of Chapter VII, as no such determination was made by the Security Council." M.E. Tzartzouras, *The Law of Humanitarian Intervention after Somalia*, 46 Revue hellénique de Droit International (1993) 197-224, at 216.

Nations, that all States shall ... immediately implement a general and complete embargo on all deliveries of weapons and military equipment to Somalia". This wording clearly implies that the decision was taken as a measure under Article 41 of the Charter.

The decision contained in resolution 794 (1992) to send in the UNITAF was taken under Chapter VII of the Charter after a less ambiguous determination that the situation in Somalia "constitutes a threat to international peace and security". This decision ought to be seen as a measure taken under Article 42 of the Charter. Interestingly, resolution 794 (1992) did provide for a role for the Secretary-General of the United Nations in the command and control of the Force. Eventually, however, the US assumed this function. The action may thus be conceived as a parallel to the Iraqi case: an enforcement action undertaken by a group of states authorized to do so by the Council. An important distinction, of course, is that self-defence was not at stake in the Somali case. The establishment of UNOSOM II was similarly a decision of the Council under Article 42 of the Charter. The wide mandate given to the troops by virtue of resolution 814 (1993), including "responsibility for the consolidation, expansion and maintenance of a secure environment throughout Somalia", clearly envisaged the use of force.[547] Pursuant to this resolution the troops did indeed become engaged in hostilities with the SNA.

3.9 Rwanda 1993-1996

3.9.1 Factual Background

In 1990, an ethnically motivated civil war broke out in Rwanda between the Hutu-dominated government forces and the Tutsi Rwandese Patriotic Front (RPF),[548] after the latter had invaded Rwanda from neighbouring Uganda. The tensions halted periodically with the signing of the Arusha Accords by both parties in August 1993. On 6 April 1994, however, an aircraft carrying both the Presidents of Rwanda and Burundi was shot down over the Rwandan capital of Kigali. This reignited the tensions between both factions and in the three months that followed, extremely brutal killings took place. The killings were predominantly by radical Hutus against Tutsis and moderate Hutus, costing an estimated 500,000-1,000,000 lives.[549] By the end of June

---

[547] See, *e.g.*, *ibid.*, 218-219.

[548] The Rwandan population is made up of approximately 85% Hutus, 14% Tutsis and 1% Twa.

[549] See Österdahl, *op. cit. supra* n.353, 261; Murphy, *op. cit. supra* n.172, 244; J. Karhilo, *The Establishment of the International Tribunal for Rwanda*, 64 NJIL (1995) 683- 713, 687.

1994 the RPF had taken control of the larger part of the Rwandan population, and the RPF has effectively been in control of the country since that date.

3.9.2.1 The Establishment of an Arms Embargo

In the preamble to resolution 812 (1993) the Council stated that it was "gravely concerned by the fighting in Rwanda and its consequences regarding international peace and security."[550] This was reiterated in resolution 846 (1993), in which the Council referred to the "adverse consequences" the fighting could have on "international peace and security."[551] These hints at a threat to the peace were taken further in resolution 918 (1994). Herein the Council first 'strongly condemned' the ongoing violence in Rwanda, and in particular "the very numerous killings of civilians which have taken place in Rwanda and the impunity with which armed individuals have been able to operate and continue operating therein." Then the Council expressed its 'deep disturbance' at "the magnitude of the human suffering caused by the conflict".[552] Subsequently the Council determined, in the preamble to Section B of resolution 918 (1994), "that the situation in Rwanda constitutes a threat to peace and security in the region." This was accompanied by the establishment of an arms embargo on Rwanda. To this effect paragraph 13 of resolution 918 (1994) states:

> that all States shall prevent the sale or supply to Rwanda by their nationals or from their territories or using their flag vessels or aircraft of arms and related matériel of all types, including weapons and ammunition, military vehicles and equipment, paramilitary police equipment and spare parts.[553]

Altogether the embargo did not prove very successful, as is exemplified by the Council's repeated calls to strictly comply with it. In resolution 997 (1995), for example, the Council:

> Affirms that the restrictions imposed under Chapter VII of the Charter of the United Nations by resolution 918 (1994) apply to the sale or supply of arms and matériel specified therein to persons in the States neighbouring Rwanda, if that sale or supply is for the purpose of the use of such arms or matériel within Rwanda.[554]

---

[550] S/Res. 812 (1993), 12 March 1993, para. 1.

[551] S/Res. 846 (1993), 22 June 1993, preamble.

[552] S/Res. 918 (1994), 17 May 1994, preamble.

[553] In para. 14, moreover, the Council "decides also to establish, in accordance with rule 28 of the provisional rules of procedure of the Security Council," a Sanctions Committee.

[554] S/Res. 997 (1995), 9 June 1995, para. 4. Similarly the Council, in the preamble to S/Res. 1013 (1995), 7 Sept. 1995, expressed "once again its grave concern at allegations of the sale and supply of arms and related matériel to former Rwandan government forces in violation of the embargo

More than a year after its imposition of the weapons embargo, the Council announced its termination. In paragraph 8 of resolution 1011 (1995) the Council, "acting under Chapter VII of the Charter of the United Nations," decided that the restrictions imposed by paragraph 13 of resolution 918 (1994) would be terminated on 1 September 1996.[555]

This notwithstanding, the Council soon thereafter directed the Secretary-General to set up an International Commission of Inquiry with the mandate to, *inter alia*, investigate violations of the arms embargo.[556] Although the Commission did find evidence of violations, in particular by Zaire,[557] the Council did not decide to take any action on the violations and the embargo ended on 1 September 1996.

3.9.2.2 The Authorization of a Multilateral Intervention

In 1993, the Council established the 'United Nations Observer Mission Uganda-Rwanda' (UNOMUR).[558] The mission was deployed on the Ugandan side of the border and was mandated to "monitor the Uganda/Rwanda border to verify that no military assistance reaches Rwanda", including the transit of "lethal weapons and ammunition across the border, as well as any other material which could be of military use."[559]

Three months later, UNOMUR was integrated within a newly established peacekeeping operation[560] under the name 'United Nations Assistance Mission for

imposed under its resolutions 918 (1994), 997 (1995) and 1011 (1995), and underlining the need for Governments to take action to ensure the effective implementation of the embargo."

555 S/Res. 1011 (1995), 16 Aug. 1995.

556 S/Res. 1013 (1995), 7 Sept. 1995, para. 1(a).

557 See the Report of the Commission to the Security Council, annexed to the letter from the Secretary-General to the Security Council, S/1996/195, 13 March 1996. *Cf.* the preamble to S/Res. 1053 (1996), 23 April 1996, in which the Council notes its deep concern as regards "the strong evidence presented by the Commission of Inquiry leading to the conclusion that it is highly probable that a violation of the arms embargo occurred, in particular by the sale of arms which took place in Seychelles in June 1994 and the subsequent two shipments of arms to Goma, Zaire from Seychelles destined for former Rwandan government forces." The third and 'final' report of the Commission is annexed to S/1997/1010, 24 Dec. 1997, but by resolution 1161 (1998), 9 April 1998, para. 1, the Council decided to 'reactivate' the Commission. For the final report of the Commission see the 'Letter Dated 18 November 1998 from the Secretary-General Addressed to the President of the Security Council', S/1998/1096, 18 Nov. 1998, Annex.

558 See S/Res. 846 (1993), 22 June 1993, para. 2.

559 *Ibid.*, para. 3.

560 See S/Res. 872 (1993), 5 Oct. 1993, adopted unanimously, para. 4. The integration did not

Rwanda' (UNAMIR), which was to oversee the observance of the Arusha Accords which had been signed between the Hutu government and the RPF in August 1993.[561] In response to the volatile environment in which the peacekeeping soldiers had to operate after the large-scale killings had resumed in April 1994, the Council first decided to adjust UNAMIR's mandate and decrease its size.[562] The following month, however, the Council reversed its position and decided to increase the number of troops to 5,500 and to expand UNIMAR's mandate.[563]

The Secretary-General, however, had considerable difficulty in acquiring troops and logistical support for UNAMIR II. In this context, France announced on 15 June 1994 that it was prepared, "along with its main European and African partners", to intervene in Rwanda to protect groups threatened by "extinction."[564] France's allies, however, did not support this interventionist course, amongst other things, because

---

change UNOMUR's terms of reference. Thus in para. 3 of resolution 891 (1993), adopted on 20 Dec. 1993, the Council "notes that the integration of UNOMUR within UNAMIR is purely administrative in nature and that it will in no way affect the mandate of UNOMUR as set out in resolution 846 (1993)." In the end UNOMUR's mandate was terminated on 21 Sept. 1994 in accordance with S/Res. 928 (1994), 20 June 1994.

561 S/Res. 872 (1993), 5 Oct. 1993, adopted unanimously, paras. 2 and 3. The mandate also included the "contribut[ion] to the security of the city of Kigali, *inter alia*, within a weapons secure area established by the parties in and around the city." *Ibid.*, para. 3(a).

562 S/Res. 912 (1994), 21 April 1994, para. 8. The adjustments, which include the mandate to "act as an intermediary between the parties" and "assist in the resumption of humanitarian relief operations", were made in conformity with the second alternative described in the 'Special Report of the Secretary-General on the United Nations Assistance Mission for Rwanda', S/1994/470, 20 April 1994. Herein the Secretary-General offered three alternatives to the Council: I) an "immediate and massive reinforcement of UNAMIR and a change in its mandate so that it would be equipped and authorized to coerce the opposing forces into a cease-fire, and to attempt to restore law and order and put an end to the killings." This option required "several thousand additional troops" and implied that "UNAMIR may have to be given enforcement powers under Chapter VII of the Charter of the United Nations." [para. 13]. II) The second option presented was that "a small group ... with necessary staff, would remain in Kigali to act as intermediary between the two parties in an attempt to bring them to an agreement on a cease-fire". [para. 15]. III) The third option would then be "the complete withdrawal of UNAMIR." [para. 19].

563 S/Res. 918 (1994), 17 May 1994, Section A, paras. 3 and 5. In para. 4 the Council, moreover, "recognizes that UNAMIR may be required to take action in self-defence against persons or groups who threaten protected sites and populations, United Nations and other humanitarian personnel or the means of delivery and distribution of humanitarian relief." The expanded mission, which was to be known as UNAMIR II, is described in the 'Report of the Secretary-General on the Situation in Rwanda', S/1994/565, 13 May 1994.

564 Statement by the French Minister for Foreign Affairs, A. Juppé, quoted in Murphy, *op. cit. supra* n.172, at 247.

France had allegedly armed the Hutu government forces,[565] its impartiality hence being questioned. The RPF, moreover, was gradually seizing control in Rwanda and strongly opposed a French intervention.[566] The Security Council, however, in view of the "time needed to gather the necessary resources for the effective deployment of UNAMIR, as expanded in resolutions 918 (1994) and 925 (1994),[567] decided to authorize an intervention under resolution 929 (1994).

In the preamble to resolution 929 (1994) the Council stressed "the strictly humanitarian character of this operation which shall be conducted in an impartial and neutral fashion", and emphasized that it "shall not constitute an interposition force between the parties." The Council then reaffirmed its concern with regard to the "continuation of systematic and widespread killings of the civilian population in Rwanda", and its recognition that the "current situation in Rwanda constitutes a unique case which demands an urgent response by the international community." Accordingly, the Council determined that "the magnitude of the humanitarian crisis in Rwanda constitutes a threat to peace and security in the region." In paragraph 1 it agreed that "a multinational operation may be set up for humanitarian purposes in Rwanda until UNAMIR is brought up to the necessary strength." Thereto, the Council:

> 2. Welcomes ... the offer by Member States ... to cooperate with the Secretary-General in order to achieve the objectives of the United Nations in Rwanda through the establishment of a temporary operation under national command and control aimed at contributing, in an impartial way, to the security and protection of displaced persons, refugees and civilians at risk in Rwanda, on the understanding that the costs of implementing the offer will be borne by the Member States concerned;
> 3. Acting under Chapter VII of the Charter of the United Nations, authorizes the Member States cooperating with the Secretary-General to conduct the operation referred to in paragraph 2 above using all necessary means to achieve the humanitarian objectives set out in subparagraphs 4 (a) and (b) of resolution 925 (1994);
> 4. Decides that the mission of Member States cooperating with the Secretary-General will be limited to a period of two months following the adoption of the present resolution, unless the Secretary-General determines at an earlier date that the expanded UNAMIR is able to carry out its mandate.[568]

---

[565] See, *e.g.*, report of the Associated Press, 'Government Probe Accused of Hiding French Role in Rwanda', 21 March 1998. Accessed at http://cnn.com on 2 April 1998.

[566] Murphy quotes their military chief as saying that: "France trained the militias and the army, and it did not condemn the murderers. France is clearly partial, and the return of its soldiers would only complicate the situation." Murphy, *op. cit. supra* n.172, at 248.

[567] S/Res. 929 (1994), 22 June 1994, preamble. The resolution was adopted by 10 votes in favour with 5 abstentions (Brazil, China, New Zealand, Nigeria, Pakistan), preamble. *Cf.* the 'Letter Dated 19 June 1994 from the Secretary-General Addressed to the President of the Security Council', S/1994/728, 20 June 1994, which discusses the possibility of a short-term deployment of UNAMIR II.

[568] In S/Res. 925 (1994), 8 June 1994, para. 4 (a) and (b) the Council reaffirms that UNAMIR will:

Pursuant to this resolution, France initiated *Opération Turquoise* on 23 June 1994.[569] Approximately 2,500 French troops, which were later accompanied by some 600 African troops, established a 'humanitarian protected zone' on the southwestern border with Zaire, which in effect primarily protected fleeing Hutus. On 19 July a new government of national unity was formed, composed of (moderate) Hutus and Tutsis. The new government was opposed to an extension of the French presence in Rwanda, hence the troops withdrew on 22 August, despite calls from various states to remain in Rwanda for a longer period.[570] UNAMIR then assumed responsibility for the safety zone, until the Council terminated its mandate on 8 March 1996.[571]

"(a) Contribute to the security and protection of displaced persons; refugees and civilians at risk in Rwanda, including through the establishment and maintenance, where feasible, of secure humanitarian areas; and (b) Provide security and support for the distribution of relief supplies and humanitarian relief operations."

569 For an account of the operation see, *e.g.*, Murphy, *op. cit. supra* n.172, 250-260.

570 See 'Progress Report of the Secretary-General on the United Nations Assistance Mission for Rwanda', S/1994/1133, 6 Oct. 1994, section V. The major problem at that time was the mass exodus of refugees to neighbouring countries, notably Zaire (an estimated 2,000,000 people, that is 25% of the total Rwandan population), with the ensuing humanitarian complications.

571 S/Res. 1029 (1995), 12 Dec. 1995, para. 1. In 1996, moreover, a civil war erupted in Zaire (now Congo). In that context Rwandan Tutsis engaged in hostilities with Hutus that had fled to Zaire and allegedly staged attacks on Tutsis in Rwanda, Burundi and Zaire. In Nov. 1996 the humanitarian situation in Zaire became alarming, which prompted Canada and the US, amongst others, to call for a multinational intervention (see, for example, 'Diary of confusion as the crisis week unfolds', Daily Telegraph, International News, 17 Nov. 1996. Accessed at http://www.telegraph.co.uk on 15 July 2000). The Security Council responded positively to these calls by adopting resolution 1080 (1996) on 15 Nov. 1996. In para. 3 of this resolution it: "Welcomes the offers made by Member States ... concerning the establishment for humanitarian purposes of a temporary multinational force to facilitate the immediate return of humanitarian organizations and the effective delivery by civilian relief organizations of humanitarian aid to alleviate the immediate suffering of displaced persons, refugees and civilians at risk in eastern Zaire". In para. 3, furthermore, the Council: "Authorizes the Member States ... to achieve, by using all necessary means, the humanitarian objectives set out". In the end no action was taken pursuant to this resolution, as the humanitarian situation quickly improved after its adoption. See, *e.g.*, T. Butcher, 'Exodus by Hutus lifts the threat of disaster', 16 Nov. 1996; L. Tunbridge, T. Butcher, 'Troops no longer needed for Zaire, says Canada', 20 Nov. 1996. Both texts accessed at http://www.telegraph.co.uk on 15 July 2000.

3.9.2.3 The International Criminal Tribunal for Rwanda[572]

During the conflict in Rwanda the Council repeatedly called upon the parties to observe the laws of war.[573] In resolution 912 (1994), furthermore, the Council mentioned the "mindless violence and carnage which are engulfing Rwanda."[574]

In the preamble to resolution 918 (1994), moreover, the Council referred to the ongoing violence in language reminiscent of the definition of genocide.[575] After first expressing "its alarm at continuing reports of systematic, widespread and flagrant violations of international humanitarian law in Rwanda, as well as other violations of the rights to life and property", the Council 'recalled' that "in this context ... the killing of members of an ethnic group with the intention of destroying such a group, in whole or in part, constitutes a crime punishable under international law."[576]

---

572 Generally see Karhilo, *op. cit. supra* n.549; P. Akhavan, *The International Criminal Tribunal for Rwanda: The Politics and Pragmatics of Punishment*, 90 AJIL (1996) 501-510; L.D. Johnson, *The International Tribunal for Rwanda*, 67 Revue Internationale de Droit Pénal (1996) 211-232; R.S. Lee, *The Rwanda Tribunal*, 9 LJIL (1996) 37-61; D. Shraga, R. Zacklin, *The International Criminal Tribunal for Rwanda*, 7 EJIL (1996) 501-518; G. Abi-Saab, *International Criminal Tribunals and the Development of International Humanitarian and Human Rights Law*. In: E. Yakpo, T. Boumedra (eds.), Liber Amicorum Mohammed Bedjaoui (1999) 649-658.

573 *Cf.* S/Res. 812 (1993), 12 March 1993, para. 8, in which the Council: "Urges both parties strictly to respect the rules of international humanitarian law" and para. 6 of S/Res. 846 (1993), 22 June 1993, in which the Council: "Urges the Government of Rwanda and the RPF strictly to respect the rules of international humanitarian law."

574 S/Res. 912 (1994), 21 April 1994, para. 6. See to the same effect S/Res. 918 (1994), 17 May 1994, para. 1.

575 Article II of the 1948 Convention on the Prevention and Punishment of the Crime of Genocide (78 UNTS 277) contains the following definition:
"In the present Convention, genocide means any of the following acts committed with intent to destroy, in whole or in part, a national, ethnical, racial or religious group as such:
(a) Killing members of the group;
(b) Causing serious bodily or mental harm to members of the group;
(c) Deliberately inflicting on the group conditions of life calculated to bring about its physical destruction in whole or in part;
(d) Imposing measures intended to prevent births within the group;
(e) Forcibly transferring children of the group to another group."

576 S/Res. 918 (1994), 17 May 1994. In an earlier statement the President of the Security Council held that: "The Security Council is appalled at continuing reports of the slaughter of innocent civilians in Kigali and other parts of Rwanda, and reported preparations for further massacres. ... The Security Council condemns all these breaches of international humanitarian law in Rwanda, particularly those perpetrated against the civilian population, and recalls that persons who instigate or participate in such acts are individually responsible. In this context, the Security Council recalls that the killing of members of an ethnic group with the intention of destroying such a group in whole or in part constitutes a crime punishable under international law." S/PRST/1994/21, 30 April

Subsequently, the Secretary-General was requested to report on "the investigation of serious violations of international humanitarian law committed in Rwanda during the conflict."[577] After this report concluded that "massacres and killings have continued in a systematic manner throughout the country",[578] the Council adopted resolution 935 (1994). Herein the Council first 'recalled' that "all persons who commit or authorize the commission of serious violations of international humanitarian law are individually responsible for those violations and should be brought to justice." The Secretary-General was then requested to establish, "as a matter of urgency", a Commission of Experts that was to gather "evidence of grave violations of international humanitarian law committed in the territory of Rwanda, including the evidence of possible acts of genocide."[579]

In its preliminary report the Commission of Experts, *inter alia*, concluded that ample evidence existed of "serious breaches of international humanitarian law"; "crimes against humanity" perpetrated by "individuals from both sides"; and acts of genocide against the Tutsi group by Hutu elements in a "concerted, planned, systematic and methodical way."[580] Accordingly, the Commission:

> considers that to enhance the fair and consistent interpretation, application and adjudication of international law on individual responsibility for serious human rights violations and to effect the most efficient allocation of resources, the jurisdiction of the International Criminal Tribunal for the former Yugoslavia should be expanded to permit cases concerning the situation in Rwanda to be brought under it.[581]

The evidence of the crimes mentioned above induced the Council to create an International Criminal Tribunal for Rwanda (ICTR)[582] under resolution 955 (1994).

1994. Indeed in the preamble to S/Res. 925 (1994), 8 June 1994, the Council noted "with the gravest concern the reports indicating that acts of genocide have occurred in Rwanda and recalling in this context that genocide constitutes a crime punishable under international law."

[577] S/Res. 918 (1994), 17 May 1994, para. 18.

[578] 'Report of the Secretary-General on the Situation in Rwanda', S/1994/640, 31 May 1994, para. 6.

[579] S/Res. 935 (1994), 1 July 1994, para. 1.

[580] 'Preliminary Report of the Independent Commission of Experts Established in Accordance with Security Council Resolution 935 (1994)', paras. 146-148. Annexed to 'Letter Dated 1 October 1994 from the Secretary-General Addressed to the President of the Security Council', S/1994/1125, 4 Oct. 1994.

[581] *Ibid.*, para. 149.

[582] Known in full as the "International Criminal Tribunal for the Prosecution of Persons Responsible for Genocide and Other Serious Violations of International Humanitarian Law Committed in the Territory of Rwanda and Rwandan citizens responsible for genocide and other such violations committed in the territory of neighbouring States, between 1 January 1994 and 31 December 1994."

This was done by the Council in the following terms:

> Expressing once again its grave concern at the reports indicating that genocide and other systematic, widespread and flagrant violations of international humanitarian law have been committed in Rwanda,
> Determining that this situation continues to constitute a threat to international peace and security,
> Determined to put an end to such crimes and to take effective measures to bring to justice the persons who are responsible for them,
> Convinced that in the particular circumstances of Rwanda, the prosecution of persons responsible for serious violations of international humanitarian law would enable this aim to be achieved and would contribute to the process of national reconciliation and to the restoration and maintenance of peace,
> Believing that the establishment of an international tribunal for the prosecution of persons responsible for genocide and the other above-mentioned violations of international humanitarian law will contribute to ensuring that such violations are halted and effectively redressed,
> ...
> Acting under Chapter VII of the Charter of the United Nations,
>
> 1. Decides hereby, having received the request of the Government of Rwanda (S/1994/1115), to establish an international tribunal for the sole purpose of prosecuting persons responsible for genocide and other serious violations of international humanitarian law committed in the territory of Rwanda and Rwandan citizens responsible for genocide and other such violations committed in the territory of neighbouring States, between 1 January 1994 and 31 December 1994 and to this end to adopt the Statute of the International Criminal Tribunal for Rwanda annexed hereto.[583]

Thus, the Council, contrary to the recommendations of the Commission of Experts, decided to establish an independent Tribunal for Rwanda, in Arusha, Tanzania, although the ICTR is linked to the ICTY. The ICTR consists of two Trial Chambers and an Appeals Chamber, the Prosecutor and the Registry.[584] The Appeals judges and the Chief Prosecutor of the ICTY perform the same functions for the ICTR.[585] The Tribunal is competent to:

> prosecute persons responsible for serious violations of international humanitarian law committed in the territory of Rwanda and Rwandan citizens responsible for such violations committed in the territory of neighbouring States, between 1 January 1994 and 31 December 1994.[586]

---

[583] S/Res. 955 (1994), 8 Nov. 1994, adopted by 13 votes in favour, with 1 abstention (China) and 1 vote against. The reference to the Rwandese request in para. 1 is somewhat ironic, as this was the only state voting against the resolution.

[584] For an overview of the ICTR's functions and work see, *e.g.*, Karhilo, *op. cit. supra* n.549; Lee, *op. cit. supra* n.572; T. Howland, W. Calathes, *The UN's International Criminal Tribunal, Is It Justice or Jingoism for Rwanda? A Call for Transformation*, 39 VJIL (1998) 135-168; Akhavan, *op. cit. supra* n.572; T. Sapru, *Into the Heart of Darkness: A Case Against the Foray of the Security Council Tribunal into the Rwandan Crisis*, 32 Texas ILJ (1997) 329-354.

[585] Arts. 12(2) and 15(3) of the Statute as contained in S/Res. 955 (1994), Annex. For a comparison of the Statutes of the ICTY and the ICTR see, *e.g.*, Johnson, *op. cit. supra* n.572.

[586] Statute, Art. 1.

These serious violations cover acts of genocide, crimes against humanity, and violations of Article 3 common to the Geneva Conventions and of Additional Protocol II.[587] The jurisdiction *ratione temporis* is confined to acts committed between 31 December 1993 and 1 January 1995,[588] whilst the territorial jurisdiction extends "to the territory of Rwanda including its land surface and airspace".[589] The jurisdiction of the Tribunal is concurrent with that of domestic jurisdictions, the former possessing primacy.[590] The rights of the accused include the *non-bis-in-idem* principle.[591]

As regards the cooperation between states and the tribunal, Article 28 of the Statute determines that: "States shall cooperate with the International Tribunal for Rwanda in the investigation and prosecution of persons accused of committing serious violations of international humanitarian law."[592]

3.9.3 Summary

The Security Council, after initially confining itself to expressions of concern regarding the situation in Rwanda, made a formal determination that the situation "constitutes a threat to peace and security in the region" in resolution 918 (1994). On this occasion, the Council imposed an arms embargo on Rwanda, which ended on 1 September 1996. Prior to this the Council had already sent two peacekeeping missions to Rwanda, UNOMUR and UNAMIR. When the increasingly volatile situation in Rwanda prevented UNAMIR from pursuing its objectives and when it became apparent that United Nations members would not rapidly contribute forces to an

---

[587] Statute, Arts. 2-4. R. Karadzic and R. Mladic are among those indicted. See the 'International Arrest Warrants and Orders for Surrender for Radovan Karadzic and Ratko Mladic', 36 ILM (1997) 96-99.

[588] The Commission had recommended a period beginning on 6 April 1994. The Rwandan delegation itself proposed a period extending from 1 Oct. 1990 to 17 July 1994. The rejection of this proposal was one of the reasons why Rwanda voted against resolution 955 (1994), together with the Tribunal's exclusion of capital punishment. See S/PV.3453, 15-16.

[589] Statute, Art. 7. The reference to Rwandan airspace was included so as to allow for the prosecution of those allegedly responsible for inciting genocide via radio broadcasts. See J.F. Metzl, *Rwandan Genocide and the International Law of Radio Jamming*, 91 AJIL (1997) 628-651.

[590] Statute, Arts. 8(1) and 8(2).

[591] Statute, Art. 9. See also Art. 20.

[592] *Cf.* Art. 28(2) of the Statute, according to which: "States shall comply without undue delay with any request for assistance or an order issued by a Trial Chamber, including, but not limited to: (a) The identification and location of persons; (b) The taking of testimony and the production of evidence; (c) The service of documents; (d) The arrest or detention of persons; (e) The surrender or the transfer of the accused to the International Tribunal for Rwanda."

expanded UNAMIR, the Security Council authorized a multilateral force to intervene in Rwanda. This force stayed in Rwanda for three months and was successful in protecting Hutu refugees, but by then the worst atrocities had already occurred. Indeed, the failure of the United Nations to prevent the genocide in Rwanda has been recognized by the Organization itself.[593] When relative stability returned to Rwanda after the victory of the RPF the Council decided to establish an international criminal tribunal for Rwanda by resolution 955 (1994).

3.9.4 Analysis: The Application of Chapter VII by the Council

The Council's determination contained in resolution 918 (1994) that the situation in Rwanda constitutes "a threat to the peace and security in the region" is to be read as an application of Article 39 of the Charter, although the terminology employed in the resolution differs slightly from that of the Charter. The decision to establish an arms embargo was made under Chapter VII of the Charter, in this case Article 41. The authorization of the intervention in Rwanda under the name Opération Turquoise by resolution 929 (1994) was a measure taken under Article 42 of the Charter.

The establishment of the ICTR must be seen as a measure under Article 41. In resolution 955 (1994) the Council held that the situation in Rwanda continued "to constitute a threat to international peace and security", and that "in the particular circumstances of Rwanda, the prosecution of persons responsible for serious violations of international humanitarian law would ... contribute to the process of national reconciliation and to the restoration and maintenance of peace." After these Article 39

---

[593] In a letter dated 18 March 1999 (S/1994/339), the Secretary-General informed the Security Council of his intention to appoint an independent inquiry into the actions of the United Nations during the 1994 genocide in Rwanda. In their reply (S/1999/340), the members of the Council expressed their support for the initiative 'in this unique circumstance'. In May 1999 the Secretary-General appointed the (three) members of the Independent Inquiry, which submitted a report on 15 Dec. 1999. In the conclusion the "Independent Inquiry finds that the response of the United Nations before and during the 1994 genocide in Rwanda failed in a number of fundamental respects. The responsibility for the failings of the United Nations to prevent and stop the genocide in Rwanda lies with a number of different actors, in particular the Secretary-General, the Secretariat, the Security Council, UNAMIR and the broader membership of the United Nations. This international responsibility is one which warrants a clear apology by the Organization and by Member States concerned to the Rwandese people." Upon receipt of the Report, the Secretary-General stated that he fully accepted the conclusions of the report and expressed his "deep remorse" for the failure of the United Nations in Rwanda. See his 'Statement on Receiving the Report of the Independent Inquiry into the Actions of the United Nations During the 1994 Genocide in Rwanda', 16 Dec. 1999.

determinations, the Council acted under Chapter VII of the Charter in establishing the international tribunal.

3.10 Haiti 1993-1996

3.10.1 Factual Background

In the first democratic elections in decades, which were observed by the United Nations, Jean-Bertrand Aristide was elected President in December 1990. The Haitian army, however, staged a *coup d'état* on 30 September 1991 and installed a repressive military regime headed by Lt. General Raoul Cédras. President Aristide subsequently went into exile and the internal situation became volatile, which *inter alia* resulted in many refugees fleeing the country.

3.10.2 Security Council Action concerning Haiti

The Security Council determined that the situation in Haiti posed a threat to international peace and security in June 1993. In the preamble to resolution 841 (1993) the Council first noted "the incidence of humanitarian crises, including mass displacements of population, becoming or aggravating threats to international peace and security." The Council, moreover, expressed its concern that the continuation of the situation in Haiti:

> contributes to a climate of fear of persecution and economic dislocation which could increase the number of Haitians seeking refuge in neighbouring Member States and convinced that a reversal of this situation is needed to prevent its negative repercussions on the region.

After these expressions of concern, the Council determined that "in these unique and exceptional circumstances, the continuation of this situation threatens international peace and security in the region." Subsequently, an oil and arms embargo were established as a measure taken under Chapter VII of the Charter,[594] the implementation

[594] See S/Res. 841 (1993), adopted unanimously, 16 June 1993, paras. 5-6. In addition, para. 8 holds that: "States in which there are funds, including any funds derived from property, (a) of the Government of Haiti or of the de facto authorities in Haiti, or (b) controlled directly or indirectly by such Government or authorities or by entities, wherever located or organized, owned or controlled by such Government or authorities, shall require all persons and entities within their own territories holding such funds to freeze them to ensure that they are not made available directly or indirectly to or for the benefit of the de facto authorities in Haiti."

of which was to be monitored by a Sanctions Committee.[595] It may be noted that after the adoption of the resolution, the President of the Council issued a declaration in which he stated that members of the Council had asked him to say that the adoption of the resolution was "warranted by the unique and exceptional situation in Haiti and should not be regarded as constituting a precedent."[596]

When an agreement was reached between President Aristide and the Commander -in- Chief of the Armed Forces R. Cédras,[597] the Council suspended the sanctions.[598] Subsequently the Council sent in a United Nations Mission in Haiti (UNMIH), which was to guide and train the Haitian police and military.[599] When the 'USS Harlan County' carrying 220 United Nations military personnel arrived in Port-au-Prince on 11 October 1993, however, armed civilians ("attachés") prevented the ship from anchoring. This prompted the Council to determine that the failure of the Haitian military authorities to fulfil their obligations under the Governors Island Agreement "constitutes a threat to peace and security in the region".[600] Consequently the sanctions that were established under resolution 841 (1993), and suspended by resolution 861 (1993), were reimposed.[601] With regard to the monitoring of the sanctions regime, moreover, the Council, on 16 October 1993, adopted resolution 875 (1993) which stated:

> Acting under Chapters VII and VIII of the Charter of the United Nations,
>
> 1. Calls upon Member States, acting nationally or through regional agencies or arrangements, cooperating

---

[595] *Ibid.*, para. 10.

[596] S/PV.3238 (1993), at 9. Quoted in N.M. Blokker, M. Kleiboer, *The Internalization of Domestic Conflict: The Role of the UN Security Council*, 9 LJIL (1996) 7-35, at 29.

[597] The agreement, known as the Governors Island Agreement, was signed on 3 July 1993 and is reproduced in S/26063.

[598] S/Res. 861 (1993), 27 Aug. 1993. Herein the Council: "Acting under Chapter VII of the Charter of the United Nations," decides in para. 1 that "the measures set out in paragraphs 5 to 9 of resolution 841 (1993) are suspended with immediate effect and requests all States to act consistently with this decision as soon as possible."

[599] S/Res. 867 (1993), 23 Sept. 1993, paras. 2-4.

[600] S/Res. 873 (1993), 13 Oct. 1993, preamble.

[601] In S/Res. 873 (1993), 13 Oct. 1993, para. 1, the Council, whilst "acting under Chapter VII of the Charter of the United Nations," decided "to terminate the suspension of the measures set out in paragraphs 5 to 9 of resolution 841 (1993) ... on 18 October 1993 unless the Secretary-General, having regard for the views of the Secretary-General of the Organization of American States, reports to the Council that the parties to the Governors Island Agreement and any other authorities in Haiti are implementing in full the agreement to reinstate the legitimate Government of President Jean-Bertrand Aristide and have established the necessary measures to enable UNMIH to carry out its mandate."

with the legitimate Government of Haiti, to use such measures commensurate with the specific circumstances as may be necessary under the authority of the Secretary-General to ensure strict implementation of the provisions of resolutions 841 (1993) and 873 (1993) relating to the supply of petroleum or petroleum products or arms and related matériel of all types, and in particular to halt inward maritime shipping as necessary in order to inspect and verify their cargoes and destinations.

In May 1994, moreover, the Council decided to extend the scope of the embargo. This was done by resolution 917 (1994), in which the Council reaffirmed "that the goal of the international community remains the restoration of democracy in Haiti and the prompt return of the legitimately elected President, Jean-Bertrand Aristide, under the framework of the Governors Island Agreement."

The Council, furthermore, determined that:

in these unique and exceptional circumstances, the situation created by the failure of the military authorities in Haiti to fulfil their obligations under the Governors Island Agreement and to comply with relevant Security Council resolutions constitutes a threat to peace and security in the region.[602]

When the sanctions did not result in a change in the behaviour of the military, the Security Council decided to authorize an international intervention in Haiti by resolution 940 (1994). After again determining in the preamble that "the situation in Haiti continues to constitute a threat to peace and security in the region," the Council:

Acting under Chapter VII of the Charter of the United Nations,

authorizes Member States to form a multinational force under unified command and control and, in this framework, to use all necessary means to facilitate the departure from Haiti of the military leadership, consistent with the Governors Island Agreement, the prompt return of the legitimately elected President and the restoration of the legitimate authorities of the Government of Haiti, and to establish and maintain a secure and stable environment that will permit implementation of the Governors Island Agreement, on the understanding that the cost of implementing this temporary operation will be borne by the participating Member States.[603]

Pursuant to this resolution a Multinational Force (MNF), which was composed of troops from 28 countries and was led by the US, landed in Haiti on 19 September 1994.[604] After negotiating with the military leadership the force succeeded in taking over control of the country peacefully,[605] and on 15 October 1994 President Aristide

---

[602] S/Res. 917 (1994), 6 May 1994, preamble. For the expanded sanctions see paras. 2-11.

[603] S/Res. 940 (1994), 31 July 1994, para. 4.

[604] For an assessment of the action see L.F. Damrosch, *et. al.*, *Agora: The 1994 U.S. Action in Haiti*, 89 AJIL (1995) 58-87.

[605] In the words of Meron: "The agreement of September 18, 1994, negotiated in Port-au-Prince between President Jimmy Carter and General Raoul Cédras, and its acceptance by the Aristide

was able to return to Haiti. This prompted the Security Council to terminate the embargo on Haiti.[606]

It had been decided that the MNF would be replaced by the existing peacekeeping operation.[607] Therefore the Security Council, after determining in paragraph 5 of resolution 975 (1995) that "a secure and stable environment, appropriate to the deployment of UNMIH as foreseen in ... resolution 940 (1994), now exists in Haiti," decided that the "full transfer of responsibility from the MNF to UNMIH" was to be "completed by 31 March 1995."[608] The mandate of the UNMIH was extended until 31 June 1996,[609] when at the request of the Haitian government a smaller UN mission was deployed in Haiti.[610]

3.10.3 Summary

The Security Council first established an oil and weapons embargo on Haiti, then suspended it when hopes of a peaceful settlement of the internal conflict were high, but reimposed and tightened the embargo when it became apparent that the military regime was not willing to reinstall the democratically elected President. When the sanctions failed to induce a behavioural change on the part of the military regime, the Council authorized a multilateral forceful intervention, which succeeded in taking control of the country peacefully. With the reinstalment of democracy thus achieved, the Council assumed responsibility for the situation in Haiti through the UNMIH, which proved successful, and was therefore replaced by a (smaller) mission in 1996.

3.10.4 Analysis: The Application of Chapter VII by the Council

The Council's involvement started with the determination in resolution 841 (1993) that the continuation of the situation in Haiti threatens international peace and security in

---

government, led to the consent-based, nonviolent, hostilities-free entry of U.S. forces and their peaceful deployment." T. Meron, *Extraterritoriality of Human Rights Treaties*, 89 AJIL (1995) 78-82, at 78.

606 S/Res. 944 (1994), 29 Sept. 1994, para. 4.

607 See para. 8 of resolution 940 (1994), which stipulates that "the multinational force will terminate its mission and UNMIH will assume the full range of its functions ... when a secure and stable environment has been established and UNMIH has adequate force capability and structure to assume the full range of its functions."

608 S/Res. 975 (1995), 30 Jan. 1995, para. 7.

609 See S/Res. 1048 (1996), 29 Feb. 1996.

610 S/Res. 1063 (1996), 28 June 1996.

the region, and that *therefore* the Council acted under Chapter VII of the Charter. This amounts to a determination under Article 39 of the Charter, and the subsequent imposition of sanctions are to be seen as measures taken under Article 41. The suspension and later reinforcement and enlargement of the sanctions have the same legal basis. When these non-forcible actions did not induce the military regime in Haiti to cooperate in re-establishing President Aristide's government, the Council decided to take measures under Article 42 of the Charter. As in Somalia, it authorized a multinational force to – if necessary, forcibly – secure a peaceful environment, that is an environment in which the democratically elected President Aristide could resume office. Indeed, according to some the authorization is a sign of an emerging right of people to democracy.[611]

3.11 Sudan 1995-2000

3.11.1 Factual Background

During a visit to Ethiopia, an attempt on the life of the Egyptian President Hosni Mubarak took place in Addis Ababa on 26 June 1995. The attempt was believed to have been committed by the Egyptian-based group Jama'a Islamiya,[612] which according to both Ethiopia and Egypt is provided with direct assistance by Sudan's security services. Three surviving assailants captured by Ethiopian police after the attempt provided incriminating information about the involvement of Sudan, including the supply of travel documents and weapons, and the harbouring of key planners of the operation. Ethiopia subsequently requested Sudan to extradite three Egyptians suspected of planning and executing the assassination attempt, to which Sudan replied

---

611 See T.M. Franck, *The Emerging Right to Democratic Governance*, 86 AJIL (1992) 46-91; O. Corten, *La Résolution 940 du Conseil De Sécurité Autorisant une Intervention Militaire en Haïti: L'émergence d'un Principe de Légitimité Démocratique en Droit International?*, 6 EJIL (1995) 116-133; W.M. Reisman, *Haiti and the Validity of International Action*, 89 AJIL (1995) 82-84; W.M. Reisman, *Humanitarian Intervention and Fledgling Democracies*, 18 Fordham JIL (1995) 794-805; M.J. Glennon, *Sovereignty and Community after Haiti: Rethinking the Collective Use of Force*, 89 AJIL (1995) 70-74. See in this context also the contributions by I.I. Lukashuk, *The United Nations and Illegitimate Regimes: When to Intervene to Protect Human Rights*, 143-158; T.M. Franck, *Intervention Against Illegitimate Regimes*, 159-176; A.M. Burley, *Commentary on Intervention Against Illegitimate Regimes*, 177-180; and V. Nanda, *Commentary on International Intervention to Promote the Legitimacy of Regimes*, 181-184. In: L.F. Damrosch, D.J. Scheffer (eds.), *Law and Force in the New International Order* (1991).

612 Indeed the Jama'a Islamiya claimed responsibility for the assassination attempt. See G. Butt, 'Militants Promise Further Attempt on Mubarak's Life', The Daily Telegraph, 5 July 1995. Accessed at http://www.telegraph.co.uk on 19 March 1998.

that it could not comply with the request as it was unable to locate them. In response, on 11 September and 19 December 1995, the Organization of African Unity (OAU) took a rare decision against a member state by calling on Sudan to extradite the three suspects believed to have been involved in the assassination attempt and to stop aiding terrorism. The Security Council subsequently seized the matter.

3.11.2 Security Council Action concerning Sudan

In the preamble to resolution 1044 (1996), adopted six months after the assassination attempt, the Council noted that "acts of international terrorism in all its forms which endanger or take innocent lives, have a deleterious effect on international relations and jeopardize the security of States." Furthermore, the Council 'recalled' the 1973 "Convention on the Prevention and Punishment of Crimes against Internationally Protected Persons, including Diplomatic Agents." Subsequently, it announced its 'conviction' that "the suppression of acts of international terrorism, including those in which States are involved, is an essential element for the maintenance of international peace and security."

In the operative part of the resolution the Council then condemned the "terrorist assassination attempt on the life of the President of the Arab Republic of Egypt in Addis Ababa, Ethiopia, on 26 June 1995"; and 'strongly deplored' the "flagrant violation of the sovereignty and integrity of Ethiopia and the attempt to disturb the peace and security of Ethiopia and the region as a whole."[613] Subsequently the Council "called upon' Sudan to extradite the three suspects, and in general to "desist from engaging in activities of assisting, supporting and facilitating terrorist activities and from giving shelter and sanctuaries to terrorist elements".[614]

When Sudan failed to comply with these calls, the Council established an embargo in resolution 1054 (1996). In the preamble it first 'determined' that the non-compliance by Sudan with the requests contained in paragraph 4 of resolution 1044 (1996) "constitutes a threat to international peace and security." Subsequently the Council, whilst "acting under Chapter VII of the Charter of the United Nations," demanded that Sudan comply with the requests covered by resolution 1044 (1996), paragraph 4, and that until such compliance was forthcoming sanctions were to be imposed on Sudan.[615]

---

[613] S/Res. 1044 (1996), 31 Jan. 1996, paras. 1 and 2.

[614] *Ibid.*, para. 4.

[615] S/Res. 1054 (1996), 26 April 1996, paras. 1-3. The measures include diplomatic sanctions and travel restrictions for officials of the Sudanese government and its armed forces.

The Sudanese government, however, again declined to meet these demands. In response the Council extended the scope of the sanctions so as to include an aerial embargo. Thereto the Council, in resolution 1070 (1996), first 'reaffirmed' that "the suppression of acts of international terrorism, including those in which States are involved is essential for the maintenance of international peace and security."[616] Subsequently it reaffirmed its determination that the non-extradition of the suspects constituted a threat to international peace and security.[617] In paragraph 3 of resolution 1070 (1996) the Council then, explicitly "acting under Chapter VII of the Charter of the United Nations", decided to impose an aerial embargo in the following terms:

> all States shall deny aircraft permission to take off from, land in, or overfly their territories if the aircraft is registered in Sudan, or owned, leased or operated by or on behalf of Sudan Airways or by any undertaking, wherever located or organized, which is substantially owned or controlled by Sudan Airways, or owned, leased or operated by the Government or public authorities of Sudan, or by an undertaking, wherever located or organized, which is substantially owned or controlled by the Government or public authorities of Sudan.

Since the suspects were not extradited, the sanctions remained in force in the period under consideration.

3.11.3 Summary

In resolution 1044 (1995) the Council determined "that the suppression of acts of international terrorism, including those in which States are involved, is an essential element for the maintenance of international peace and security." Although the assassination attempt was condemned as a "flagrant violation of the sovereignty and integrity of Ethiopia" and "an attempt to disturb the peace and security of Ethiopia and the region as a whole", at this stage the Council confined itself to calling upon the government of Sudan to extradite the suspects. When this call was disregarded, the Council adopted resolution 1054 (1995). Herein it explicitly determined that the non-compliance by Sudan with the requests to extradite "constitutes a threat to international peace and security", and limited diplomatic sanctions were accordingly established. These sanctions were broadened with the adoption of resolution 1070 (1996), which additionally established an aerial embargo on Sudan.

---

[616] S/Res. 1070 (1996), 16 Aug. 1996, preamble.
[617] *Ibid.*

3.11.4 Analysis: The Application of Chapter VII by the Council

In the three resolutions on Sudan described above, the Council quite neatly followed the Charter provisions. While at first merely hinting at an 'attempted disturbance' of "the peace and security of Ethiopia and the region as a whole" in resolution 1044 (1995), the non-compliance by Sudan with the Council's request to extradite was unequivocally termed a threat to peace and security in resolution 1054 (1995). Following this Article 39 determination, the Council imposed sanctions under Article 41, a course of action which was repeated in resolution 1070 (1996).

3.12 Sierra Leone 1997-2000

3.12.1 Factual Background

The former British colony of Sierra Leone gained independence in 1961. After a period of democracy the army staged a coup and overthrew the elected government in 1967. The country has been ruled by the military since that day, although the 1991 constitution called for general multi-party elections to be held in 1992. The Revolutionary United Front (RUF), however, pre-empted this and installed V.E.M. Strasser as Head of State in 1992. Strasser was subsequently ousted by a RUF rival in 1996. General elections following this coup were won by A.T. Kabbah. Despite a peace agreement brokered by the OAU between the newly elected government and the RUF, a civil war between President Kabbah and the RUF erupted from 1997 onwards. The RUF gained control of the country and forced Kabbah to flee in May 1997, but Kabbah was able to return in March 1998 after military intervention by the Military Observer Group (ECOMOG) of the Economic Community of West African States (ECOWAS). RUF leader Sankoh was sentenced to death in October 1998, but after RUF troops took control of the capital Freetown in 1999 he was freed and granted amnesty by Kabbah as part of a Peace Accord signed in Lome, Togo, on 7 July 1999. The Accord also provided for shared governance by Kabbah and the RUF, and cease-fire monitoring by United Nations peacekeepers.

3.12.2 Security Council Action concerning Sierra Leone

After condemning the RUF military coup that took place in May 1997,[618] the Council determined that "the situation in Sierra Leone constitutes a threat to international peace and security in the region" in resolution 1132 (1997). By that same resolution, the Council established an arms and oil embargo and imposed travel restrictions on members of the military junta.[619] In paragraph 8 of resolution 1132 (1997), moreover, the Council "acting under Chapter VIII of the Charter" authorized ECOWAS "to ensure strict implementation" of the arms and weapons embargo. In the same paragraph, the Council stated that this could include: "where necessary and in conformity with applicable international standards ... halting inward maritime shipping in order to inspect and verify their cargoes and destinations, and calls upon all States to cooperate with ECOWAS in this regard."

After President Kabbah returned from exile in March 1998, the Council terminated the oil embargo[620] and narrowed the scope of the prohibition to sell arms to non-governmental forces in June 1998.[621]

In July 1998, furthermore, the Council established a small peacekeeping mission, the United Nations Observer Mission in Sierra Leone (UNOMSIL).[622] The ECOWAS was to provide security for UNOMSIL. UNOMSIL was replaced by the United Nations Mission in Sierra Leone (UNAMSIL) in 1999, a mission that was to be comprised of "a maximum of 6,000 military personnel."[623] On 1 May 2000, RUF forces captured 7 members of UNAMSIL after a dispute concerning the disarmament of the rebels. From that day onwards, RUF and UNAMSIL forces have been engaged in hostilities and some 400 peacekeepers are believed to have been held hostage by the RUF.[624] In response the Council enlarged the mission to 13,000 military personnel[625] and established a prohibition on the import of non-certified rough diamonds from Sierra

---

[618] See the 'Statements of the President of the Security Council', S/PRST/1997/29, 27 May 1997; S/PRST/1997/36, 11 July 1997; and S/PRST/1997/42, 6 Aug. 1997.

[619] S/Res. 1132 (1997), 8 Oct. 1997, paras. 5-6. A monitoring Committee was established by para. 10 thereof.

[620] S/Res. 1156 (1998), 16 March 1998, para. 2.

[621] S/Res. 1171 (1998), 5 June 1998, paras. 1-3.

[622] S/Res. 1181 (1998), 13 July 1998.

[623] See S/Res. 1270 (1999), 22 Oct. 1999, paras. 8-9.

[624] See the 'Fourth report of the Secretary-General on the United Nations Mission in Sierra Leone', S/2000/455, 19 May 2000, paras. 56-79.

[625] S/Res. 1299 (2000), 19 May 2000, para. 1.

Leone.[626] On 15 July 2000, moreover, troops from Nigeria, Ghana and India freed 222 UNAMSIL peacekeepers and 11 military observers[627] in an action endorsed by the Security Council.[628] By that date President Kabbah had already sent a letter to the Secretary-General of the United Nations, in which he asked the United Nations to assist in the establishment of a court to try RUF members "for crimes against the people of Sierra Leone and for the taking of United Nations peacekeepers as hostages."[629] The court would not be a criminal tribunal similar to the ICTY or ICTR, but rather a national court assisted by the United Nations.[630] In resolution 1315 (2000), the Council endorsed this request and requested the Secretary-General to negotiate an agreement to that effect with Sierra Leone.[631]

3.12.3 Summary

The Council imposed an arms and oil embargo on Sierra Leone by resolution 1132 (1997) when the RUF took control of the country and "authorized" ECOWAS to ensure the strict implementation of the embargoes. The sanctions were eased in 1998, when progress towards national unity seemed to have been made with the return of President Kabbah. Peacekeeping forces were sent in and soon became involved in hostilities with rebellious forces, which induced the Council to impose additional

---

626 S/Res. 1306 (2000), 5 July 2000, para. 1.

627 See 'Newly freed U.N. peacekeepers airlifted to safety in Sierra Leone', 16 July 2000. Accessed at http://cnn.com on 24 July 2000.

628 See the Presidential Statement of 17 July 2000, S/PRST/2000/24, in which the "Security Council expresses its full support for the decision taken by the Secretary-General to mount a military operation by the United Nations Mission in Sierra Leone (UNAMSIL) to relieve its surrounded peacekeepers and military observers at Kailahun."

629 'Fifth report of the Secretary-General on the United Nations Mission in Sierra Leone', S/2000/751, 31 July 2000, para. 9.

630 See *ibid.*, para. 10. See also B. Crossette, 'Sierra Leone Asks U.N. for Role in War Court', NY Times, 21 June 2000, accessed at http://www.nytimes.com on 15 Aug. 2000; and A. La Guardia, 'Help us make RUF leader face justice', Daily Telegraph, 21 June 2000, accessed at http://www.dailytelegraph.co.uk on 15 Aug. 2000.

631 S/Res. 1315 (2000), 14 Aug. 2000, para. 1. The agreement between the Secretary-General and Sierra Leone would probably not require an enabling Chapter VII resolution, as the government of Sierra Leone voluntarily asked for assistance. In the preamble to resolution 1315 (2000), however, the Council opened the door to a mandatory resolution by "reaffirming the importance of compliance with international humanitarian law [and] that persons who commit or authorize serious violations of international humanitarian law are individually responsible and accountable". Furthermore the Council 'recognized' that "a credible system of justice and accountability ... would contribute to ... the restoration and maintenance of peace."

sanctions aimed against RUF forces and to increase the size of the peacekeeping mission.

3.12.4 Analysis: The Application of Chapter VII by the Council

The decision to impose a weapons and oil embargo contained in resolution 1132 (1997), and a prohibition on the import of rough diamonds in resolution 1306 (2000), are evidently measures taken under Chapter VII of the Charter, *i.e.* Article 41. The exact basis of the "authorization" given to ECOWAS to ensure the implementation of the measures, including the halting of ships in order to inspect their cargo, is less clear. Particularly if one considers that states are "called upon" to "cooperate with ECOWAS in this regard." This language is reminiscent of resolution 221 (1966) in the Rhodesian case and resolution 665 (1990) in the case of Iraq.[632] Although resolution 221 (1966) explicitly referred to "the use of force if necessary" to stop the tanker *Joanna V*, and resolution 665 (1990) to "maritime forces in the area" to inspect ships, the halting of ships in order to verify their cargo could include the use of force if a ship requested to halt does not comply. The authorization contained in paragraph 8 of resolution 1132 (1997) therefore has to be based on Article 42 of the Charter.

3.13 Afghanistan 1998-2000

3.13.1 Factual Background

On 7 August 1998 bombings of the US embassies in Nairobi, Kenya and Dar es Salaam, Tanzania, killed 224 people in total. The US suspected Usama Bin Laden of involvement in the bombings, a suspicion that materialized in a formal indictment in November 1998.[633] On 20 August 1998, the US military, moreover, struck several sites in Afghanistan and Sudan in retaliation for the bombings.[634] In 1998, Usama Bin Laden was believed to reside in Afghanistan, a country torn by civil war in which the

---

[632] See *supra*, note 252, respectively note 302.

[633] United States District Court, Southern District of New York, Indictment S(2) 98 Cr. 1023 (LBS).

[634] The sites were allegedly connected to a 'terrorist network' associated with Usama Bin Laden. See J. McIntyre, A. Koppel, 'U.S. Missiles Pound Targets in Afghanistan, Sudan', 21 Aug. 1998. Accessed at http://www.cnn.com on 18 Jan. 2000. For an analysis of the attacks see J. Lobel, *Colloquy – The Use of Force to Respond to Terrorist Attacks: The Bombing of Sudan and Afghanistan*, 24 Yale JIL (1999) 537-557; L.M. Campbell, *Defending Against Terrorism: A Legal Analysis of the Decision to Strike Sudan and Afghanistan*, 74 Tulane Law Review (2000) 1067-1096.

Muslim-oriented Taliban effectively controls 90% of the territory. The US asked the Taliban to extradite Usama Bin Laden.

3.13.2 Security Council Action concerning Afghanistan

In resolution 1189 (1998) the Security Council expressed its 'deep disturbance' with regard to "the indiscriminate and outrageous acts of international terrorism that took place on 7 August 1998 in Nairobi, Kenya and Dar-es-Salaam, Tanzania."[635] The Council held that such acts "have a damaging effect on international relations and jeopardize the security of States" and that "the suppression of acts of international terrorism is essential for the maintenance of international peace and security."[636] In paragraph 5 of resolution 1189 (1998), moreover, the Council: "Calls upon all States to adopt, in accordance with international law and as a matter of priority, effective and practical measures for security cooperation, for the prevention of such acts of terrorism, and for the prosecution and punishment of their perpetrators."

When the Taliban refused to extradite Usama Bin Laden, the Council adopted resolution 1214 (1998). In the preamble to this resolution the Security Council states that it is:

> Deeply disturbed by the continuing use of Afghan territory, especially areas controlled by the Taliban, for the sheltering and training of terrorists and the planning of terrorist acts, and reiterating that the suppression of international terrorism is essential for the maintenance of international peace and security.[637]

In paragraph 13 of resolution 1214 (1998), moreover, the Security Council: "Demands also that the Taliban stop providing sanctuary and training for international terrorists and their organizations, and that all Afghan factions cooperate with efforts to bring indicted terrorists to justice."

These demands were not complied with by Afghanistan, which prompted the Security Council to take further measures nearly a year later. In October 1999, the Council adopted resolution 1267 (1999), in which the Council determined that the "failure of the Taliban authorities to respond to the demands in paragraph 13 of resolution 1214 (1998) constitutes a threat to international peace and security."[638]

Explicitly "acting under Chapter VII of the Charter of the United Nations", the Council then demanded that:

---

[635] S/Res. 1189 (1998), 13 Aug. 1998, preamble.

[636] *Ibid.*

[637] S/Res. 1214 (1998), 8 Dec. 1998.

[638] S/Res. 1267 (1999), 15 Oct. 1999, preamble.

> the Taliban turn over Usama bin Laden without further delay to appropriate authorities in a country where he has been indicted, or to appropriate authorities in a country where he will be returned to such a country, or to appropriate authorities in a country where he will be arrested and effectively brought to justice.[639]

If the Taliban did not do so by 14 November 1999, 'all states' were to implement the following measures:

> (a) Deny permission for any aircraft to take off from or land in their territory if it is owned, leased or operated by or on behalf of the Taliban ... unless the particular flight has been approved in advance... on the grounds of humanitarian need, including religious obligation such as the performance of the Hajj;
> (b) Freeze funds and other financial resources, including funds derived or generated from property owned or controlled directly or indirectly by the Taliban, or by any undertaking owned or controlled by the Taliban ... and ensure that neither they nor any other funds or financial resources so designated are made available, by their nationals or by any persons within their territory, to or for the benefit of the Taliban or any undertaking owned or controlled, directly or indirectly, by the Taliban, except as may be authorized... on a case-by-case basis on the grounds of humanitarian need.[640]

The response of the Taliban regime was negative. On 19 December 1999, for example, the Taliban-controlled newspaper *Hewad* stated that "Osama is our guest and a fellow Muslim. Afghan people will never hand him over to the Americans to stand trial before a court headed by Jews or Christians."[641]

Although the Taliban at a later stage softened the tone of their language, Usama Bin Laden was not extradited and therefore the sanctions became effective as of 14 November 1999.

3.13.3 Summary

The Council first demanded that the Taliban "cooperate with efforts to bring indicted terrorists to justice" in resolution 1214 (1998). When the Taliban refused to comply with this demand, it determined that this non-compliance constituted a threat to international peace and security in resolution 1267 (1999). Accordingly, the Council imposed an aerial embargo and financial sanctions specifically aimed at (members of) the Taliban.

---

[639] S/Res. 1267 (1999), 15 Oct. 1999, para. 2.

[640] S/Res. 1267 (1999), 15 Oct. 1999, para. 4. The exceptions mentioned in para. 4 were to be authorized by a Sanctions Committee of the Security Council, established under para. 6 of the same resolution.

[641] See 'Taliban vow to protect bin Laden', Associated Press, 20 Dec. 1999. Accessed at http://www.cnn.com on 16 Jan. 2000.

3.13.4 Analysis: The Application of Chapter VII by the Council

Although the Council "demanded" that the "Taliban stop providing sanctuary and training for international terrorists and their organizations" in resolution 1214 (1998), and 'reiterated' that the "suppression of international terrorism is essential for the maintenance of international peace and security", the resolution did not contain an Article 39 determination. Without such a determination, the demand contained in resolution 1214 (1998) cannot be deemed binding, notwithstanding the quite strong language in which it is phrased. The legal situation changed with the adoption of resolution 1267 (1999), in which the Council did determine that the non-compliance with the demands constituted a threat to international peace and security. The Council accordingly took binding measures under Article 41 of the Charter, which include an aerial embargo and the requirement to freeze Taliban-owned funds.

3.14 Ethiopia-Eritrea 1998-2000

3.14.1 Factual Background

Eritrea became one of the six provinces of 'Italian East Africa' after Ethiopia and Italy signed the Treaty of Wichale in 1899. Subsequently Eritrea came under British administration in 1941 and joined the Ethiopian Empire in 1962. From then on, however, Eritrea forcefully strived for secession. Independence was granted by Ethiopia in 1993, after rebellious forces (including Eritrean secessionists) had ousted the Ethiopian socialist government and a referendum indicated that the vast majority of the Eritrean population favoured independence. Eritrea was subsequently admitted to the United Nations on 28 May 1993.[642] The good neighbourly relations between both countries deteriorated in 1997, however, when a dispute evolved around the exact demarcation of the Ethiopian-Eritrean border. The dispute escalated into a border war on 6 May 1998. Although the parties agreed to a cease-fire in June 1998, the fighting resumed in 1999 and continued until a peace agreement brokered by the OAU was signed on 18 June 2000.[643]

---

[642] A/Res. 47/230.

[643] For the provisions of the agreement see the 'Report of the Secretary-General on Ethiopia and Eritrea', S/2000/643, 30 June 2000, paras. 2-9.

3.14.2 Security Council Action concerning Ethiopia-Eritrea

Although it may be safely said that the fighting between Ethiopia and Eritrea constituted a manifest breach of, or at least threat to, international peace and security, the Council withheld this judgment until May 2000. It initially condemned the hostilities and demanded their cessation,[644] accompanied by a 'strong urge' for "all States to end immediately all sales of arms and munitions to Ethiopia and Eritrea."[645] This urging of all states was replaced by stronger language in resolution 1298 (2000). Herein the Council determined that "the situation between Eritrea and Ethiopia constitutes a threat to regional peace and security." Subsequently the Council, "acting under Chapter VII of the Charter", decided to establish a weapons embargo on both countries.[646]

3.14.3 Analysis: The Application of Chapter VII by the Council

At first the Council's actions were confined to condemnations of the hostilities between Eritrea and Ethiopia. In resolution 1227 (1999), moreover, the Council 'urged' states not to sell arms to either country. This wording and the absence of a determination under Article 39 implies that the call was taken under Chapter VI of the Charter. This changed with the adoption of resolution 1298 (2000), in which the Council, explicitly acting under Chapter VII of the Charter, decided to impose a weapons embargo, a measure taken under Article 41 of the Charter.

3.15 Categorization and Analysis of Functions Assumed by the Council

The Iraqi occupation of Kuwait and the successful liberation of Kuwait achieved in a campaign that was 'authorized' by a Security Council that was not paralyzed by the veto of its permanent members, led to optimism that the Council would at last be able to effectively maintain international peace and security. Indeed the case studies above show that the Council dealt with a comparatively large number of cases during the 1990s, compared to the Cold War era.

---

644 See S/Res. 1177 (1998), 26 June 1998, para. 1 and S/Res. 1227 (1999), 10 Feb. 1999, paras. 1-2.

645 S/Res. 1227 (1999), 10 Feb. 1999, para. 7.

646 See S/Res. 1298 (2000), 17 May 2000, para. 6. A Committee responsible for monitoring the embargo was established by para. 8 of the same resolution.

With this increasingly activist Council the number of resolutions rose significantly,[647] and the number of decisions taken under Chapter VII of the Charter has risen accordingly. In taking these decisions, the Council has assumed various new functions and taken innovative measures. This paragraph will categorize and analyze these new functions and measures. The following does not purport to extensively describe all aspects and possible implications of the Council's actions. It will describe the main categories and new functions assumed by the Council in its 'activist' period. The categorization will be made according to the causes the Council identified as appropriate for taking measures under Chapter VII of the Charter. The second part takes a look at the modalities those measures have taken.

3.15.1 Causes of Security Council Action

The Council has enlarged its scope of action by expanding the concept of threats to the peace and breaches of the peace under Article 39. These causes for action will be considered in subparagraph 1 below.

3.15.1.1 Humanitarian Concerns[648]

It is safe to state that the original Charter scheme envisaged Council actions in cases of inter-state use of force.[649] In this scheme peace is defined as the absence of inter-state use of force. Indeed, in the cases of Iraq and Yugoslavia, the Council dealt with such 'classical' uses of force. Perhaps the most striking development in the Council's application of Chapter VII, however, is that the Council has consistently treated internal conflicts with (grave) consequences for the populations involved as threats to

---

647 Between 1946 and 1975 the Council adopted 384 resolutions, an average of 13 per year. Between 1976 and 1989 the Council adopted 262 resolutions, or 19 per year. Between 1990-1995 this figure rose to 389 resolutions, or 78 per year, and in the years 1996-1999 the Council adopted 248 resolutions, or 62 per year.

648 Generally see Bothe, *op. cit. supra* n.168; R. Cryer, *The Security Council and Article 39: A Threat to Coherence?*, 1 Journal of Armed Conflict (1996) 161-195, 172-188; L.E. Fielding, *Taking a Closer Look at Threats to the Peace: The Power of the Security Council to Address Humanitarian Crises*, 73 University of Detroit Mercy Law Review (1996) 551-568; R. Gordon, *United Nations Intervention in Internal Conflicts: Iraq, Somalia, and Beyond*, 15 MJIL (1994) 519-589; M. Herdegen, *Die Befugnisse des UN-Sicherheitsrates: Aufgeklärter Absolutismus im Völkerrecht?* (1998), at 15; Malanczuk, *op. cit. supra* n.31, 385 ff.

649 See Kooijmans, *op. cit. supra* n.510, 333; Frowein, *op. cit. supra* n.124, 608; B. Graefrath, *International Crimes and Collective Security*. In: K.C. Wellens (ed.), International Law: Theory and Practice (1998) 237-252; M. Koskenniemi, *The Place of Law in Collective Security*, 17 MJIL (1996) 455-490, 459.

international peace and security. In the cases of Southern Rhodesia, South Africa, Somalia, Liberia; Northern Iraq, Haiti, and Rwanda, human rights abuses and their consequences for the populations involved triggered the invocation of Article 39. In the 1960s and 1970s this led to strong allegations of violations of the right of non-interference in matters belonging to the domestic jurisdiction of the states against which action was being taken. At present, such concerns are much less strong, and a practice has developed according to which the humanitarian repercussions of a domestic conflict justifies action by the Council under the provisions of Chapter VII of the Charter.[650]

This development has been gradual and in certain respects somewhat ambiguous. In several cases the Council went to great lengths to establish an international dimension with regard to the situations it was dealing with under Chapter VII. In the Kurdish case, for example, the Council referred to the "massive flow of refugees towards and across international frontiers" and to "cross-border incursions" to justify its determination that the situation threatens "international peace and security *in the region*."[651] Several commentators, however, have noted the artificial nature of these references as far as an international dimension is concerned. In the context of Somalia, for example, Kirgis submits that "there was little evidence that the strife between clans in Somalia, devastating though it was for the people of that country, actually posed a serious threat to stability in neighboring states, at least in the short term."[652]

Kooijmans also holds that in the Somalian case "the determination of a threat to the peace ... seems to be mainly motivated by humanitarian concern although there is a slight reference to the consequences on the stability and peace in the region."[653]

In other cases the Council, in what appears to be an effort to prevent any precedential value arising from its decisions, emphasized the uniqueness of the prevailing circumstances which necessitated unique measures. Thus in resolution 929 (1994) on Rwanda, for example, the Council 'recognized' that "the current situation in Rwanda constitutes a unique case which demands an urgent response by the international community."[654]

---

[650] See Murphy, *op. cit. supra* n.3, 229-233; Frowein, *op. cit. supra* n.124, 611.

[651] S/Res. 688 (1991), emphasis added.

[652] Kirgis, *op. cit. supra* n.129, at 513.

[653] Kooijmans, *op. cit. supra* n.133, at 115. See to a similar effect, *e.g.*, Gordon, *op. cit. supra* n.648, 554; Mwagiru, *op. cit. supra* n.511, 42.

[654] *Cf.* S/Res. 794 (1992) on Somalia, in which the Council 'recognized' "the unique character of the present situation in Somalia and mindful of its deteriorating, complex and extraordinary nature, requiring an immediate and exceptional response." Similarly, S/Res. 841 (1993) on Haiti refers to

These cautious formulations notwithstanding, the application by the Council of Article 39 undisputably conveys a shift "from the protection of sovereigns to the protection of people."[655] Thus Reisman observes that:

> Since the white minority government of Rhodesia declared its independence and "sovereign" right to suppress the black majority, it has been settled UN law that gross violations of human rights – which the Rhodesian Government insisted were entirely "domestic" – can constitute threats to the peace and can justify action under chapter VII.[656]

In a similar way Franck submits, in the context of resolution 688 (1991) dealing with the Kurds in Iraq, that: "The Kurdish crisis provides an indication of an evolution in the thinking of the Security Council and the Secretary-General regarding the legitimacy of United Nations intervention in situations of extremely aggravated civil war and civil oppression."[657] The same conclusion is reached by Schrijver. In a survey of economic sanctions taken by the Council, Schrijver concludes that in two cases (Iraq and Yugoslavia) the Council tried to "halt aggression of one State against another and thus to maintain the international *status quo*." Subsequently, he observes that in a majority of cases the Council wanted to alter the conditions in which populations of targeted countries had to live: "In six cases (Southern Rhodesia, South Africa, Somalia, Liberia, Haiti and Angola) the true objective rather seems to be to enforce a change of the *status quo* at domestic level."[658]

3.15.1.2 Extradition of Alleged Terrorists

In the Lockerbie case the Council first, in resolution 731 (1992), 'urged' Libya to extradite the Libyan nationals allegedly responsible for the Lockerbie bombing. Libya refused, which prompted the Council to determine that the non-extradition of alleged terrorists by Libya constituted a threat to international peace and security in resolutions 748 (1992)[659] and 833 (1993). This course of action was repeated in the cases of Sudan

---

"unique and exceptional circumstances."

[655] W.M. Reisman, *Sovereignty and Human Rights in Contemporary International Law*, 84 AJIL (1990) 866-876, at 872.

[656] Reisman, *op. cit. supra* n.611, at 83.

[657] T.M. Franck, *The Security Council and 'Threats to the Peace': Some Remarks on Remarkable Recent Developments*. In: J.R. Dupuy, The Development of the Role of the Security Council (1993) 83-110, at 106.

[658] Schrijver, *op. cit. supra* n.510, at 144.

[659] Indeed, resolution 748 (1992) is unique in the sense that it is the first in which a terrorist act and the subsequent non-extradition of the individuals allegedly responsible for it, are characterized as a threat to international peace and security. See F. Beveridge, *The Lockerbie Affair*, 41 ICLQ (1992)

and Afghanistan. In resolution 1044 (1996) the Council 'called upon' Sudan to "extradite to Ethiopia for prosecution the three suspects sheltering in the Sudan and wanted in connection with the assassination attempt" on President Hosni Mubarak. In resolution 1054 (1996) the Council held "that non-compliance by the Government of Sudan with the[se] requests ... constitutes a threat to international peace and security."[660] Again, in resolution 1214 (1998) the Council 'demanded' that the "Taliban stop providing sanctuary and training for international terrorists and their organizations, and that all Afghan factions cooperate with efforts to bring indicted terrorists to justice." In resolution 1267 (1999) the Council held that the subsequent "failure of the Taliban authorities to respond to the[se] demands ... constitutes a threat to international peace and security."

These cases display "a marked increase in support of the categorisation of terrorism as a threat"[661] to international peace and security. It is remarkable in these cases that the acts of terrorism themselves are not categorized under Article 39, but that the Council considers the non-extradition of those allegedly responsible for the acts as a threat to the peace.

3.15.1.3 Preventive Measures

The annexation of Kuwait by Iraq was determined to be a breach of international peace and security by the Council in resolution 660 (1990). Indeed the annexation can be seen as a textbook example of aggression, and in this context the Council's invocation of Article 39 has not been called into doubt. Kuwait was liberated by a coalition of states in an action "authorized" by the Council under resolution 678 (1990), and the extensive conditions for a cease-fire were imposed by resolution 687 (1991). Part of these conditions, such as the disarmament of Iraq, may be seen as being based on a preventive concept of international peace and security: as long as the Iraqi regime is in force, international peace and security is threatened. The means to curtail this threat is *inter alia* to remove the military capacities of the regime. Hence the Council went beyond reinstalling the *status quo ex ante* by imposing the conditions of the cessation of hostilities.

907-920, 912; Tomuschat, *op. cit. supra* n.7, 44; and T. Stein, *Das Attentat von Lockerbie vor dem Sicherheitsrat der Vereinten Nation und dem Internationalen Gerichtshof*, 31 Archiv des Völkerrechts (1993) 206-229, 222.

660 A determination that was reaffirmed in S/Res. 1070 (1996).

661 Cryer, *op. cit. supra* n.648, at 184.

3.15.1.4 Quasi-Judicial Determinations

The Security Council will necessarily have to engage in legal appreciations and determinations in the discharge of its functions and powers related to the maintenance of international peace and security. This is part of what may be called the quasi-judicial power of the Council. This power has been employed by the Council in several situations. Cases not mentioned in this chapter include, for example, the determination in 1970 by the Council that the presence of South Africa in Namibia was illegal,[662] or that "the policy and practices of Israel in establishing settlements in the Palestinian and other Arab territories occupied since 1967 have no legal validity."[663]

Cases described in this chapter *inter alia* include the determination of the illegality of the proclamation of independence of Southern Rhodesia,[664] and the illegality of the annexation of Kuwait by Iraq in 1990.[665] In its post-1990 practice the Council has extended this power of legal appreciation.[666] Firstly, it has consistently condemned violations of humanitarian law.[667] Secondly, it has determined that Iraq was liable for

---

662 S/Res. 276 (1970), 30 Jan. 1970. In para. 2 the Council: "Declares that the continued presence of the South African authorities is illegal and that consequently all acts taken by the Government on behalf of or concerning Namibia after the termination of the Mandate are illegal."

663 S/Res. 446 (1979), 22 March 1979, para. 1.

664 In S/Res. 217 (1965) the Council: "Condemns the usurpation of power by a racist settler minority in Southern Rhodesia and regards the declaration of independence by it as having no legal validity."

665 See S/Res. 662 (1990), para. 1, in which the Council: "Decides that annexation of Kuwait by Iraq under any form and whatever pretext has no legal validity, and is considered null and void."

666 See Gowlland-Debbas, *op. cit. supra* n.2, 63.

667 *E.g.* S/Res. 670 (1990), in which the Council: "Reaffirms that the Fourth Geneva Convention applies to Kuwait and that as a High Contracting Party to the Convention Iraq is bound to comply fully with all its terms and, in particular, is liable under the Convention in respect of the grave breaches committed by it, as are individuals who commit or order the commission of grave breaches"; S/Res. 764 (1992) on Bosnia and Herzegovina, in which the Council 'reaffirmed' "that all parties are bound to comply with the obligations under international humanitarian law and in particular the Geneva Conventions of 12 August 1949, and that persons who commit or order the commission of grave breaches of the Conventions are individually responsible in respect of such breaches"; S/Res. 794 (1992) on Somalia, in which the Council: "Strongly condemns all violations of international humanitarian law occurring in Somalia, including in particular the deliberate impeding of the delivery of food and medical supplies essential for the survival of the civilian population, and affirms that those who commit or order the commission of such acts will be held individually responsible in respect of such acts"; S/Res. 912 (1994) on Rwanda, in which the Council "calls upon all concerned ... to respect fully international humanitarian law"; S/Res. 950 (1994) on Liberia, para. 7. Generally see S.D. Bailey, *The Security Council*. In: P. Alston (ed.), The United Nations

all direct losses and damages related to the invasion and occupation of Kuwait,[668] that the statements of Iraq repudiating its foreign debts "were null and void"[669] and has recalled Iraq's obligation to respect diplomatic immunities.[670]

Thus, although a determination of illegality is not essential for taking measures under Chapter VII of the Charter,[671] the Council increasingly seems to take measures under Chapter VII based on a prior finding of illegality and with the goal of remedying that illegality. Indeed, a trend can be discerned toward what has been called the enforcement of international obligations.[672] Thus Schachter observes that Article 41:

> was not meant to provide sanctions for enforcing international legal obligations as such ... In practice, however, the Council has generally applied Article 41 sanctions against a state that has not complied with a Charter requirement or significant legal obligation.[673]

3.15.2 The Modalities of Chapter VII Measures

The case studies above reveal various ways in which the Council has used Chapter VII in order to maintain international peace and security. These will be examined below.

---

and Human Rights: A Critical Appraisal (1995) 304-336, 312-315.

[668] Thus in para. 16 of S/Res. 687 (1991), for example, the Council: "Reaffirms that Iraq ... is liable under international law for any direct loss, damage, including environmental damage and the depletion of natural resources, or injury to foreign Governments, nationals and corporations, as a result of Iraq's unlawful invasion and occupation of Kuwait."

[669] In para. 17 of S/Res. 687 (1991) the Council: "Decides that all Iraqi statements made since 2 August 1990 repudiating its foreign debt are null and void."

[670] Thus in the preamble to S/Res. 667 (1990) the Council: "Recall[s] the Vienna Conventions of 18 April 1961 on diplomatic relations and of 24 April 1963 on consular relations, to both of which Iraq is a party" and "consider[s] that the decision of Iraq to order the closure of diplomatic and consular missions in Kuwait and to withdraw the immunity and privileges of these missions and their personnel is contrary to the decisions of the Security Council, the international Conventions mentioned above and international law."

[671] See Gowlland-Debbas, *op. cit. supra* n.2, 77.

[672] Gowlland-Debbas (*op. cit. supra* n.2) refers, at 57, to "the evolving function of the Security Council in the *enforcement* of international obligations." *Cf.* para. 61 of the *First Report of the International Law Association (ILA) Study Group on the Law of State Responsibility*, 8 June 2000, in which it is stated that: "The peace and security mechanisms of the Charter have increasingly become a part of an emerging regime relating to collective responses to violations of norms considered of fundamental importance to the international community, at least when these are signalled out as constituting threats to or breaches of international peace and security."

[673] O. Schachter, *United Nations Law*, 88 AJIL (1994) 1-23, at 12. See also Herdegen, *op. cit. supra* n.648, 18-24.

3.15.2.1 Determinations under Article 39

The Council has consistently referred to threats or breaches of international peace and security before deciding on Chapter VII measures, although the formulations have been inconsistent.[674] They range from determinations that certain situations constitute a 'breach' or 'threat' to international peace and security, to determinations that the international peace in the region is threatened,[675] or to mere referrals to earlier resolutions in which an Article 39 determination was made.[676] Moreover, sometimes the Council refers to a 'disturbance'[677] or 'endangerment'[678] of the peace, rather than a 'threat' or 'breach'. Also the 'consequences' of certain actions at times provided the basis for a determination under Article 39.[679] A common course of action followed by the Council is to hold that the 'continuation' of certain practices may threaten international peace and security, followed by a later resolution in which the practice is qualified as a threat to international peace and security.

The Council is not required to make express reference to Article 39 when deciding that a situation poses a threat to, or breach of, international peace and security.[680] Indeed in making such determinations the Council has seldom explicitly mentioned Article 39 of the Charter.[681] It usually states that it is "acting under Chapter VII of the Charter" after determining that international peace and security is threatened. These formulations indicate that the Council was making its determination under Article 39.

Notwithstanding the different formulations employed by the Council, it has consistently made a determination under Article 39 in one form or another, before taking further measures under Chapter VII. As observed by Kirgis, this practice "by

---

[674] According to Freudenschuß the Council's terminology even reveals a "complete inconsistency". Freudenschuß, *op. cit. supra* n 1, at 523.

[675] The Council refers to 'regional peace and security' in, for example, S/Res. 688 (1991) on Iraq; S/Res. 812 (1993) and 918 (1994) on Rwanda; S/Res. 788 (1992) on Liberia; S/Res. 733 (1992) on Somalia; and S/Res. 841 (1993) on Haiti.

[676] *E.g.* resolution 678 (1990). In the preamble thereto, the Council 'recalls' and 'reaffirms' its "resolutions 660 (1990) of 2 August (1990), 661 (1990) of 6 August 1990, 662 (1990) of 9 August 1990, 664 (1990) of 18 August 1990, 665 (1990) of 25 August 1990, 666 (1990) of 13 September 1990, 667 (1990) of 16 September 1990, 669 (1990) of 24 September 1990, 670 (1990) of 25 September 1990, 674 (1990) of 29 October 1990 and 677 (1990) of 28 November 1990."

[677] S/Res. 311 (1972) on South Africa.

[678] S/Res. 567 (1985) on South Africa.

[679] *E.g.* S/Res. 688 (1991) on the Kurds in Iraq.

[680] Frowein, *op. cit. supra* n.124, 613.

[681] An example is provided by S/Res. 232 (1966) on Southern Rhodesia, in which the Council states that it is: "Acting in accordance with Articles 39 and 41 of the Charter."

now amounts to an authoritative interpretation of chapter VII to the effect that an Article 39 determination must be made in advance of, or at the time of, enforcement action."[682]

3.15.2.2 Measures under Article 41 of the Charter

The Council has taken various enforcement measures under Article 41. The most common forms may be categorized as follows.

3.15.2.2.1 Sanctions

In most of the cases studied above, the Council imposed economic sanctions and these sanctions have been broad in their range. Thus states were prohibited to import certain designated goods[683] or all goods[684] originating from the targeted state.

A common sanction instrument has also been the prohibition on the export of strategic goods to targeted states. The foremost examples are the establishment of arms and oil embargoes. A prohibition to export arms to targeted states or regions occurred in nine of the twelve cases described above.[685] Oil embargoes were established in two cases, Angola and Haiti.[686] Furthermore, financial sanctions, which typically include the freezing of funds,[687] have been imposed in five cases. Aerial sanctions, moreover, have also been imposed in five cases.[688] These financial and aerial sanctions have regularly been accompanied by the imposition of travel restrictions aimed at specific

---

[682] Kirgis, *op. cit. supra* n.129, at 512. See also *infra*, paragraph 4.2.3.1.

[683] *E.g.* S/Res. 232 (1966), para. 2(a), in which states were prohibited to import "asbestos, iron ore, chrome, pig-iron, sugar, tobacco, copper, meat and meat products and hides, skins and leather originating in Southern Rhodesia".

[684] Thus in para. 3(a) of S/Res. 661 (1990) the Council decided that all states were to prevent "the import into their territories of all commodities and products originating in Iraq or Kuwait exported therefrom after the date of the present resolution."

[685] In the case of Southern Rhodesia: S/Res. 232 (1966), para. 2(d); South Africa: S/Res. 418 (1977), para. 2; Libya: S/Res. 748 (1992), para. 5(a); Liberia: S/Res. 788 (1992), para. 8; Angola: S/Res. 864 (1993), para. 19; former Yugoslavia: S/Res. 713 (1991), para. 6; Somalia: S/Res. 733 (1992), para. 5; Rwanda: S/Res. 918 (1994), para. 13; Haiti: S/Res. 841 (1993), para. 5.

[686] See S/Res. 864 (1993), para. 19 (Angola) and S/Res. 841 (1993), para. 5 (Haiti).

[687] See S/Res. 661 (1990), para. 4, on Iraq; S/Res. 883 (1993), para. 3, on Libya; S/Res. 1173 (1998), para. 11, on Angola; S/Res. 917 (1994), para. 4, on Haiti; S/Res. 1267 (1999), para. 4(b), on Afghanistan.

[688] See S/Res. 748 (1992), paras. 4 and 6(b), on Libya; S/Res. 1127 (1997), para. 4(d), on Angola; S/Res. 757 (1992), para. 7, on Yugoslavia; S/Res. 1070 (1996), para. 3, on Sudan.

targets within a country. This has occurred in Angola,[689] Sudan,[690] Haiti[691] and Afghanistan.[692] Financial sanctions and travel restrictions are targeted at specific non-state actors who have been held responsible for actions that threaten international peace and security.[693] The latter sanctions may be described as "targeted" or "smart" sanctions. Their imposition is indicative of the growing unease among the membership of the United Nations with the effects of sanctions on the population of the countries against which the sanctions are directed, populations that usually have little say in the formation of the state's policies that threaten international peace and security.[694] Indeed, the Security Council seems to have been susceptible to this criticism, for in 1995 the permanent members announced that: "further collective actions in the Security Council within the context of any future sanctions regime should be directed to minimize unintended adverse side-effects of sanctions on the most vulnerable segments of targeted countries."[695]

3.15.2.2.2 The Establishment of Subsidiary Organs

In all cases the Council established Sanctions Committees as subsidiary organs of the Council. These committees are responsible for the monitoring of the sanctions. In three cases, however, the Council established as subsidiary organs institutions with the power to adjudicate on violations of international law and make final legal determinations. In relation to the violations of humanitarian law in Yugoslavia and

---

689 S/Res. 1127 (1997), para. 4(a) and 4(b).

690 S/Res. 1054 (1996), para. 3.

691 S/Res. 917 (1994), para. 3.

692 S/Res. 1267 (1999), para. 4(b).

693 On which see, *e.g.*, Kooijmans, *op. cit. supra* n.510.

694 See, *e.g.*, the 'Annual Report of the Secretary-General on the work of the Organization', A/54/1, 31 Aug. 1999, paras. 124-126; and his opening remarks to the 'International Peace Academy Seminar on Sanctions', contained in Press Release SG/SM/7360, 17 April 2000. In the latter document the Secretary-General summarizes the unease as follows: "just as we recognize the importance of sanctions as a way of compelling compliance with the will of the international community, we also recognize that sanctions remain a blunt instrument, which hurt large numbers of people who are not their primary targets." *Loc. cit.*, at 2. See on the prospects of 'smarter' sanctions also the final reports of the 1998 and 1999 seminars on 'targeted financial sanctions' sponsored by the Swiss government, available at http://www.smartsanctions.ch.

695 'Letter from the Permanent Members of the Security Council on the Humanitarian Aspects of Sanctions', S/1995/300, 13 April 1995.

Rwanda it established the ICTY[696] and ICTR.[697] Furthermore, subsequent to the determination by the Council that Iraq is liable for all direct losses ensuing from Iraq's purported annexation of Kuwait, the Council established the UNCC.[698] This is a new development that has been described by Malanczuk as follows:

> It remains a fact that the method adopted by the Security Council is unprecedented in the history of international law and at variance from normal settlement practices usually adopted after the cessation of hostilities and the forms of claims settlement adopted by sovereign states.[699]

The Council, moreover, decided to establish the United Nations Iraq-Kuwait Boundary Demarcation Commission which was to demarcate the boundary between Iraq and Kuwait.

By establishing these organs the Council has extended its legislative powers. It may be noted that in a general sense, the Council "legislates in that its decisions potentially bind all states."[700] By establishing the organs mentioned above, however, the Council went farther than merely declaring the illegality of certain actions, but also created the instruments to remedy them. This amounts to a considerable extension of its legislative powers.[701]

3.15.2.3 Measures under Article 42

Without ever explicitly mentioning the Article, the Council took measures under Article 42 of the Charter on several occasions. The common denominator in these cases is that the Council "authorizes"[702] or "calls upon"[703] states to use "all necessary means"[704] to enforce the implementation of relevant resolutions.[705] The more precise

---

696 S/Res. 827 (1993).

697 S/Res. 955 (1994).

698 S/Res. 692 (1991).

699 Malanczuk, *op. cit. supra* n.2, at 139.

700 Caron, *op. cit. supra* n.4, at 562. A more strict definition of legislative authority within the UN system is quoted by Kirgis and runs as follows: "Legislative acts have three essential characteristics: they are unilateral in form, they create or modify some element of a legal norm, and the legal norm in question is general in nature, that is, directed to indeterminate addressees and capable of repeated application in time." E. Yemin, *Legislative Powers in the United Nations and Specialized Agencies* (1969), at 6. Quoted by Kirgis, *op. cit. supra* n.129, at 520.

701 See K. Zemanek, *Is the Security Council the Sole Judge of Its Own Legality?*. In: E. Yakpo, T. Boumedra (eds.), Liber Amicorum Mohammed Bedjaoui (1999) 629-645, 630.

702 S/Res. 678 (1990) on Iraq, S/Res. 940 (1994) on Haiti, and S/Res. 929 (1994) on Rwanda.

703 S/Res. 794 (1992) on Somalia.

704 *Cf.* "to use all necessary means", S/Res. 678 (1990), para. 2; "to use all necessary means", S/Res.

formulation would therefore be that the Council, under Article 42 of the Charter, authorized states to take measures in pursuance of Security Council objectives related to the maintenance of international peace and security. Given the absence of agreements concluded under Article 43 this should not come as a surprise.[706] It may be noted that the authorizations "to use all necessary means" give a considerable amount of discretion to the states acting pursuant to that authorization.[707]

Indeed, forces acting pursuant to Security Council authorizations have generally been under national command and control rather than that of the United Nations.[708] Although attempts were made in the case of Somalia to establish the forces under the control of the Secretary-General, decisions were "in fact largely taken by the Americans."[709] Moreover, Article 47 of the Charter, which provides for a role for the Military Staff Committee in, *inter alia*, the "employment and command of forces placed at its disposal", has fallen into desuetude.[710] In light of this and the recent practice of the Council, it is not to be expected that the Security Council will readily assume the role of military commander.[711] Indeed, the permanent members of the Council are

---

794 (1992), para. 10; "such measures as may be necessary", S/Res. 929 (1994), para. 3; "to use all necessary means", S/Res. 940 (1994), para. 4. S/Res. 221 (1966) on Southern Rhodesia is more explicit. Herein the Council "calls upon" the UK to prevent "by the use of force if necessary" vessels arriving at Beira that carry oil destined for Southern Rhodesia.

705 An exception is S/Res. 678 (1990), para. 2, in which states were authorized not only to "uphold and implement resolution 660 (1990) and all subsequent relevant resolutions" but also to "restore international peace and security in the area."

706 After the Gulf War some optimism existed that Art. 43 agreements could finally be concluded. Thus Secretary-General Boutros Boutros-Ghali, in his 'Agenda for Peace', recommended "that the Security Council initiate negotiations in accordance with Article 43". A/47/277, 17 June 1992, para. 43. No efforts have been made, however, to negotiate such agreements. See Houck, *op. cit. supra* n.155, 6.

707 Thus Quigley notes that: "The formulation that the Security Council has used in issuing authorizations makes it clear that the states are left to decide whether or take military action. Starting with the Iraqi resolution, the Council has not mentioned military force as the action it was authorizing, but speaks rather of "all necessary means" or words to that effect. This formulation leaves it to the member states to decide whether military force, or some measures short of it, might bring about the desired result." J. Quigley, *The 'Privatization' of Security Council Enforcement Action: A Threat to Multilateralism*, 17 MJIL (1996) 249-283, at 262.

708 See C. Walter, *Security Council Control over Regional Action*, 1 Max Planck Yearbook of United Nations Law (1997) 129-193, 176-190; Wolfrum, *op. cit. supra* n.168.

709 Freudenschuß, *op. cit. supra* n.1, at 527.

710 During the Gulf War the Soviet Union in particular attempted to revitalize the Military Staff Committee, with limited success, however. Indeed, Schachter observes that the Committee "has had some meetings to discuss military problems raised by the Council resolutions on Iraq but its 'advice', if any, has not been disclosed." Schachter, *op. cit. supra* n.162, at 74.

711 *Cf.* the Secretary-General pointing out that the United Nations Secretariat could not command

resistant to placing their troops under 'foreign' command.[712]

It has furthermore been suggested that standing forces, that could be rapidly deployed in crisis situations, be made available to the United Nations.[713] An initiative has been undertaken by several countries to establish such a force, the Multinational United Nations Stand-by Forces High Readiness Brigade (SHIRBRIG).[714] Although supported by the Secretary-General,[715] the creation of the force has been criticized by several members of the United Nations as reaffirming "the existing tendency to set it up as a new privileged formation of those Member States which had wide capacities to finance their participation in it."[716]

---

and control an enforcement action in Somalia because the Secretariat was already overstretched and did not have adequate capabilities to undertake an operation of this size. 'Letter of the Secretary-General to the Security Council', S/24868, 29 Nov. 1992.

712 C. Conetta, C. Knight, *Vital Force: A Proposal for the Overhaul of the UN Peace Operations System and for the Creation of a UN Legion* (1995), 4; C. Greenwood, *International Humanitarian Law and United Nations Military Operations*, 1 Yearbook of International Humanitarian Law (1998) 3-34, 13. *Cf.* the Executive Summary of the Presidential Decision Directive 25 (PDD-25) on 'Administration Policy on Reforming Multilateral Peace Operations', signed by President Clinton on 3 May 1994, reproduced in 33 ILM (1994) 798-813. Herein the US government announces that it will never relinquish "command" over United States military personnel, but that personnel may be placed under the "operational control" of a non-U.S. commander for limited and defined purposes. *Loc. cit.*, 808.

713 For an overview of these proposals see, *e.g.*, D.A. Leurdijk, *Rapid Deployment: A Capacity Gap*. In: E. Denters, N. Schrijver (eds.), Reflections on International Law from the Low Countries (1998) 301-314; Conetta, Knight, *op. cit. supra* n.712, 67-69; G. Wirick, *The Prospects for a United Nations Rapid Reaction Capability*, March 1996. Accessed at http://www.unac.org/unreform [as wirick.html] on 20 July 2000.

714 See, *e.g.*, the 'Letter dated 29 February 1996 from the Permanent Representative of Denmark to the United Nations addressed to the Secretary-General', S/1996/166, 5 March 1996. A report by a "military working group with participation from Argentina, Austria, Belgium, Canada, Czech Republic, Finland (observer), Ireland (observer), the Netherlands, New Zealand, Norway, Poland and Sweden" is annexed to this letter, which deals with the establishment of a 'Multinational United Nations Stand-by Forces High Readiness Brigade.' The letter states that the "report will serve as a basis for a further elaboration among these countries on the modalities for establishment of a cooperation on a Multinational United Nations Stand-by Forces High Readiness Brigade." See also the 'Report of the Panel on United Nations Peace Operations', annexed to the 'Identical letters dated 21 August 2000 from the Secretary-General to the President of the General Assembly and the President of the Security Council', A/55/305-S/2000/809, 21 Aug. 2000, paras. 84-169. Herein the Panel recommends the establishment of "rapid and effective deployment capacity" by the United Nations.

715 See, for example, 'Peacekeeping in the Twenty-first Century', address by the Secretary-General to the 'Standby High Readiness Brigade Ministerial Meeting', Press Release SG/SM/7339 PKO/87, 27 March 2000.

716 'Concern over High Readiness Brigade Expressed at Special Committee on Peacekeeping Operations', Press Release GA/PK/152, 31 March 1998, statement by the representative of Ukraine

4.

Sources and Content of the Legal Limits to the Council's Powers

4.1 Introduction to the Problem

As seen in the previous chapter, the Security Council has taken a remarkably activist stance since 1990, beginning with the Kuwait crisis. In numerous situations the Council has acted under Chapter VII of the Charter, and as indicated in paragraph 3.15 above, several of these situations fall outside the traditional understanding of threats to international peace and security. In deciding upon measures to restore the peace, moreover, the Council has taken various innovative measures. These measures at time have severe consequences for the entities against which they are imposed, which include both states and non-state actors. The comprehensive sanctions regime imposed on Iraq, the travel restrictions on Sudanese officials and members of the Sudanese armed forces, the aerial embargo on Libya and the weapons embargo on the territory of former Yugoslavia as well as the establishment of the ICTY and ICTR are amongst the cases in question. In addition, these measures established far-reaching obligations for the members of the United Nations, which are responsible for the implementation of the measures. Such measures can, for example, have strong detrimental effects on the economy of a member state implementing the measures.[717] Great hardship,

---

to the United Nations, at 5. The concerns reside with members of the Non-Aligned Movement in particular.

717 See, *e.g.*, 'Report of the Secretary-General on Implementation of provisions of the Charter related to assistance to third States affected by the application of sanctions', A/53/312, 27 Aug. 1998; J. Carver, J. Hulsmann, *The Role of Article 50 of the UN Charter in the Search for International Peace and Security*, 49 ICLQ (2000) 528-577.

moreover, may be incurred on the populations of the targeted countries.[718]

The increasing number and scope of measures has led to concern about the limits to the powers of the Security Council under Chapter VII of the Charter.[719] At times it seemed that the Council was free to do as it wished, and more in particular the US as the only remaining superpower seemed to be in a position to use the Security Council as an instrument by which to implement its national foreign policy. This has even led to concern amongst the permanent members of the Council itself.[720]

It has been observed that "once a Chapter VII situation arises", the Security Council is of the opinion that it can take "any and all actions that it considers useful and suitable for dealing with the situation or any of its consequences, whether those actions are of a military, administrative, regulatory, or even primarily judicial nature."[721] This state of affairs induced a debate as to the legal limits, if any, on the powers of the Council under Chapter VII of the Charter.

As seen in chapter 2, the Council's powers under Chapter VII are extensive. Once the Council has determined that a situation poses a threat to international peace and security, it can impose legally binding measures on the members of the United Nations. This means that member states are obliged to carry out the measures, including economic sanctions. As observed by Schrijver, moreover, collective sanctions imposed by international organizations "cannot but override other principles and rules of international law such as non-interference in internal affairs, sovereignty, the duty to co-operate, non-discrimination and freedom of trade and navigation."[722]

The question ensuing from such Council interference with existing rights and duties of states, is whether the Council is 'free to do whatever it wants', and that hence

---

[718] See W.M. Reisman, D.L. Stevick, *The Applicability of International Law Standards to United Nations Economic Sanctions Programmes*, 9 EJIL (1998) 86-141.

[719] For an overview of these concerns see, *e.g.*, Alvarez, *op. cit. supra* n.5; Caron, *op. cit. supra* n.4; W.B.L. Kapinga, *The United Nations System and Collective Uses of Force under the New World Order*, ASICL, 5th Annual Congress (1993) 6-20, 7-15; M. Koskenniemi, *The Police in the Temple Order, Justice and the UN: A Dialectical View*, 6 EJIL (1995) 325-348; K. Dicke, *National Interest vs. the Interest of the International Community – A Critical Review of Recent UN Security Council Practice*. In: J. Delbrück, New trends in International Lawmaking - International 'Legislation' in the Public Interest (1997) 145-169; Dupuy, *op. cit. supra* n.46, 28-30.

[720] See, *e.g.*, the French reaction to 'U.S. unilateralism', International Herald Tribune, 3 Feb. 1999, 1 and 8. See also *infra*, paragraph 6.1.

[721] P.C. Szasz, *Centralized and Decentralized Law Enforcement: The Security Council and the General Assembly Acting under Chapters VII and VIII*. In: J. Delbrück, Allocation of Law Enforcement Authority in the International System (1995) 17-38, at 33.

[722] Schrijver, *op. cit. supra* n.510, at 124. To the same effect see Gill, *op. cit. supra* n.5, 61-62; Akande, *op. cit. supra* n.104, 320; and Gardam, *op. cit. supra* n.172, 297.

one must conclude that "what the Council says *is* the law."[723] Or alternatively, whether international law circumscribes the Council's powers under Chapter VII. This leads to the central operative question examined in this work. In short, the question is whether *legal* limits exist to the Council's authority under Chapter VII of the Charter.[724]

Before assessing these possible limits, a distinction will be made between the sources from which they could be derived.[725] This distinction is two-fold. One source is the Charter, which is the constituent treaty of the United Nations from which the Council derives its powers and hence may also provide for limits on those powers. The other source may be rules from general international law,[726] that is rules from extra-Charter sources that could provide a limit on the Council's authority under Chapter VII. During the course of the argument, however, it will become apparent that the distinction cannot always be strictly maintained, due to the considerable overlap and interaction between the two sources.

In addition to identifying the possible sources providing limitations, one must also look at the content of these limitations, that is to identify the actual standards to which Security Council actions must conform.

4.2 Charter-based Constraints

It is a truism to state that as an organ deriving its powers from a constituent treaty, the Council must abide by that same treaty. This has been affirmed by the Appeals Chamber of the ICTY in the following terms:

> The Security Council is an organ of an international organization, established by a treaty which serves as a constitutional framework for that organization. The Security Council is thus subjected to certain constitutional limitations, however broad its powers under the constitution may be. Those powers cannot, in any case, go beyond the limits of the jurisdiction of the Organization at large, not to mention other specific limitations or

---

723 Koskenniemi, *op. cit. supra* n.719, at 327. *Cf.* A. Randelzhofer, *Great Powers*, 9 EPIL (1986) 142-166. At 144 Randelzhofer submits that: "Once the unanimity of the five Great Powers is given, the UN Charter gives them the legal basis for a far-reaching reign and provides for only scarce limitations to secure the sovereign independence of the other States."

724 See also *supra*, the text accompanying note 14.

725 See K. Doehring, *Unlawful Resolutions of the Security Council and their Legal Consequences*, 1 Max Planck Yearbook of United Nations Law (1997) 91-109, 101-108; F.P. King, *Sensible Scrutiny: The Yugoslavia Tribunal's Development of Limits on the Security Council's Powers under Chapter VII of the Charter*, 10 Emory ILR (1996) 509-591, 542-543; A.M. Gunn, *Council and Court: Prospects in Lockerbie for an International Rule of Law*, 52 University of Toronto Faculty of Law Review (1994) 206-258, 226.

726 The term "general" international law is used here to denote "rules and principles that are applicable to a large number of states", as opposed to "regional" international law, that "applies only to certain groups of states." See Malanczuk, *op. cit. supra* n.31, 2. See on the scope of application of international law generally J.I. Charney, *Universal International Law*, 87 AJIL (1993) 529-551.

those which may derive from the internal division of power within the Organization. In any case, neither the text nor the spirit of the Charter conceives of the Security Council as *legibus solutus* (unbound by law).[727]

The assumption that the United Nations Charter provides simultaneously for the powers of the Council and for the limits to those powers, is in itself more or less free from controversy. As early as 1948, this was recognized by the International Court of Justice when it held that:

The political character of an organ cannot release it from the observance of the treaty provisions established by the Charter when they constitute limitations on its powers and criteria for its judgment. To ascertain whether an organ has freedom of choice for its decisions, reference must be made to the terms of the constitution.[728]

Disagreement arises, however, when one tries to identify and define the contents of these limitations. The open-texture of the Charter,[729] in particular, hinders the identification of the Articles and rules contained in the Charter and the correct interpretation of these rules.[730]

Before turning to the provisions of the Charter that might provide for limitations on the Council's powers under Chapter VII, one may first recall the 'enabling' provisions and those emphasizing the members' obligations under the Charter, in addition to the specific powers granted to the Council under Articles 39-42. Thus, the first purpose of the United Nations, mentioned in Article 1(1) of the Charter, is "to maintain international peace and security, and to that end: to take effective collective measures for the prevention and removal of threats to the peace". Article 2(2) provides that all members of the organization "shall fulfil in good faith the obligations assumed by them in accordance with the present Charter", and Article 2(5) that the members "shall give the United Nations every assistance in any action it takes in accordance with the present Charter." Moreover, according to Article 24(1) member states "confer on the Security Council primary responsibility for the maintenance of international peace and security, and agree that in carrying out its duties under this responsibility the Security Council acts on their behalf." Furthermore, as seen earlier, under Article 25 members "agree to accept and carry out the decisions of the Security Council in

---

727 Appeals Chamber Decision on the Tadić Jurisdictional Motion, *Prosecutor v. Dusko Tadić a/k/a "Dule"*, Case No. IT-94-1-AR72, 2 Oct. 1995, para. 28.

728 *Conditions of Admission of a State to Membership in the United Nations*, Adv. Op., ICJ Rep. (1948), at 64.

729 See, *e.g.*, Reisman, *op. cit. supra* n.7; and Watson, *op. cit. supra* n.7. Watson observes at 34 that: "The Bill of Rights may seem hopelessly vague to students of the U.S. Constitution, but it is a model of clarity and detail compared with the corresponding provisions of the U.N. Charter."

730 On the interpretation of the Charter see *supra*, chapter 1, paragraph 1.4 in particular.

accordance with the present Charter." This is reaffirmed by Article 49, which holds that "the Members of the United Nations shall join in affording mutual assistance in carrying out the measures decided upon by the Security Council." Article 103, moreover, stipulates that: "In the event of a conflict between the obligations of the Members of the United Nations under the present Charter and their obligations under any other international agreement, their obligations under the present Charter shall prevail." The Charter thus emphasizes the loyalty of its members towards the organization,[731] and at a minimum provides for its primacy *vis-à-vis* other treaty obligations.[732]

4.2.1 Purposes and Principles of the United Nations

As mentioned above, the Charter provides the constitutional framework within which the Council operates. A general limitation on the powers of an organ of an international organization is that it must act in accordance with the object and purpose of that organization.[733]

In addition to this general rule, Article 24, paragraph 2 of the Charter expressly stipulates that in discharging its duties the Council "shall act in accordance with the Purposes and Principles of the United Nations." This was interpreted to mean the following during the San Francisco Conference:

> Wide freedom of judgment is left as regards the moment [the Security Council] may choose to intervene and the means to be applied, with sole reserve that it should act 'in accordance with the purposes and principles of the [United Nations].'[734]

The purposes and principles are laid down in Articles 1 and 2 of the Charter.[735] On first reading they may appear to be very loosely formulated, reflecting a political programme rather than strictly defined legal rules. Thus Gill observes that they "are extremely broad in scope and hardly synonymous in most respects with specific rules

---

731 See Doehring, *op. cit. supra* n.725, 105-106.

732 See R. Bernhardt, *Article 103*. In: B. Simma, *et. al.* (eds.), The Charter of the United Nations (1994) 1117-1125.

733 *E.g.* Kelsen, *op. cit. supra* n.51, 230 ff.

734 Statement of the Special Rapporteur of Committee III/3, 11 UNCIO Docs. at 785. Quoted by the Trial Chamber in the Trial Chamber Decision on the Defence Motion on Jurisdiction, *Prosecutor v. Dusko Tadić a/k/a "Dule"*, Case No. IT-94-1-T, 10 Aug. 1995, at 5.

735 The preamble and Art. 55 also refer to the purposes of the United Nations. As observed by Goodrich and Hambro, however, the "fact that the words 'Purposes and Principles' are used in capitalized form [in Art. 24(2)] suggests that the reference is to the specific provisions of Articles 1 and 2 respectively." Goodrich, Hambro, *op. cit. supra* n.164, at 207.

of international treaties and general international law."[736] This non-specific phrasing notwithstanding, from the inclusion of Article 24 (2) it follows that "the legally binding nature of the purposes is undoubtedly clear, since they are expressly described as the object of legal protection."[737] The inclusion of Article 24(2) reaffirms that the Council is bound to respect them. In this respect Delbrück's contention that "Art. 24(2) second sentence, turns out to be legally rather meaningless ... since the conclusion that an organ may act only within the limits of the powers granted to the organization for which it functions, is self-evident"[738] must be dismissed. Although Delbrück correctly refers to the tautological nature of the second sentence of Article 24(2), the inclusion of the article strengthens the Council's duty to act in accordance with the purposes and principles of the Charter. Without this Article, a *prima facie* reading of the Charter could lead to the conclusion that the purposes and principles are too vague to provide for concrete legal limits to the Council's authority, as argued by some. This position is, for example, held by Martenczuk, who maintains that:

> the purposes and principles of the United Nations as laid down in Articles 1 and 2 of the Charter are extremely vague and general in nature ... [T]he standard of review of Security Council resolutions cannot be sought in the purposes and principles of the United Nations.[739]

It is submitted here that the inclusion of Article 24(2) necessitates a closer look at the purposes and principles of the Charter, and that such an exercise does reveal that they contain rules binding on the Council. This is in line with Suy, who contends that: "The Council is bound by the Purposes and Principles of the Organization and discharges its duties on the basis of the specific powers granted by the Charter."[740]

In a similar fashion Gowlland-Debbas submits that: "The substantive limits are to be found in Article 24(2), according to which the Council is bound to act in accordance with the purposes and principles of the United Nations."[741] Fassbender also maintains that: "The values and goals set out by the Charter in its preamble and first two articles are ... standards of legality (or constitutionality) for legal acts passed by UN organs."[742]

---

736 Gill, *op. cit. supra* n.5, at 73. See to the same effect Reisman, *op. cit. supra* n.7, 93.

737 K. Doehring, *Self-Determination*. In: B. Simma, *et. al.* (eds.), The Charter of the United Nations (1994) 56-72, at 57.

738 Delbrück, *op. cit. supra* n.107, at 404.

739 B. Martenczuk, *The Security Council, the International Court and Judicial Review: What Lessons from Lockerbie?*, 10 EJIL (1999) 517-547, at 537.

740 E. Suy, *International Organization*, 43 NILR (1996) 237-244, at 243.

741 Gowlland-Debbas, *op. cit. supra* n.2, at 91.

742 Fassbender, *op. cit. supra* n.46, at 316. See also Gill, *op. cit. supra* n.5, 72-74; Shaw, *op. cit. supra*

On closer reading, then, there are several purposes and principles which may provide limitations on the Council's powers. These are provided by Articles 1 and 2 and the preamble of the Charter in general; and Articles 1(2), 1(3), 2(1), 2(2) and 2(7) in particular.

4.2.1.1 Article 1(2): Self-Determination

Article 1(2) states that the United Nations is "to develop friendly relations among nations based on respect for the principle of equal rights and self-determination of peoples".[743] Although the exact content and scope of the notion 'self-determination of peoples' is difficult to define,[744] it follows from Article 1(2) that the Council may not violate the right of self-determination.[745] This right includes "the right to freely determine its political status as well as its economic, social and cultural structure. This would mean that each nation has a sovereign right to decide for itself its political structure."[746]

From this it can be inferred that the right of self-determination "precludes the imposition of any form of government by the United Nations on the population of a State or other entity"[747] against the will of the people concerned. Indeed the Council, when intervening in a state (Somalia, Yugoslavia), has generally sought the cooperation of conflicting parties in reaching a settlement that could restore international peace and security. The exceptions are provided by Rhodesia, South Africa and Haiti, in

---

n.16, 877; R.St.J. MacDonald, *Changing Relations between the International Court of Justice and the Security Council of the United Nations*, 31 CYIL (1993) 3-32, 26-29.

743 *Cf.* Art. 55, which refers to "the creation of conditions of stability and well-being which are necessary for peaceful and friendly relations among nations based on respect for the principle of equal rights and self-determination of peoples"

744 Generally see Doehring, *op. cit. supra* n.737, 63-72; H. Hannum, *Rethinking Self-Determination*, 34 VJIL (1993) 1-69; V.P. Nanda, *Self-Determination Under International Law: Validity of Claims to Secede*, 13 Case W. Res. J. International Law (1981) 257-280; Dixon, *op. cit. supra* n.40, 145-147; K.J. Partsch, *Self-Determination*. In: R. Wolfrum (ed.), United Nations: Law, Policies and Practice (1995) 1171-1179.

745 M. Bedjaoui, *The New World Order and the Security Council: Testing the Legality of its Acts* (1994), 34-35.

746 R.C. Hingorani, *Modern International Law* (1984), at 264. *Cf.* the *Western Sahara* case, Adv. Op., ICJ Rep. (1975), in which the court held at para. 55 that "the application of the right of self-determination requires a free and genuine expression of the will of the peoples concerned."

747 Gill, *op. cit. supra* n.5, at 75. *Cf.* Herdegen, *op. cit. supra* n.648, at 29: "Beim Wiederafbau von Staaten nach dem Zerfall einer einheitlichen Staatsgewalt hat der Sicherheitsrat das Selbstorganisationsrecht des jeweiligen (Staats)Volkes im Sinne der Selbstbestimmung nach innen zu beachten."

which cases the Council expressly targeted the governments in office and thus seemed to have aimed at a change in the national *status quo*. Since the governing elites were not supported by their peoples, however, the Council cannot be said to have violated their right of self-determination. Indeed, the case can be made that the elites violated the right of internal self-determination of its peoples.[748] A difficult case could arise when a people freely elects a leadership that pursues 'aggressive' wars. Would the Council be entitled to strive for the removal of that leadership as a measure for enforcing peace? This difficult question bears on the classic paradox in democratic theory: what if a people democratically decides to abolish democracy?[749] It would seem that in such a case the Council should target the aggressive policies of the regime in question, rather than removing the regime itself.

The principle of self-determination does not preclude the transitional taking over of a state's administration, as happened for example in Cambodia,[750] provided the

[748] *Cf.* the preamble to S/Res. 417 (1977), in which the Council affirms "the right to the exercise of self-determination by all the people of South Africa as a whole, irrespective of race, colour or creed." See also resolutions 460 (1979) and 463 (1980), in which the Council reaffirmed "the inalienable right of the people of Zimbabwe to self-determination". On 24 Oct. 1970, moreover, the General Assembly adopted resolution 2625 (XXV) (reproduced in 9 ILM (1970) 1292-1297), which contained a 'Declaration on Principles of International Law concerning Friendly relations and Co-operation among States in accordance with the Charter of the United Nations.' Herein a state is defined as complying with the "principle of self-determination" if the state possesses "a government representing the whole people belonging to the territory without distinction as to race, creed or colour." See on the topic of self-determination in the context of South Africa and Rhodesia R. Emerson, *Self-Determination*, 65 AJIL (1971) 459-475, 466-468. In the context of Haiti one might refer to Kirgis, who mentions: "The internal self-determination freedom to choose one's own form of government, or even more sharply, the right to a democratic form of government, as in Haiti." F.L. Kirgis, *The Degrees of Self-Determination in the United Nations Era*, 88 AJIL (1994) 304-310, at 307.

[749] This is what happened in Algeria in the early 1990s, when the first multi-party elections were held since Algeria gained independence in 1962. In December 1991 the Islamic opposition party (the FIS), which purported to establish an Islamic state, won 188 out of 231 parliamentary seats up for election. The second round was scheduled for January 1992, in which the 199 seats remaining would be allocated. The FIS was thus heading for an absolute majority in Parliament. Subsequently, the military leaders cancelled the second round and "nullified the first-round results in January 1992." L. Addi, *Algeria's Tragic Contradictions*, 7 Journal of Democracy (1996) 94-107, at 94. Addi notes that since then: "Algeria has plunged into murderous strife that already has claimed more than 60,000 lives." *Ibid.* On the situation in Algeria see also the 'Report of the Panel Appointed by the Secretary-General of the United Nations to Gather Information on the Situation in Algeria in Order to Provide the International Community with Greater Clarity on That Situation', submitted to the Secretary-General on 10 Sept. 1998.

[750] On the 'United Nations Transitional Authority in Cambodia' (UNTAC) see, *e.g.*, UNDPI, *op. cit. supra* n.388, 447-481; M.W. Doyle, A. Suzuki, *Transitional Authority in Cambodia*. In: T.G. Weiss (ed.), The United Nations and Civil Wars (1995) 127-149; N.T. Vu, *The Holding of Free and Fair Elections in Cambodia: The Achievement of the United Nations' Impossible Mission*, 16 MJIL (1995) 1177-1241.

Security Council does not impose a long-term administrative authority not chosen by the population.[751]

4.2.1.2 Article 1(3): Respect for Human Rights

Article 1(3) of the Charter provides that one of the purposes of the organization is to promote and encourage "respect for human rights and for fundamental freedoms for all without distinction as to race, sex, language, or religion".[752] This purpose probably provides for the most far-reaching limitation on the Council's discretion under Chapter VII. From Article 1(3) it follows that "the Security Council must take account of the impact of sanctions upon the population of 'target' countries and ensure that UN civil and military personnel observe human rights standards in the conduct of their operations."[753]

Indeed, the majority view is that the Council must evaluate the impact of its decisions on the human rights of the people affected by those decision. Although individual hardship will occur by necessity when economic sanctions are taken by the Council, the Council must evaluate the necessity and proportionality of its measures in relation to the threat to the peace which provides for the basis of its actions. In fact, the humanitarian impact of Security Council sanctions has become a topical issue both within[754] and outside[755] the UN, specifically in the context of the ongoing sanctions against Iraq. This debate induced the Secretary-General to state in his 1998 annual report to the General Assembly that:

> The international community should be under no illusion: ... humanitarian and human rights policy goals cannot easily be reconciled with those of a sanctions regime. It cannot be too strongly emphasized that sanctions are a tool of enforcement and, like other methods of enforcement, they will do harm. This should

---

[751] Gill, *op. cit. supra* n.5, 75.

[752] *Cf.* Art. 55(c), according to which the United Nations shall promote "universal respect for, and observance of, human rights and fundamental freedoms for all without distinction as to race, sex, language, or religion."

[753] Gill, *op. cit. supra* n.5, at 78.

[754] See, *e.g.*, Annual Reports of the Secretary-General on the Work of the Organization, A/53/1, 27 Aug. 1998, paras. 62-64.; and A/54/1, 31 Aug. 1999, paras. 124-126.

[755] See, *e.g.*, C. Bruderlein, Special Advisor to the Office for the Coordination of Humanitarian Affairs (OCHA), *Coping with Humanitarian Impact of Sanctions: An OCHA Perspective*, Dec. 1998; R. Garfield, *The Impact of Economic Sanctions on Health and Well-being*, Relief and Rehabilitation Network Paper No. 31, Nov. 1999; Reisman, Stevick, *op. cit. supra* n.718.

be borne in mind when the decision to impose them is taken, and when the results are subsequently evaluated.[756]

Respect for human rights also means that in establishing subsidiary (judicial) organs, the Council must conform to "the rule of law." This issue has been dealt with by the ICTY in the *Tadić* case, in which the Appeals Chamber affirmed the Appellant's plea that the ICTY must be "established by law." This plea was affirmed by the Chamber, according to which "established by law" means that "it must be established in accordance with the proper international standards; it must provide all the guarantees of fairness, justice and even-handedness, in full conformity with internationally recognized human rights instruments."[757]

Interestingly, the prosecution in the *Tadić* case, which might be said to have had an interest in minimizing the limitations on the Council's powers, maintained that: "It is part of international law that a fair trial of accused persons will be rendered. We would submit that the Security Council would not or should not take steps or measures which fly in the face of that."[758]

This confirms that in exercising its functions under Chapter VII, the Council must respect human rights, particularly when exercising its legislative powers. In this context one may refer to King, who has correctly observed that a distinction may be made:

> between situations when the Security Council creates an institution as a Chapter VII measure responsive to an ongoing threat to the peace and to situations when the Council takes rapid action in response to an immediate or unanticipated threat to the peace. Review of the Council's actions seems more reasonable in the former situation, when there is likely to be less concern for speed and secrecy and when there may be some expectation of an effective judicial remedy.[759]

4.2.1.3 Article 2(1): Sovereign Equality

Article 2(1) provides that the United Nations is based on the "principle of the sovereign equality of all its Members." From this some observers have inferred that the

---

[756] 'Annual Report of the Secretary-General on the Work of the Organization', A/53/1, 27 Aug. 1998, para. 64.

[757] Appeals Chamber Decision on the Tadić Jurisdictional Motion, *Prosecutor v. Dusko Tadić a/k/a "Dule"*, Case No. IT-94-1-AR72, 2 Oct. 1995, para. 44. See also Trial Chamber Decision on the Defence Motion on Jurisdiction, *Prosecutor v. Dusko Tadić a/k/a "Dule"*, Case No. IT-94-1-T, 10 Aug. 1995, para. 8.

[758] Quoted by King, *op. cit. supra* n.725, at 565.

[759] *Ibid.*, at 576.

Council may not violate a state's political independence or territorial integrity.[760] As indicated above, however, the Council's actions under Chapter VII will inevitably affect matters falling within the sovereign competence of a state, for example the right to free trade. The concept of sovereignty, moreover, has gradually eroded, rendering it less relevant today.[761] At first sight, therefore, an argument to the effect that a state's sovereignty may not be violated seems of little or no use. The correct interpretation of the article would seem to be, however, that the Council's actions may only temporarily affect a state's sovereignty as long as that state's actions threaten international peace and security. A measure by the Council that permanently infringes on a State's sovereignty is unwarranted. Thus, the Council would not have the power to, for example, decide to abolish a state.[762] It could be argued that the United Nations Iraq-Kuwait Boundary Demarcation Commission did permanently infringe on Iraq's sovereignty, by delimiting rather than demarcating the Iraq-Kuwait border. By (reluctantly) accepting the Commission's conclusions, however, Iraq can no longer protest against the boundary established by the Commission by virtue of the principle of estoppel.[763]

4.2.1.4 Article 2(2): Good Faith

Article 2(2) provides that "all Members, in order to ensure to all of them the rights and benefits resulting from membership, shall fulfil in good faith the obligations assumed by them in accordance with the present Charter." It thus integrates the principle of good faith "into the law of the Charter."[764] Albeit the obligation refers to members in the first place, the obligation extends to the organs of the United Nations as well.[765] In any event, the obligations of the members to act in good faith would also apply in their specific capacity as a member of an organ of the United Nations.

The principle of good faith is inherent in the rule of *pacta sunt servanda* in the law

[760] See Schachter, *op. cit. supra* n.162, 75.

[761] See, *e.g.*, Malanczuk, *op. cit. supra* n.31, 17-18. Note that Malanczuk prefers the term 'independence' rather than 'sovereignty'. See on the present content of 'sovereignty' also Reisman, *op. cit. supra* n.655; and J.S. Barkin, B. Cronin, The State and the Nation: Changing Norms and the Rules of Sovereignty in International Relations, 48 International Organization (1994) 107-130.

[762] Generally see S.P. Subedi, *The Doctrine of Objective Regimes in International Law and the Competence of the United Nations to Impose Territorial or Peace Settlements on States*, 37 GYIL (1994) 162-205.

[763] See Post, *op. cit. supra* n.316.

[764] J.P. Müller, *Article 2(2)*. In: B. Simma, *et. al.* (eds.), The Charter of the United Nations (1994) 89-97, at 93.

[765] *Ibid.*, 93-94.

of treaties, meaning that treaties are binding on the parties and shall be executed in good faith by them.[766] Good faith not only applies to the execution and interpretation of treaties, but also to execution of rights and obligations, regardless of their source.[767] Indeed, the principle of good faith is one of the foundations of international law as such.[768]

This means that the Security Council must exercise its responsibilities in good faith. In the words of Bermejo Perez: "there exist limits to the Security Council's actions under Chapter VII, which are the principles and purposes of the Charter and the principle of good faith in fulfillment of the maxim *pacta sunt servanda*."[769] The corollary of the principle of good faith is the doctrine of abuse of rights.[770] If the Council is obliged to act in good faith, that means that it may neither abuse its rights or powers, nor that it may act arbitrarily. In this sense, Gowlland-Debbas has argued that "limits to what may appear to be an unlimited discretionary power may be found in the doctrine of abuse of rights arising from failure by States to exercise their rights in good faith and with due regard to the consequences of such exercise."[771]

---

[766] *Cf.* Art. 26 of the Vienna Convention on the Law of Treaties, which is headed *Pacta sunt servanda:* "Every treaty in force is binding upon the parties to it and must be performed by them in good faith." On the historical origins of the rule see, *e.g.*, M. Lachs, *Pacta Sunt Servanda*, 7 EPIL (1984) 364-371, 364-366; H. Wehberg, *Pacta Sunt Servanda*, 53 AJIL (1959) 775-786, 775-782. Both authors argue that it dates back to "time immemorial".

[767] A. D'Amato, *Good Faith*, 7 EPIL (1984) 107-109, 107. *Cf.* the *Nuclear Tests* case (Australia v. France), ICJ Rep. (1974), 253 ff., para. 46: "One of the basic principles governing the creation and formation of legal obligations, *whatever* their source, is the principle of good faith. Trust and confidence are inherent in international co-operation, in particular in an age when this co-operation in many fields is becoming increasingly essential. Just as the very rule of *pacta sunt servanda* in the law of treaties is based on good faith, so also the binding character of an international obligation assumed by unilateral declaration" (first emphasis added). *Cf.* also GA Res. 2625 (XXV), 24 Oct. 1970, according to which: "Every State has the duty to fulfil in good faith its obligations under the generally recognized principles and rules of international law."

[768] Thus Virally maintains that "good faith presents itself as an absolute necessary ingredient to the operation of the whole international legal order, namely, to the creation and performance of law." M. Virally, *Review Essay: Good Faith in Public International Law*, 77 AJIL (1983) 130-134, at 133. *Cf.* Wehberg, according to whom adherence to a view that does not recognize the validity of the rule of *pacta sunt servanda* "would amount to denying the existence of international law in general." Wehberg, *op. cit. supra* n.766, at 782.

[769] M.P. Bermejo Perez, *International Justice and the United Nations Security Council: Towards Meaningful Reform*, 16 Thesaurus Acroasium (1997) 859-882, at 882.

[770] Generally see A.C. Kiss, *Abuse of Rights*, 7 EPIL (1984) 1-5; V. Paul, *The Abuse of Rights and Bona Fides in International Law*, 28 Österreichische Zeitschrift für öffentliches Recht und Völkerrecht (1977) 107-130; Taylor, *op. cit. supra* n.9; H. Lauterpacht, 1 *International Law* (1970), 383-386; B. Cheng, *General Principles of Law as Applied by International Courts and Tribunals* (1987), 121-136.

[771] Gowlland-Debbas, *op. cit. supra* n.2, at 94. Similarly, Bowett maintains that the Security Council

This means the actions decided upon by the Council should objectively relate to the maintenance of international peace and security. In the *Tadić* case the Trial Chamber of the ICTY formulated this as follows: "It is a matter of logic that if the Security Council acted arbitrarily or for an ulterior purpose it would be acting outside the purview of the powers delegated to it in the Charter."[772] Consider the possibility of a Council decision to impose economic sanctions against a state in financial debt to several states, based on a reasoning that the non-payment of debts results in a climate prone to disrupt international peace and security. If it were to be established that the targeted state was in substantial financial debt to the permanent members of the Council themselves, and that the sanctions were merely established by the members to 'get their goods back', a claim that the Council abused its rights would indeed be viable.

Acting in good faith would also require that the measures decided upon in order to restore the peace should be necessary and proportional.[773] Some would also submit that the Council must act in a consistent manner.[774] This does not appear to be a feasible position. As observed by one commentator:

"cannot, in principle, act arbitrarily and unfettered by any restraints." D.W. Bowett, *The Law of International Institutions* (1982), at 33. See to the same effect M.N. Shaw, *The Security Council and the International Court of Justice: Judicial Drift and Judicial Function*. In: A.S. Muller, D. Raič, J.M. Thuránszky (eds.), The International Court of Justice: Its Future Role after Fifty Years (1997) 219-259, 226; Cryer, *op. cit. supra* n.648, 169; Alvarez, *op. cit. supra* n.5, 26; T.M. Franck, *The United Nations as Guarantor of International Peace and Security: Past, Present and Future*. In: C. Tomuschat (ed.), The United Nations at Age Fifty: A Legal Perspective (1995) 25-38, 37; Delbrück, *op. cit. supra* n.107, 404; Gunn, *op. cit. supra* n.725, 228-229; A. Leporatti, *Some Aspects of the Relationship between the International Court of Justice and the Security Council in the Light of Recent Cases: In Particular, are there Limitations to the Security Council's Powers?*, 16 Thesaurus Acroasium (1997) 725-732, 729.

772 Trial Chamber Decision on the Defence Motion on Jurisdiction, *Prosecutor v. Dusko Tadić a/k/a "Dule"*, Case No. IT 94 1 T, 10 Aug. 1995, at 8

773 Thus Marauhn holds that "mandatory measures decided upon by the Security Council have to be proportional. To this extent, the powers of the Security Council are limited." Marauhn, *op. cit. supra* n.320, at 786. So also Kirgis submits that "the Security Council in a chapter VII situation should respect the principle of proportionality – or what might better be described as the principle of avoiding excessive disproportionality." Kirgis, *op. cit. supra* n.129, at 517; and Bothe holds that "Il est ... possible de conclure que le principe de la proportionalité constitue en effet un principe générale qui limite l'exercise de certains pouvoirs de l'autorité publique." M. Bothe, *Les Limits des pouvoirs du Conseil de Sécurité*. In: J.R. Dupuy (ed.), The Development of the Role of the Security Council (1993) 67-81, at 78.

774 *E.g.* Herdegen, *op. cit. supra* n.648, at 31.

> As a political body, the Security Council ... operates with a high degree of discretion; it acts neither necessarily nor regularly in all the situations that would seem to call for action, but operates, instead in a selective way. In addition, the Council is not bound to use uniform criteria in seemingly similar situations.[775]

In the *Tadić* case, moreover, the Trial Chamber held that:

> Certainly the International Tribunal is the first of its kind to be created. However, the fact that the Security Council has not taken a similar step in other, earlier cases cannot in itself be of any relevance in determining the legality of its action in this case.[776]

The argument might have been applicable if the Charter had not provided for the right of veto for the permanent members. As the situation prior to 1990 shows, the veto will preclude the Council from acting if a permanent state considers its interests threatened. In the current usage of the veto a consistent pattern is discernible. The three Western members support an active role for the Council, whilst China and Russia fear that an active Council will create precedents that could turn against them.[777] In this configuration it is difficult to achieve consistency in the Council's decision-making. A recent example is provided by NATO's military intervention in Kosovo.[778] Although the Security Council condemned the violence in the province and determined that it posed a threat to international peace and security in the region, Russia and China blocked further (military) action by the Council.[779] This prompted

---

[775] S. Boelaert-Suominen, *Iraqi War Reparations and the Laws of War: A Discussion of the Current Work of the United Nations Compensation Commission with Specific Reference to Environmental Damage During Warfare*, 50 Zeitschrift für öffentliches Recht (1996) 225-316, 251-252. See to the same effect Herdegen, *op. cit. supra* n.648, 31; Gowlland-Debbas, *op. cit. supra* n.2, 71. *Cf.* also Koskenniemi, who observes that "collective security under the U.N. Charter system ... involves little automation. Under the Charter, the decision whether and how to react is vested with the Council, which itself has broad discretion." Koskenniemi, *op. cit. supra* n.649, at 457.

[776] Trial Chamber Decision on the Defence Motion on Jurisdiction, *Prosecutor v. Dusko Tadić a/k/a "Dule"*, Case No. IT-94-1-T, 10 Aug. 1995, at 12. In this the Trial Chamber followed the Prosecutor, who had submitted that as "a political organ of the United Nations, the Security Council is not called upon to repress serious violations of international humanitarian law on a consistent and uniform legal basis." 'Prosecutor's Response to the Motion of the Defence on the Jurisdiction of the Tribunal', quoted by King, *op. cit. supra* n.725, at 566.

[777] *Cf.* the statement of the Chinese President Jiang Zemin during the second meeting of the Security Council at the level of Heads of State and Government on 7 Sept. 2000. He stated that: "History has proven that the success of United Nations peacekeeping operations depends on observance of the purposes and principles of the United Nations Charter, particularly respect for State sovereignty, non-interference in the internal affairs of recipient countries, neutrality and non-use of force except in self-defence". See Press Release SC/6919, 7 Sept. 2000.

[778] On which see *supra*, the text accompanying notes 467-469.

[779] See Cassese, *op. cit. supra* n.468, 25.

three permanent members to take action without a clear mandate by the Security Council.

By itself, therefore, the selectivity argument would not constitute an abuse of rights. It could, however, contribute to a plea that the Council has acted arbitrarily.[780] One would then have to demonstrate that the Council had consistently regarded a course of action as not being in breach of, or not posing a threat to, international peace and security. If the Council would suddenly reverse this practice and consider such actions as requiring action under Chapter VII, it could contribute to the plea that the Council was acting with ulterior motives.

From the inclusion of Article 2(2) in the Charter it follows that the criterion of good faith, and its corollary known as abuse of rights, is a criterion for the legality of a Security Council decision. These principles, however, are not clearly defined. Thus Cryer submits that: "Another possible limit on the council is the doctrine of abuse of power. ... Although it seems that this could become a feasible limit, it needs more entrenchment and clarification to become fully accepted."[781]

Indeed, it has been observed that the duty imposed on the Council by virtue of the good faith notion is of a rather general and broad nature.[782] Hence Judge Morelli in the *Certain Expenses* case held that:

> It is only in especially serious cases that an act of the Organization could be regarded as invalid, and hence an absolute nullity. Examples might be a resolution which had not obtained the required majority, or a resolution vitiated by a manifest *excès de pouvoir* (such as, in particular, a resolution the subject of which had nothing to do with the purposes of the Organization).[783]

It thus appears that the abuse of rights must be manifest, self-evident, or "gross".[784] Such an abuse would occur when the action was manifestly disproportionate or unnecessary as regards its aim, the restoration of international peace.[785] Of course,

---

[780] See *contra*, however, King, *op. cit. supra* n.725, at 569.

[781] Cryer, *op. cit. supra* n.648, at 169.

[782] *Cf.* Shaw: "the doctrines of good faith and abuse of rights may have some relevance as constraints of a rather general nature." Shaw, *op. cit. supra* n.771, at 226.

[783] *Certain Expenses* case, ICJ Rep. (1962), at 223.

[784] See Alvarez, who refers to the "test of 'manifest irregularity' or 'abuse of power/discretion' ..." Alvarez, *op. cit. supra* n.5, at 26; and Franck, who mentions a possible "gross abuse of discretion" by the Council. Franck, *op. cit. supra* n.771, at 37. *Cf.* R. Bernhardt, Ultra Vires *Activities of International Organizations*. In: J. Makarczyk (ed.), Theory of International Law at the Threshold of the 21st Century (1996) 599-609, 604.

[785] On proportionality see J. Delbrück, *Proportionality*, 7 EPIL (1984) 396-400. At 399 Delbrück notes that in the taking of "coercive economic sanctions ... a due relation between means and ends has to be observed, lest the coercive measures become illegal as a prohibited act of intervention into the

neither the principle of good faith nor the notion of gross or manifest abuse of rights are strictly defined legal concepts. In addition, supplying general rules for what constitutes an abuse of rights is nearly impossible. One would have to look at the particular circumstances of each case in order to determine whether the Council has acted *mala fides*.

Since the question whether the Council has acted in good faith is measured against its responsibility for the maintenance of international peace and security, Article 2(2) is intimately related to the Council's interpretation of international peace and security, and the general acceptability thereof. This aspect, the limits to the Council's freedom of making interpretations under Article 39, will be elaborated upon below.[786]

4.2.1.5 Article 2(7): Domestic Jurisdiction

Some commentators contend that Article 2(7) substantially limits the Council's powers. Thus Franck, for example, submits that: "the 'Greenwich foot' by which the actions taken by the Security Council in the name of 'collective' security are judged is Article 2(7) of the Charter."[787] Nowadays this contention is not tenable, however. The text of Article 2(7) itself provides that the "principle shall not prejudice the application of enforcement measures under Chapter VII." Moreover, as seen above, the domain exclusively reserved to States has been restricted, and on several occasions the Council has taken enforcement measures in essentially internal conflicts. With the exception of the South African and Rhodesian cases this interpretation of Article 2(7) has not

---

internal affairs of the State addressed by the measures." It is true that the Charter itself explicitly excludes enforcement measures taken by the Council by virtue of Chapter VII in its domestic jurisdiction clause (Article 2(7), on which see *infra*, paragraph 4.2.1.5). This, however, does not warrant the conclusion that 'coercive economic sanctions *authorized or ordered for by the Security Council* cannot constitute a prohibited intervention in the internal affairs of a State.' The Council's actions (*i.e* the taking of economic sanctions), and their subsequent implementation, will only be legal if the measures correspond to the threat they are addressing. *Cf.* Delbrück's contention that: "In view of the increasingly widespread recognition of the principle of proportionality in international law there is hardly any breach of it where the applicability of the principle could be denied." *Ibid.* In this context one might also refer to the 2nd Report of the Committee of the International Law Association (ILA) on *Accountability of International Organisations*, submitted to the ILA 2000 conference. Para. 29 thereof holds that: "Any action of an organ of an IO or of a treaty-organ is undertaken in order to achieve the objectives laid down in the constituent instrument. The principle of proportionality has to be interpreted and applied in relationship with other relevant principles such as good governance, the principle of constitutionality and the concept of functional necessity in order to constitute a relevant framework for the exercise of power."

786 See *infra*, paragraphs 4.2.3.1 and 5.3.5.

787 Franck, *op. cit. supra* n.109, at 219.

been seriously questioned, and the plea of non-interference in internal matters is therefore increasingly difficult to sustain.[788]

4.2.1.6 Articles 1 and 2 Generally: International Humanitarian Law

The applicability of international humanitarian law in United Nations enforcement actions has been contested in the legal doctrine.[789] Indeed, the United Nations is not, and probably cannot be, a party to the Geneva Conventions and other treaties concerning international humanitarian law. At present, however, there seems to be consensus that international humanitarian law is both applicable in cases of enforcement action *stricto sensu*, that is action taken by troops under a unified UN command, and in cases where national forces act pursuant to Security Council authorizations.[790] In this sense Bothe maintains: "The fact that the UN is not a state and does not possess certain organs which a state normally possesses is no excuse for not applying the law of war."[791] Gill, moreover, submits that:

> Once the UN authorizes Member States to carry out military enforcement measures, [the] duty rests both upon ... States ... and ... the Security Council itself to ensure that Member States carry out the UN mandate in accordance with applicable ... humanitarian law.[792]

In a similar fashion Shaw contends that: "One cannot easily envisage it being acceptable that the Council should by decision consciously breach the norms of the law of armed conflict."[793]

This understanding seems to be consistent with the Charter and the practice of the Security Council. As the preamble and Articles 1 and 2 indicate, the primary objective of the United Nations is the maintenance of international peace and security. The Council, moreover, has repeatedly recognized that violations of international

---

[788] See Cryer, *op. cit. supra* n.648, 170. See also *supra*, paragraph 3.15.1.1.

[789] See Schachter, *op. cit. supra* n.356, 465-467; Gill, *op. cit. supra* n.5, 79; Bothe, *op. cit. supra* n.388, 600; F. Seyersted, *United Nations Forces in the Law of Peace and War* (1966), 197-209; Greenwood, *op. cit. supra* n.712, 3-4.

[790] See Schachter, *op. cit. supra* n.356, 465-467; Gill, *op. cit. supra* n.5, 80. Both Schachter and Gill refer to the fact that during *Operation Desert Storm* the coalition forces went to considerable lengths to demonstrate that their actions were in conformity with international humanitarian law.

[791] Bothe, *op. cit. supra* n.388, at 600. *Cf.* Greenwood, *op. cit. supra* n.712, 15-17.

[792] Gill, *op. cit. supra* n.5, at 78. *Cf.* Gardam, *op. cit. supra* n.172, 318-319.

[793] Shaw, *op. cit. supra* n.771, at 230. To the same effect Reisman and Stevick submit that "we take it as unexceptional that when the community of nations applies coercion in defence of public order, it is subject to the same laws of war or humanitarian law that have been prescribed for others." Reisman, Stevick, *op. cit. supra* n.718, at 127. *Cf.* Schachter, *op. cit. supra* n.162, 75-76.

humanitarian law have repercussions on international peace and security. A rather awkward conclusion would ensue from the assumption that the Council itself can employ measures of which it has indicated that they threaten international peace and security.[794] Indeed, in its practice the Council has authorized the use of force (partially) based on non-observance of humanitarian law, for instance in the cases of Yugoslavia, Somalia and Rwanda. It would be illogical for the Council to initiate action based – partially at least – on non-compliance with international humanitarian law, and then in implementing that action not comply with that same law. Indeed, according to Gill:

> Humanitarian law ... forms part of the core values and principles of the Organization ... In founding the UN as primary repository of collective security, the Member States could not, in transferring or conferring the power to wage war and conduct military operations as an instrument of international peace and security by means which would violate these fundamental precepts. The Member States could not attribute to the Organization a power which they themselves did not and do not possess.[795]

Moreover, international humanitarian law applies whenever an international or internal armed conflict takes place. In the *Tadić* case the Appeals Chamber of the ICTY formulated this principle as follows:

> an armed conflict exists whenever there is a resort to armed force between States or protracted armed violence between governmental authorities and organized armed groups or between such groups within a State. International humanitarian law applies from the initiation of such armed conflicts and extends beyond the cessation of hostilities until a general conclusion of peace is reached; or, in the case of internal conflicts, a peaceful settlement is achieved.[796]

In other words, the Council has to ensure that armed forces acting pursuant to its decisions or authorizations respect at least the core principles of international humanitarian law. Part and parcel thereof are *inter alia* the principle of proportionality,[797] the duty to distinguish between civilian and military targets, and the prohibition on causing unnecessary suffering to combatants.[798] This was recognized by

---

[794] The counter argument that an authorization by the Council to use force will also necessarily have detrimental effects on international peace and security is not valid, for the ensuing actions are based on the illegality of the action which is sought to be remedied by the authorized action. It is thus a lawful resort to the use of force (*jus ad bellum*).

[795] Gill, *op. cit. supra* n.5, at 82.

[796] Appeals Chamber Decision on the Tadić Jurisdictional Motion, *Prosecutor v. Dusko Tadić a/k/a "Dule"*, Case No. IT-94-1-AR72, 2 Oct. 1995, para. 70.

[797] See Schachter, *op. cit. supra* n.356, 460 and 466; Alvarez, *op. cit. supra* n.5, 27; Delbrück, *op. cit. supra* n.785, 398.

[798] *Cf.* the Adv. Op. by the International Court of Justice on the *Legality of the Threat or Use of Nuclear Weapons*, issued 8 July 1996. In para. 78 the Court refers to the "cardinal principles" of humanitarian law: "The first is aimed at the protection of the civilian population and civilian objects

the United Nations Secretary-General in a Bulletin issued on 6 August 1999.[799] Herein he "promulgates" that the "fundamental principles and rules of international humanitarian law set out in the present bulletin are applicable to United Nations forces ... in enforcement actions, or in peacekeeping operations when the use of force is permitted in self-defence." These principles and rules include a duty to "make a clear distinction at all times between civilians and combatants and between civilian objects and military objectives",[800] and a prohibition on the use of weapons or "methods of warfare which may cause superfluous injury or unnecessary suffering."[801] The Bulletin, moreover, holds that "members of the military personnel of a United Nations force are subject to prosecution in their national courts" in case they violate international humanitarian law.[802]

4.2.1.7 Interim Conclusions

From the above it follows that several purposes and principles of the United Nations provide limitations on the Council's powers under Chapter VII of the Charter. Specifically, Articles 1(2) on self-determination, 1(3) on human rights, 2(1) on sovereign equality, 2(2) on good faith and 2(7) on domestic jurisdiction, could provide for limitations on the Council's powers. A closer look at these Articles reveals that

---

and establishes the distinction between combatants and non-combatants; States must never make civilians the object of attack and must consequently never use weapons that are incapable of distinguishing between civilian and military targets. According to the second principle, it is prohibited to cause unnecessary suffering to combatants: it is accordingly prohibited to use weapons causing them such harm or uselessly aggravating their suffering. In application of that second principle, States do not have unlimited freedom of choice of means in the weapons they use." In the *Tadić* case, moreover, the ICTY held that the customary laws of war include "the regime of protection established under Common Article 3 [of the 1949 Geneva Conventions] applicable to armed conflicts not of an international character, as a reflection of elementary considerations of humanity, and which is applicable to armed conflicts in general". Trial Chamber, *Prosecutor v. Dusko Tadić a/k/a "Dule"*, Case No. IT-94-1, Opinion and Judgment, 7 May 1997, para. 609.

799 Secretary-General's Bulletin on 'Observance by United Nations Forces of International Humanitarian Law', ST/SGB/1999/13, 6 Aug. 1999.

800 *Ibid.*, section 5.1

801 *Ibid.*, section 6. It may be noted that, conversely, United Nations forces are also protected by international humanitarian law. In order to provide for additional protection for these forces the United Nations adopted the 'Convention on the Safety of United Nations and Associated Personnel' on 9 Dec. 1994. For an assessment of the Convention see E.T. Bloom, *Protecting Peacekeepers: The Convention on the Safety of United Nations and Associated Personnel*, 89 AJIL (1995) 621-631. See also Greenwood, *op. cit. supra* n.712.

802 *Ibid.*, section 4.

Articles 1(2), 1(3) and 2(2) in particular provide for the outer limits of legal Security Council action. Articles 1 and 2, in conjunction with the preamble, warrant the conclusion that the Council is bound by international humanitarian law.

The domestic jurisdiction clause contained in Article 2(7) has gradually eroded in UN practice, a practice in which less and less matters are treated as matters falling within the exclusive domestic jurisdiction of states. Moreover, Article 2(7) itself makes an exception for enforcement measures by the Council. A plea that the Council cannot interfere in a situation because that situation falls within the domestic jurisdiction of a targeted state, is therefore difficult to sustain. In a similar way, the concept of sovereignty, mentioned in Article 2(1), has lost ground in international relations. The terms employed in Article 2(1), moreover, seem too general to provide for specific limitations. Furthermore, since the imposition of sanctions will necessarily infringe upon states' sovereignty, an argument to the effect that the Council cannot interfere in matters belonging to the sovereignty of a state would render the provisions of Articles 41 and 42 redundant. The inclusion of Article 2(1) in the Charter, however, does preclude the Council from permanently infringing upon a state's sovereignty against the will of that state.

From Article 1(2) it follows that the Council should exercise its responsibilities in good faith. Article 1(3), moreover, implies that the Council should evaluate the impact of its actions against the human rights of the population of a targeted state. The imposition of sanctions, however, will nearly always detrimentally affect a state's population. Such sanctions will have to pass a test of proportionality: only if the Council's actions are proportionate in relation to the threat or breach of the peace, can they be said to be legal. The picture is different with regard to the limits provided by Articles 1(2) and Articles 1 and 2 in conjunction with the preamble. Contrary to human rights, which will at times have to be affected by Security Council enforcement measures, the right to self-determination and the core principles of international humanitarian law may not be violated under any circumstance.

4.2.2 Procedural Limits: Articles 27(3), 31 and 24(3) of the Charter

According to Article 27(3) a decision on non-procedural matters can be vetoed by a permanent member, whilst for it to be validly adopted it would require an additional affirmative vote of four out of nine non-permanent members. This requirement of unanimity among the permanent members effectively worked as a limit to the Council's powers prior to 1990.[803] In fact, as seen in chapter 3, during that period there were

[803] For an overview of the usage of the veto see A.V. Patil, *The UN Veto in World Affairs, 1946-1990:*

only two cases (South Africa and Southern Rhodesia) in which the Council was able to take enforcement measures under Chapter VII. This provision thus works as a limit to the Council's powers, albeit that the current US dominance in international affairs has led to concerns about the effectiveness of this limit in the early 1990s.[804]

Article 31 provides that:

Any Member of the United Nations which is not a member of the Security Council may participate, without vote, in the discussion of any question brought before the Security Council whenever the latter considers that the interests of that Member are specially affected.

This formula has been incorporated in Article 37 of the Provisional Rules of Procedure of the Security Council.[805] From this it has been inferred that if the Council is deciding on measures against a state under Chapter VII "quite certainly, the government of that country must be heard in accordance with Rule 37 of the Rules of Procedure of the Security Council. No sanctions may be imposed out of the blue."[806] Although this statement is correct in principle, it would be difficult to maintain that Article 31 of the Charter, in conjunction with Article 37 of the Provisional Rules of Procedure, amounts to a strict legal rule, in the sense that a decision taken by the Council without the participation of a specially affected state would automatically be invalid. The language of Article 31 and Rule 37 is permissive rather than obligatory, and it would seem that in the event the Council has strong indications that the participation of a state "whose interest is specially affected" would not alter the course of the decisions made it would not be obliged to invite that state. In its practice, however, the Council has abided by Article 31 quite scrupulously.[807]

Article 24(3) of the Charter stipulates that "the Security Council shall submit annual and, when necessary, special reports to the General Assembly for its consideration." It has been maintained that this article "could be considered as limiting or qualifying the discretionary powers of the Security Council".[808] Indeed from this duty to report

---

A Complete Record and Case Histories of the Security Council's Veto (1992).

804 See *infra*, paragraph 6.1.

805 Provisional Rules of Procedure of the Security Council, as amended 21 Dec. 1982. Article 37 holds that: "Any Member of the United Nations which is not a member of the Security Council may be invited, as the result of the decision of the Security Council to participate, without vote, in the discussion of any question brought before the Security Council when the Security Council considers that the interests of that Member are specially affected."

806 Tomuschat, *op. cit. supra* n.7, at 46.

807 See Bailey, Daws, *op. cit. supra* n.51, 154-161.

808 Nkala, *op. cit. supra* n.239, at 174. *Cf.* Suy, *op. cit. supra* n.740, 243.

to the General Assembly it has been argued that the Security Council is subordinate to the General Assembly.[809] However, as observed by Delbrück, the General Assembly "does not possess of any right to sanction decisions or acts" of the Security Council.[810] Therefore, one cannot but agree with Nkala, when he states that the limitation provided for by Article 24(3) is more "apparent than real."[811]

4.2.3 The provisions of Chapter VII

A distinction can be made between the determination that a situation poses a threat to, or a breach of international peace and security (Article 39), and the measures decided upon by the Council pursuant to that determination (Articles 41 and 42). The extent of, and limits to, the discretion accorded to the Council in making a determination under Article 39, and acting on that determination pursuant to Articles 41 and 42, will be considered below.

4.2.3.1 Seizure by the Council Under Article 39

Crucial to Chapter VII is Article 39, which holds that the Council shall determine whether an act of aggression or a threat to – or breach of – international peace and security has occurred. Such a determination opens the door to the extensive powers of the Council under Articles 41 and 42 of the Charter.

The first question that arises in this respect is whether Article 39 provides for a procedural limit. In other words, is an Article 39 determination a necessary precondition for taking further action under Chapter VII? The answer must be in the affirmative. Although the Council's terminology relating to its determinations under Article 39 has not always been very been consistent,[812] the provisions of Article 39 are unambiguous in that such a determination is necessary before the Council may take further (enforcement) measures under Chapter VII. Thus Gowlland-Debbas, for example, observes that "before applying mandatory measures of Articles 41 and 42 of the Charter, the Council has to make a preliminary finding under Article 39."[813]

---

809 See Delbrück, *op. cit. supra* n.107, 404.

810 *Ibid.*, at 405.

811 Nkala, *op. cit. supra* n.239, at 174.

812 See *supra*, paragraph 3.15.2.1.

813 Gowlland-Debbas, *op. cit. supra* n.2, at 61. See to the same effect Schrijver, *op. cit. supra* n.510, 144; Frowein, *op. cit. supra* n.124, 612-613. See further Bailey, Daws, *op. cit. supra* n.51, 271; J.A. Frowein, *Legal Consequences for International Law Enforcement in Case of Security Council Inaction*. In: J. Delbrück

This is substantiated by the practice of the Council, which has consistently referred to the impact of situations on international peace and security, albeit in somewhat inconsistent terms. The conclusion following from this is that decisions contained in a resolution that does not include a prior determination under Article 39, cannot be considered binding decisions under Chapter VII of the Charter. In this sense Article 39 is to be regarded as a procedural limit on the Council's authority under Chapter VII. It may be recalled that decisions under Article 39 are non-procedural and hence subject to the voting requirements of Article 27(3).

The more important issue relates to the extent of the Council's freedom to determine whether an action or a situation falls within the category of 'threats to the peace', 'breaches of the peace', or 'acts of aggression.' This question has given rise to sharp debates. Doubts and concerns as to the validity of – implicit or explicit – Council determinations under Article 39, have been expressed in nearly all the cases in which the Council has taken enforcement measures under Chapter VII. These concerns were particularly strong with regard to the sanctions taken against Iraq, Libya and (former) Yugoslavia. In the context of Libya, for example, it may be recalled that the Security Council determined in resolution 748 (1992) that Libya's non-compliance with resolution 731 (1992), which incorporates the American and British requests for the extradition of those suspected of the bombing, constituted a threat to international peace and security. Several commentators have expressed doubts as to the validity of this decision. Thus Graefrath submits that:

> it remains absolutely unclear why or how the failure to renunciate terrorism by concrete actions ... or the failure to surrender suspects, or the refusal of compensation claims which are not established under any legal procedure, could constitute a threat to the peace.[814]

And in a similar fashion Weller holds that:

> the widening of Council jurisdiction to tackle prospective cases of 'terrorism' is to be encouraged, as these can indeed under certain circumstances be considered 'threats to international peace and security.' But the use of that label retroactively to deal with a case which, when it occurred some three years earlier was not considered a threat to international peace and security is not likely to encourage this tender trend.[815]

With regard to the sanctions against Iraq, moreover, it has been submitted that by guaranteeing the inviolability of the boundary between Iraq and Kuwait in resolution

---

(ed.), The Future of International Law Enforcement: New Scenarios – New Law? (1993) 111-124, 114.

[814] Graefrath, *op. cit. supra* n.7, at 196.

[815] Weller, *op. cit. supra* n.7, at 323.

687 (1991), the Council had engaged in "a preventive act not covered by Article 39 of the Charter which requires an actual, not a potential danger."[816]

An often-quoted passage by Judge Shahabuddeen in the *Lockerbie* case aptly describes the problem at hand:

> The question now is whether a decision of the Security Council may override the legal rights of States, and, if so, whether there are any limitations on the power of the Council to characterize a situation as one justifying the making of a decision entailing such consequences. Are there any limits to the Council's power of appreciation? In the equilibrium of forces underpinning the structure of the United Nations within the evolving international order, is there any conceivable point beyond which a legal issue may properly arise as to the competence of the Security Council to produce such overriding results? If there are any limits, what are those limits and what body, if other than the Security Council, is competent to say what those limits are?[817]

The Charter does not contain a definition of international peace and security, nor of aggression. As seen above,[818] it was decided to give the Council a large degree of freedom in deciding whether or not a situation falls within one of these three categories. Proposals to include a definition of aggression in the Charter, for example, were defeated as being incompatible with the Council's freedom, and as being inconsistent with the need for an effective Council. From this it follows that the Council has a very wide margin of appreciation in making determinations under Article 39.[819] Nearly all commentators subscribe to this view. Shaw, for example, refers to the extremely "wide discretion to exercise its judgement as to whether an Article 39 situation exists" granted to the Council by the Charter.[820] And in a similar vein Zemanek observes that: "Since the Security Council determines itself whether one of these situations [mentioned in Article 39] exists, and has successfully warded off attempts to define them precisely, it has a wide discretionary power."[821]

---

816 Zemanek, *op. cit. supra* n.701, at 630.

817 *Questions of Interpretation and Application of the 1971 Montreal Convention Arising from the Aerial Incident at Lockerbie* (Prov. Measures), Libya v. US, Sep. Op. Shahabuddeen, ICJ Rep. (1992), at 142.

818 See *supra*, the text accompanying notes 131-139.

819 See also *infra*, paragraph 5.3.5.

820 Shaw, *op. cit. supra* n.771, at 226.

821 Zemanek, *op. cit. supra* n.701, at 635. Similar views are held by King, who holds that: "The Council's decision on whether a situation constitutes a threat to the peace is particularly difficult to circumscribe." King, *op. cit. supra* n.725, at 581; Judge Weeramantry, who contends that "the determination under Article 39 of the existence of any threat to the peace, breach of the peace or act of aggression, is one entirely within the discretion of the Council". *Questions of Interpretation and Application of the 1971 Montreal Convention Arising from the Aerial Incident at Lockerbie* (Prov. Measures), Libya v. UK, Diss. Op. Weeramantry, ICJ Rep. (1992), at 66; Herdegen, who submits that: "Im Einklang mit der Entstehungsgeschichte und dem historischen Willen der Gründerväter der Vereinten Nationen versteht die herrschende Völkerrechtslehre Art. 39 der Charta als Ermächtigung mit großem Gestaltungsspielraum im Hinblick auf die Konkretisierung der

The leeway available to the Council has also been (provisionally) affirmed by the International Court of Justice in the *Lockerbie* case. Herein the Court affirmed the *prima facie* validity of the resolution,[822] notwithstanding some concerns expressed by individual judges as to whether the non-extradition of the suspects by Libya warranted a Council determination under Article 39.[823] If any conclusions may be drawn from the case as it has developed until now, it would be that the Council enjoys a large degree of discretion in making a determination under Article 39.[824]

Another challenge to the validity of a Council determination under Article 39 was raised in the *Tadić* case. Herein the Appeals Chamber of the ICTY dealt with the objection of the defence as to the jurisdiction of the Tribunal.[825] After finding that the ICTY was competent to examine the validity of its establishment,[826] quite a remarkable

---

unbestimmten Rechtsbegriffe dieser Vorschrift." M. Herdegen, *Der Sicherheitsrat und die autoritative Konkretisierung des VII Kapitels der UN-Charter*. In: U. Beyerlin, *et. al.* (eds.), Recht zwischen Umbruch und Bewahrung (1995) 103-109, at 107-108; Schachter, who states that the determination by the Council under Article 39 "is generally considered discretionary and final." Schachter, *op. cit. supra* n.673, at 12; Akehurst, submitting that "a threat to the peace is whatever the Security Council says is a threat to the peace." M. Akehurst, *A Modern Introduction to International Law* (1987), at 219. Similarly, Reisman notes that the "United Nations system was essentially designed to enable the Permanent Five, if all agree, to use Charter obligations and the symbolic authority of the organization as they think appropriate to maintain or restore international peace, as they define it." Reisman, *op. cit. supra* n.133, at 418. And Kooijmans refers to "the complete discretion the Security Council has with regard to the interpretation of the three concepts 'threat to the peace', 'breach of the peace' and 'act of aggression'." Kooijmans, *op. cit. supra* n.133, at 111; whilst Bothe maintains that with regard to the concept of peace and threats thereto "il est difficile de trouver des limites." Bothe, *op. cit. supra* n.773, at 72.

822 See *Questions of Interpretation and Application of the 1971 Montreal Convention Arising from the Aerial Incident at Lockerbie* (Prov. Measures), Libya v. US, ICJ Rep. (1992), para. 42.

823 Bedjaoui, for example, observes that "no small number of people may find it disconcerting that the horrific Lockerbie bombing should be seen today as an urgent threat to international peace when it took place over three years ago." Diss. Op. Bedjaoui, *Questions of Interpretation and Application of the 1971 Montreal Convention Arising from the Aerial Incident at Lockerbie* (Prov. Measures), Libya v. US, Diss. Op. Bedjaoui, ICJ Rep. (1992), at 153.

824 For a detailed assessment of the case see *infra*, paragraphs 5.3.4.4-5.3.4.4.9.

825 Appeals Chamber Decision on the Tadić Jurisdictional Motion, *Prosecutor v. Dusko Tadić a/k/a "Dule"*, Case No. IT-94-1-AR72, 2 Oct. 1995. For a review of this decision see King, *op. cit. supra* n.725.

826 The Chamber first held in para. 12. that "if the International Tribunal were not validly constituted, it would lack the legitimate power to decide in time or space or over any person or subject-matter ... This issue is a preliminary to and conditions all other aspects of jurisdiction." It then concluded that the *compétence de la compétence* principle is part of every international tribunal's 'incidental' jurisdiction (*ibid.*, para. 18); that the Statute did not contain a limitative provision in this respect (para. 19); that "the question before the Appeals Chamber is whether the International Tribunal, in exercising this 'incidental' jurisdiction, can examine the legality of its establishment by

decision in itself,[827] the Chamber gave its decision on the following question: "Was there really a threat to the peace justifying the invocation of Chapter VII as a legal basis for the establishment of the International Tribunal?"[828]

The Appeals Chamber held that the text of Article 39 shows that the Security Council "exercises a very wide discretion under this Article."[829] As seen above, however, in exercising its responsibilities the Council is obliged to respect the purposes and principles of the Charter. This was stated by the Chamber in the following terms: "the determination that there exists such a threat is not a totally unfettered discretion, as it has to remain, at the very least, within the limits of the Purposes and Principles of the Charter."[830]

Thus the conclusion to be drawn is that the Council enjoys a very wide discretion, but that in making a determination under Article 39 it is limited by the purposes and principles of the Charter. As was determined above this means, amongst other things, that the Council should act in good faith and may not abuse its rights or act arbitrarily. In this context one might refer to the *Namibia* case, in which Judge Fitzmaurice remarked that "the Security Council can act in the preservation of peace and security, provided the threat said to be involved is not a mere figment or pretext."[831] And in the

---

the Security Council, solely for the purpose of ascertaining its own 'primary' jurisdiction over the case before it" (para. 20); that the case law of the International Court of Justice supports an affirmative answer to this question (para. 21); and that hence "the International Tribunal has jurisdiction to examine the plea against its jurisdiction based on the invalidity of its establishment by the Security Council" (para. 22).

[827] At an earlier stage the Trial Chamber had refused to examine the legality of its establishment, *inter alia* on the grounds that "The broad discretion given to the Security Council in the exercise of its Chapter VII authority itself suggests that decisions taken under this head are not reviewable." Trial Chamber Decision on the Defence Motion on Jurisdiction, *Prosecutor v. Dusko Tadić a/k/a "Dule"*, Case No. IT-94-1-T, 10 Aug. 1995, para. 7 at 5. On judicial review see *infra*, paragraphs 5.3.5-5.3.9.

[828] Appeals Chamber Decision on the Tadić Jurisdictional Motion, *Prosecutor v. Dusko Tadić a/k/a "Dule"*, Case No. IT-94-1-AR72, 2 Oct. 1995, para. 27.

[829] *Ibid.*, para. 28.

[830] *Ibid.*, para. 29. So also Judge Sidhwa, in his separate opinion, held that: "All exercise of discretionary power is subject to the rules of fairness and reasonableness and to the jurisdictional limits provided, or which fairly and inherently can be assumed out of the objects and purposes that call for its exercise and the surrounding circumstances that create its need." *Ibid.*, Sep. Op. Sidhwa, para. 21.

[831] *Legal Consequences for States of the Continued Presence of South Africa in Namibia (South West Africa) notwithstanding Security Council Resolution 276*, Adv. Op., ICJ Rep. (1971), at 293. At 294, moreover, he states that "limitations on the powers of the Security Council are necessary because of the all too great ease with which any acutely controversial international situation can be represented as involving a latent threat to peace and security, even where it is really too remote genuinely to be

same case Judge Gross maintained that: "To assert that a matter may have a distant repercussion on the maintenance of peace is not enough to turn the Security Council into a world government."[832]

This position is supported by most commentators. Thus Franck observes that the Council may only take enforcement measures in matters that would otherwise fall under the domestic jurisdiction of a state (Article 2(7) of the Charter), if the Council"has discovered a *bona fide* 'threat to the peace, breach of the peace, or act of aggression'."[833] And Shaw submits that with regard to determinations under Article 39 "the Council would appear to possess the fullest discretion or widest latitude limited only by inherent notions of good faith and non-abuse of rights."[834] Similarly, Brownlie observes that:

> A determination of a threat to the peace as a basis for action necessary to remove the threat to the peace, cannot be used as a basis for action which – if the evidence so indicates – is for collateral and independent purposes, such as the overthrow of a government or the partition of a State.[835]

One may thus conclude that the Council's latitude to determine whether a situation poses a threat to international peace and security is very great, but is nevertheless limited by the obligation to act in good faith. Inherent to the issue of the extent of the Council's powers of appreciation under Article 39, however, is the political question doctrine. In short, this relates to whether there are any legal standards according to which the Council's determinations made under Article 39 can be judged, or whether this is a matter of policy which lies beyond legal scrutiny. This question will be addressed below.[836]

4.2.3.2 Measures Under Articles 41 and 42

The next question related to the powers of the Council under Chapter VII concerns the range of measures the Council may employ under Articles 41 and 42, once an Article 39 determination has been made. Again the text of the Charter appears to grant the Council great leeway in this respect. This was affirmed by the ICTY in the *Tadić* case.

---

one."

832 *Ibid.*, at 340.

833 Franck, *op. cit. supra* n.109, at 221.

834 Shaw, *op. cit. supra* n.771, at 234.

835 I. Brownlie, *The Decisions of Political Organs of the United Nations and the Rule of Law*. In: R.St.J. MacDonald (ed.), Essays in Honour of Wang Tieya (1994) 91-102, at 96.

836 See *infra*, paragraph 5.3.5.

In that case the Appeals Chamber addressed the contention made by the defence that the establishment of the tribunal "was never contemplated by the framers of the Charter as one of the measures to be taken under Chapter VII, as witnessed by the fact that it figures nowhere in the provisions of that Chapter, and more particularly in Articles 41 and 42."[837] Whilst observing in general terms that "Articles 41 and 42 leave to the Security Council such a wide choice as not to warrant searching, on functional or other grounds, for even wider and more general powers than those already expressly provided for in the Charter",[838] the Chamber concluded that "the measures set out in Article 41 are merely illustrative examples which obviously do not exclude other measures. All the Article requires is that they do not involve the use of force."[839]

The Chamber, moreover, rejected the contention of the defence that:

> the Security Council is constitutionally inherently incapable of creating a judicial organ, as it is conceived in the Charter as an executive organ, hence not possessed of judicial powers which can be exercised through a subsidiary organ.[840]

In a somewhat concise manner the Chamber concluded that the Security Council was not "usurping for itself part of a judicial function which does not belong to it" but that the Council had:

> resorted to the establishment of a judicial organ in the form of an international criminal tribunal as an instrument for the exercise of its own principal function of maintenance of peace and security, *i.e.*, as a measure contributing to the restoration and maintenance of peace in the former Yugoslavia.[841]

Thus under Articles 41 and 42 the Council also enjoys a wide discretion. In the words of King, the "conclusion that emerges ... is that the language of Article 41 provides no specific limits on the types of measures the Security Council can take in response to a threat to the peace."[842]

Similar to a determination under Article 39, however, the Council would be bound by the purposes and principles of the Charter when taking action under Articles 41

---

[837] Appeals Chamber Decision on the Tadić Jurisdictional Motion, *Prosecutor v. Dusko Tadić a/k/a "Dule"*, Case No. IT-94-1-AR72, 2 Oct. 1995, para. 32. *Cf.* Zemanek, *op. cit. supra* n.701. Zemanek maintains at 631 that "in establishing International Criminal Tribunals for the former Yugoslavia and for Rwanda, the Security Council exercised again legislative powers which are not evident from the Charter."

[838] Appeals Chamber Decision on the Tadić Jurisdictional Motion, *Prosecutor v. Dusko Tadić a/k/a "Dule"*, Case No. IT-94-1-AR72, 2 Oct. 1995, para. 31.

[839] *Ibid.*, para. 35.

[840] *Ibid.*, para. 32.

[841] *Ibid.*, para. 38.

[842] King, *op. cit. supra* n.725, at 588.

and 42 of the Charter. As seen above this *inter alia* implies a duty to act in good faith, meaning that one should determine "whether the responsive measure selected by the Security Council was commensurate with the threat to the peace it had identified."[843] In this context Brownlie observes that the concepts of "purpose and necessity" are relevant to the Council's choice of measures under Articles 41 and 42 particularly because it "cannot be *ex hypothesi* necessary to select a method of implementation which is incompatible with general international law."[844] And Shaw also takes note of the "extensive" discretion afforded the Security Council under the Charter scheme "as regards actions taken consequent upon the determination in order to maintain or restore international peace and security." At the same time, however, he maintains that:

> the more subsidiary such measures are and the further away from the initial action taken in the exercise of the primary responsibility to restore international peace and security, the stronger grows the case for the application of international legal principles.[845]

The purposes and principles of the Charter, moreover, require the Council to weigh the impact of its decisions on the human rights of a targeted population, and to respect the right of self-determination and international humanitarian law in deciding on measures under Articles 41 and 42.[846] In the context of Article 42, this means that the Council should abide by the humanitarian laws of war, including the principles of proportionality and necessity.[847] Note that the principle of proportionality is not only applicable to the *jus in bello*, but also to the *jus ad bellum*.[848] That is, measures taken under Article 42 should be proportionate to the threats to the peace which they address. If, for example, the Security Council issues an authorization to "use all necessary means" to secure the compliance of a state with its obligations under the 1989 Universal Postal Convention to "forward always by the quickest routes which it uses for its own items, closed mails and à découvert letter-post items which are passed to it", this might conceivably lead to doubts as to the proportionality of the

[843] *Ibid.*, at 587. This is not the same as testing their effectiveness in restoring international peace and security, for as the Appeals Chamber of the ICTY held: "it would be a total misconception of what are the criteria of legality and validity in law to test the legality of such measures *ex post facto* by their success or failure to achieve their ends." Appeals Chamber Decision on the Tadić Jurisdictional Motion, *Prosecutor v. Dusko Tadić a/k/a "Dule"*, Case No. IT-94-1-AR72, 2 Oct. 1995, para. 39.

[844] Brownlie, *op. cit. supra* n.835, at 96. See also Zemanek, *op. cit. supra* n.701, 639.

[845] Shaw, *op. cit. supra* n.771, at 234-235.

[846] See *supra*, paragraphs 4.2.1.1 and 4.2.1.6.

[847] Kirgis, *op. cit. supra* n.129, at 517. See also *supra*, paragraph 4.2.1.6.

[848] See J.G. Gardam, *Proportionality and Force in International Law*, 87 AJIL (1993) 391-413, 391.

authorization.[849] The proportionality principle also implies that the Council may not inflict punishment on a state for its past behavior. Doubts have been cast on the Council's compliance with this requirement in the case of Iraq.[850]

4.2.3.3 Article 51: Self-Defence

It may be recalled that Article 51 holds that:

> Nothing in the present Charter shall impair the inherent right of individual or collective self-defence if an armed attack occurs against a Member of the United Nations, until the Security Council has taken measures necessary to maintain international peace and security.

The correct interpretation of this Article in relation to the authority of the Council under Chapter VII is that the right of self-defence by a state can only be curtailed to the extent that the Council orders effective actions against the aggressor state. In other words, if the Council fails to take action that brings an end to the basis for self-defence, the right must be considered to remain in effect.[851] The problems associated with ineffective measures is described by Shaw in the following terms:

> Ineffective collective security measures coupled with a presumed overriding of the inherent right to self-defence represents the worst of both worlds and in terms of political reality is likely simply to be ignored as states placed in such a position seek to disregard such sanctions in practice often with the connivance of third states.[852]

Article 51 provides for a limit to the Council's powers: ineffective measures can result in lawful non-compliance with those measures.[853] It has, for example, been maintained

---

[849] Dicey once said that: "If a legislature decided that all blue-eyed babies should be murdered, the preservation of blue-eyed babies would be illegal; but legislators must go mad before they could pass such a law, and subjects be idiotic before they could submit to it." A.V. Dicey, *Introduction to the Study of the Law of the Constitution* (1959), at 81. Quoted by H.G.A. Wright, *Sovereignty of the People – the New Constitutional Grundnorm*, 26 Federal Law Review, no. 1 (1998). Accessed at http://law.anu.edu.au on 15 Aug. 2000. The above course of action would indeed be mad, but sometimes extreme examples help illustrate the problem at hand.

[850] Graefrath and Mohr submit that: "International legal sanctions, even if responding to the crime of aggression, cannot have the function of inflicting punishment, neither on the State nor on the people of Iraq." Graefrath, Mohr, *op. cit. supra* n.357, at 136.

[851] See B. Conforti, *Le Pouvoir Discrétionnaire du Conseil de Sécurité en Matière de Constatation d'une Menace Contre la Paix, d'une Rupture de la Paix ou d'un Acte d'Agression*. In: J.R. Dupuy, The Development of the Role of the Security Council (1993) 51-60, at 55; Herdegen, *op. cit. supra* n.648, at 28; Gill, *op. cit. supra* n.5, 91-104; Lavalle, *op. cit. supra* n.367, 62; M. Halberstam, *The Right to Self-defense once the Security Council takes Action*, 17 MJIL (1996) 229-248, 248.

[852] Shaw, *op. cit. supra* n.771, at 232.

[853] On such non-compliance see also *infra*, text accompanying note 931.

that by imposing a weapons embargo on the whole territory of the former Yugoslavia by resolution 713 (1991) the Council "impaired the inherent right of Bosnia-Herzegovina under Article 51 of the Charter to defend itself effectively against attacks."[854] Indeed, after the so-called 'safe areas' Srebrenica and Zepa were overrun in July 1995 the US Senate and House of Representatives passed a Bill that required the US lift the arms embargo against Bosnia-Herzegovina,[855] but President Clinton vetoed these proposals on 11 August 1995.[856]

4.2.4 Miscellaneous Charter Provisions

Article 7(1) establishes the principal organs of the United Nations, and Article 92 holds that the International Court of Justice shall be the "principal judicial organ of the United Nations." From this it has been inferred that the Council should not intervene in the Court's judicial domain.[857] The issue has arisen in the *Lockerbie* and *Bosnia* cases, and relates to the litispendence principle, which will be addressed below.[858]

After determining the limits to the Council' authority under Chapter VII contained in its constituent instrument, it is now time to turn to the question of extra-Charter limitations.

4.3 Extra-Charter Constraints

In addition to the Charter, general international law may provide limitations to the Council's enforcement authority. The following will examine possible constraints

---

854 Zemanek, *op. cit. supra* n.701, at 630. *Cf.* the Application of Bosnia-Herzegovina in the *Bosnia* case, that "under the circumstances set forth above, Bosnia and Herzegovina has the sovereign right to defend Itself and its People under United Nations Charter Article 51 and customary international law, including by means of immediately obtaining military weapons, equipment, supplies and troops from other States." *Application of the Convention on the Prevention and Punishment of the Crime of Genocide*, Bosnia and Herzegovina v. Yugoslavia (Serbia and Montenegro), Application instituting proceedings, filed 20 March 1993, para. 35.

855 See S. Robinson, 'US Senate votes to lift Bosnian arms embargo', available at http://www.telegraph.co.uk.

856 See 'Clinton vetoes arms embargo', 11 August 1995. Available at http://www.cnn.com.

857 *E.g.* Graefrath, *op. cit. supra* n.7.

858 The litispendence principle regulates the allocation of jurisdiction when two or more organs are seized of the same dispute. The applicability of the principle in the relations between the International Court of Justice and the Security Council will be considered *infra*, paragraphs 5.3.2.1-5.3.4.5.

stemming from the sources of international law as defined in Article 38(1) of the Statute of the International Court of Justice.[859]

4.3.1 Treaty Law

As Article 38(1) lists international conventions as the first source of international law, the first question dealt with here is whether the Council ought to respect treaty law in force between states when acting under Chapter VII. May the Council, for example, order the closing down of a pipeline by State B in order to prevent State A from exporting oil through that pipeline, notwithstanding a treaty between both states by which State B has undertaken to take all measures within its legal powers to ensure that the pipeline remains operative at all times? Article 103 of the Charter seems to settle this issue. In full it reads:

> In the event of a conflict between the obligations of the Members of the United Nations under the present Charter and their obligations under any other international agreement, their obligations under the present Charter shall prevail.

Thus the Charter expressly provides for the primacy of the Charter over other treaty-based obligations. Therefore, reference to the incompatibility of a Security Council resolution with rights enjoyed under other treaties could in itself not invalidate a Council resolution.[860] It has been argued that Article 103 does not relate to *rights* enjoyed under treaty law, since it only refers to possible conflicts of obligations.[861] This, however, appears to be an incorrect and excessively legalistic interpretation of the article, the purpose of which is to ensure that the Charter has a higher rank than other treaties.[862] Obligations and rights are, moreover, two sides of the same coin.[863]

---

[859] Which reads: "The Court, whose function is to decide in accordance with international law such disputes as are submitted to it, shall apply:
(a) international conventions, whether general or particular, establishing rules expressly recognized by the contesting states;
(b) international custom, as evidence of a general practice accepted as law;
(c) the general principles of law recognized by civilized nations ...".

[860] Reisman even states that: "The synergy of Articles 25 and 103 ... trumps *all* contrary non-Charter legal obligations." Reisman, *op. cit. supra* n.7, at 93 [emphasis added].

[861] See Shaw, *op. cit. supra* n.771, 229-232.

[862] Bernhardt, *op. cit. supra* n.732, 1119. *Cf.* Art. 30(1) of the 1969 Vienna Convention on the Law of Treaties, according to which "the rights and obligations of States parties to successive treaties relating to the same subject-matter" shall be determined by the provisions of the 1969 Vienna Convention "subject to Article 103 of the Charter of the United Nations."

[863] Shaw, *op. cit. supra* n.771, 230.

An exception to this primacy of the Charter is provided by provisions of treaties that codify the law of treaties, notably provisions contained in the 1969 Vienna Convention on the Law of Treaties.[864] Another hypothetical exception would be provided by a treaty that codifies *jus cogens*.[865]

Within the legal doctrine, moreover, it remains controversial whether non-member states of the United Nations are bound to comply with Security Council decisions.[866] The controversy is based on Article 2(6) of the Charter, which provides that: "The Organization shall ensure that states which are not Members of the United Nations act in accordance with these Principles so far as may be necessary for the maintenance of international peace and security." Indeed, decisions issued by the Security Council under its responsibility for the maintenance of international peace and security are generally addressed to "all States".[867] If this practice and Article 2(6) were to be interpreted to the effect that non-members are obliged to implement measures taken by the Council under Chapter VII, they could be required to implement economic sanctions against a state in contravention of their existing treaty obligations towards that state. In general, however, treaties are only binding between the parties. Therefore, a non-member of the United Nations cannot be obliged to, for example, disregard its treaty obligations with a state that is targeted by the Council under Chapter VII of the Charter. As observed by Vitzthum, however, the "practical importance of the problem of the relationship between the UN and non-members has been substantially reduced" in view of the "almost complete universality" of its membership.[868]

4.3.2 Customary International Law

A second possible source is provided by customary international law. This relates to the question whether the Council has to respect customary international law in exercising its responsibilities under Chapter VII. In general, the answer must be in the negative. Both treaties and custom are accorded the same hierarchy as sources of

---

[864] See *infra*, the text accompanying notes 872-875.

[865] The obligation to abide by treaties which codify *jus cogens* would rest on the *jus cogens* nature of the norms codified rather than on the treaty-nature of the obligation. Therefore, this issue will be addressed in the context of *jus cogens*. See *infra*, page 197 ff.

[866] For an overview of this problem see W.G. Vitzthum, *Article 2(6)*. In: B. Simma, *et. al.* (eds.), The Charter of the United Nations (1994) 131-139.

[867] For examples see *supra*, chapter 3.

[868] Vitzthum, *op. cit. supra* n.866, at 132-133. As of 1 July 2000 the most notable non-members were Switzerland, Taiwan, Tuvalu and the Vatican City.

international law.[869] It would therefore be illogical to presume that the obligations of states under the Charter must prevail over those enjoyed under treaty law (Article 103), but not over those under customary international law.[870] This notwithstanding, there are some exceptions to the primacy of the Charter over customary law. One of these is provided by the customary rules of the law of treaties. As an international instrument created by states, the United Nations Charter is governed by the law of treaties. As seen in paragraph 4.2.1.4 above, moreover, Article 2(2) of the Charter itself provides for the exercise of its responsibilities by the Council in good faith. However, this obligation would also be incumbent upon the Council absent this provision in the Charter. Thus the maxim *pacta sunt servanda*, which forms part of customary international law,[871] applies to the members of the Council. The existence of limitations to an organ's freedom to interpret its own powers under its constituent treaty has, for example, been confirmed by the International Court of Justice in its advisory opinion in the *IMCO* case.[872] The opinion was given pursuant to the request of the Assembly of the IMCO, and revolved around the correct interpretation of Article 28(a) of its constituent instrument, which reads as follows:

> The Maritime Safety Committee shall consist of fourteen Members elected by the Assembly from the Members governments of those nations having an important interest in maritime safety, of which not less than eight shall be the largest ship-owning nations, and the remainder shall be elected so as to ensure adequate representation of Members, governments of other nations with an important interest in maritime safety, such as nations interested in the supply of large numbers of crews or in the carriage of large numbers of berthed and unberthed passengers, and of major geographical areas.[873]

The Assembly had not elected Liberia and Panama to sit on the Committee, although they rated third and eighth on a list of total gross registered tonnage. This led to the question of the meaning of the words "largest ship-owning nations". In its opinion the Court rejected the argumentation that the Assembly had discretionary power to determine which nations were or were not the largest ship-owning nations, and concluded that "the Maritime Safety Committee of the Inter-Governmental Maritime Consultative Organization, which was elected on 15 January 1959, is not constituted

---

[869] If one were to establish a difference in rank between the two sources, treaties would probably be prioritized. See M. Akehurst, *The Hierarchy of the Sources of International Law*, 47 BYIL (1974-1975) 273-285, 274-275; Dixon, *op. cit. supra* n.40, 21. An exception is provided by *jus cogens*, on which see *infra*, page 197 ff.

[870] See *contra*, however, Gardam, *op. cit. supra* n.172, 304.

[871] Wehberg, *op. cit. supra* n.766, 782-783.

[872] *Constitution of the Maritime Safety Committee of the Inter-Governmental Maritime Consultative Organization*, Adv. Op. 8 June 1960, ICJ Rep. (1960), 150 ff.

[873] The text of the constituent treaty of the IMCO is reproduced in 53 AJIL (1959) 516 ff.

in accordance with the Convention for the establishment of the Organization."[874] This decision shows that the member states of an organ of an international organization have to abide by the customary rules of the law of treaties, in particular the rules on treaty interpretation.[875] Consequently, an organ of an organization, being the sum of its member states, does not possess unfettered discretion in determining the extent of its powers, but has to abide by those same customary rules of the law of treaties in interpreting and exercising its powers.

There are additional exceptions to the primacy of the Charter *vis-à-vis* customary international law, and the foremost are the peremptory norms of international law. These norms, also referred to as *jus cogens*, are norms from which derogation is not possible under any circumstance. Article 53 of the 1969 Vienna Convention on the Law of Treaties defines such norms as follows:

> a peremptory norm of general international law is a norm accepted and recognized by the international community of States as a whole as a norm from which no derogation is permitted and which can be modified only by a subsequent norm of general international law having the same character.[876]

This non-derogatory character means that all subjects of international law, including the Security Council, have to abide by them.[877] This was recognized by Judge Lauterpacht in the following terms:

---

[874] ICJ Rep. (1960), at 171. For a discussion of the case see, *e.g.*, Amerasinghe, *op. cit. supra* n.66, 43-44.

[875] Therefore, the members are also bound to respect the provisions on interpretation and fulfilment in good faith of treaties contained in 1969 Vienna Convention on the Law of Treaties, to the extent to which those provisions have codified, or have become, customary international law.

[876] On the origins of the concept of *jus cogens* and the drafting history of Article 53 see, *e.g.*, E. Schwelb, *Some Aspects of International Jus Cogens as Formulated by the International Law Commission*, 61 AJIL (1967) 946-975; A. Verdross, *Jus Dispositivum and Jus Cogens in International Law*, 60 AJIL (1966) 55-63; A. von Verdross, *Forbidden Treaties in International Law: Comments on Professor Garner's Report on the 'Law of Treaties'*, 31 AJIL (1937) 571-577; R.D. Kearny, R.E. Dalton, *The Treaty on Treaties*, 64 AJIL (1970) 495-561, 535-538. *Cf.* Article 19 of the ILC's Draft Articles on State Responsibility, which distinguishes between international delicts and international crimes in a way that resembles Article 53 of the Vienna Convention. According to draft Article 19(2) "An internationally wrongful act which results from the breach by a State of an international obligation so essential for the protection of fundamental interests of the international community that its breach is recognised as a crime by that community as a whole constitutes an international crime." Whilst adopted on first reading in 1980, the article proved to be quite controversial on second reading, and in 1998 the ILC decided that "draft article 19 would be put to one side for the time being" in order not to frustrate the work on the other draft articles. See the 'Report of the ILC on the work of its fiftieth session', A/53/10, para. 331. For an assessment of draft article 19 see, *e.g.*, D.W. Bowett, *Crimes of State and the 1996 Report of the International Law Commission on State Responsibility*, 9 EJIL (1998) 163-173; G. Abi-Saab, *et. al.*, *Symposium on State Responsibility*, 10 EJIL (1999) 339-460.

[877] See Paust, *op. cit. supra* n.164, 139-140.

The relief which Article 103 of the Charter may give the Security Council in case of conflict between one of its decisions and an operative treaty obligation cannot – as a matter of simple hierarchy – extend to a conflict between a Security Council resolution and *jus cogens*.[878]

The *jus cogens* standard may appear question-begging at first, since at present there is no consensus on which norms have acquired a peremptory status.[879] The protection of certain basic values, however, is inherent to any legal thinking. Thus in the context of the (in)validity of treaties, Sinclair has observed:

Whatever their doctrinal point of departure, the majority of jurists would no doubt willingly concede to the sceptics that there is little or no evidence in positive international law for the concept that nullity attaches to a treaty concluded in violation of *jus cogens*. But they would be constrained to admit that the validity of a treaty between two States to wage a war of aggression against a third State or to engage in acts of physical or armed force against a third State could not be upheld; and, having made this admission, they may be taken to have accepted the principle that there may exist norms of international law so fundamental to the maintenance of an international legal order that a treaty concluded in violation of them is a nullity.[880]

In a similar vein, Doehring maintains that "one may tolerate the disregard of dispositive norms of international law if otherwise the peace among states could not be preserved. But this cannot be true regarding peremptory norms losing their legal nature when not respected."[881]

The ensuing question is which legal rules can be classified as constituting *jus cogens*. There are various candidates in this respect, the foremost being the prohibition on the unlawful use or threat of force, the prohibition on genocide, and the duty to respect basic human rights.[882] These "classic" examples coincide with the examples of obligations *erga omnes* given, in *obiter dicta*, by the International Court of Justice in the

---

[878] Sep. Op. Lauterpacht, *Convention on the Prevention and Punishment of the Crime of Genocide* case (Prov. Measures), Bosnia and Herzegovina v. Yugoslavia (Serbia and Montenegro), ICJ Rep. (1993), at 440. Similarly Herdegen contends: "Da die Regelungskompetenzen des Sicherheitsrates ebenso wie die von ihm neubegründeten Verpflichtungen für Staaten vertraglicher Natur sind, dürfen sie nicht den Rahmen des zwingender Völkerrecht (*ius cogens*) entspringen." Herdegen, *op. cit. supra* n.648, at 27. *Cf.* Bedjaoui, who holds that "the Charter, like any other treaty, may not exist in contradiction to international law, or at any rate in opposition to certain imperative and inviolable norms of international law." Bedjaoui, *op. cit. supra* n.745, at 34.

[879] Thus Malanczuk, for example, submits that "at present, very few rules pass this [Art. 53 of the VCLT] test." Malanczuk, *op. cit. supra* n.31, at 58. See also Shaw, *op. cit. supra* n.16, 97.

[880] Sinclair, *op. cit. supra* n.16, 222.

[881] Doehring, *op. cit. supra* n.725, at 99. *Cf.* Cryer, *op. cit. supra* n.648, 170.

[882] See the commentary of the ILC on what has become Article 53 of the Vienna Convention on the Law of Treaties, in which examples are given of "some of the most obvious and best settled rules of *jus cogens*", including the unlawful use of force, trade in slaves, piracy and genocide. 2 YBILC (1966), at 248.

Barcelona Traction case.[883] Herein the Court stated that there exist "obligations of a State towards the international community as a whole" and that accordingly, "in view of the importance of the rights involved, all States can be held to have a legal interest in their protection; they are obligations *erga omnes*."[884]

The Court then stated that:

> such obligations derive, for example, in contemporary international law, from the outlawing of acts of aggression, and of genocide, as also from the principles and rules concerning the basic rights of the human person, including protection from slavery and racial protection.[885]

Hence, according to this classification,[886] the first *jus cogens* norm is the outlawing of aggression. This means that the Council may not commit or support acts of aggression.[887] It also means that the Council may not interfere with the customary right of self-defence, the other side of aggression's coin.[888] This right has entered into the Charter in the form of Article 51 and has been dealt with above.[889] Suffice it here to mention, therefore, that the Council cannot abrogate the right of self-defence under both Article 51 and customary law, unless it takes measures that are effective in maintaining or restoring international peace and security.

The second candidate is the prohibition on genocide.[890] The consequence of this norm is that the Council has to ensure that its actions do not interfere with the prohibition on genocide. Of course one could hardly envisage the Council ordering or authorizing genocidal acts. The problem lies with the Council taking measures in the maintenance of international peace and security which effectively contribute to ongoing acts of genocide. This is exactly what has been contended in the *Bosnia* case by Bosnia-Herzegovina, that by establishing a weapons embargo on the territory of the

---

883 See M. Ragazzi, *The Concept of International Obligations Erga Omnes* (1997), 49-50 (on the relationship between obligations *erga omnes* and *jus cogens* norms see *ibid.*, 189-214); I. Brownlie, *Principles of Public International Law* (1990), 513, Shaw, *op. cit. supra* n.10, 97.

884 *Barcelona Traction* (Belgium v. Spain), ICJ Rep. (1970), 3 ff., para. 33.

885 *Ibid.*, para. 34.

886 Although the International Court of Justice has never explicitly declared a rule of international law as having the character of *jus cogens*, the Court and its individual members have referred to *jus cogens* in various areas of the law. See Ragazzi, *op. cit. supra* n.883, n.12 at 46.

887 If the Council unlawfully orders or authorizes the use or threat of force, for example because it has abused its rights, it could be claimed that such use of force constitutes aggression.

888 Shaw, *op. cit. supra* n.771, at 230.

889 See *supra*, paragraph 4.2.3.3.

890 *Cf.* Shaw, *op. cit. supra* n.771, at 230; Doehring, *op. cit. supra* n.725, 105.

former Yugoslavia by resolution 713 (1991), the Council contributed to the ongoing acts of genocide by the Federal Republic of Yugoslavia.[891]

The third category of *jus cogens* norms is formed by the "basic rights of the human person." Human rights standards to which the Council's actions must conform are provided by the prohibition of torture and slavery, and of discrimination such as apartheid.[892] Also the right of self-determination is included amongst them,[893] and the humanitarian laws of war.[894] As seen above, the Council is obliged to respect these human rights as they are included in the purposes and principles of the Charter. Therefore, the conclusion must be that the Council is obliged to respect basic human rights under the Charter as well as a matter of *jus cogens*. The same holds true for humanitarian law.

In addition to the *jus cogens* norms, there is another exception on the Council's freedom to interpret and exercise its powers under Chapter VII related to customary international law. When the Council is exercising its quasi-judicial authority, it must

---

891 On the Bosnian argumentation see Scott, *et. al.*, *op. cit. supra* n.7.

892 Gill, *op. cit. supra* n.5, at 79. In this context one might also refer to Doehring, who observes that "states cannot dispose of those rights whose true holders are the individuals even under international law." Doehring, *op. cit. supra* n.725, at 102. See also *Legal Consequences for States of the Continued Presence of South Africa in Namibia (South West Africa) Notwithstanding Security Council Resolution 276 (1970)*, Adv. Op., ICJ Rep. (1971), para. 122 at 55, in which the Court held that states were obliged to "abstain from invoking or applying" existing bilateral treaties concerning Namibia, or concluded on behalf of Namibia, in their dealings with South Africa. It then stated that: "With respect to multilateral treaties, however, the same rule cannot be applied to certain general conventions such as those of a humanitarian character, the non-performance of which may adversely affect the people of Namibia." *Cf.* Watson, *op. cit. supra* n.7, who maintains at 37 that: "It is quite reasonable to conclude that the U.N. Charter, itself a treaty, does not authorize acts that violate peremptory norms of international law. Precisely what these norms are is a matter of dispute. It is generally agreed, however, that states cannot enter into treaties to commit genocide, to perpetuate slavery, to engage in illegal aggression, or to perpetuate apartheid. The test is whether a very large majority of states believes that a practice is unacceptable in any circumstances." To a similar effect see Herdegen, *op. cit. supra* n.648, 27.

893 According to Doehring: "No state is entitled to disregard or even to abolish this right which belongs to the body of international peremptory norms." Doehring, *op. cit. supra* n.725, at 102. See also Doehring, *op. cit. supra* n.737, 70-71. *Cf.* the statement of the International Court of Justice that: "In the Court's view, Portugal's assertion that the right of peoples to self-determination, as it evolved from the Charter and United Nations practice, has an *erga omnes* character, is irreproachable. The principle of self-determination of peoples has been recognized by United Nations Charter and in the jurisprudence of the Court; it is one of the essential principles of international law." *Case Concerning East Timor* (Portugal v. Australia), ICJ Rep. (1995), para. 29 at 102 [references omitted].

894 Gowlland-Debbas notes on *jus cogens* and *erga omnes* obligations that they "include the protective norms of the Geneva Conventions as attested by many of their provisions ensuring their application in all circumstances." Gowlland-Debbas, *op. cit. supra* n.2, at 93. See also Herdegen, *op. cit. supra* n.648, at 27.

abide by general international law, including customary international law.[895] Thus Shaw has observed that in the context of:

> resolutions which in effect amount to a determination or characterization of a legal situation ... one must question the competence of the Security Council to alter unilaterally the principles of international law ... it is able to go no further than reaffirm existing international law and suggest a particular application in a particular situation.[896]

In this quasi-judicial sphere the Council may only apply the law, it may not change it. This follows from the fact that the Council cannot choose to ignore the rules which it is supposedly enforcing itself. The same holds true for subsidiary organs created by the Council. With regard to the establishment and the working procedures of the United Nations Compensation Commission (UNCC), it has been maintained that the Council ignored this limitation and that it modified the customary rules of state responsibility.[897]

4.3.3 General Principles of Law

Analogous to the position of customary and conventional international law, it must be concluded that as a matter of hierarchy there are no general principles of law by which the Council must abide. It is assumed that general principles of law[898] rank lower than treaty and customary law.[899] The purposes and principles of the United Nations, however, do incorporate some of these principles, notably good faith and proportionality.[900] Moreover, when the Council delegates its Chapter VII powers, for

---

895 Kirgis, *op. cit. supra* n.129, at 531.

896 Shaw, *op. cit. supra* n.771, at 234-235. *Cf.* Herdegen, according to whom "der Sicherheitsrat nicht von sich aus neue völkerrechtliche Pflichten schaffen kann." Herdegen, *op. cit. supra* n.648, at 24.

897 See Kirgis, *op. cit. supra* n.129, 529; Malanczuk, *op. cit. supra* n.2. See also, generally, Gowlland-Debbas, *op. cit. supra* n.2.

898 For a discussion of these principles see, *e.g.*, H. Mosler, *General Principles of Law*, II EPIL (1995) 511-527.

899 Akehurst, *op. cit. supra* n.869, 279. This source was essentially included to fill any gaps in the law that the International Court of Justice might encounter. See Malanczuk, *op. cit. supra* n.31, 48. Writing in 1981, however, Jennings remarked that such gaps have become rare: "the problem today is that we have so much material to marshall somehow under Article 38(a) and (b) [of the Court's Statute], that we hardly know how best to start." R.Y. Jennings, *What is International Law and How do we Tell It when we see It?*, 37 SJIR (1981) 59-88, at 72.

900 The International Court of Justice has applied the principle of proportionality in several contexts. See, *e.g.*, the *Case concerning the Gabcíkovo-Nagymaros Project* (Hungary v. Slovakia), Merits, ICJ Rep. (1997), para. 85, on the element of proportionality in the taking of countermeasures; *Maritime Delimitation in the Area between Greenland and Jan Mayen*, Merits, ICJ Rep. (1993), paras. 64-66,

example through the establishment of subsidiary organs, the Council can only confer those powers that it possesses itself.[901] These powers must have been granted to the Council through the Charter, either explicitly or as implied powers.[902] This relates to the general principle of law embodied in the maxim *nemo dat quod non habet* – one cannot give what one does not possess.

4.4 Conclusions

As an organ deriving its powers from the United Nations Charter, the Council is bound to comply with its provisions. This conclusion is in itself not controversial. Problems arise, however, when determining the exact content of these provisions. As seen above, however, the purposes and principles of the Charter, which are formulated quite loosely, do have a legally defined content. This leads to the conclusion that the Council must respect the right of self-determination (Article 1(2)), human rights (Article 1(3)), and humanitarian law (Articles 1 and 2 in general) in exercising its powers under Chapter VII. Moreover, Article 2(2) stipulates that in this exercise the Council should act in good faith. The notion of good faith simultaneously provides for the main limitations to the Council's powers to make a determination under Article 39 that a situation poses a threat to international peace and security. As in the case of determinations under Article 39, the Council enjoys a very wide margin of discretion in deciding on measures under Articles 41 and 42. The main limitations to be found in this respect are, once again, Articles 1(2), 1(3) and 2(2).

As regards the limitations imposed by general international law, it has been shown that the Council is not *a priori* bound to respect the rights and obligations of states under operative international conventions; Article 103 of the Charter specifically provides for this. As an organ created by a treaty, however, the Council should comply with the conventional law of treaties, *i.e.* the Vienna Convention on the Law of Treaties.

In a similar way, the Council is not bound to respect customary international law beforehand, with two important exceptions. Peremptory norms of general international law, *jus cogens* in short, may not be set aside by the Council. These norms are certain

---

on proportionality in the context of maritime delimitation; the *Nicaragua* case, Merits, ICJ Rep. (1986), 14, and the Adv. Op. on the *Legality of the Threat or Use of Nuclear Weapons*, ICJ Rep. (1996), paras. 40-44, on the requirement of proportionality when acting in self-defence.

901 See N. Blokker, *Is the Authorization Authorized? Powers and Practice of the UN Security Council to Authorize the Use of Force by 'Coalitions of the Able and Willing'*, 11 EJIL (2000), 541-568, 552-555.

902 See Schermers, Blokker, *op. cit. supra* n.51, 153; D. Sarooshi, *The United Nations and the Development of Collective Security: The Delegation by the UN Security Council of its Chapter VII Powers* (1999), 20.

'fundamental' human rights, such as the prohibition on genocide, the right of self-determination, the right of self-defence and the prohibition on torture. When the Council is exercising its quasi-judicial authority, moreover, it is obliged to apply the law and not to change it according to its own wishes. This requires respect for customary international law.

5.

Illegal Council Decisions: Consequences and the Remedies Available

5.1 Who Determines whether Council Decisions are *ultra vires*?[903]

As seen in chapter 4, a resolution adopted by the Council under Chapter VII of the Charter may be invalid on several grounds. If the Council does not respect the purposes and principles of the Charter, or if a decision violates *jus cogens*, the decision is illegal.[904] This leads to the question of who is entitled to pass judgment on the

903 Generally see J.E. Alvarez, *Legal Remedies and the United Nations' à la Carte Problem*, 12 MJIL (1991) 229-311; N. Angelet, *Protest Against Security Council Decisions*. In: K.C. Wellens (ed.), International Law: Theory and Practice (1998) 277-285, 278; E. Osieke, *The Legal Validity of 'Ultra Vires' Decisions of International Organizations*, 77 AJIL (1983) 239-256; J.S. Watson, *Autointerpretation, Competence, and the Continuing Validity of Article 2(7) of the UN Charter*, 71 AJIL (1977) 60-83; E. Zoller, *The 'Corporate Will' of the United Nations and the Rights of the Minority*, 81 AJIL (1987) 610-634.

904 For practical purposes, the terms 'invalidity" and 'illegality' are used interchangeably in this volume. Strictly speaking, however, they are not synonymous. While an illegal decision is necessarily invalid, an invalid decision is not necessarily illegal. A hypothetical example of an invalid but not illegal decision would be an Article 39 determination by the Security Council that a breach of the peace had occurred following reports that the territory of State A had been violated by an invasion by State B. If it would later turn out that the invasion was conducted by troops of State A in disguise, the decision would be invalid, as it was based on factual assumptions that proved to be erroneous. In this case the decision would not be illegal since the Council did not breach a legal rule which is binding on it, it merely made an error in judgment.

validity of Council decisions.[905] Two categories may be identified in this respect. The first is formed by individual member states, the second by the International Court of Justice.

5.2 The Right of Member States to Challenge Council Decisions

In the history of the United Nations, doubts as to the legality of Security Council resolutions have been cast by individual member states on various occasions. It should come as no surprise that these doubts are primarily expressed by states which are especially affected by the Council's decisions. Thus the Council's handling of Southern Rhodesia prompted Portugal and South Africa to address several letters to the Council in which they contested the legality of the Council's handling of the case.[906] Another example is provided by Iraq's persistent non-cooperation with the UNSCOM[907] and its protests against the procedure of the UNCC.[908] In the case of Libya, moreover, two regional organizations declared that they would no longer comply in full with the sanctions regime established against that country by the Council, prior to the lifting of the sanctions.[909] This issue is not unique to the Council, similar questions have arisen with regard to other principal organs of the United Nations. Mention may be made of the non-payment by, amongst others, the Soviet Union and the US of contributions determined by the General Assembly,[910] and of the non-acceptance by

---

905 See R. Bernhardt, *op. cit. supra* n.784, 603-608.

906 See, *e.g.*, L. Gross, *Voting in the Security Council: Abstention in the Post-1965 Amendment Phase and Its Impact on Article 25 of the Charter*, 62 AJIL (1968) 315-334, 316-318.

907 See the Council's condemnations of Iraq's refusal to cooperate with UNSCOM in, *e.g.*, S/Res. 1205 (1998), 5 Nov. 1998; S/Res. 1137 (1997), 12 Nov. 1997; S/Res. 1060 (1996), 12 June 1996; and S/Res. 707 (1991), 15 Aug. 1991.

908 See, *e.g.*, S/AC.26/1993/None No. 14 and S/AC.26/1993/None No. 17.

909 The Organization of African Unity (OAU) Heads of State, in a resolution adopted on 8 June 1998, called upon African nations to suspend compliance with UN Security Council sanctions against Libya immediately for religious, humanitarian or OAU-related Libyan flights, and to ignore sanctions entirely beginning in September 1998 if the US and UK had not by then agreed to one of Libya's third country trial options. Moreover, the foreign ministers of the League of Arab States adopted a resolution on 21 Sept. 1997, in which they, *inter alia*, invited "Arab countries to undertake measures to ease the severity of the embargo imposed on Libya until a final, peaceful, and just solution to the crisis is reached"; "to lift measures freezing Libyan accounts involving money, the source of which is other than the selling or exporting of oil"; and to exempt from sanctions Libyan "flights related to participation of the Libyan political leadership and official delegations in regional and international meetings."

910 See Zoller, *op. cit. supra* n.903, 614-615; J.E. Alvarez, *Financial Responsibility*, In: C.C. Joyner (ed.), The United Nations and International Law, 1997, 409-431, 413-415.

the US of the 1986 judgment of the International Court of Justice in the *Nicaragua* case.[911]

These protests lead to the question "to what extent do member states of the United Nations have discretion to claim that their interpretation of the Charter is the correct one?"[912] From the outset it must be stated that according to international law as it stands today, absent any treaty provisions that hold otherwise,[913] states themselves determine the legality of their acts and those of other subjects of international law. A classic formulation of this states that "each State establishes for itself its legal situation *vis-à-vis* other States."[914] In cases where a state's rights have been violated, the right of last resort would be self-help, that is the resort to measures of self-help, such as reprisals.[915]

It is hardly disputable that a state has a right to challenge the validity of acts of international organizations.[916] In the context of the Security Council Angelet has noted that "the right to protest flows from the fact that the Council has not been granted the right to modify the UN Charter",[917] a submission corroborated by the *IMCO* opinion of the International Court of Justice.[918] Such protests can be lodged during the decision-making process or after the actual adoption of a decision. Thus, a member can pass judgment on the legality of Security Council resolutions for itself. It is another matter, however, whether non-compliance with a Council decision by the protesting state is lawful. The main conflict inherent in this issue is the tension between a members state's rights and its obligations towards the organization. Put

---

[911] After the Court had decided in 1984 that it had jurisdiction to entertain Nicaragua's application, the US withdrew from the proceedings before the Court. On 27 June 1986, the Court rendered its decision on the merits. Subsequently, by a letter dated 17 Oct. 1986 (UN Doc. S/18415), Nicaragua requested an emergency meeting of the Security Council "to consider the non compliance with the Judgment of the International Court of Justice dated 27 June 1986". A draft resolution, introduced on 28 Oct. 1986 and calling for immediate compliance with the Court's judgment, was vetoed by the US, which claimed that the Court had issued a decision that it "had neither the jurisdiction nor the competence to render". See A. Tanzi, *Problems of Enforcement of Decisions of the International Court of Justice and the Law of the United Nations*, 6 EJIL (1995) 539-572, 544-547.

[912] Zoller, *op. cit. supra* n.903, at 621.

[913] For example, settlement of dispute provisions within a treaty.

[914] *Case concerning the Air Service Agreement of 27 March 1946 between the United States of America and France*, 18 Reports of International Arbitral Awards (1978), para. 81 at 443.

[915] Malanczuk, *op. cit. supra* n.31, 3-4.

[916] Osieke, *op. cit. supra* n.903, 240.

[917] Angelet, *op. cit. supra* n.903, at 282.

[918] See *supra*, the text accompanying notes 872-875.

differently, the organization cannot function without the loyalty of its members. In other words, if a right to pass judgment on the legality of Security Council decisions would reside with individual member states, the binding character of these decisions would be undermined and Article 25 of the Charter would become a dead letter.[919] On the other hand, a member state must be entitled to the protection of its rights under international law against what has been called the 'tyranny of the majority'.[920] If the Council takes a decision that is illegal under international law, a remedy against that decision must be available. The tension between a state's duty to comply with its obligations under the Charter, *i.e.* to comply with a Council decision, and its right to challenge the validity of Council decisions, has been described by Lauterpacht as follows:

> We are faced here by a fundamental conflict between the principle that an illegal act is null *ab initio* and the principle that the mere assertion by an interested party that the act is unlawful should not be conclusively determinative of the question. There is no legal principle which can, by itself, resolve this conflict.[921]

The debate concerning the non-payment of UN contributions by individual member states may provide some insight in this regard. On the one side stand those who argue that withholding of payments "is an inherent right of UN membership."[922] Their position is summarized by Alvarez in the following terms:

> since no effective remedy exists for breach ... it would be politically impossible and unwise to attempt to create a remedy requiring a member State to pay for an act to which it objects; international law permits unilateral withholding by member States when, in the judgment of these members, the UN has acted illegally.[923]

Others deny the existence of such a right. They maintain that "to arrogate to the member states a general right to reject a properly adopted decision on the basis of a unilateral determination that it is *ultra vires* would be tantamount to making the members the judge in their own cause."[924]

To this it has been replied, however, that the same holds for the organization itself. Thus Watson correctly observes that it is "as much a violation of that principle [*nemo iudex in sua causa*] for the Organization to make the decision as it is for the state

[919] See Angelet, *op. cit. supra* n.903, 278.

[920] See Alvarez, *op. cit. supra* n.903, 272.

[921] E. Lauterpacht, *The Legal Effect of Illegal Acts of International Organizations*. In: D.W. Bowett, *et. al.*, Cambridge Essays in International Law: Essays in Honour of Lord McNair (1965) 88-121, at 115.

[922] Zoller, *op. cit. supra* n.903, at 632.

[923] Alvarez, *op. cit. supra* n.903, at 231.

[924] Osieke, *op. cit. supra* n.903, at 255. Alvarez also contends that "the issue must be initially determined by an entity which is not a judge in its own cause." Alvarez, *op. cit. supra* n.903, at 283.

concerned to do so, since the Organization is likewise an interested party."[925]

Indeed, being a judge in one's own cause is consistent with the state of international law as it still stands today.[926] It is therefore not possible to deny a member the right to determine whether a decision of an organization is invalid, based solely on the objection that this would make the member a judge in its own cause, although the potential for abuse is very real in such cases. The more convincing argument is that granting a state the right to unilaterally reject a Security Council decision would seriously hamper the effectiveness of the organization.[927] If it were left to the individual member states to judge the validity of acts of the organization and hence whether or not to abide by those acts, the organization could no longer function effectively. This is all the more true for the decisions of a highly politicized organ such as the Security Council, whose decisions can and will have far-reaching effects as far as the addressees are concerned. The most a member state can do against a decision it considers illegal is to protest. Such a protest can be lodged prior to, during or after the decision is taken. When doing so the protestor should indicate the legal defects of the contested decision and establish a *prima facie* case.[928] In this context it must be noted that the principles of acquiescence, estoppel, severability and lapse of time *ex tempore* can invalidate a challenge to the legality of a decision.[929] If a *prima facie* case is established, the organization could then consider the claim, if necessary by referring the case to the International Court of Justice for an advisory opinion. The organization could also deem the matter to be settled or simply ignore the protest. The practical options available to the protesting state in case its claim is rejected would then be non-compliance with the decision, with the risk of sanctions being incurred against it by the Council, or in extreme cases withdrawal from the organization by the protesting state.[930]

---

[925] Watson, *op. cit. supra* n.903, at 64.

[926] *Cf.* O. Schachter, *The Quasi-Judicial Role of the Security Council and the General Assembly*, 58 AJIL (1964) 960-965, 960; Charney, *op. cit. supra* n.726, 530; Zemanek, *op. cit. supra* n.701, 612-613.

[927] *Cf.* Pollux, according to whom the "easiest, the most primitive, and the most unsatisfactory solution is to say that each individual Member has the right to decide for itself how to interpret the Charter." Pollux, *The Interpretation of the Charter*, 23 BYIL (1946), at 56.

[928] Alvarez, *op. cit. supra* n.903, 310-311; Angelet, *op. cit. supra* n.903. *Cf.* Doehring, *op. cit. supra* n.725, 106.

[929] Osieke, *op. cit. supra* n.903, 247; Doehring, *op. cit. supra* n.725, 103.

[930] See Lauterpacht, *op. cit. supra* n.921, 118. *Cf.* Crawford, according to whom: "The only redress a dissatisfied minority Member would have [in such a case] is withdrawal from the Organisation, an option expressly not conferred, although understood to be available as a last resort." J. Crawford, *The Charter of the United Nations as a Constitution*. In: H. Fox (ed.), The Changing Constitution of the United Nations (1997) 3-16, at 11.

An exception to the obligation to comply with Council decisions is based on Article 51 of the Charter. If a state is under attack and the Council has taken measures that are ineffective in protecting the victim state, such as the imposition of an arms embargo, that state or its allies may lawfully ignore the Council's measures. Although such non-compliance would be in violation of member states' obligations under Article 25 of the Charter, this obligation is outweighed by the a state's right to survival. In this context one might refer to the reasoning employed by the International Court of Justice in the *Legality of the Threat or Use of Nuclear Weapons* case. Herein the Court first concluded that "the threat or use of nuclear weapons would generally be contrary to the rules of international law". Then, however, the Court stated that it "conclude definitively whether the threat or use of nuclear weapons would be lawful or unlawful in an extreme circumstance of self-defence, in which the very survival of a State would be at stake."[931]

Thus, with the exception of cases in which their survival is at stake, member states are bound to comply with allegedly illegal decisions of the Council, and their options are generally limited to protesting.[932] If a state would decide not to comply with a decision, this would amount to a violation of its obligations under the Charter. The Organization could penalize the state for this non-compliance. It might also be possible, however, for a state to lodge a protest against the decision in contentious proceedings before the International Court of Justice, or to mobilize the General Assembly and other authorized bodies in order to obtain a request for an advisory opinion related to the legality of Security Council decisions. The role the Court can play in reviewing the legality of Security Council decisions will be addressed below.

5.3 Review by the International Court of Justice

The remainder of this chapter is concerned with the possible role of the International Court of Justice in reviewing the validity or legality of Security Council decisions. Before assessing that role, it is necessary to provide an overview of the jurisdiction of the International Court of Justice and (preliminary) objections thereto. After that overview, the applicability of the principle of *litispendence* as a preliminary objection to the exercise of jurisdiction by the Court will be examined,[933] as well as the applicability of the political question doctrine. These paragraphs will be concluded

931 International Court of Justice, *Legality of the Threat or Use of Nuclear Weapons*, Adv. Op., 8 July 1996., operative part E.

932 See Weller, *op. cit. supra* n.7, 324.

933 The litispendence principle regulates the allocation of jurisdiction when two or more organs are seized of the same dispute. The principle will be addressed *infra*, in paragraphs 5.3.2.1.-5.3.4.4.9.

with an assessment of the feasibility and *de lege lata* possibilities of the Court's exercise of a power of judicial review.

5.3.1.1 The Jurisdiction of the Court in Contentious Proceedings

Under its present Statute only states may be parties in contentious proceedings at the International Court of Justice.[934] Distinct from, *i.e.*, the Permanent Court of Arbitration, individuals, corporations and international organizations do not have any *locus standi* in contentious proceedings.[935] As a corollary of the 'sovereignty' of states, the judicial settlement of disputes through the World Court is based on the consent of the parties.[936] This consensual basis of the Court's jurisdiction has been affirmed by the Court on various occasions. For instance, in the *Peace Treaties* case the Court held that: "The consent of States, parties to a dispute, is the basis of the Court's jurisdiction in contentious cases."[937]

Also in the *Monetary Gold* case the International Court of Justice stated:

> To adjudicate upon the international responsibility of Albania without her consent would run counter to a well-established principle of international law embodied in the Court's Statute, namely that the Court can only exercise jurisdiction over a State with its consent.[938]

States may express their consent to appear before the Court in several forms. Thereto Article 36(1) of the Statute provides that: "The jurisdiction of the Court comprises all cases which the parties refer to it and all matters specially provided for in the Charter of the United Nations or in treaties and conventions in force."

The wording 'all cases which the parties refer to it' relates to cases in which the parties have agreed to have recourse to the International Court of Justice in order to

---

[934] Art. 34(1) of the ICJ Statute.

[935] The former two, however, may be granted diplomatic protection by their states on the basis of their nationality. On this see, *e.g.*, the *Mavromaatis Palestine Concessions case* (Jurisdiction), PCIJ Rep. (1924), Ser. A, no. 2, 12; the *Nottebohm case* (Second Phase), ICJ Rep. (1955), 16-17; and the *Barcelona Traction case* (Second Phase), ICJ Rep. (1970), 42.

[936] The term World Court employed hereinafter refers to both the Permanent Court of International Justice and its successor, the International Court of Justice.

[937] ICJ Rep. (1950), at 71. And in the *Minority Schools* case the Permanent Court of International Justice held that "the Court's jurisdiction depends on the will of the Parties." PCIJ Rep. (1928), Ser. A, Judg. no. 12, at 22.

[938] ICJ Rep. (1954), at 32. To the same effect also the *Eastern Carelia* Advisory Opinion: "It is well established in international law that no State can, without its consent, be compelled to submit its disputes with other States either to mediation or arbitration, or to any other kind of pacific settlement." PCIJ Rep. (1923), Ser. B, no. 5, at 27.

settle their dispute. This may take several forms. The traditional method is the conclusion of a 'special agreement' or *compromis*, by which the parties define their dispute and agree to refer it to the Court for decision.[939] However, various new methods of expressing consent to be bound to the jurisdiction of the Court have developed.[940] Thus a state may, for example, agree to adjudication by taking part in the initiation of the proceedings in response to a unilateral application.[941] The "matters specially provided for" refer to provisions in conventions other than the United Nations Charter,[942] which hold that in the event of a dispute concerning the interpretation or application of the conventions, the parties to the dispute may refer the matter to the International Court of Justice. An example of such provisions is Article 14(1) of the 1971 Montreal Convention for the Suppression of Unlawful Acts Against the Safety of Civil Aviation:

> Any dispute between two or more Contracting States concerning the interpretation or application of this Convention which cannot be settled through negotiation, shall, at the request of one of them, be submitted to arbitration. If within six months from the date of the request for arbitration the Parties are unable to agree

---

[939] See S. Rosenne, *The Law and Practice of the International Court: 1920-1996* (1997), 663-665.

[940] See *Ibid.*, 573-586. *Cf.* the *Corfu Channel* case (Prel. Objections): "while the consent of the parties confers jurisdiction on the Court, neither the Statute nor the Rules require that this consent should be expressed in any particular form." ICJ Rep. (1948), at 27.

[941] Brownlie, *op. cit. supra* n.883, 722. *Cf.* the *Corfu Channel* case, in which the Court ruled that the Albanian government, by its letter of 2 July 1947, had voluntary accepted the jurisdiction of the Court, thereby waiving its right to raise an objection against the admissibility of the application. The letter reads, *inter alia*, that: "the United Kingdom was not entitled to bring the case before the International Court of Justice by unilateral application, without concluding a special agreement with the Albanian Government." However, Albania "is prepared notwithstanding this irregularity to appear before the Court." *Corfu Channel* case (Prel. Objections), ICJ Rep. (1948), at 27.

[942] According to Akehurst "there are *no* 'matters specially provided for in the Charter of the United Nations'. The explanation of this paradox is that Article 36(1) of the Statute of the Court was drafted at a time when it looked as if the Charter would provide for compulsory jurisdiction; the San Francisco Conference subsequently rejected proposals to provide for compulsory jurisdiction in the Charter, but forgot to delete the cross-reference in the Statute." Akehurst, *op. cit. supra* n.821, at 246-247. See to the same effect Brownlie, *op. cit. supra* n.883, 721-722. Both authors refer to the *Corfu Channel* case, in which seven judges – in a joint declaration – rejected the argument of the UK that a recommendation of the Council to refer a dispute to the Court is sufficient to establish the Court's jurisdiction in the case. See ICJ Rep. (1948), 15. See Rosenne, *op. cit supra* n.939, 692-695, according to whom the joint declaration referred to above is not conclusive of the issue. For an opposite view one might refer to Mosler. In his commentary on the jurisdiction of the Court under Art. 36(1) of the Statute, he maintains that the 'matters specially provided for in the UN Charter' refer to Arts. 36(3), 92, 96, 102, and 103. See H. Mosler, *Article 92*. In: B. Simma (ed.), The Charter of the United Nations (1994) 973-1001, 988.

on the organization of the arbitration, any one of those Parties may refer the dispute to the International Court of Justice by request in conformity with the Statute of the Court.[943]

In addition, states may deposit a declaration with the Secretary-General of the United Nations by which they "recognize as compulsory, *ipso facto* and without special agreement, in relation to any other State accepting the same obligation, the jurisdiction of the Court." According to Article 36(2) of the Court's Statute, also known as the optional clause, this jurisdiction covers:

all legal disputes concerning-
(a) the interpretation of a treaty;
(b) any question of international law;
(c) the existence of any fact which, if established, would constitute a breach of an international obligation;
(d) the nature or extent of the reparation to be made for the breach of an international obligation.

Suffice it here to mention that by recognizing the jurisdiction of the Court under Article 36(2) of the Statute, the "declarant state [is] bound to accept jurisdiction *vis-à-vis* any other declarant so far as the acceptances coincide."[944]

5.3.1.2 Jurisdiction of the Court in Advisory Proceedings

In addition to being a forum for the settlement of disputes between states, the Charter of the United Nations provides for a specific institutional role of the Court. According to Article 96 of the Charter:

1. The General Assembly or the Security Council may request the International Court of Justice to give an advisory opinion on any legal question.
2. Other organs of the United Nations and specialized agencies, which may at any time be so authorized by the General Assembly, may also request advisory opinions of the Court on legal questions arising within the scope of their activities.

Individual States are thus not entitled to request an advisory opinion, although in practice they do appear in court to submit their views on the legal issues at hand.[945] It is interesting to note that according to Article 102(2) and 102(3) of the Rules of Court the request for an advisory opinion may relate "to a legal question actually pending

---

[943] Reproduced in 10 ILM (1971) 1151 ff.

[944] Brownlie, *op. cit. supra* n.883, at 725. Article 36(3) provides that the optional clause declarations "may be made unconditionally or on condition of reciprocity on the part of several or certain States, or for a certain time." For an analysis of Art. 36(2) and 36(3) see Rosenne, *op. cit. supra* n.939, 732-745. See also Akehurst, *op. cit. supra* n.821, 247; and N. Singh, *The Role and Record of the International Court of Justice* (1989), 14-23.

[945] See Rosenne, *op. cit. supra* n.939, 1728-1733.

between two or more States". Article 102(3) stipulates that in these cases Article 31 of the Statute applies, *i.e.* that if the Bench does not include a judge of the nationality of one of the parties, the party may request that such a judge be included. At first sight these provisions are incompatible with the consensual basis of the Court's jurisdiction. In the two cases where the Court was confronted with a request pursuant to Article 102 of the Rules of Court, however, it ruled that the issues at hand did not relate to legal questions "actually pending between two or more States."[946] In the *Western Sahara* case, moreover, the Court held that it would not render an opinion if that opinion "would have the effect of circumventing the principle that a State is not obliged to allow its disputes to be submitted to judicial settlement without its consent."[947]

The advisory opinions are legally non-binding.[948] In practice, however, they have far-reaching effects, for one could hardly imagine a State or an organ pursuing a course of action knowing that such a course is illegal under international law.[949] The Court can thus clarify and set the legal parameters within which the United Nations and its specialized agencies can act.

It is as yet unsettled whether the decision to request an advisory opinion by the General Assembly is an 'important' question under Article 18(2) of the Charter, which would necessitate a qualified majority. With regard to the Security Council, it is also not clear whether the decision of the Council is a 'procedural matter' that requires a simple majority under Article 27(2), or an 'other matter' that requires the affirmative votes of the permanent members of the Council under Article 27(3).[950]

---

[946] The *Namibia* Advisory Opinion, ICJ Rep. (1971), and the *Western Sahara* Advisory Opinion, ICJ Rep. (1975). See Rosenne, *op. cit. supra* n.939, 1152-1156.

[947] *Western Sahara* Advisory Opinion, ICJ Rep. (1975), at 25. Indeed, the Permanent Court of International Justice declined to entertain a request made by the Council in the *Status of Eastern Carelia* case (PCIJ Rep. (1923), Ser. B, no. 5), because that would have essentially amounted to deciding on a dispute pending between Finland and Russia. See on this, *e.g.*, D. Bowett, *The Court's Role in Relation to International Organizations*. In: V. Lowe, M. Fitzmaurice, (eds.), Fifty Years of the International Court of Justice (1996) 181-192, 183-184; J. Herbst, *Rechtskontrolle des UN–Sicherheitsrates* (1999), 406-408.

[948] Unless decided otherwise by the requesting organ. See H. Mosler, *Article 96*. In: B. Simma, *et. al.* (eds.), The Charter of the United Nations (1994) 1008-1017, 1015. The example given by Mosler are opinions reviewing judgments of the Administrative Tribunal of the International Labour Organization (ILO).

[949] *Cf.* Herdegen, who observes that: "An objection to the validity of a Security Council resolution will claim hardly rebuttable plausibility once it finds clear support in a ruling of the ICJ." Herdegen, *op. cit. supra* n.5, at 147.

[950] See M. Schröder, *International Court of Justice*. In: R. Wolfrum (ed.), United Nations: Law, Policies and Practice (1995) 673-685, 682-683.

5.3.1.3 The Court's *Compétence de la Compétence*

As a result of the requirement of consent, the Court does not possess any jurisdiction beforehand:[951] it will have to determine for each separate case whether the dispute, if any,[952] falls within its jurisdiction. The competence to decide on this question is attributed to the Court by customary law[953] and its Statute.[954] This means the Court has jurisdiction to decide on its own jurisdiction,[955] otherwise known as the *compétence de la compétence*.[956] At first sight this principle contradicts the consensual basis of the jurisdiction of the Court, but is considered necessary for the effective exercise thereof. It is argued that if it were left to the parties to a dispute to decide the extent of their dispute and the jurisdiction of the tribunal, the likelihood of reaching an agreement would be minimal and adjudication would subsequently be rendered impossible.[957]

---

[951] Proposals by smaller states for a compulsory jurisdiction of the ICJ were not adopted at the San Francisco UNCIO. See Akehurst, *op. cit. supra* n.821, 245 and Rosenne, *op. cit. supra* n.939, 727-732.

[952] See the *Mavromaatis Palestine Concessions case (Jurisdiction)*, in which the PCIJ defined a legal dispute as "a disagreement on a point of law or fact, a conflict of legal views or of interests between two persons." PCIJ Rep. (1924), Ser. A, no. 2, at 11.

[953] In the *Nottebohm case* (Preliminary Objection) the Court stated that: "Since the *Alabama* case, it has been generally recognized, following the earlier precedents, that, in the absence of any agreement to the contrary, an international tribunal has the right to decide on its own jurisdiction and has the power to interpret for this purpose the instruments which govern that jurisdiction." ICJ Rep. (1953), 119. And at 120: "Article 36(6) of the Statute suffices to invest the Court with power to adjudicate on its jurisdiction in the present case. But even if this were not the case, the Court 'whose function it is to decide in accordance with international law such disputes as are submitted to it' ... should follow in this connection what is laid down by general international law. The judicial character of the Court and the rule of general international law referred to above [at 119] are sufficient to establish that the Court is competent to adjudicate on its own jurisdiction in the present case."

[954] See Arts. 53(2) and 36(6) of the Statute, the latter providing that: "In the event of a dispute as to whether the Court has jurisdiction the matter shall be decided by the decision of the Court."

[955] This is a form of 'incidental' jurisdiction, which is distinct from the 'principal' jurisdiction of the Court. Principal jurisdiction refers to the jurisdiction of the Court to hear the merits of a case, whereas incidental jurisdiction includes all other matters, such as the competence to decide on questions of jurisdiction and admissibility, as well as the power to indicate interim measures of protection under Art. 41 of the Statute. See Rosenne, *op. cit. supra* n.939, 596-602.

[956] The origins of the principle are commonly traced back to the 1794 *Jay Treaty*; the 1797 *Betsy*; and the 1872 *Alabama* cases. See Rosenne, *op. cit. supra* n.939, 846-862; and I.F.I. Shihata, *The Power of the International Court to Determine its Own Jurisdiction: Compétence de la Compétence* (1965), 11-24.

[957] See Fitzmaurice, *op. cit. supra* n.28, 436 and 451-454; Shihata, *op. cit. supra* n.956, 24-27.

5.3.1.4 Preliminary Objections to the Exercise of Jurisdiction

A general distinction may be made between objections to the jurisdiction of a tribunal and objections to the admissibility of a claim.[958] The former plea purports to establish the incompetence of the tribunal to rule on the admissibility or merits of the claim. In the latter plea, the jurisdiction of the tribunal is not contested, but it is argued that the claim is invalid on grounds which are distinct from the jurisdiction or the 'ultimate merits' of the case. Objections to jurisdiction are thus abstract and general, related to the competence of the tribunal to hear a – class of – dispute(s). In objections to admissibility this general competence of the tribunal is not denied, but rather the competence of the tribunal to try the specific case due to a defect in the claim. In other words, it is not the existence of jurisdiction that is disputed, but rather the exercise thereof.[959] Such objections can be based on, for instance, undue delay in presenting the claim, the non-exhaustion of legal remedies, domestic jurisdiction or the nationality of the claimant.[960]

It is, however, not always possible to maintain a sharp distinction between preliminary objections and the merits of the case. Under certain circumstances an examination of the merits by the Court will be necessary to determine whether the objections are well founded. Thereto the Rules of Court provide for a joinder of the objections to the merits.[961] This provision was first incorporated in the 1936 amendment of the Rules of the Permanent Court of International Justice, and first applied in the *Certain German Interests in Polish Upper Silesia* case. In a frequently quoted passage from that judgment the Court stated that:

> The Court cannot in its decision on this objection in any way prejudge its future decision on the merits. On the other hand, however, the Court cannot on this ground alone declare itself incompetent; for, if it were to do so, it would become possible for a Party to make an objection to the jurisdiction – which could not be dealt with without recourse to arguments taken from the merits – with the effect of precluding further proceedings simply by raising it in *limine litis*; this would be quite inadmissible.[962]

Thus, if the objection is not "exclusively of a preliminary nature" and cannot be settled

---

[958] Brownlie, *op. cit. supra* n.883, 719; Mosler, *op. cit. supra* n.942, 998; Singh, *op. cit. supra* n.944, 371-372. In addition, Rosenne mentions objections to the receivability of a claim. See Rosenne, *op. cit. supra* n.939, n.34 at 853.

[959] See Rosenne, *op. cit. supra* n.939, 853.

[960] Brownlie, *op. cit. supra* n.883, 719; Akehurst, *op. cit. supra* n.821, 248; Singh, *op. cit. supra* n.944, 371.

[961] See Art. 79(7) of the Rules.

[962] PCIJ Rep. (1925), Ser. A, no. 6, at 15.

without having recourse to an examination of the merits of the case, it will be joined with the merits and pronounced on in the judgment. If the objection is upheld the proceedings will be discontinued.

5.3.2.1 The Principle of Litispendence

It is sometimes maintained that the Court cannot and should not exercise jurisdiction over a matter in contentious proceedings because the principle of litispendence precludes this. The following will explain the origins and content of the principle, and examine the case law of the Permanent International Court of Justice and the International Court of Justice in order to ascertain its views on the applicability of litispendence as an obstacle to the exercise of jurisdiction by the Court.

5.3.2.2 Origins of the Principle

The principle of litispendence evolved within domestic legal systems and has a twofold function therein: firstly the circumvention of conflicting judgments, and secondly, the avoidance of a proliferation of pending cases on the same issue.[963] As such, the doctrine is concerned with the distribution of jurisdiction within a state, specifically between municipal courts. The French expression is *exception de litispendance*, which is raised when multiple proceedings are instituted on the same matter. The Latin equivalent is *lis alibi pendens*, which refers to a 'suit pending elsewhere' in the Anglo-American language.[964] In municipal law, the principle refers to a situation in which an identical matter is pending between the same parties before organs possessing jurisdiction of identical or similar character. Thus in municipal law the plea of litispendence may be invoked if the following three conditions are met: there is (i) an identical matter, (ii) pending between the same parties, (iii) before organs possessing similar jurisdiction.[965]

---

[963] See T.J.H. Elsen, *Litispendence between the International Court of Justice and the Security Council* (1986), at 1; and D.R. Reichert, *Problems with Parallel and Duplicate Proceedings: The Litispendence Principle and International Arbitration*, 8 Arbitration International (1992) 237-255, 239. The present context mainly relates to the former function, the prevention of conflicting judgments.

[964] See Reichert, *op. cit. supra* n.963, 239; and Elsen, *op. cit. supra* n.963, n.1 at 1.

[965] See Elsen, *op. cit. supra* n.963, 3; and D. Ciobanu, *Litispendence between the International Court of Justice and the Political Organs of the United Nations*. In: L. Gross (ed.), The Future of the International Court of Justice (1976) 209-275, 215.

5.3.2.3 Litispendence in International Law

With the post World War I increase in international organization the possibility of concurrent jurisdiction in inter-state relations became greater.[966] But in contrast to domestic legal systems, the applicability – or, more specifically, the conditions under which the principle is to be applied – is seriously questioned on the international plane. This results from the distinctive nature of inter-state relations, which hampers a direct transfer of the municipal concept of litispendence to international law. Thus the fulfilment of the first condition, that of the identical nature of the matter, is hindered by the fact that in international relations questions commonly involve both legal and political aspects.[967] It is therefore not uncommon to argue that a question raised before a judicial organ is in fact political ('non-justiciable') and *vice versa*.[968] Moreover, parties to a dispute may refer to different sources of international law in order to establish a legal claim. The question then arises whether a claim based on, for example, customary international law is identical to a similar claim based on treaty provisions.[969]

It is not difficult to ascertain whether the same parties are engaged in proceedings, therefore the second condition is not very problematic. Difficulties may conceivably arise, however, when third parties intervene in the first proceedings and abstain from intervention in the second proceedings or *vice versa*. Additional problems may occur when a state exercises diplomatic protection.[970]

---

[966] *E.g.* Verzijl, writing on the League of Nations era, points out that: "lately, ... the possibility of the occurrence of cases of purely inter-State litispendence has greatly increased owing to the remarkable multiplication of the number of international tribunals or other bodies invested with the power of decision." J.H.W. Verzijl, *The Jurisprudence of the World Court* (1965), at 24. Reisman also observes that: "in modern international law, the rapid proliferation of institutions has already begun to generate an incipient doctrine of *lis alibi pendens* to deal with such conflicts [of jurisdiction]." Reisman, *op. cit. supra* n.7, at 87.

[967] See Ciobanu, *op. cit. supra* n.965, 216-217.

[968] See on this *infra*, paragraph 5.3.5.

[969] This occurred in the *Nicaragua* case, in which Nicaragua contended that by resorting to force the US had violated both the customary non-use of force principle and Article 2(4) of the UN Charter. See *Case Concerning Military and Paramilitary Activities in and against Nicaragua* (Merits), Nic. v. US, ICJ Rep. (1986), para. 23 at 22. The Court ruled that the non-use of force in international relations is indeed governed by both customary law and Article 2(4) of the Charter (*ibid.*, paras. 188-193 at 99-103), but could decide only on the basis of the former, since a US reservation to its 'optional clause' declaration excluded disputes arising under multilateral treaties.

[970] Consider the possibility of an international treaty conferring the right to bring a claim to a tribunal on individuals, and a state in relation to the subject matter of that claim bringing an action before another international body or tribunal. Are the parties identical in both proceedings? In fact

The third criterion is that of 'organs possessing similar jurisdictions'. Doctrinally, the question of its applicability is as yet undecided. It is significant that the formulation of this criterion varies considerably. Thus, for example, Elsen refers to "courts of the same character";[971] Reichert to "equally competent jurisdictions";[972] Klein to "Jurisdiktionshomogenität";[973] Ténékidès to "juridictions d'ordre national";[974] and Ciobanu to "organs possessing jurisdiction of the same character".[975]

The question arises whether the jurisdiction of, say, an *ad hoc* international arbitral tribunal is 'similar' to that of a permanent international court, such as the International Court of Justice. Furthermore, given the fact that the municipal concept of litispendence is concerned with the regulation of jurisdiction between domestic courts, is it justified to extrapolate it to the jurisdiction of political and judicial bodies?[976]

This brief overview reveals that on the international level the application of the principle of litispendence, analogous with its content in domestic law, is confronted with numerous problems.[977] Indeed it has been observed that:

> because of the peculiar nature of inter-State relations, one could hardly find a single case in which at least one of the three conditions of litispendence ... would not be absent, and the missing condition invoked as a preliminary defense.[978]

---

this situation occurred in the *Upper Silesia* case, in which the PCIJ answered this question in the negative. See *infra*, paragraph 5.3.3.3.

971 Elsen, *op. cit. supra* n.963, at 3.

972 Reichert, *op. cit. supra* n.963, at 239.

973 E. Klein, *Paralleles Tätigwerden von Sicherheitsrat und Internationalem Gerichtshof bei friedensbedrohenden Streitigkeiten*, 43 ZaöRV (1983) 467-491, at 476.

974 G. Ténékidès, *L' Exception de Litispendance devant les Organismes Internationaux*, 26 RGDIP (1929) 502-527, at 503.

975 Ciobanu, *op. cit. supra* n.965, at 218.

976 For a negative answer one might, *e.g.*, refer to Delbrück, according to whom: "The Court has to decide exclusively on the basis of international law ..., whereas the SC has to decide primarily according to political criteria. Considering this basic difference between the procedures of the SC and the ICJ, no objection of *lis pendens* or *res judicata* may be raised against the ICJ acting simultaneously (or prior to or after the SC) in a case pending before the SC." Delbrück, *op. cit. supra* n.107, 403. See to the same effect Bedjaoui, *op. cit. supra* n.745, 67-70.

977 In this context one might refer to Verzijl, who observes that "in general ... the direct transfer of traditional notions from the sphere of substantive and procedural private law to that of international law is objectionable." Verzijl, *op. cit. supra* n.966, at 24. Rosenne also submits that "there may be a fault of logic in approaching problems of international law and international administration by the standards of municipal law and municipal practices, and danger in drawing hasty analogies from the latter." Rosenne, *op. cit. supra* n.939, at 1603-1604.

978 Ciobanu, *op. cit. supra* n.965, 216.

Introducing the principle on the international level would, therefore, require its content to be changed according to the specific nature of international relations. Indeed, several authors submit that in the international sphere, litispendence has assumed characteristics different from its domestic counterpart.[979] It remains to be seen if the World Court follows these submissions.

5.3.2.4 Classification of Litispendence as a Preliminary Objection

The principle of litispendence is a preliminary objection related to the admissibility of a claim.[980] If invoked by a party – normally the defendant – it does not relate to the jurisdiction of the Court in general but rather to the exercise of its jurisdiction in the specific case. It is argued that the Court may not assert its jurisdiction because the case is already pending before another forum.

5.3.3.1 The World Court's Case law relevant to Litispendence

Both the Permanent Court of International Justice and the International Court of Justice have been confronted with pleas raising the *lis alibi pendens* issue. The case law of both courts will be examined below in order to ascertain whether the principle *a priori* excludes the Court from reviewing, in contentious cases, decisions taken by the Council.

5.3.3.2 The League of Nations and the Permanent Court

Following the First World War a Peace Conference was held in Paris from January to April 1919. The Conference formulated the Covenant of the League of Nations,[981] adopted it on 28 April, and decided that the Covenant was to be incorporated in the

---

[979] See, *e.g.*, Elsen, *op. cit. supra* n.963, 12-14; Ciobanu, *op. cit. supra* n.965, 216; Ténékidès, *op. cit. supra* n.974, 503; Verzijl, *op. cit. supra* n.966, 24-25.

[980] Thus, for example, in the *Polish Upper Silesia* case the Court examined the objection of litispendence under the heading "admissibility of the suit." PCIJ Rep. (1925), Ser. A., no. 6, 18. See also Elsen, *op. cit. supra* n.963, 2. According to Ciobanu, however, the classification of the principle of litispendence as a preliminary objection is not yet settled: "the ... question as to whether the objection *lis pendens* refers to the jurisdiction of the organs or to the admissibility, receivability or examinability of the claim ... did not find a generally acceptable answer in either the International Court of Justice or the political organs of the United Nations." Ciobanu, *op. cit. supra* n.965, at 227.

[981] For an analysis of the drafting of the Covenant see, *e.g.*, Walters, *op. cit. supra* n.87, 25-38.

Peace Treaties[982] so as to ensure its performance.[983] The League of Nations, therefore, officially came into existence when the Treaty of Versailles entered into force on 10 January 1920.[984]

The principal organs of the League were the Assembly, the Council and the Secretariat.[985] In addition, the Assembly adopted a draft Statute for the Permanent Court of International Justice in 1920, on which occasion the Assembly decided that member states had to individually ratify an instrument by which they agreed to be bound by the Statute. The Statute was incorporated as a separate protocol to the Covenant, making it "both an internal League instrument and a part of an international treaty."[986] The Statute entered into force in September 1921, by which time the majority of members had ratified it.

The Council was composed of representatives of the 'Allied and Associated Powers' on a permanent basis,[987] and of representatives of four members to be "selected by the Assembly from time to time by its discretion."[988] It was charged with the broad responsibility of dealing "with any matter within the sphere of the League or affecting the peace of the world."[989] The Covenant provided for two forms of action by the Council in the discharge of the latter part of this responsibility. Article 11(1) provided that the League "shall take any action that may be deemed wise and effectual to safeguard the peace of nations" in case of "any war or threat of war." This was

---

982 The four Peace Treaties were concluded between the Principal Allied and Associated Powers (the United Kingdom, France, Italy, Japan and the United States) and others, on the one hand, and Germany, Bulgaria, the Serb-Croat-Slovene State, and Hungary on the other. The Treaty of Versailles with Germany was concluded on 28 June 1919; of St. Germain with the Serb-Croate-Slovene State on 10 Sept. 1919; of Neuilly with Bulgaria on 27 Nov. 1919; and of Trianon with Hungary on 4 June 1920.

983 See Elsen, *op. cit. supra* n.963, 15. According to Bowett "the inclusion of the Covenant within the four Peace Treaties led to certain legal difficulties and to a partial identification of the League with the victor States, even though it later came to be recognised as a treaty independent of the Peace Treaties and the League admitted to membership former enemy States." Bowett, *op. cit. supra* n.771, at 20.

984 Walters, *op. cit. supra* n.87, 38.

985 Art. 2 of the League Covenant.

986 Elsen, *op. cit. supra* n.963, at 17.

987 France, Italy, Japan and the UK.

988 Art. 4 (1) of the Covenant. This composition was altered more than once. In 1926 Germany acquired a permanent seat, whilst the number of non-permanent members was increased to six in 1922, to nine in 1926 and to eleven in 1936.

989 Art. 4(4) of the Covenant.

dependent upon a member of the League requesting a meeting of the Council on the matter. In addition, paragraph 2 of Article 11 mentioned:

the friendly right of each Member of the League to bring to the attention of the Assembly or the Council any circumstance whatever affecting international relations which threatens to disturb international peace or the good understanding between nations upon which peace depends.

The second form of action concerned "any dispute likely to lead to a rupture" between members of the League.[990] Article 12 held that in such events the members would "in no case resort to war" but would submit them to either arbitration, judicial settlement or enquiry by the Council. Disputes "suitable for submission to arbitration or judicial settlement"[991] were defined in Article 13(2).[992] The forum for considering such disputes was to be the Permanent Court of Justice "or any other tribunal agreed on by the parties to the dispute or stipulated in any convention existing between them."[993] In case of an enquiry by the Council, it first endeavoured "to effect a settlement of the dispute."[994] If this failed, the Council would vote on and publish a report "containing a statement of the facts of the dispute and the recommendations which are deemed just and proper in regard thereto."[995] If adopted unanimously, the members of the League agreed not to go to war with any party to the dispute that complied with the recommendations of the report.[996] A similar report adopted by majority vote, however, entitled the members to "reserve to themselves the right to take such action as they shall consider necessary for the maintenance of right and justice."[997]

The two procedures briefly described above clearly overlapped. According to Article 11, the Council could act in case of any war or threat of war, or any circumstance whatsoever which threatened to disturb the international peace. This

---

990 Art. 12 of the Covenant.

991 Art. 13(1) of the Covenant. The quoted passage continues "and which cannot be satisfactorily settled through diplomacy", suggesting a bias towards political rather than judicial settlement.

992 The categorization reappears in Art. 36(2) of the PCIJ Statute, which in turn was reproduced in Art. 36(2) of the Statute of the International Court of Justice. For the text of Art. 36(2) see *supra*, page 213.

993 Art. 13(2) of the Covenant.

994 Art. 15(3) of the Covenant.

995 Art. 15(4) of the Covenant.

996 Art. 15(6) of the Covenant.

997 Art. 15(7) of the Covenant. The decisions of the Council were not legally binding, or in an indirect manner at the most. See also Art. 16(2), holding that "it shall be the duty of the Council to *recommend* what effective military, naval or air force the Members shall contribute to the armed forces to be used to protect the covenants of the League" (emphasis added), in case a member had resorted to war in disregard of its obligations under Arts. 12, 13 or 15 of the Covenant.

partially coincided with the powers of other bodies. Firstly, with those of the Assembly under Article 11(2); secondly, and in the present context more importantly, with those of the Permanent Court of Justice or any other tribunal agreed on by the parties under Articles 12 and 13; and thirdly, with other international bodies, such as the Conference of Ambassadors or Mixed Arbitral Tribunals.[998]

The design of the Covenant regarding the maintenance of peace and security thus included the possibility of two or more organs simultaneously dealing with the same matter. This implies that conflicts of jurisdictions and judgments could occur. The next sections will examine the concurrent jurisdiction between the League Council and the Permanent Court of International Justice, and the views of the Permanent Court thereon.[999] But before that is addressed, the classical case with regard to litispendence will be examined, the *Polish Upper Silesia* case. This is the first and only case in which the World Court explicitly addressed the issue of litispendence in the international context.

5.3.3.3 The Permanent Court on Litispendence: Polish Upper Silesia

In the *Case Concerning Certain German Interests in Polish Upper Silesia (Jurisdiction)* the question arose whether the Permanent Court of Justice or the Germano-Polish Arbitral Tribunal[1000] was the appropriate forum to consider a dispute that had arisen between Germany and Poland. The dispute arose from the following facts.[1001] In March 1915, Germany had concluded a contract with a private company,[1002] by which the company

---

[998] Several Mixed Arbitral Tribunals were established under the Peace Treaties. The Conference of Ambassadors, moreover, was installed by the Allied Supreme Council in 1991 in order to ensure the implementation of the Peace Treaties. See H. Blomeyer-Bartenstein, *Conference of Ambassadors*, 7 EPIL (1984) 48-49, 49.

[999] As this chapter is predominantly concerned with the role of the International Court of Justice in remedying illegal Security Council decisions, the attitude of the Council towards concurrent jurisdiction will not be considered in detail. The Council of the League of Nations was confronted with pleas bearing on litispendence on at least four occasions. See on this Elsen, *op. cit. supra* n.963, 28-36, where he discusses the 1921 *Albanian Border Dispute*, the 1921 *Corfu Incident*, the 1927 *Hungarian Optants Dispute* and the *Cruiser Salamis* case. At 36 he concludes that: "the Council proved willing to defer its jurisdiction to other organs already engaged in the settlement of the controversy. However ... the Council kept the situation under surveillance, aware of its responsibilities under the Covenant for the maintenance of peace."

[1000] Established by Art. 304 (and Annex) of the 1919 Treaty of Versailles.

[1001] See PCIJ Rep. (1925), Ser. A, no. 6, 8-11.

[1002] The Bayerische Stickstoffwerke AG.

undertook to establish and manage a nitrate factory, and Germany committed itself to acquiring the necessary lands at Chorzow. On 20 January 1920, the company[1003] was entered in the land register as the owner of the factory. The Polish government, however, enacted a liquidation law on 14 July 1920, according to which all the assets of Germany located in the territory ceded to Poland were transferred to the Polish treasury. The law, moreover, declared null and void any transactions regarding such assets made after 11 November 1918. Pursuant to this law, the Polish state was entered as the owner of the factory on 1 July 1922. This prompted the German company to institute proceedings against Poland at the Germano-Polish Arbitral Tribunal on 15 November 1922, claiming the restoration of the factory and compensation. According to Germany the Polish actions[1004] constituted wrongful acts in violation of, amongst other things, the Geneva Convention concerning Upper Silesia.[1005] The German government therefore filed an application with the Permanent Court of Justice on 15 May 1925. The application was based on Article 23 of the Geneva Convention, which read as follows:

1. Should differences of opinion respecting the construction and application of Articles 6 to 22 arise between the German and Polish Governments, they shall be submitted to the Permanent Court of International Justice.
2. The jurisdiction of the Germano-Polish Mixed Arbitral Tribunal derived from the stipulations of the Treaty of Peace of Versailles shall not hereby be prejudiced.

In its preliminary objections, the Polish government contended that in regard to the factory at Chorzow "the application could not be entertained until the Germano-Polish Mixed Arbitral Tribunal had given Judgment."[1006] At this stage Limburg, the Polish agent, did not explicitly refer to litispendence, but he did attempt to establish that the parties in the two suits were identical.[1007] In its response Germany submitted that the two proceedings involved completely different parties, a private company and the German state; that the Polish objections were therefore unfounded and that the Court was consequently entitled to consider the case.[1008]

1003 In effect, the Oberschlesische Stickstoffwerke which was closely linked to Bayerische Stickstoffwerke AG, to which Germany had conveyed the factory in December 1919.

1004 In addition to the seizing of the factory Poland had notified the owners of several large estates that it intended to expropriate their lands. The notification included a prohibition on selling the estates. See PCIJ Rep. (1925), Ser. A, no. 6, 10-11.

1005 The Geneva Convention concerning Upper Silesia, between Germany and Poland, 15 May 1922.

1006 PCIJ Rep. (1925), Ser. A, no. 6, at 7.

1007 PCIJ, Ser. C, no. 9-1, at 123.

1008 *Ibid.*, 164-165.

During the pleadings Limburg raised the issue of litispendence.[1009] He argued that Germany controlled the private company, that it had been confronted with a choice between the Arbitral Tribunal and the Permanent Court of Justice and that by choosing the former it had forfeited its right to institute proceedings at the latter. The German counsel, Kaufmann, countered by stating that:

> Même si l'on applique en droit international les principes développés par le droit interne, l'exceptio litis pendentis n'est pas fondée dans l'espèce. Pour cette exception soit justifée, il faut, en effet, que les parties en cause, la nature et l'objet du litige soient les mêmes; or, les trois conditions ne sont pas remplies dans notre cause.[1010]

According to Kaufmann, the two proceedings not only involved different parties, but also had different objectives: the action at the Tribunal was aimed at the restitution of the unlawfully expropriated goods, whereas the Permanent Court of Justice was asked to interpret the Geneva Convention concerning Upper Silesia.[1011]

In its judgment the Permanent Court of Justice rejected the Polish objections to the exercise of its jurisdiction. The Court stated that formally the plea of litispendence was not forwarded:

> The Polish Government ... does not really advance the plea generally known as litispendance. In point of fact this word does not occur in the Polish reply; it has only been used in the statements of Counsel, and chiefly, it would seem, as a convenient expression.[1012]

The Court, however, did proceed to elaborate upon the concept of litispendence. It considered that:

> If, however, the plea were to be examined in accordance with the principles generally accepted in regard to *litispendance*, the Court would undoubtedly arrive at the conclusion that it is not well-founded. It is a much disputed question in the teachings of legal authorities and in the jurisprudence of the principal countries whether the doctrine of *litispendance*, the object of which is to prevent the possibility of conflicting judgments, can be invoked in international relations, in the sense that the judges of one State, in the absence of a treaty, refuse to entertain any suit pending before the courts of another State, exactly as they would be bound to do if an action on the same subject had at some previous time been brought in due form before another Court of their own country.
>
> There is no occasion for the Court to devote time to this discussion in the present case, because it is clear that the essential elements which constitute litispendance are not present. There is no question of two identical actions: the action still pending before the Germano-Polish Mixed Arbitral Tribunal at Paris seeks the restitution to a private company of the factory of which the latter claims to have been wrongfully deprived; on

---

1009 "Le Gouvernement polonais, tout en excipant de l'incompétence de la Cour, a soulevé en outre dans sa Réponse exceptionelle la litispendance." *Ibid.*, at 52.

1010 *Ibid.*, at 82.

1011 *Ibid.*, 83-84.

1012 PCIJ Rep. (1925), Ser. A, no. 6, at 19-20.

the other hand, the Permanent Court of International Justice is asked to give an interpretation of certain clauses of the Geneva Convention. The parties are not the same, and, finally, the Mixed Arbitral Tribunals and the Permanent Court of International Justice are not courts of the same character.[1013]

In rendering this judgment, the Court restrictively interpreted the principle of litispendence. After observing that the principle is concerned with the prevention of conflicting judgments, it held that the criteria attached to it had not been met: the plea lacked the necessary identity of parties, actions and jurisdiction. This decision has attracted both support and criticism by the international legal community.[1014] It has been pointed out that, taking the prevention of conflicting judgments into account, the denial of the first two criteria is disputable. For even if the denial holds true formally, materially the parties and actions coincided.[1015] Moreover, the observation that the Court and the Germano-Polish Arbitral Tribunal are not "juridictions du même ordre"[1016] remains quite equivocal, for no explanation whatsoever is provided.

5.3.3.4 The League Council and the Court Concurrent Jurisdiction

The issue in the case discussed above was whether the Permanent Court of International Justice and the Germano-Polish Arbitral Tribunal could simultaneously exercise jurisdiction. In addition, the Permanent Court considered the problem of

---

1013 *Ibid.*, at 20.

1014 Thus Seidl-Hohenveldern submits: "As for the Polish contention of litispendence ... the PCIJ ... *rightly* held this contention not to be well founded." (emphasis added). I. Seidl-Hohenveldern, *German Interests in Polish Upper Silesia Cases*, 2 EPIL (1981) 111-114, at 113. Verzijl, on the contrary, maintains that: "This superficial motivation of a decision on the objection of alleged litispendence, raised in *inter-State* proceedings, with reasons directly taken from the *national* laws of procedure appears very unconvincing if one takes into consideration the difference between national and international conditions which undeniably exist also in this respect." Verzijl, *op. cit. supra* n.966, at 24. Elsen is also critical of the decision in that: "The Court's observations on the first two criteria are at least susceptible of comprehension on the basis of formal argumentation. Unfortunately, this is not the case with respect to its observations on the third requirement." Elsen, *op. cit. supra* n.963, at 25. Ciobanu remarks that: "The Court might have erred, but sometimes, *error communis facit jus*." Ciobanu, *op. cit. supra* n.965, at 215.

1015 *Cf.* Verzijl, *op. cit. supra* n.966, at 25: "it is indeed not possible to deny the identity of the parties simply because in connection with a wrong done to a private person in one action it is this person himself who acts and in another action the State to which he belongs." Moreover: "just as the decision on an action for restitution of a property often depends upon the interpretation of a disputable treaty provision which the action is intended to elicit, so the request for the interpretation of the treaty provision will often directly aim at and achieve such a restitution, because the request was caused precisely by the complaint of the wronged private person." *Ibid.*

1016 The French equivalent for "courts of the same character."

concurrent jurisdiction between itself and the League Council on three occasions. Although the doctrine of litispendence was not explicitly addressed in these cases, the opinion and judgments indicate the attitude of the Court towards overlapping jurisdictions. They will therefore be considered, in short, below.

5.3.3.4.1 Settlers of German Origin

In 1923, the Council requested an advisory opinion whereby the Court was, *inter alia*, asked to determine whether the Council was competent to consider a dispute that had arisen between Poland and Germany regarding the holdings of settlers of German origin. In its opinion, the Court took the Minorities Treaty into account.[1017] It held that the dispute had been brought to the attention of the Council in accordance with Article 12 (2) of that treaty.[1018] The Court then rejected the Polish contention that the Council was not competent to consider the case. It held that:

> the fact that a question brought before the Court by the Council under Paragraph 2 might conceivably be brought before the Court by a single Power as an international difference under Paragraph 3, cannot be accepted as a reason for preventing the Council from discharging its duties under Paragraph 2.[1019]

This implies, in turn, that the fact that a situation was considered by the Council could not bar the institution of proceedings before the Permanent Court of International Justice in accordance with Article 12, paragraph 3, of the Minorities Treaty. A plea of

---

1017 Particularly Art. 12(2) and (3), which read: "Poland agrees that any Member of the Council of the League of Nations shall have the right to bring to the attention of the Council any infraction, or any danger of infraction, of any of these obligations, and that the Council may thereupon take such action and give such direction as it may deem proper and effective in the circumstances. Poland further agrees that any difference of opinion as to questions of law or fact arising out of these Articles between the Polish Government and any one of the Principal Allied and Associated Powers or any other Power, a Member of the Council of the League of Nations, shall be held to be a dispute of an international character under Article 14 of the Covenant of the League of Nations. The Polish Government hereby consents that any such dispute shall, if the other party thereto demands, be referred to the Permanent Court of International Justice. The decision of the Permanent Court shall be final and shall have the same force and effect as an award under Article 13 of the Covenant."

1018 PCIJ Rep. (1923), Ser. B., no. 6, at 22.

1019 *Ibid.*, at 23. *Cf.* the Court's statement at 22: "the matter having been brought to the attention of the Council, the Council ... may at once proceed to 'take such action and give such directions as it may deem proper and effective in the circumstances'. This stipulation clearly makes it proper for the Council to exercise its power under Article 14 of the Covenant to request the advice of the Court on points of law, on the determination of which its actions may depend."

inadmissibility based on litispendence would therefore have been rejected by the Court.[1020]

5.3.3.4.2 Rights of Minorities in Upper Silesia (Minority Schools)

In 1928, the German and Polish governments faced each other in court once again. Germany had filed an application on 2 January, based on Article 72(3) of the Geneva Convention concerning Upper Silesia.[1021] The dispute had started when local Polish authorities declared null and void several entries of children in the registers of certain minority schools. Germany contested this action and brought[1022] the matter to the attention of the Council under Articles 149-157 of the Geneva Convention. The Council considered the question at four meetings in 1927. On 12 March, it adopted a resolution by which an enquiry was initiated that was to assist the local authorities in determining the validity of entries. The German government was, however, not satisfied with this outcome and applied to the Court in order to "clear up the legal questions of principle governing the admission of children to German minority schools."[1023] The Polish government raised preliminary objections against the jurisdiction of the Court and to the admissibility of the claim, arguing, *inter alia*, that the matter had already been settled by the Council by its resolution of 12 March. In its judgment the Court held:

> The Court's jurisdiction depends on the will of the Parties ... Article 36 of the Statute ... establishes this principle in the following terms: 'The jurisdiction of the Court comprises all cases which the parties refer to it and all matters specially provided for in treaties and conventions in force.' This principle only becomes inoperative in those exceptional cases in which the dispute which States might desire to refer to the Court *would fall within the exclusive jurisdiction reserved to some other authority*. That, however, is not the position in the present suit; for the jurisdiction possessed by the Council of the League of Nations under Articles 147 and 149 of the Geneva Convention to decide upon individual or collective petitions, is entirely distinct from, and in no respect restricts, the Court's jurisdiction to hear and determine disputes between States ... The Court's position, in regard to jurisdiction, cannot be compared to the position of municipal courts, amongst which jurisdiction is apportioned by the State, either *ratione materiae* or in accordance with a hierarchical system.[1024]

And with regard to the Polish contention that the dispute had ended through the intervention of the Council, it considered that:

1020 Elsen, *op. cit. supra* n.963, 39.

1021 15 March 1922.

1022 In effect the *Deutsche Volksbund*.

1023 PCIJ Rep. (1928), Ser. A, Judg. no. 12, at 15.

1024 *Ibid.*, at 22-23 (first emphasis added).

the Agent for the Polish Government also raised the objection that, by virtue of Articles 149 and 157 of the Convention, 'the matter had been settled by the Council of the League of Nations which is the final authority as regards measures to be taken', and that its decision could not be subject to revision by the Court of International Justice. ... The Court cannot consider this plea as being well founded. ... The situation arising from the co-existence of these powers [of the Council under the Geneva Convention] and of the jurisdiction conferred upon the Court by Article 72, paragraph 3, has not been defined by the Convention. But in the absence of any special regulation in this respect, the Court thinks it appropriate to recall its earlier observations, namely, that *the two jurisdictions are different in character*.[1025]

5.3.3.4.3 Interpretation of the Statute of the Memel Territory

This case was brought before the Court by France, Italy, Japan and the United Kingdom. The applicants asked the Court to decide whether certain acts of the Lithuanian government were in conformity with the Statute of the Memel territory.[1026] The defendant raised preliminary objections based on Article 17 of the Memel Convention.[1027] According to Lithuania, "the two paragraphs of Article 17 relate to two distinct phases of one and the same procedure, and ... accordingly, *all disputes, before being referred to the Court, must be submitted to the Council for examination.*"[1028] The questions raised in points five and six of the application had not been brought to the attention of the Council and the Lithuanian agent therefore contended that the Court was not competent to decide on these points.

The Court did not consider the Lithuanian arguments to be well-founded:

It should be noted, in the first place, that the proceedings before the Council, contemplated by paragraph I of Article 17, are quite different from the judicial proceedings before the Court to which the second paragraph

---

1025 *Ibid.*, at 29 (emphasis added).

1026 The Statute was annexed to the Memel Convention of 8 May 1924. Reproduced in 29 LNTS, 87 ff.

1027 Which provided that: "The High Contracting Parties declare that any Member of the Council of the League of Nations shall be entitled to draw the attention of the Council to any infraction of the provisions of the present Convention. In the event of any difference of opinion in regard to questions of law or of fact concerning these provisions between the Lithuanian Government and any of the Principal Allied Powers members of the Council ..., such difference shall be regarded as a dispute of an international character under the terms of Article 14 of the Covenant of the League of Nations. The Lithuanian Government agrees that all disputes of this kind shall, if the other party so requests, be referred to the Permanent Court of International Justice. There shall be no appeal from the Permanent Court's decision, which shall have the force and value of a decision rendered in virtue of Article 13 of the Covenant."

1028 PCIJ Rep. (1932), Ser. A/B, no. 47, at 8. And further in the text, at 8-9, the Court held that "it must be concluded that paragraph 2 of Article of the Convention of Memel regards recourse to the Permanent Court of International Justice as a procedure only to be employed after a failure of the procedure before the Council of the League of Nations, under paragraph I of the same Article 17."

> of Article 17 relates. ... It is to be observed that there is nothing in the text of Article 17 to show that it was the intention of the Parties to make proceedings before the Council a condition precedent to proceedings before the Court.
>
> The actual text of Article 17 shows that the two procedures relate to different objects. The object of the procedure before the Council is the examination of an 'infraction of the provisions of the Convention', which presupposes an act already committed, whereas the procedure before the Court is concerned with 'any difference in opinion in regard to questions of law or fact'. Such difference of opinion may arise without any infraction having been noted. It is true that one and the same situation may give rise to proceedings either before the Council under the first paragraph, or before the Court under the second; but that will not always be the case, and this suffices to prove that the two procedures are not necessarily connected with one another.[1029]

In addition to the differences in object between the two proceedings, the Court observed a difference in parties entitled to institute proceedings. It noted that any member of the Council could bring the dispute before the Council, whereas only one of the Principal Allied Powers which was a member of the Council could bring the case before the Court.[1030] Accordingly, the Court considered that:

> If the principle of the unity of proceedings were to be adopted, it would follow that a case could not be proceeded with before the Court, under paragraph 2 of Article 17, if it had been brought before the Council, under paragraph I, by a Member of the Council other than one of the Principal Allied Powers which signed the Convention.[1031]

5.3.3.5 Conclusions: The Permanent Court on Litispendence

The Court interpreted the principle of litispendence in a formalistic and restrictive manner in the jurisdictional phase of the *Case Concerning Certain German Interests in Polish Upper Silesia*. In the first place, it held that the very existence of the principle on the international plane is a much disputed question in the legal community. It also held that the private company and the German state were different parties; that the actions were not identical; and that the Mixed Arbitral Tribunal and itself were not courts of the same character. Thus the Court indicated that the plea of litispendence, albeit not formally advanced by Poland, would have been rejected.

The same unwillingness on the part of the Court to renounce its jurisdiction is reflected in the three other cases in which it was argued that the matters brought before the Court fell within the jurisdiction of the League Council, and that the Court was therefore not competent to decide on these matters. By its Advisory Opinion on *Certain Settlers of German Origin*, the Court laid down that the fact that a dispute was

1029 *Ibid.*, at 9.

1030 *Ibid.*, at 10.

1031 *Ibid.*

pending before the Court, did not by itself bar further consideration of the matter by the Council, and *vice versa*. In the *Minority Schools* judgment, the Court considered its jurisdiction to be complementary to that of the Council and that the two jurisdictions were "different in character." This difference was reaffirmed in the *Interpretation of the Memel Statute* case.

Thus the Permanent Court of International Justice, confronted with pleas to that effect, did not consider the co-existence of powers between itself and the Council to be an obstacle to the exercise of its jurisdiction. It considered the functions of the Council and Court to be different and complementary, and saw no problem in the two bodies discharging these functions simultaneously. The following will now address the case-law of the successor of the Permanent Court of International Justice, the International Court of Justice, in order to determine its views on litispendence between itself and the Security Council of the United Nations.

5.3.4.1 Concurrent Jurisdiction within the United Nations

In general, four categories of concurrent jurisdiction between bodies acting in the United Nations can be identified.[1032] These are the concurrent jurisdictions between: the United Nations taken as a whole and States;[1033] the United Nations, or any of its organs, and other international organizations;[1034] the political organs of the United Nations and the International Court of Justice, its principal judicial organ; and the political organs of the United Nations.[1035] A special case concerning the third category

---

1032 D. Ciobanu, *Preliminary Objections Related to the Jurisdiction of the United Nations Political Organs* (1975), 50.

1033 *Cf.* the *Reparation for Injuries Suffered in the Service of the United Nations* case, Adv. Op., 11 April 1949, wherein the Court, having determined that the United Nations possessed the capacity to bring international claims, examined the question of "how action by the United Nations [is] to be reconciled with such rights as may be possessed by the State of which the victim is a national." (ICJ Rep. (1949), at 185). It ruled that both the organization and the State of which the victim is a national could exercise diplomatic protection. However, the Court did not lay down a general principle governing such cases: "in such a case there is no rule of law which assigns priority to the one or to the other, or which compels either the State or the Organization to refrain from bringing an international claim." *Ibid.*

1034 For the Security Council see, *e.g.*, T.J. Kahng, *Law, Politics, and the Security Council* (1969), 57-70.

1035 See, *e.g.*, *Conditions of Admission of a State to Membership in the United Nations*, Adv. Op., 28 May 1948. In this case the General Assembly requested an opinion from the Court on the conformity of the Council's practice of imposing additional conditions on membership of the UN, with Article 4 of the Charter. The Court held that this practice was incompatible with the said article (ICJ Rep. (1948), 65). See also Article 12(1) of the Charter, which holds that the General Assembly will abstain

will be examined below, *i.e.* the concurrent exercise of jurisdiction by the International Court of Justice and the Security Council. This means that the jurisdiction of the principal judicial organ of the United Nations, the International Court of Justice, will be compared to that of a principal political organ, the Security Council.

The potential coincidence of their jurisdiction becomes apparent when one compares, for example, Article 36(1) of the Charter with Article 36(2) of the Court's Statute. The former states that the Security Council may make recommendations on any dispute or situation, the continuance of which is likely to endanger international peace and security. Under Chapter VII of the Charter, moreover, the Council may take binding measures in order to maintain international peace and security. Article 36(2) of the Court's Statute provides that states may recognize as compulsory the jurisdiction of the International Court of Justice in their legal disputes. Thus, under the Charter both organs may be simultaneously seized of a dispute, with the ensuing possibility of conflicting decisions being taken.

5.3.4.2 The International Court of Justice on Concurrent Jurisdiction

There have been several occasions on which the International Court of Justice and the Security Council both have dealt with the same matter. The cases in which this fact was taken into account by the Court will be presented here in chronological order.

5.3.4.2.1 The Aegean Continental Shelf Case

The first case in which the Court considered the issue of concurrent jurisdiction was the *Aegean Sea Continental Shelf Case* (Interim Protection).[1036] In a dispute over this shelf, Greece had instituted proceedings against Turkey on 10 August 1976, at the same time requesting the indication of provisional measures. In addition, Greece brought the matter before the Security Council, which discussed the issue on 12, 13 and 25 August, and adopted resolution 395 (1976) on the latter occasion. Resolution 395 urged the Greek and Turkish governments "to do everything in their power to

---

from making recommendations on matters under consideration by the Security Council, "unless the Security Council so requests."

1036 In an earlier case, the *Anglo-Iranian Oil Co.* (Jurisdiction), UK v. Iran, the counsel for Iran had contested the admissibility of the claim, *inter alia* on the ground that the matter was already being dealt with by the Council. The Court, however, did not consider this objection as it declined to exercise jurisdiction on other grounds. See the Judgment of 22 July, ICJ Rep. (1952), 113-115.

reduce the present tensions in the area so that the negotiating process may be facilitated" and called for the resumption of "direct negotiations over their differences". The resolution, moreover, reiterated to the governments "the principles of the Charter of the United Nations concerning the peaceful settlement of disputes"; and the need "to respect each other's international rights and obligations and to avoid any incident which might lead to the aggravation of the situation".

In its judgment on the provisional measures, the Court took "cognizance of the fact that, simultaneously with the proceedings before it in respect of the request for interim measures for protection, the United Nations Security Council also has been seized of the dispute."[1037] After citing the relevant provisions of resolution 395 (1976), the Court considered that:

> Both Greece and Turkey, as Members of the United Nations, have expressly recognized the responsibility of the Security Council for the maintenance of international peace and security; ... in the above-mentioned resolution, the Security Council has recalled to them their obligations under the United Nations Charter with respect to the peaceful settlement of disputes, ... these obligations are clearly imperative in regard to their present dispute ... and it is not to be presumed that either State will fail to heed its obligations under the Charter of the United Nations or fail to heed to the recommendation of the Security Council addressed to them with respect to their present dispute. ... Accordingly, it is not necessary for the Court to decide the question whether Article 41 of the Statute confers upon it the power to indicate interim measures of protection for the sole purpose of preventing the aggravation or extension of a dispute.[1038]

This is an interesting judgment insofar as the Court did not consider it necessary to indicate interim measures in order to avoid an aggravation of the situation. The Court considered the obligations of the parties under the Charter and the actions of the Security Council, which has the primary responsibility for the maintenance of international peace and security, a sufficient bar to such aggravation, and hence did not use its power under Article 41 of the Statute. This *could* imply that the Court recognizes the principle of litispendence in its relationship with the Security Council, but the decision remains silent on the issue. The answer to this question may possibly be found in the separate grounds given by the judges to motivate their decision.

In addition to the dissenting judge *ad hoc*, eight of the twelve judges who concurred with the decision issued separate opinions. They reflect the different views held by the judges on the role of the Court alongside the Security Council in the settlement of disputes. Judge Jiménez de Aréchaga, the President of the Court, for example, noted that "the Court's specific power under Article 41 of the Statute is directed to the

---

1037 *Aegean Sea Continental Shelf Case* (Interim Protection), 11 Sept. 1976, ICJ Rep. (1976), para. 37 at 12.

1038 *Ibid.*, paras. 41-42 at 13.

preservation of rights 'sub-judice' and does not consist in a police power over the maintenance of international peace and security."[1039]

Judge Lachs, on the other hand, stated that:

there was in my view no statutory bar to [the Court's] spelling out the legal consequences of the Security Council's resolution and the official statements of the representatives of the two States. The pronouncements of the Council did not dispense the Court, an independent judicial organ, from expressing its own view on the serious situation in the disputed area.[1040]

Judge Tarazi specifically elaborated upon the role of the Court in the United Nations system. He stressed that:

at the same time it requested the Court to indicate interim measures, Greece turned to the Security Council to request it to examine the situation which it had already described in the Application. This was not an example of the simultaneous use of two parallel remedies, inasmuch as the Security Council, unlike the Court, is a political organ. The rule *electa una via* did not have to be applied.[1041]

According to Tarazi "the present Court, while maintaining its independence, should not fail to take into account this basic truth, namely that it is an integral part of the United Nations."[1042] In the United Nations "the Security Council bears an essential responsibility for the maintenance of international peace and security. The Court, if the circumstances so require, ought to collaborate in the accomplishment of this fundamental mission."[1043]

These opinions warrant the conclusion that despite their non-indication of provisional measures, the judges did not adhere to the principle of litispendence, with the possible exception of Jiménez de Aréchaga. The majority position may be summarized by Judge Elias' observation that "both organs are competent each in its own sphere to deal with the matter submitted to it and come to its own conclusions thereon."[1044] The case was eventually dismissed, as the Court found that the two instruments relied upon by Greece as conferring jurisdiction were invalid.[1045]

1039 Sep. Op. Jiménez de Aréchaga, *ibid.*, at 16.

1040 Sep. Op. Lachs, *ibid.*, at 20.

1041 Sep. Op. Tarazi, *ibid.*, at 33.

1042 *Ibid.*

1043 *Ibid.*

1044 Sep. Op. Elias, *ibid.*, at 27.

1045 See the Judgment of 19 Dec. 1978, ICJ Rep. (1978).

5.3.4.2.2 United States Diplomatic and Consular Staff in Tehran

The second case related to the seizure by an armed group of several hundred people of the United States embassy in Tehran on 4 November 1979. The group, which had emanated from a demonstration against the United States' decision to admit the former Shah to its territory, subsequently took all the personnel of the embassy hostage.[1046] Since the Iranian government did not respond to American requests for action, the United States instituted proceedings at both the Security Council and the International Court of Justice. The Council met on 27 November and 4 December 1979, adopting Resolution 457 (1979) on the latter occasion. Resolution 457 (1979) noted that the level of tension between Iran and the United States could have grave consequences for international peace and security; called for the immediate release of the personnel of the embassy; requested the Secretary-General to lend his good offices for the immediate implementation of the resolution and to take all appropriate measures to that end; and provided that the Security Council would remain actively seized of the matter.

The United States applied to the Court on 29 November 1979, whereby the Court was asked to adjudge and declare that the seizure of the embassy and the subsequent inaction of the Iranian government violated several treaties in force;[1047] that all hostages were to be released; that the United States was entitled to reparation; and that the Iranian government was to surrender the responsible persons for prosecution in the United States. On the same day, the United States requested the indication of provisional measures.

Iran chose not to participate in the proceedings at the Court. In a letter to the Court, it stated that the question of the hostages "represents only a marginal and secondary aspect of an overall problem" and that "the Court cannot examine the American Application divorced from its proper context, namely the whole political dossier of the relations between Iran and the United States over the last 25 years."[1048]

1046 For the facts of the case see the *Case Concerning United States Diplomatic and Consular Staff in Tehran* (Merits), US v. Iran, ICJ Rep. (1980), paras. 14-24.

1047 The 1961 Vienna Convention on Diplomatic Relations (500 UNTS 95 ff.); the 1963 Vienna Convention on Consular Relations (596 UNTS 262 ff.); the 1973 Convention on the Prevention and Punishment of Crimes against Internationally Protected Persons (13 ILM (1974) 43 ff.); the 1955 Treaty of Amity, Economic Relations, and Consular Rights between the United States and Iran (248 UNTS 93 ff.); and the United Nations Charter.

1048 Letter from the Iranian Minister for Foreign Affairs, dated 9 December 1979. Reproduced in *Case Concerning United States Diplomatic and Consular Staff in Tehran* (Prov. Measures), US v. Iran, Order of 15 Dec. 1979, ICJ Rep. (1979), 10-11.

According to Iran, moreover, the Islamic revolution was a "revolution of a whole oppressed nation" and "any examination of the numerous repercussions thereof is a matter essentially and directly within the national sovereignty of Iran."[1049]

In its decision on interim measures, the Court held that "the two considerations advanced by the Government in its letter ... cannot ... be accepted as constituting any obstacle to the Court's taking cognizance of the case."[1050] After noting that *prima facie* jurisdiction existed, it granted the provisional measures requested by the United States.[1051]

Iran, again, did not appear at the Court when the merits of the case were examined. It reiterated its objections to the admissibility of the claim by a letter dated 16 March 1980.[1052] When the proceedings commenced, the Security Council had adopted the aforementioned resolution 457 (1979), and resolution 461 (1979).[1053] Pursuant to these resolutions, the Secretary-General visited Tehran and, on 20 February 1980, announced the establishment of a Commission which would engage in a fact-finding mission in Iran. A draft resolution sponsored by the United States calling for an economic embargo against Iran failed to be adopted due to a negative vote by the Soviet Union.[1054]

As in its decision on provisional measures, the Court rejected the Iranian objections to the admissibility of the claim in its judgment on the merits.[1055] Prior to the examination of the merits, however, the Court:

1049 *Ibid.*

1050 *Ibid.*, para. 26 at 16. The contention that the question of the hostages was of 'secondary' or 'marginal' importance was rejected by the Court, *inter alia* by reference to S/Res. 457 (1979), which noted that the tension between the two states could have grave consequences for international peace and security. See *ibid.*, para. 23.

1051 These included restoring the embassy to the possession and exclusive control of the US, the release of all hostages, and an order that both sides were to abstain from taking any action that could aggravate the tension or render the dispute more difficult to solve.

1052 Reproduced in *Case Concerning United States Diplomatic and Consular Staff in Tehran,* (Merits), US v. Iran, ICJ Rep. (1980), para. 10 at 8. This letter closely resembles the letter of 9 Dec. 1979.

1053 Adopted on 31 Dec. 1979, this resolution reiterated the calls on the Iranian government made in resolution 457 (1979).

1054 UN Doc. S/13735, 13 Jan. 1980. The draft resolution received 10 votes in favour, 2 against, with 2 abstentions.

1055 See *Case Concerning United States Diplomatic and Consular Staff in Tehran,* (Merits), US v. Iran, ICJ Rep. (1980), paras. 33-38 and 81-82, at 18-20, respectively 37-38.

thought it right to examine, *ex officio*, whether its competence to decide the present case, or the admissibility of the present proceedings, might possibly have been affected by the setting up of the Commission by the Secretary-General of the United Nations on 20 February 1980.[1056]

In doing so, the Court considered that:

In the preamble to this second resolution the Security Council expressly took into account the Court's Order of 15 December 1979 indicating provisional measures; and it does not seem to have occurred to any member of the Council that there was or could be anything irregular in the simultaneous exercise of their respective functions by the Court and the Security Council. Nor is there in this any cause for surprise. Whereas Article 12 of the Charter expressly forbids the General Assembly to make any recommendation with regard to a dispute or situation while the Security Council is exercising its functions in respect of that dispute or situation, no such restriction is placed on the functioning of the Court by any provision of either the Charter or the Statute of the Court. The reasons are clear. It is for the Court, the principal judicial organ of the United Nations, to resolve any legal questions that may be in issue between parties to a dispute; and the resolution of such legal questions by the Court may be an important, and sometimes decisive, factor in promoting peaceful settlement of the dispute. ... It follows that neither the mandate given by the Security Council to the Secretary-General in resolutions 457 and 461 of 1979, nor the setting up of the Commission by the Secretary-General, can be considered as constituting any obstacle to the exercise of the Court's jurisdiction in the present case.[1057]

These statements by the Court seem quite unequivocal. On its own initiative, it decided to examine the question whether prior action of the Security Council precluded it from exercising its jurisdiction. The Court concluded that with regard to the seizure of a dispute by both the Security Council and the International Court of Justice, there does not appear to be anything irregular in the "simultaneous exercise of their respective functions." It thus reaffirmed the position taken by the majority in the *Aegean Continental Shelf* case. The conclusion to be drawn from this is that reference to litispendence as an objection to the admissibility of a claim before the Court will not be successful. To this effect Elsen, for example, states that:

the Hostages case taught that even in disputes allegedly involving a threat to international peace the Court will not defer to the Security Council. Deferral to the Security Council would be considered as an abandonment of its responsibilities under the Charter as the principal judicial organ of the United Nations.[1058]

1056 *Ibid.*, para. 39 at 20-21.

1057 *Ibid.*, paras. 40 and 44, at 21 and 23-24. The Court seems to have concurred with the argument forwarded by the American counsel, Mr. Owen, that: "There is absolutely nothing in the United Nations Charter or in this Court's Statute to suggest that action by the Security Council excludes action by the Court, even if the two actions might in some respects be parallel." ICJ Pleadings, *U.S. Diplomatic and Consular Staff in Tehran*, at 29.

1058 Elsen, *op. cit. supra* n.963, at 63. To the same effect Klein submits: "Kein Organ hat sich in seinem *procedure* von dem Vorgehen des anderen Organs behindert gesehen." Klein, *op. cit. supra* n.973, at 474. See also Bedjaoui, *op. cit. supra* n.745, 64.

5.3.4.2.3 The Nicaragua Case

The most extensive elaboration by the Court on its role in the settlement of disputes alongside the Security Council was made in the *Nicaragua* case. Nicaragua had instituted proceedings against the United States on 9 April 1984. In its application, the Nicaraguan government requested the Court to adjudge and declare that the United States was in violation of international law[1059] by embarking on certain military and paramilitary actions conducted in Nicaragua and the waters off its coasts.[1060] In order to immediately put an end to these actions Nicaragua simultaneously requested interim measures of protection. Prior to this litigation the Security Council had seized the matter. On 19 May 1983, it adopted resolution 530 (1983), in which it recalled the Charter principles governing the peaceful settlement of disputes and reaffirmed "the right of Nicaragua and of all other countries of the area to live in peace and security, free from outside interference." A later draft resolution condemning, and calling for an immediate end to, the mining of the main ports of Nicaragua was, however, vetoed by the United States.[1061]

The interim measures were indicated by an order of 10 May 1980. Herein the Court unanimously held that: "The United States of America should immediately cease and refrain from any action restricting, blocking or endangering access to or from Nicaraguan ports, and in particular, the laying of mines."[1062]

Furthermore, by fourteen votes to one the Court decided that:

> The right to sovereignty and to political independence possessed by the Republic of Nicaragua, like any other State of the region, or of the world, should be fully respected and should not in any way be jeopardized by any military and paramilitary activities which are prohibited by the principles of international law, in particular the principle that States should refrain in their international relations from the threat or use of force against

---

[1059] The treaty provisions invoked by Nicaragua in its application include Art. 2(4) of the UN Charter; Arts. 18 and 20 of the OAS Charter; Art. 8 of the Convention on Rights and Duties of States; and Art. I(3) of the Convention concerning the Duties and Rights of States in the Event of Civil Strife. Moreover, Nicaragua contended that the US had breached various obligations under general and customary law, such as the principles of non-intervention; the non-use of force; and respect for the freedom of the high seas.

[1060] The conducting of armed attacks by air, land and sea; aerial trespassing into Nicaraguan airspace; incursions into Nicaraguan territorial waters; and the support of movements forcefully resisting the Nicaraguan government. See *Case Concerning Military and Paramilitary Activities in and against Nicaragua* (Prov. Measures), Nic. v. US, ICJ Rep. (1984), 170-171.

[1061] See UN Doc. S/16463.

[1062] *Case Concerning Military and Paramilitary Activities in and against Nicaragua* (Prov. Measures), Nic. v. US, ICJ Rep. (1984), at 187.

the territorial integrity or political independence of any State, and the principle concerning the duty not to intervene in matters within the domestic jurisdiction of a State.[1063]

In rendering this decision, the Court rejected the United States' contention that "in the circumstances of this case ... questions regarding the use of force during hostilities are more properly committed to resolution by the political organs of the United Nations and of the Organization of American States."[1064]

The next phase of the case concerned the question of jurisdiction[1065] and the admissibility of the application. The United States contested this admissibility on five grounds, three of which directly or indirectly bear on the present subject. According to the United States all the allegations made by Nicaragua in effect constituted a single claim, namely that it was engaged in the unlawful use of armed force or had committed acts of aggression against Nicaragua. This claim constituted:

a matter which is committed by the Charter and by practice to the competence of other organs, in particular the United Nations Security Council. All allegations of this kind are confided to the political organs of the Organization for consideration and determination ... Article 24 of the Charter ... confers upon the Security Council 'primary responsibility for the maintenance of international peace and security.' The provisions of

---

1063 *Ibid.*

1064 *Ibid.*, para. 37 at 185. The US disputed the admissibility of the request for provisional measures on two alternative grounds. Firstly, that such measures would directly implicate the rights and interests of other Central American states involved in the ongoing regional settlement efforts (the Contadora process), and that these "other Central American States are indispensable parties in whose absence the Court cannot properly proceed" (*ibid.*, para. 35 at 184). Secondly, that "Contadora itself is a properly instituted regional process seeking to resolve complex and interrelated social, political and economic issues, as well as security matters underlying the current turmoil in Central America. This Court cannot take cognizance of Nicaragua's Application or indicate the interim measures Nicaragua requests without detrimentally affecting that process in unpredictable and irremediable ways." *Ibid.*, para. 36 at 184-185.

1065 One of the main jurisdictional issues was whether the 1929 declaration, by which Nicaragua without reservations accepted the optional clause under the PCIJ Statute, was a declaration "still in force" in accordance with Art. 36(5) of the present Statute. This was because the instrument of ratification had not been deposited at the League of Nations, although the Nicaraguan Foreign Minister had announced this in a telegram sent in 1939. The Court eventually held that "having regard to the origins and generality of the statements to the effect that Nicaragua was bound by its 1929 Declaration, it is right to conclude that the constant acquiescence of that State in those affirmations constitutes a valid mode of manifestation of its intent to recognize the compulsory jurisdiction of the Court under Article 36, paragraph 2, of the Statute, and that accordingly Nicaragua is vis-à-vis the United States, a State accepting 'the same obligation' under that Article." *Case Concerning Military and Paramilitary Activities in and against Nicaragua* (Jurisdiction of the Court and Admissibility of the Application), Nic. v. US, 26 Nov. 1984, ICJ Rep. (1984), para. 47 at 412-413.

the Charter dealing with the ongoing use of force contain no recognition of the possibility of settlement by judicial, as opposed to political means.[1066]

Secondly, the United States observed that Nicaragua had approached the Security Council on 4 April 1984. The draft resolution which was then presented, which failed to be adopted, corresponded to the claims submitted by Nicaragua to the Court. The United States, therefore, contended that: "Since Nicaragua's Application in effect asks the Court for a judgment in all material respects identical to the decision which the Security Council did not take, it amounts to an appeal from an adverse consideration in the Security Council."[1067]

Lastly, the United States maintained that the ongoing conflict involved the use of force and that the Court could not deal effectively with it "without overstepping proper judicial bounds."[1068] For:

The resort to force during ongoing armed conflict lacks the attributes necessary for the application of the judicial process, namely a pattern of legally relevant facts discernible by the means available to the adjudicating tribunal, established in conformity with applicable norms of evidence and proof, and not subject to further material evolution during the course of, and subsequent to, the judicial proceedings. It is for reasons of this nature that ongoing armed conflict must be entrusted by political processes.[1069]

The Court dismissed the American objections. With regard to the contention that "the matter was essentially one for the Security Council since it concerned a complaint by Nicaragua involving the use of force",[1070] the Court cited the *Hostages* case in order to establish that "the fact that a matter is before the Security Council should not prevent it being dealt with by the Court and that both proceedings could be pursued *pari parsu*."[1071]

The Court went further, however, and cited Article 24 of the Charter, which confers on the Security Council "primary responsibility for the maintenance of international peace and security." The Court then stated that:

The Charter accordingly does not confer *exclusive* responsibility upon the Security Council for the purpose. While in Article 12 there is a provision for a clear demarcation of functions between the General Assembly and the Security Council, in respect of any dispute or situation, that the former should not make any recommendation with regard to that dispute or situation unless the Security Council so requires, there is no similar provision anywhere in the Charter with respect to the Security Council and the Court. The Council has

---

1066 *Ibid.*, para. 89 at 431-432.

1067 *Ibid.*, para. 91 at 432-433.

1068 *Ibid.*, para. 99 at 436-437.

1069 *Ibid.*

1070 *Ibid.*, para. 93 at 433-434.

1071 *Ibid.*

functions of a political nature assigned to it, whereas the Court exercises purely judicial functions. *Both organs can therefore perform their separate but complementary functions with respect to the same events.*[1072]

Furthermore, the Court held that:

until the Security Council makes a determination under Article 39, a dispute remains to be dealt with by the methods of peaceful settlement provided under Article 33, including judicial settlement; and even after a determination under Article 39, there is no necessary inconsistency between Security Council action and adjudication by the Court.[1073]

As to the objection that the Court was in effect being asked to reverse a Security Council decision, the Court remarked that it:

is not asked to say that the Security Council was wrong in its decision, nor that there was anything inconsistent with law in the way in which the members of the Council employed their right to vote. The Court is asked to pass judgment on certain legal aspects of a situation which has also been considered by the Security Council, a procedure which is entirely consonant with its position as the principal judicial organ of the United Nations.[1074]

The Court, moreover, referred to the *Corfu Channel* case to show that "the Court has never shied away from a case brought before it merely because it had political implications or because it involved serious elements of the use of force."[1075] On the last argument that the Court would overstep "proper judicial bounds" by adjudicating the conflict, it ruled that:

it is the litigant seeking to establish a fact who bears the burden of proving it; and in cases where evidence may not be forthcoming, a submission may in the judgment be rejected as unproved, but is not to be ruled out as inadmissible *in limine* on the basis of an anticipated lack of proof.[1076]

In rendering this judgment, the Court upheld and reaffirmed its position in the *Hostages* case. According to the Court, the Council and itself may simultaneously deal with a dispute, even after the Security Council has acted under Chapter VII of the

---

1072 *Ibid.*, para. 95 at 434-435 (latter emphasis added). *Cf.* the *Certain Expenses* case, in which the Court, after citing Art. 24 of the Charter, stated that in regard to the powers of the General Assembly "this responsibility is 'primary', not exclusive." *Certain Expenses of the United Nations*, ICJ Rep. (1962), at 162.

1073 *Ibid.*, para. 90 at 432.

1074 *Ibid.*, para. 98 at 436.

1075 *Ibid.*, para. 94 at 434. Prior to this passage, however, the Court had already held that "the complaint of Nicaragua is not about an ongoing armed conflict between it and the United States, but one requiring, and indeed demanding, the peaceful settlement of disputes between the two States. Hence, it is properly brought before the principal judicial organ of the Organization for peaceful settlement." *Ibid.*

1076 *Ibid.*, para. 101 at 437-438.

Charter. In such cases the invocation of litispendence will not be successful since in the view of the Court both organs perform "separate but complementary functions." In other words the two organs do not possess 'similar jurisdictions', and thus the third condition attached to the concept of litispendence will not be met.[1077]

5.3.4.2.4 The Bosnian Genocide Case

The facts of this case are as follows. On 20 March 1993 Bosnia-Herzegovina instituted proceedings against the Federal Republic of Yugoslavia (Serbia and Montenegro). In its application[1078] Bosnia-Herzegovina, *inter alia*, asked the Court to adjudge and declare that Yugoslavia had committed acts of genocide and was in violation of customary and treaty law regarding the non-use of force.[1079] As seen above, the Security Council had imposed a weapons embargo on Yugoslavia by resolution 713 (1999).[1080] In view of the actions of Serbia and Montenegro, however, the applicant asked the Court to determine that it "has the sovereign right to defend Itself and its People under United Nations Charter Article 51 and customary international law, including by means of immediately obtaining military weapons, equipment, supplies and troops from other States."[1081]

Consequently, the Court was asked to declare that resolution 731 (1992) "must be

---

1077 See Bedjaoui, *op. cit. supra* n.745, 64.

1078 The application was based on the 1948 Convention on the Prevention and Punishment of the Crime of Genocide. Article IX thereof provides that: "Disputes between the Contracting Parties relating to the interpretation, application or fulfilment of the present Convention, including those relating to the responsibility of a State for genocide or for any of the other acts enumerated in Article III, shall be submitted to the International Court of Justice at the request of any of the parties to the dispute." On 31 March 1993 the Agent of Bosnia-Herzegovina filed a letter, submitting that it afforded an additional basis for the jurisdiction of the Court. This letter by Serbia and Montenegro, dated 8 June 1992, was addressed to the President of the Arbitration Commission of the International Conference for Peace in Yugoslavia. It contained a reply to three questions submitted to the FRY by the Arbitration Commission in respect of the legal consequences of the dissolution of Yugoslavia. In response to the question "on what basis and by what means should the problem of succession of States arising between the different States emerging from the Socialist Federal Republic of Yugoslavia be settled?", Serbia and Montenegro submitted that "all legal disputes which cannot be settled by agreement between FR Yugoslavia and the former Yugoslav republics should be taken to the International Court of Justice, the principal judicial organ of the United Nations." See *Case Concerning Application of the Convention on the Prevention and Punishment of the Crime of Genocide* (Provisional Measures), Order 8 April 1993, ICJ Rep. (1993), paras. 27-32 at 16-18.

1079 *Ibid.*, paras. 1-2 at 4-7.

1080 See *supra*, paragraph 3.6.

1081 *Case Concerning Application of the Convention on the Prevention and Punishment of the Crime of Genocide* (Prov. Measures), ICJ Rep. (1993), para. 2, at 6.

construed in a manner that shall not impair the inherent right of individual or collective self-defence of Bosnia and Herzegovina".[1082]

On the same day on which the application was filed, Bosnia and Herzegovina requested interim measures of protection. These would, in the first place, be to the effect that Serbia and Montenegro had to immediately cease and desist from all acts of genocide and the use of force in and against Bosnia-Herzegovina. In addition, the Court was asked to rule that "under the current circumstances, the Government of Bosnia and Herzegovina has the right to seek and receive support from other States in order to defend Itself and its People, including by means of immediately obtaining military weapons, equipment, supplies."[1083]

In other words, Bosnia-Herzegovina asked the Court to declare that the arms embargo imposed by the Security Council was contrary to international law, and that it consequently had no legal effect. Yugoslavia, on the other hand, contended that "so long as the Security Council is acting under Article 25 of the Charter, it would be premature and inappropriate for the Court to indicate provisional measures, and certainly provisional measures of the type which have been requested."[1084]

The Court rejected the Bosnian requests with regard to its self-defence. It ruled that its jurisdiction *ratione materiae* was confined to Article IX of the Genocide Convention,[1085] and consequently the Court held that it could only rule on the measures requested "which fall within the scope of the Genocide Convention."[1086] At the same time it duly noted that it did not follow Yugoslavia's contention that the Court ought to defer to the Council. It repeated its observation made in the Nicaragua

---

1082 *Ibid.* The Court was subsequently asked to determine that "resolution 713 (1991) and all subsequent Security Council resolutions referring thereto or reaffirming thereof must not be construed to impose an arms embargo upon Bosnia and Herzegovina, as required by Articles 24(1) and 51 of the United Nations Charter and in accordance with the customary doctrine of *ultra vires*." *Ibid.*

1083 *Ibid.*, para. 3, at 8.

1084 *Ibid.*, para. 33 at 18-19.

1085 According to the Court "it is by no means clear ... whether the letter of 8 June 1992 was intended as an 'immediate commitment' ... binding on Yugoslavia, to submit unconditionally the unilateral submission to the Court of a wide range of legal disputes ...; or whether it was intended as a commitment solely to submission to the Court of the three questions raised by the Chairman of the Committee; or as no more than the enunciation of a general policy of favouring judicial settlement, which did not embody an offer or commitment." *Ibid.*, para. 31 at 18 (reference omitted).

1086 *Ibid.*, para. 35 at 19. Bosnia and Herzegovina subsequently dropped the self-defence argument during the proceedings.

case to the effect that: "Both organs can therefore perform their separate but complementary functions with respect to the same events."[1087]

5.3.4.3 Interim Conclusions

The examination of the cases above reveals a consistent pattern. According to the Court, a parallel seizure of a dispute by itself and the Security Council does not preclude it from exercising jurisdiction. This follows from the independence of both organs, which is confirmed by the observation that neither the Charter nor the Court's Statute place any restriction on the functioning of the Court in respect of a dispute already dealt with by the Council. Moreover, the Court maintains that both organs perform different functions and are therefore not to be considered as organs possessing similar jurisdiction. Although the doctrine as such did not appear in the proceedings before the Court, it may be inferred from the foregoing that the Court rejects the applicability of litispendence in its relationship with the Council. In this it reaffirms the jurisprudence of the Permanent Court of International Justice. According to one author, this "well points up to the functional parallelism of two principal organs of the United Nations, each of which has competence, under the combined Charter and Statute, to deal with the same 'dispute', but with different functions."[1088]

In the next case under review, the *Lockerbie* case, the Court was also confronted with a plea of inadmissibility based on a prior seizure of the dispute by the Security Council. It differs from the cases discussed above in that it is the first in which the Council and Court were seized by different parties to the same dispute.

5.3.4.4 The Lockerbie case

After US and UK investigations suggested that two Libyan nationals were responsible for the bombing of Pan Am Flight 103 on 21 December 1988, the Security Council adopted resolution 731 (1992) which called for the extradition of the suspects.[1089] Libya refused and instituted proceedings against the US and the UK at the International Court of Justice on 3 March 1992. The application was based on Article 14(1) of the 1971 Montreal Convention, which, according to Libya, is "the only appropriate

---

1087 *Ibid.*, para. 33 at 19.

1088 Rosenne, *op. cit. supra* n.939, at 155.

1089 For the facts of the case and the Security Council actions see *supra*, paragraph 3.3.

convention in force between the Parties."[1090] In its application, Libya asserted that it had taken all necessary steps to try the suspects, as provided for by Articles 5 and 8 of the Montreal Convention.[1091] Libya subsequently asked the Court to adjudge and declare:

(a) that Libya has fully complied with all of its obligations under the Montreal Convention;
(b) that the United States has breached, and is continuing to breach, its legal obligations to Libya under Articles 5(2), 5(3), 7, 8(2), and 11 of the Montreal Convention; and
(c) that the United States is under a legal obligation immediately to cease and desist from such breaches and from the use of any and all force or threats against Libya, including the threat of force against Libya, and from all violations of the sovereignty, territorial integrity, and the political independence of Libya.[1092]

The United States contested the admissibility of the Libyan claim, contending that "the Security Council was actively seized of the situation which was the subject of the Application and ... therefore the Court should not indicate provisional measures."[1093]

In addition to the filing of the application instituting proceedings against the United States and the United Kingdom, Libya requested the indication of interim measures of protection.[1094] According to Libya these measures were:

urgently required in order to cause the United States to abstain from any action capable of having a prejudicial effect on the Court's decision in the case and to refrain from taking any step that might aggravate or extend the dispute, as would surely happen if sanctions were imposed against Libya or force were employed.[1095]

1090 See *Questions of Interpretation and Application of the 1971 Montreal Convention Arising from the Aerial Incident at Lockerbie* (Request for the Indication of Provisional Measures), Libya v. US, Order of 14 April 1992, ICJ Rep. (1992) [hereinafter *Lockerbie (Prov. Measures)*], para. 3 at 115. Both orders on provisional measures are practically identical.

1091 Article 5(2) stipulates that: "Each Contracting State shall likewise take such measures as may be necessary to establish its jurisdiction over the offences mentioned in [the Convention], in the case where the alleged offender is present in its territory and it does not extradite him pursuant to Article 8". Moreover, according to Article 5(3): "This Convention does not exclude any criminal jurisdiction exercised in accordance with national law." Article 8(2) provides that: "If a Contracting State which makes extradition conditional on the existence of a treaty receives a request for extradition from another Contracting State with which it has no extradition treaty, it may at its option consider this Convention as the legal basis for extradition in respect of the offences. Extradition shall be subject to the other conditions provided by the law of the requested State."

1092 *Lockerbie (Prov. Measures)*, para. 7 at 117-118.

1093 *Ibid.*, para. 25 at 122.

1094 The measures requested would: "(a) ... enjoin the United States from taking any action against Libya calculated to coerce or compel Libya to surrender the accused individuals to any jurisdiction outside of Libya; and (b) ... ensure that no steps are taken that would prejudice in any way the rights of Libya with respect to the legal proceedings that are the subject of Libya's Application."

1095 *Lockerbie (Prov. Measures)*, para. 10 at 118. During the proceedings Libya explicitly referred to the possibility of the imposition of sanctions by the Security Council, and requested the Court

Three days after the oral hearings on the request had closed, however, the Security Council adopted resolution 748 (1992) under Chapter VII of the Charter, in which it demanded that Libya extradite the suspects.

As could have been expected, the United States considered resolution 748 (1992) an "additional reason" to maintain its original submission "that the request for the indication of provisional measures should be denied."[1096] In response to an invitation of the Court to make observations on the consequences of resolution 748 (1992), the agent of the United States, in a letter of 7 April 1992, stated that "in order to avoid any conflict with the Security Council the Court should decline the request to indicate provisional measures in this case."[1097] Libya, on the other hand, contended that:

> the risk of contradiction between the resolution and the provisional measures requested of the Court by Libya does not render the Libyan request inadmissible, since there is in law no competition or hierarchy between the Court and the Security Council, each exercising its own competence.[1098]

5.3.4.4.1 The 1992 Order on Provisional Measures

Confronted with resolution 748 (1992), the Court rendered the following decision:

> both Libya and the United States, as Members of the United Nations, are obliged to accept and carry out the decisions of the Security Council in accordance with Article 25 of the Charter; ... the Court, which is at the stage of proceedings on provisional measures, considers that prima facie this obligation extends to the decision contained in resolution 748 (1992); and ... in accordance with Article 103 of the Charter, the obligations of the Parties in that respect prevail over their obligations under any other international agreement, including the Montreal Convention ...
>
> the Court, while thus not at this stage called upon to determine definitely the legal effect of Security Council resolution 748 (1992), considers that, whatever the situation previous to the adoption of that resolution, the rights claimed by Libya under the Montreal Convention cannot now be regarded as appropriate for protection by the indication of provisional measures ...
>
> furthermore, an indication of the measures requested by Libya would be likely to impair the rights which appear prima facie to be enjoyed by the United States by virtue of Security Council resolution 748 (1992).[1099]

The Court accordingly, by eleven votes to five, found "that the circumstances of the case are not such as to exercise its power under Article 41 of the Statute to indicate provisional measures."[1100] It was, however, cautious to note that:

---

to indicate that the US was to refrain from taking any initiative within the Security Council to the effect that the Court could no longer exercise jurisdiction. See *ibid.*, paras. 32-33 at 124.

1096 *Lockerbie (Prov. Measures)*, para. 35 at 125.

1097 Quoted in Diss. Op. Bedjaoui, *Lockerbie (Prov. Measures)*, at 154.

1098 *Lockerbie (Prov. Measures)*, para. 39 at 126.

1099 *Ibid.*, paras. 42-44 at 126-127.

1100 *Ibid.*, at 127. Voting in favour: Oda, Jennings, Lachs, Ago, Schwebel, Ni, Evensen, Tarassov,

in order to pronounce on the present request for provisional measures, the Court is not called upon to determine any of the other questions which have been raised before it in the present proceedings, including the question of its jurisdiction to entertain the merits of the case; and ... the decision given in these proceedings in no way prejudges any such question, and leaves unaffected the rights of the Government of Libya and the Government of the United States to submit arguments in respect of any of these questions.[1101]

Since this decision raises important constitutional questions and contains sparse grounds for the decision, the separate and dissenting opinions will be examined in the next paragraphs in order to determine the legal reasoning behind the judgment.

5.3.4.4.2 Libya's Rights under the Montreal Convention

A majority acknowledged that, in view of the incorporation of the *aut dedere, aut judicare* principle in the Montreal Convention, Libya was not obliged to extradite its accused nationals. Thus the four judges who issued a joint declaration, maintained that "the Montreal Convention, which in our opinion was applicable in this case, did not prohibit Libya from refusing to extradite the accused to the United Kingdom or the United States."[1102] The only dissenter in this respect was Judge Oda, according to whom: "The rights of which Libya claims protection ... cannot ... be assumed to be rights under the Montreal Convention and to fall within the scope of the Application, but are rather sovereign rights under general international law."[1103]

5.3.4.4.3 Resolution 731 (1992) and the Court Proceedings

Resolution 731 (1992) did not appear to interfere with the proceedings before the Court. The judges who had pronounced on its legal basis considered it a non-binding recommendation issued by the Council under Chapter VI of the Charter.[1104] Therefore, the resolution neither affected the rights enjoyed by Libya under the Montreal

Guillaume, Shahabuddeen, and Aguilar Mawdsley (with the exception of Jennings, Ago and Schwebel issuing separate opinions or declarations). Against: Bedjaoui, Weeramantry, Ranjeva, Ajibola, and El-Kosheri (all attaching dissenting opinions). El-Kosheri was added to the bench as Judge *ad hoc* upon Libya's request pursuant to Art. 31(2) of the Court's Statute.

1101 *Ibid.*, para. 45 at 127.

1102 Joint Declaration by Evensen, Tarassov, Guillaume and Aguilar Mawdsley, *Lockerbie (Prov. Measures)*, at 136-137. See also *ibid.*, Diss. Opinions Ajibola, 186-187; Bedjaoui, 148; Ni, 134-135; Shahabuddeen, 140; Weeramantry, 179; and Judge Ranjeva in his Diss. Op. in the order on prov. measures in the Libya v. UK case, ICJ Rep. (1992), 72.

1103 Declaration Oda, *Lockerbie (Prov. Measures)*, at 131.

1104 See, *e.g.*, *Lockerbie (Prov. Measures)*, Diss. Opinions Weeramantry, 176-177; Ajibola, 192; and Bedjaoui, 152.

Convention,[1105] nor confronted the Court with problems arising from their concurrent jurisdiction.[1106]

5.3.4.4.4 Concurrent Jurisdiction between the Council and the Court

In view of the *prima facie* validity of resolution 748 (1992), several judges commented on both the problem of concurrent jurisdiction ensuing from its adoption, as well as the need for cooperation between the two organs. The problem posed by the adoption of resolution 748 (1992) is cogently presented by Judge Ni:

> The question arises whether the Security Council and the Court can now exercise their respective functions at the same time in respect of the dispute. ... It can be urged on behalf of the Security Council that under Article 24 of the United Nations Charter, Members of the United Nations confer on the Security Council primary responsibility for the maintenance of international peace and security, in order to ensure prompt and effective action by the United Nations. But on the other hand, it can also be argued that it is provided in Article 92 of the United Nations Charter that the International Court of Justice shall be the principal judicial organ of the United Nations which is given the power, under Article 36 of the Court's Statute, to settle "all legal disputes concerning: (a) the interpretation of a treaty; (b) any question of international law.[1107]

1105 Ranjeva, for example, states on the consequences of resolution 731 (1992) that: "The nature of the Security Council does not confer upon its recommendatory acts the legal effect of *res judicata*." Diss. Op. Ranjeva, *Lockerbie (Prov. Measures)*, at 73.

1106 On the impact of Security Council recommendations on the Court's competence Weeramantry, for instance, remarks that: "This Court will not place itself in a position of confrontation with the Security Council where that organ has already exercised its powers ... But in areas not covered by its binding decisions under Chapter VII, the Court is free to use its influence and authority to serve the purposes of international peace in which it has as much interest as any organ of the United Nations. The furtherance and preservation of peace are not the exclusive preserve of one organ but the common goal of all." Diss. Op. Weeramantry, *ibid.*, at 180. With regard to the competence of the Security Council and the ICJ at this stage, Ranjeva asserts that: "The adage *una via electa* does not apply when it comes to governing two rights of action which are different in nature, namely one before the Court and the other in the Security Council. In the judicial field, it is the judicial course, based upon international law, which prevails in case of conflict." Diss. Op. Ranjeva, *ibid.*, at 73.

1107 Declaration Ni, *Lockerbie (Prov. Measures)*, at 132. See also Lachs, who notes that "the Council, by moving into the terrain of Chapter VII of the Charter, decided certain issues pertaining to the Lockerbie disaster with binding force. Hence problems of jurisdiction and the operation of the *sub judice* principle came into the foreground as never before." Sep. Op. Lachs, *Lockerbie (Prov. Measures)*, at 138. And according to Shahabuddeen "several cases demonstrate, in one way or another, that the Court is not precluded from acting by the mere circumstance that the matter in contest is also under consideration by another organ of the United Nations. In this case, it happens that the decision which the Court is asked to give is one which would directly conflict a decision of the Security Council. That is not an aspect which can be overlooked." Sep. Op. Shahabuddeen, *Lockerbie (Prov. Measures)*, at 140-141.

After recalling the Court's jurisprudence in this respect (the *Hostage* and *Nicaragua* cases), Ni argues that the complementarity of the functions of the Security Council and the Court:

> should not be overlooked. Although both organs deal with the same matter, there are different points of emphasis. ... These functions may be correlated with each other. What would be required between the two is co-ordination and co-operation, not competition or mutual exclusion.[1108]

Judge Bedjaoui also observes that the *Lockerbie* case poses questions with regard to the relationship between the Court and the Council. He notes that:

> if the concomitant exercise of concurrent but not exclusive powers has thus far not given rise to serious problems, the present case, by contrast, presents the Court not only with the grave question of the possible influence of the decision of a principal organ on the consideration of the same question by another organ, but also, more fundamentally, with the question of the possible inconsistency between the decisions of two organs and of how to deal with such a delicate situation.[1109]

With regard to this possible inconsistency, Bedjaoui identifies two different disputes pending between Libya and the United States and United Kingdom.[1110] The first, which was brought before the Court by Libya, concerns a "very precise legal dispute"[1111] concerning the question whether Libya is under an international obligation to extradite two of its nationals. The second is concerned with an action by the United States and the United Kingdom at the Security Council against Libya, which they accuse "of being implicated in terrorism in general and in the Lockerbie bombing in particular."[1112] He then states that:

> The respective missions of the Security Council and the Court are thus on two different planes, have different objects and require specific methods of settlement consistent with their own respective powers ... But the difficulty in the present case lies in the fact that the Security Council not only has decided to take a number

---

1108 *Ibid.*, at 134. See also Ranjeva, who holds that "the new elements in international relations call for greater clarification of United Nations law on the one hand as regards the line of demarcation between the fields respectively covered by Chapters VI and VII of the Charter ..., and, on the other hand, a new characterization of situations from the standpoint of the relevant provisions of the Charter." Diss. Op. Ranjeva, *Lockerbie (Prov. Measures)*, at 77.

1109 Diss. Op. Bedjaoui, *ibid.*, at 143. He furthermore remarks, at 145, that "it is as a rule not the Court's role to exercise appellate jurisdiction in respect of decisions taken by the Security Council in the fulfilment of its fundamental mission of maintaining international peace and security, no more than it is the role of the Security Council to take the place of the Court, thereby impairing the integrity of its international judicial function."

1110 See *ibid.*, 143-144.

1111 *Ibid.*, at 144.

1112 *Ibid.*

> of political measures against Libya, but has also demanded from it the *extradition of its two nationals. It is this specific demand of the Council that creates an overlap with respect to the substance of the legal dispute with which the Court must deal.*[1113]

Weeramantry concurs with Bedjaoui in that: "This case has raised as perhaps no case has done in the past, certain questions of importance and interest concerning the respective functions of this Court and the Security Council."[1114] According to Weeramantry, both organs "are complementary to each other, each performing the special role allotted to it by their common instrument of creation."[1115] And with regard to the parallel seizure of a matter by the two organs, he maintains that:

> where the Security Council is addressing a situation with direct implications for the matter brought before the Court, the Court should examine whether its actions would conflict with the actions that the Security Council has taken or is considering and, where the circumstances permit, should seek to reinforce the actions of the Council.[1116]

In contrast to the views expressed above, El-Kosheri does not seem to locate a problem arising out of the simultaneous exercise of jurisdiction by both organs. He submits that as the principal judicial organ of the United Nations, the Court "exercises a function fundamentally different in nature and operating methods from that conferred upon the Security Council."[1117]

1113 *Ibid.* (emphasis in the original).

1114 Diss. Op. Weeramantry, *Lockerbie (Prov. Measures)*, at 163. He additionally observes that this case is of "special importance" since "the Court and the Council have been approached by opposite parties to the dispute, each claiming a form of relief consistent with its own position." *Ibid.*, at 169.

1115 *Ibid.*, at 165. As regards these roles he remarks that "there is not among the United Nations organizations the same strict principle of separation of powers one sometimes finds in municipal systems. ... Nor is there a hierarchical arrangement of the organs of the United Nations, and each organ is *par inter pares*. As a judicial organ, it will be the Court's duty from time to time to examine and determine from a strictly legal point of view matters which may at the same time be the subject of determination from an executive or political point of view by another principal organ of the United Nations." *Ibid.*

1116 *Ibid.*, at 169.

1117 Diss. Op. El-Kosheri, *ibid.*, at 201.

5.3.4.4.5 The Pre-eminence of Resolution 748 (1992)

Except for El-Kosheri and possibly Ni,[1118] all judges acknowledged the pre-eminence of resolution 748 (1992) by virtue of Articles 25 and 103 of the Charter.[1119] In this way Oda observed that:

> Since a decision of the Security Council properly taken in the exercise of its competence, cannot be summarily reopened, and since it is apparent that resolution 748 (1992) embodies such a decision, the Court has at present no choice but to acknowledge the pre-eminence of that resolution.[1120]

The four judges issuing a joint declaration agreed on the conclusive effect which resolutions 731 (1992) and 748 (1992) had on the proceedings before the Court. They claimed that, in the light of the decisions contained in these documents:

> the Court, pronouncing on a request for the indication of provisional measures submitted by Libya in order to preserve the legal situation existing prior to the adoption of the Security Council resolutions, was fully justified in noting that the changes that had occurred in that situation and holding, accordingly, that the circumstances of the case were not such as to require the exercise of its power to indicate such measures.[1121]

In a similar fashion, Ranjeva submits that the adoption of resolution 748 (1992)

1118 Judge Ni voted against the request for provisional measures "on the *sole ground* of non-fulfilment of the temporal requirement provided in Article 14(1) of the 1971 Montreal Convention without having to decide at the same time on the other issues". Sep. Op. Ni, *Lockerbie (Prov. Measures)*, at 135. Art. 14(1) provides for a six-month waiting-period following a request for arbitration, before the parties involved in a dispute concerning the interpretation of the Convention may have recourse to the International Court of Justice. For the text of the Article see *supra*, page 213. He continued by stating that: "Consequently, in my view the Applicant will not be prevented from seeking a remedy of this Court in accordance with the provisions of the 1971 Montreal Convention, if the dispute months later still subsists and if the Applicant so desires." *Ibid.* He thus did not address the impact of resolution 748 (1992) on the proceedings before the Court.

1119 In his opinion Bedjaoui raised an interesting procedural point: "Unless formal (and adversary) procedures were instituted by the Parties to the dispute, the Court, it would appear, was not obliged to take into account a resolution passed after the closure of the proceedings and to apply it, retroactively as it were, to the case which had been submitted to it." Diss. Op. Bedjaoui, *Lockerbie (Prov. Measures)*, at 151. He nevertheless followed the Court, which "deemed it better itself to take the initiative of eliciting the observations of the Parties on this point, during the deliberations." *Ibid.*

1120 Declaration Oda, *Lockerbie (Prov. Measures)*, at 129. See to the same effect Lachs: "In the present case the Court was faced with a new situation which allowed no room for further analysis nor the indication of effective interim measures." *Lockerbie (Prov. Measures)*, at 139. So also Shahabuddeen, who stated that: "Whatever might have been the previous position, resolution 748 (1992) of the Security Council leaves the Court with no conclusion other than that to which it has come." Sep. Op. Shahabuddeen, *ibid.*, at 140.

1121 Joint Declaration by Evensen, Tarassov, Guillaume and Aguilar Mawdsley, *Lockerbie (Prov. Measures)*, at 137.

brought about a "fundamental change in the legal circumstances since the filing of the Application", which "without there being any change in the factual circumstances of the case, prevented the Court, the principal judicial organ, from exercising its legal function to settle the dispute between the Parties to the full extent of its powers."[1122]

Weeramantry is in agreement with the pre-eminence of the Council's decision. He concludes that Libya is *prima facie* "bound by the provisions of that resolution even if they should conflict with the rights Libya claims under the Montreal Convention."[1123] The potential conflict between Libya's rights under the Montreal Convention and resolution 748 (1992) is analyzed by Bedjaoui in even sharper terms. He maintains that "Security Council resolution 748 (1992) has annihilated those rights [claimed for protection] of Libya."[1124]

The only judge not adhering to the pre-eminence of resolution 748 (1992) was El-Kosheri. He submitted that in view of the *ultra vires* character of paragraph 1 of resolution 748 (1992), that decision cannot interfere with the proceedings pending before the Court. In his own words: "I am of the opinion, with all due respect, that paragraph 1 of resolution 748 (1992) should not be considered to have any legal effect on the jurisdiction of the Court, even on a prima facie basis."[1125]

5.3.4.4.6 Jurisdiction of the Court alongside Resolution 748 (1992)

Despite the near consensus on the *prima facie* validity and effects of resolution 748 (1992) on the measures requested by Libya, different answers were given to the question whether the Court possessed some form of residual jurisdiction with regard to the indication of provisional measures. It may first be noted that, on the concurring side, several judges were cautious to remark that the non-indication of interim measures did not mean that the Court was stepping down in face of the decisions contained in resolution 748 (1992). Thus Judge Lachs stated that the "Order made should not ... be seen as an abdication of the Court's powers; it is rather a reflection of the system within which the Court is called upon to render justice."[1126]

1122 Diss. Op. Ranjeva, *ibid.*, at 74.

1123 Diss. Op. Weeramantry, *Lockerbie (Prov. Measures)*, at 177.

1124 Diss. Op. Bedjaoui, *ibid.*, at 156. According to Reisman: "The English translation curiously escalates Judge Bedjaoui's 'abolis' to 'annihilated'." Reisman, *op. cit. supra* n.7, n.18 at 87. However, he seems to have overlooked the fact that the French original of the passage quoted in the text above reads "la résolution 748 (1992) ... a annihilé ces droits de la Libye." In other words, it is Bedjaoui himself who employs this strong terminology.

1125 Diss. Op. El-Kosheri, *Lockerbie (Prov. Measures)*, at 212.

1126 Sep. Lachs, *ibid.*, at 139.

This is affirmed by Judge Shahabuddeen, according to whom the Court's rejection of the measures requested for by Libya "is the result not of imposition of superior authority – there is none".[1127] These observations notwithstanding, the judges voting in favour saw no further room for the Court to indicate interim measures.[1128] In this they distinguish themselves from the dissenters, who all thought it appropriate for the Court to indicate general measures *proprio motu*. Such measures would have been indicated, under Article 41(1) of the Statute and Article 75 of the Rules of Court,[1129] in order to prevent an aggravation of the dispute. In this way Judge Ajibola submitted that the Court "should indicate provisional measures *proprio motu* under Article 75 of the Rules of Court against both Parties to ensure non-use of force or aggravation or extension of the dispute pending the Court's judgment on the merits."[1130] According to Ajibola such measures would not run contrary to the decision of the Security Council as contained in resolution 748 (1992) "since the resolution does not condone the use of any force."[1131] Similarly, Weeramantry suggests that:

> it does not necessarily follow that the binding nature of resolution 748 (1992) renders it inappropriate for the Court to indicate provisional measures. ... There still seems to be room, while preserving full respect for resolution 748 (1992) in all its integrity, for the Court to frame an appropriate measure *proprio motu*.[1132]

This course of action is also recommended by Judges Bedjaoui and Ranjeva. But they

---

1127 Sep. Op. Shahabuddeen, *Lockerbie (Prov. Measures)*, at 140. At the same place he submitted that the non-indication of provisional measures "results not from any collision between the competence of the Security Council and that of the Court, but from a collision between the obligations of Libya under the decision of the Security Council and any obligations which it may have had under the Montreal Convention. The Charter says that the former prevail."

1128 *Cf.* Lachs in his Sep. Op., *ibid.*, at 139: "In the present case the Court was faced with a new situation which allowed no room for further analysis nor the indication of *effective* interim measures." (Emphasis added).

1129 Article 41(1) of the Statute reads: "The Court shall have the power to indicate, if it considers that circumstances so require, any provisional measures which ought to be taken to preserve the respective rights of either party." Article 75 of the Rules, moreover, provides that:
"(1) The Court may at any time decide to examine *proprio motu* whether the circumstances of the case require the indication of provisional measures which ought to be taken or complied with by any or all of the parties.
(2) When a request for provisional measures has been made, the Court may indicate measures that are in whole or in part other than those requested, or that ought to be taken or complied with by the party which has itself made the request."

1130 Diss. Op. Ajibola, *Lockerbie (Prov. Measures)*, at 193.

1131 *Ibid.*, at 195.

1132 Diss. Op. Weeramantry, *ibid.*, at 177. The measures proposed by Weeramantry would be aimed at preventing "such aggravation or extension of the dispute as might result in the use of force by either parties." *Ibid.*, at 181.

additionally submitted that the Court should have issued an order in which its integrity *vis-à-vis* the Council would have been preserved and reaffirmed. Thus Bedjaoui observed that in view of the 'annihilation' by resolution 748 (1992) of the rights claimed for protection by Libya, the indication of provisional measures would not have "any useful effect."[1133] Despite this, he stated that:

> the facts of the case do indeed justify the effective exercise of that power [to indicate interim measures], while I would point out that its *effects* have been nullified by resolution 748 (1992). This means that I arrive, concretely, at the same result as the Court ... with the important difference that I am not led to reject the request for provisional measures, but rather to say that its *effects* have ceased to exist.[1134]

In a comparable statement Ranjeva claims that the Court:

> should have pronounced on the merits of the request, the object of which has disappeared owing to the effects of resolution 748 (1992), and should also have acknowledged its inability to rule owing to supervening circumstances external to the dispute and subsequent to the filing of the Application, at the same time calling upon the Parties to avoid all escalation. This solution, which although uncomfortable nevertheless accords with the description of the development of the proceedings, seems to me a useful one.[1135]

El-Kosheri is less cautious. In view of his submission that paragraph one of resolution 748 (1992) "should not be considered to have any legal effect on the jurisdiction of the Court", he concluded that the Court should have indicated interim measures, even if these would have run contrary to the prior action of the Council. Indeed, according to the Judge:

> the circumstances of the case required the indication of provisional measures, particularly since there was extreme urgency for the Court to act in order to avoid the coming into force of the sanctions adopted by the Security Council under certain paragraphs of resolution 748 (1992), a decision taken by the Security Council in the exercise of its powers under Chapter VII, hence outside the scope of the legal issue before the Court.[1136]

He accordingly concluded his opinion with the submission that the Court could have indicated *proprio motu* interim measures of protection to the effect that: "Pending a final decision of the Court, the two suspects ... should be placed under the custody of

---

1133 Diss. Op. Bedjaoui, *ibid.*, at 157.

1134 *Ibid.*

1135 Diss. Op. Ranjeva, *ibid.*, at 76. According to Ranjeva an appeal to the parties to refrain from taking any action which could aggravate the situation was required all the more since "the circumstances were a source of [great] concern, owing to the direct reference to Chapter VII of the Charter. The question of the opinion of the Security Council was no longer limited to a dispute between the Parties in contention, but concerned the collective security of all States and all peoples." *Ibid.*

1136 Diss. Op. El-Kosheri, *Lockerbie (Prov. Measures)*, at 215.

the governmental authorities in another State that could ultimately provide a mutually agreed and appropriate forum for their trial."[1137]

5.3.4.4.7 The 1998 Judgment on Preliminary Objections

Six years later, on 27 February 1998, the Court ruled on the preliminary objections raised by the defendants. As seen above, the Security Council had by then adopted another resolution on the matter. Herein the Council reiterated its position that the:

> failure by the Libyan Government to demonstrate by concrete actions its renunciation of terrorism, and in particular its continued failure to respond fully and effectively to the requests and decisions in resolutions 731 (1992) and 748 (1992), constitute a threat to international peace and security.[1138]

During the proceedings, the defendants raised several preliminary objections to the (exercise of) the jurisdiction of the Court. Thus the US contested the admissibility of the claim by arguing that Libya, by seizing the Court:

> was endeavouring to "undo the Council's actions". The United States argues that, even if Libya could make valid claims under the Montreal Convention, these are "superseded" by the relevant decisions of the Security Council under Chapter VII of the Charter, which impose different obligations.[1139]

Interestingly enough, the Court rejected this argument by reference to its jurisdiction *ratione temporis*. According to the Court:

> The date, 3 March 1992, on which Libya filed its Application, is in fact the only relevant date for determining the admissibility of the Application. Security Council resolutions 748 (1992) and 883 (1993) cannot be taken into consideration in this regard, since they were adopted at a later date.[1140]

In the operative part of the judgment the Court hence: "(2) *(a)* by twelve votes to three, *rejects* the objection to admissibility derived by the United States from Security Council resolutions 748 (1992) and 883 (1993)."

In the decision on preliminary objections the Court also dealt with the related contention that: "Libya's claims have become moot because Security Council resolutions 748 (1992) and 883 (1993) have rendered them without object; any

---

1137 Diss. Op. El-Kosheri, *ibid.*, at 216. Prior to this passage he maintained that "the two Libyans suspected to be the authors of the Lockerbie massacre, could not possibly receive a fair trial, neither in the United States or in the United Kingdom, nor in Libya."

1138 S/Res. 883 (1993), 11 Nov. 1993.

1139 *Case Concerning Questions of Interpretation and Application of the 1971 Montreal Convention Arising from the Aerial Incident at Lockerbie* (Prel. Objections), Libya v. US, 27 Feb. 1998, ICJ Rep. (1998), [hereinafter *Lockerbie (Prel. Objections.)*] para. 40.

1140 *Lockerbie (Prel. Objections)*, para. 43.

judgment which the Court might deliver on the said claims would thenceforth be devoid of practical purpose."[1141] On this the Court observed that:

By maintaining that Security Council resolutions 748 (1992) and 883 (1993) have rendered the Libyan claims without object, the United States seeks to obtain from the Court a decision not to proceed to judgment on the merits, which would immediately terminate the proceedings. However, by requesting such a decision, the United States is requesting, in reality, at least two others which the decision not to proceed to judgment on the merits would necessarily postulate: on the one hand a decision establishing that the rights claimed by Libya under the Montreal Convention are incompatible with its obligations under the Security Council resolutions; and, on the other hand, a decision that those obligations prevail over those rights by virtue of Articles 25 and 103 of the Charter.[1142]

According to the Court, the objection was not "exclusively of a preliminary nature." In its own words:

The Court ... has no doubt that Libya's rights on the merits would not only be affected by a decision not to proceed to judgment on the merits, at this stage in the proceedings, but would constitute, in many respects, the very subject-matter of that decision. The objection raised by the United States on that point has the character of a defence on the merits.[1143]

In the operative part of the judgment the Court therefore:

(3) by ten votes to five, *declares* that the objection raised by the United States according to which the claims of Libya became moot because Security Council resolutions 748 (1992) and 883 (1993) rendered them without object, does not, in the circumstances of the case, have an exclusively preliminary character.

5.3.4.4.8 Assessment of the Lockerbie case

At the beginning of the proceedings on provisional measures the Court was confronted with resolution 731 (1992). Herein the Council had *urged* "the Libyan Government immediately to provide a full and effective response to those requests so as to contribute to the elimination of international terrorism", and decided to remain seized of the matter. Several comments have been made on the propriety of this resolution. Not only has its procedural validity been questioned,[1144] but it has also been observed that the resolution prejudges the accusations towards Libya. Thus Beveridge, for instance, submits that:

by endorsing the demand for compensation the Security Council apparently endorses the view that Libya has breached international law and should make reparations. Since the object of the previous demand was to allow

---

1141 *Ibid.*, para. 45.

1142 *Ibid.*, para. 49.

1143 *Ibid.*, para. 49.

1144 See *supra*, note 289.

criminal trials to proceed this could be regarded as prejudicial (in the strict sense of the word).[1145]

According to the respondents, resolution 731 (1992) precluded the exercise of jurisdiction by the Court, since this could and would run contrary to the Council's actions on the matter. The Court seems to have rejected this objection: the judgment and individual opinions indicate that resolution 731 (1992) is to be considered a non-binding recommendation, delivered by the Council by virtue of Chapter VI of the Charter.[1146] Hence the resolution could not affect the rights and duties of the parties to the dispute under the Montreal Convention. With regard to these rights and duties, almost all judges asserted that under this Convention, Libya was not obliged to extradite its accused nationals. Libya had accordingly been entitled to reject the extradition claim made by the United States and United Kingdom. By virtue of its non-binding nature this right was not affected by resolution 731 (1992).

The legal situation changed when resolution 748 (1992) came into play. Not satisfied with Libya's reaction to resolution 731 (1992), and confronted with its application at the International Court of Justice, the Security Council decided to invoke Chapter VII of the Charter in order to ensure Libya's compliance with the previous demands for extradition and compensation.[1147] The resolution, which was adopted three days after the closure of the oral proceedings on provisional measures, has been criticized on several grounds. Firstly, as was the case with resolution 731, it seems that the Council prejudged the question of Libya's responsibility by endorsing the various requests for extradition and compensation.[1148]

1145 Beveridge, *op. cit. supra* n.659, at 911.

1146 Indeed, Reisman seems to be alone in viewing resolution 731 (1992) "at least *in posse*, as normatively strong enough to override other treaty or customary rights even though couched in recommendatory language. ... The belated and nervous appearance of resolution 748 (1992) and its incorporation *eo nomine* of resolution 731 (1992) merely served to make explicit the latter's implicit Chapter VII undertones." Reisman, *op. cit. supra* n.7, at 89.

1147 According to Beveridge "it was the alleged involvement of the Libyan State which was relied on to lift the dispute out of the area of State jurisdiction and to justify action by the Security Council." Beveridge, *op. cit. supra* n.659, at 909. See also Stein, *op. cit. supra* n.659, 219.

1148 Thus Harper, for example, maintains that the request for compensation was "unusual and seemingly premature, given that there had not yet been a trial of the alleged terrorists nor any adjudication of the Libyan government's involvement in the bombing." K. Harper, *Does the United Nations Security Council Have the Competence to Act as Court and Legislature?*, 27 NYUJILP (1994) 103-157, at 123. Graefrath also submits that: "Resolution 748 (1992) is based on an assumption of guilt that would be rejected by any judge in any court of a democratic state. This ... raises the question of fair trial procedures as a general principle of law within Security Council practice." Graefrath, *op. cit. supra* n.7, at 197. For an opposite view one might refer to Tomuschat, according to whom: "Extradition of major criminals is a legitimate concern within the framework of a strategy aimed at combating terrorism." Tomuschat, *op. cit. supra* n.7, at 44.

It has been observed, in the second place, that the Council's determination that Libya's (in-)action amounts to a threat to international peace and security involves a rather flexible and unconventional interpretation of Article 39 of the Charter. Hence Graefrath submits that:

> it remains absolutely unclear why or how the *failure* to renunciate terrorism by concrete actions ... or the *failure* to surrender suspects, or the refusal of compensation claims which are not established under any legal procedure, could constitute a threat to the peace.[1149]

In a similar fashion Judge Bedjaoui observes that "no small number of people may find it disconcerting that the horrific Lockerbie bombing should be seen *today* as an *urgent* threat to international peace when it took place *over three years ago*."[1150]

These observations notwithstanding, the Court affirmed the *prima facie* validity of the decisions contained in resolution 748 (1992) in its decision on provisional measures. It decided that, by virtue of Articles 25 and 103 of the Charter, the obligations arising out of these decisions prevailed over any rights previously enjoyed by Libya under the Montreal Convention.

5.3.4.4.9 The Lockerbie case and Litispendence

The *Lockerbie* case in its provisional measures stage is the first case in which the Court was obliged to defer to the Council. This deferral was made by reference to the Charter provisions which establish the primacy of decisions of the Security Council *vis-à-vis* the Montreal Convention, the instrument relied upon by Libya to confer jurisdiction on the Court. According to this reasoning, the fact that a matter is pending before the Council does not, in and of itself, preclude the Court from ruling on that dispute. It rather means that valid binding decisions of the Security Council may not be contradicted by the Court.[1151] Thus, the Court formally upheld its jurisprudentially

---

1149 Graefrath, *op. cit. supra* n.7, at 106.

1150 Diss. Op. Bedjaoui, *Lockerbie (Prov. Measures)*, at 153. *Cf.* Weller: "the widening of Council jurisdiction to tackle prospective cases of 'terrorism' is to be encouraged, as these can indeed under certain circumstances be considered 'threats to international peace and security.' But the use of that label retroactively to deal with a case which, when it occurred some three years earlier was not considered a threat to international peace and security is not likely to encourage this tender trend." Weller, *op. cit. supra* n.7, at 323

1151 In this respect the observation made by Delbrück that "from the point of view that they have to pay due respect for each other, the Security Council and the ICJ have to take each other's decisions into consideration" (Delbrück, *op. cit. supra* n.107, at 403) seems to be an understatement. Indeed, his submission that "neither the UN Charter nor the ICJ Statute provide for any such restrictions [arising out of the pendency of a dispute at the Council] on the freedom of the ICJ to

defined position that the doctrine of litispendence is not applicable in its relationship with the Security Council.[1152]

Materially, however, the *Lockerbie* decision on provisional measures could be interpreted as a recognition of the applicability of the principle of litispendence in the relationship between the Council and the Court. It may be recalled that Judges Bedjaoui and Ranjeva suggested that the Court should have indicated provisional measures requested by Libya, simultaneously noting that the effect of these measures had been nullified by resolution 748 (1992). Furthermore, the dissenting judges all submitted that the Court should have indicated general provisional measures under Article 75 of the Rules of Court. Such orders would have preserved the Court's role alongside the Council in the preservation of international peace and security and could have provided an escape from the strait-jacket imposed by resolution 748 (1992). By rejecting both approaches, the majority failed to take the opportunity to definitively assert its jurisdiction *vis-à-vis* the Council. The judgment of the Court could be read as an implicit recognition of the primacy and finality of the Council's decisions over the Court's jurisdiction.[1153]

Such an outcome is certainly not acceptable to all, however. Thus Reisman, for example, in commenting on the *Lockerbie (Provisional Measures)* decision maintains that: "As international constitutional law, such a formalistic approach is unsatisfactory, for it precludes, in blanket fashion, the exercise of judicial jurisdiction *whenever* and *simply because* the Council is in a Chapter VII decision mode."[1154]

The next phase of the case, moreover, could provide a different picture. As seen above, the judgment on the provisional measures emphasized that the obligation to accept and carry out the decisions of the Security Council under Article 25 *prima facie* extends to resolution 748 (1992), whilst the Court was not *at this stage* called upon to definitely determine the legal effect of the resolution. As the hurdle of preliminary

act" (*ibid.*) seems to have been proven incorrect by the *Lockerbie (Prov. Measures)* judgment.

1152 See to the same effect V. Gowlland-Debbas, *The Relationship between the International Court of Justice and the Security Council in the Light of the Lockerbie Case*, 88 AJIL (1994) 643-677, 658.

1153 *Cf.* Gill, who submits that "in the event that a dispute posed a threat to peace or the maintenance of security, and the Council should act under Chapter VII of the Charter, I would agree with Judge Alvarez who stated in the *Anglo Iranian Oil. Co.* case that 'if a case submitted to the Court should constitute a threat to world peace, the Security Council may seize itself of the case and put an end to the Court's jurisdiction.'" T.D. Gill, *Litigation Strategy at the International Court* (1989), at 27-28. Interestingly enough Gill, writing in 1989, states that: "Needless to say, no instance has ever occurred in which the Council has ever had the occasion to put an end to the Court's jurisdiction, nor would it be likely to exercise this power unless there existed very pressing reasons to do so." *Ibid.*, at 28.

1154 Reisman, *op. cit. supra* n.7, at 90.

objections has at least temporarily been taken, the Court could, if it pronounces itself on the merits of the case, review the validity of the underlying Security Council resolutions. In the words of Tomuschat:

> because of [the] intimate connection with the subject matter, resolution 748 cannot remain outside the scope of examination by the Court. The outcome of this dispute hinges on the legal effect of that resolution in the specific relationship between the litigant parties.[1155]

Whether or not the Court is competent to review Security Council decisions will be addressed below.[1156]

5.3.4.5 Conclusions: the World Court on Litispendence

From the beginning, the World Court has rejected objections to the exercise of its jurisdiction based on the principle of litispendence. In the classic *Polish Upper Silesia* case the Permanent International Court of Justice interpreted the doctrine in such a restrictive manner that any future application seemed to be precluded. Indeed, since then the plea has never been expressly invoked before the World Court. However, on several occasions it has been confronted with preliminary objections closely related to the principle of litispendence. These objections attempted to establish the inability of the Court to rule on the ground that the dispute at stake was already being dealt with by the Council. The Court, with the exception of the 1992 *Lockerbie (Provisional Measures)* decision, consistently dismissed these objections.

The litispendence plea may be invoked when (i) an identical matter is pending between (ii) the same parties (iii) before organs possessing similar jurisdiction. According to the case-law of the Permanent International Court of Justice (the *German Settlers, Minority Schools* and the *Memel Statute* cases) the League Council and the Court were jurisdictions 'different in character.' They were not therefore considered to be organs possessing similar jurisdictions, and consequently the third condition attached to litispendence could not have been met.

The International Court of Justice confirmed the difference in character between the jurisdiction of the Security Council and the Court. Its position has been that the Council and the Court are independent organs exercising 'separate but complementary' functions. The reasoning followed in this position is that the Court will adjudicate a matter on the basis of international law, whilst the Council bases its decisions primarily on political considerations. Thus the Court would not only have

1155 Tomuschat, *op. cit. supra* n.7, at 48.

1156 *Infra*, paragraphs 5.3.5-5.3.7.2.

denied the fulfilment of the third condition, but also of the first condition: the identity of matters.

According to the International Court of Justice, the independence of the Court and the Council does not mean that both organs should not cooperate in respect of a matter of which they are simultaneously seized. It means that the Court will not decline to exercise jurisdiction for the sole reason that the dispute brought to its attention is pending before the Council. This approach has been adopted by the Court in the *Hostages, Nicaragua,* and *Bosnia* cases. During the preliminary phase of the *Lockerbie* case, however, the Court was obliged to revise this position. Herein it decided that, by virtue of Articles 25 and 103 of the Charter, the prior action taken by the Council pursuant to Chapter VII prevailed over the conventional law on which the applicant based its case. The Court, therefore, no longer possessed the capacity to indicate provisional measures in order to preserve the rights claimed by the applicant under the Montreal Convention. It furthermore declined to indicate general provisional measures which would prevent an escalation of the dispute. The Court thus seems to have departed from its earlier judgment in the *Nicaragua* case, in which it had held that even after a determination under Article 39 there would not necessarily be inconsistency between action on the part of the Security Council and adjudication by the Court. Indeed, it seems to have applied the *Minority Schools* criterion, according to which the Court's jurisdiction is only affected in those exceptional cases in which the dispute would fall within the "exclusive jurisdiction reserved to some other authority." This notwithstanding, the Court did consider itself competent to pronounce on the merits of the case. Whether this also implies that the Court can and should review the underlying resolutions of the Council will be addressed below. Prior to that, however, another possible obstacle to the exercise of jurisdiction by the Court in cases in which it is called upon to interpret and apply Security Council decisions will be examined, namely the 'political question doctrine'

5.3.5 The 'Political Question Doctrine'

The above has shown that the seizure of a matter by the Security Council does not in itself preclude the Court from adjudging the same matter, and that the Court thus does not adhere to the principle of litispendence. However, there are additional objections to the Court exercising its jurisdiction in matters already dealt with by the Council. According to the 'political question doctrine', the Court should and could not pronounce on certain aspects of a case because these questions relate to the political sphere. The foremost category of disputes deemed non-justiciable are those involving the use of force.[1157] The doctrine is summarized by Akande in the following terms:

> The doctrine of inherent limitations of the judicial function in international law classified disputes into those that were justiciable and those that were non-justiciable, disputes as to rights as opposed to disputes arising out of conflict of interests, and legal in contradistinction to political disputes (all these being different ways of saying the same thing).[1158]

And in the *Tadić* case the Trial Chamber of the ICTY described the doctrine with the following quote:

> Prominent on the surface of any case held to involve a political question is found a textually demonstrable constitutional commitment of the issue to a co-ordinate political department; or a lack of judicially discoverable and manageable standards for resolving it; or the impossibility of deciding without an initial policy determination of a kind clearly for nonjudicial discretion; or the impossibility of a court's undertaking independent resolution without expressing lack of the respect due co-ordinate branches of government; or an unusual need for unquestioning adherence to a political decision already made; or the potentiality of embarrassment from multifarious pronouncements by various departments on one question.[1159]

Certain provisions of the Charter and the Statute of the International Court of Justice could be interpreted as validating this assertion. Thus Article 36(3) of the Charter holds that the Council, in making recommendations for the settlement of disputes, should take into consideration that *legal* disputes should as a general rule be referred to the International Court of Justice. Under Article 96, moreover, the General Assembly and Security Council and duly authorized organs may request the International Court of Justice to give an opinion on any *legal* question. And according to Article 36(2) of the Statute, State Parties to the Statute can recognize *ipso facto* the jurisdiction of the Court in all *legal* disputes.

It is sometimes maintained that decisions taken by the Security Council pursuant to its responsibility for the maintenance of international peace and security are not reviewable by a judicial body due to the political nature of the decisions involved. Indeed, in the *Tadić* case the Trial Chamber of the ICTY confirmed the existence of and actually applied the political question doctrine in relation to the powers of the Security Council under Chapter VII. The Chamber held that:

1157 See Schachter, *op. cit. supra* n.162, 228-241; C. Greenwood, *The International Court of Justice and the Use of Force*. In: V. Lowe, M. Fitzmaurice (eds.), Fifty Years of the International Court of Justice (1996) 373-385.

1158 D. Akande, *The Role of the International Court of Justice in the Maintenance of International Peace*, 8 AJICL (1996) 592-616, at 593. On the origins of the doctrine see, *e.g.*, Bedjaoui, *op. cit. supra* n.745, 20; and Gowlland-Debbas, *op. cit. supra* n.1152, 648-653.

1159 *Baker v. Carr*, 369 U.S. 186, 217 (1962). Quoted in the Trial Chamber Decision on the Defence Motion on Jurisdiction, *Prosecutor v. Dusko Tadić a/k/a "Dule"*, Case No. IT-94-1-T, 10 Aug. 1995, para. 24.

> The making of a judgement as to whether there was such an emergency in the former Yugoslavia as would justify the setting up of the International Tribunal under Chapter VII is eminently one for the Security Council and only for it; it is certainly not a justiciable issue but one involving considerations of high policy and of a political nature. As to whether the particular measure of establishing the International Tribunal is, in fact, likely to be conducive to the restoration of peace and security is, again, pre-eminently a matter for the Security Council and for it alone and no judicial body, certainly not this Trial Chamber, can or should review that step.[1160]

The arguments stemming from the Charter and the Statute must, however, be dismissed. As observed by Akande, the categorization in Article 36 of disputes includes "any question of international law".[1161] He correctly submits that "in so far as international law covers questions relating to peace among nations, as it clearly does, the Court has jurisdiction over such matters."[1162] Similarly, Rosenne notes that "modern legal doctrine does not take kindly to the idea that the law cannot always provide an answer to any question properly put to it."[1163] An analysis of the case law of the International Court of Justice furthermore reveals that the Court has seldom shied away from exercising jurisdiction because of the political implications of its judgment or opinion. The *Nicaragua, Certain Expenses* and *Nuclear Weapons* cases are demonstrative of this. Quite the contrary, the Court has repeatedly stressed that the political nature of a dispute does not render it inadmissible before the Court.[1164] Thus in its 1988 judgment in the *Border and Transborder Armed Actions* case the Court stressed that:

> political aspects may be present in any legal dispute brought before it. The Court, as a judicial organ, is however only concerned to establish, first, that the dispute before it is a legal dispute in the sense of a dispute capable of being settled by the application of principles and rules of international law and secondly, that the court has jurisdiction to deal with it, and that jurisdiction is not fettered by any circumstances rendering the application inadmissible.[1165]

Furthermore, in the Preliminary Objection phase of the Advisory Opinion requested by the World Health Organization on the *Legality of the Threat or Use of Nuclear*

1160 Trial Chamber Decision on the Defence Motion on Jurisdiction, *Prosecutor v. Dusko Tadić a/k/a "Dule"*, Case No. IT-94-1-T, 10 Aug. 1995, para. 23.

1161 See Akande, *op. cit. supra* n.1158, 596, and in particular his reference to H. Lauterpacht's *The Function of Law in the International Community* (1933).

1162 *Ibid.*, at 597.

1163 Rosenne, *op. cit. supra* n.939, at 1001.

1164 According to Gill "it is no exaggeration to state that the Court has never rejected a dispute because it contained 'political' aspect. This is one element in the Court's jurisprudence which could be termed as constant." Gill, *op. cit. supra* n.1153, at 169.

1165 *Case Concerning Border and Transborder Armed Actions* (Jurisdiction and Admissibility), Nic. v. Honduras, Judgment of 20 Dec. 1988, ICJ Rep. (1988), para. 52.

Weapons the Court found that "the political nature of the motives which may be said to have inspired the request and the political implications that the opinion given might have are of no relevance in the establishment of its jurisdiction to give such an opinion."[1166]

The Appeals Chamber in the aforementioned *Tadić* case also rejected the political question doctrine, and thus reversed the earlier decision of the Trial Chamber. According to the Appeals Chamber:

> The doctrines of "political questions" and "non-justiciable disputes" are remnants of the reservations of "sovereignty", "national honour", etc. in very old arbitration treaties. They have receded from the horizon of contemporary international law, except for the occasional invocation of the "political question" argument before the International Court of Justice in advisory proceedings and, very rarely, in contentious proceedings as well.
>
> The Court has consistently rejected this argument as a bar to examining a case. It considered it unfounded in law. As long as the case before it or the request for an advisory opinion turns on a legal question capable of a legal answer, the Court considers that it is duty-bound to take jurisdiction over it, regardless of the political background or the other political facets of the issue.[1167]

This is in accordance with legal doctrine. Most commentators agree that the dichotomy between political (non-justiciable) and legal disputes is an artificial one that is no longer valid in international law.[1168] Indeed, if one accepts that the Council must have certain privileges so as to be able to function effectively, the same must hold true for the Court.[1169] Since it follows from the nature of its jurisdiction ("any question of international law") that the Court will frequently have to deal with highly sensitive and politicized issues, it would seriously undermine the functioning of the Court to honour the plea of non-justiciable disputes. This is not to say that the Court might at times

---

1166 *Legality of the Use by a State of Nuclear Weapons in Armed Conflict* (Prel. Objections), Judgment of 8 July 1996, para. 17. See to the same effect the Court's Advisory Opinion requested by the General Assembly on the *Legality of the Threat or Use of Nuclear Weapons*, 8 July 1996, para. 13.

1167 Appeals Chamber Decision on the Tadić Jurisdictional Motion, *Prosecutor V. Dusko Tadića/k/a "Dule"*, Case No. IT-94-1-AR72, 2 Oct. 1995, para. 24.

1168 Thus Higgins submits that "there is little reality in any definition of a political, or legal, question; what is relevant is the distinction between a political method and a legal method of solving disputes." R. Higgins, *Policy Considerations and the International Judicial Process*, 17 ICLQ (1968) 58-84, at 74. See also Akande, *op. cit supra* n.1158, 597-599; T. Sugihara, *The Judicial Function of the International Court of Justice with Respect to Disputes Involving Highly Political Issues*. In: A.S. Muller, D. Raič, J.M. Thuránszky (eds.), The International Court of Justice: Its Future Role after Fifty Years (1997) 117-138, 127-129 and 138; Watson, *op. cit. supra* n.7; K. Roberts, *Second-guessing the Security Council: The International Court of Justice and its Powers of Judicial Review*, 7 Pace International Law Review (1995) 281-327, 322; D. Bowett, *The Impact of the Security Council Decisions on Dispute Settlement Procedures*, 5 EJIL (1994) 89-101, 94.

1169 *Cf.* Gill, *op. cit. supra* n.1153, 169.

choose not to exercise jurisdiction as a matter of judicial prudence. That, however, is principally a different issue. Rather than denying the existence of jurisdiction in such a case, the Court considers it inappropriate to exercise it. That would be a form of judicial propriety.

The question is thus not whether the issue is political but rather whether it is capable of being solved by the application of legal principles and norms. In the words of Gowlland-Debbas: "the distinction between a legal and a political dispute lies not in its inherent nature but in the distinction between a political and legal method of solving the dispute."[1170]

As regards the powers of the Security Council under Chapter VII, there appears to be one category of decisions that is not suitable for judicial scrutiny. This category is formed by the determinations by the Council under Article 39 that a threat to the peace or a breach of the peace exists. Thus Malanczuk, for example, submits that:

> it is difficult to conceive that a determination of the Council under Article 39 that there is a threat to international peace is as such reviewable – because it would mean that the Court would have to substitute the Council's political judgement by a political judgement of its own for which it is not qualified.[1171]

Kooijmans also maintains that:

> The determination of a threat to the peace is a political judgment, albeit that the Charter reminds the Council that it shall act in accordance with the purposes and principles of the United Nations, and it is a political judgment based on facts in a field where the Council has been given primary responsibility. Asking the Court to subject this political decision to legal scrutiny is not inviting it to undertake an essentially judicial task, namely the "interpretation of a treaty provision"; it amounts to a request to review the political evaluation made by the Council.[1172]

A similar conclusion is reached by Akande, according to whom:

> the view that Article 39 determinations of the Security Council are final and non-reviewable is one which is perfectly acceptable ... These questions are not properly suited to determination by a judicial body as there

---

[1170] Cowlland Debbas, *op. cit. supra* n.1152, at 652. *Cf.* Akande, *op. cit supra* n.1158, who submits at 602 that "the essential question is ... whether a particular question is capable of a legal answer." Similarly, Higgins maintains that: "A dispute is a 'legal' dispute if it is to be resolved by authoritative legal decision, no matter what the component elements of that dispute are." Higgins, *op. cit. supra* n.1168, at 74.

[1171] P. Malanczuk, *Reconsidering the Relationship between the ICJ and the Security Council*. In: W.P. Heere (ed.), International Law and The Hague's 750th Anniversary (1999) 87-99, at 98.

[1172] P.H. Kooijmans, *The International Court of Justice: Where does It Stand?*. In: A.S. Muller, D. Raič, J.M. Thuránszky (eds.), The International Court of Justice: Its Future Role after Fifty Years (1997) 407-418, at 416. *Cf.* D.W. Bowett, *Judicial and Political Functions of the Security Council and the International Court of Justice*. In: H. Fox (ed.), The Changing Constitution of the United Nations (1997) 73-88; R. Lapidoth, *Some Reflections on the Law and Practice Concerning the Imposition of Sanctions by the Security Council*, 30 Archiv des Völkerrechts (1992) 114-127, 114-116.

are no clear legal standards as to what constitutes a threat to the peace or a breach of the peace. ... Therefore such questions are not fit for the International Court not because of any supposed inherent limitations of the international judicial function but because they are not questions to which international law, which the Court is charged to apply by Article 38 of its Statute, provides an answer.[1173]

In the *Kanyabashi* case the Rwanda Tribunal affirmed the non-justiciability of determinations of the Council under Article 39 in the following terms:

Although bound by the provisions of Chapter VII of the UN Charter and in particular Article 39 of the Charter, the Security Council has a wide margin of discretion in deciding when and where there exists a threat to international peace and security. By their very nature, however, such discretionary assessments are not justiciable since they involve the consideration of a number of social, political and circumstantial factors which cannot be weighed and balanced objectively by this Trial Chamber.[1174]

The Charter provides the Council with a wide discretion in this respect. The obligation of the Council to abide by the object and purpose of the Charter does not pose a limitation in this regard. Furthermore, chapter 3 has shown that the Council has interpreted threats and breaches to the peace in a dynamic way.[1175] Determinations by the Council under Article 39 are therefore not subject to judicial scrutiny unless an act of bad faith by the Council can be established,[1176] or in the "exceptional – and

---

1173 Akande, *op. cit. supra* n.104, at 338. *Cf.* Lauterpacht in his Sep. Op. in the *Application of the Convention on the Prevention and Punishment of the Crime of Genocide (Bosnia and Herzegovina v. Yugoslavia)* case, Prov. Measures, Order of 13 Sept. 1993, submitting that the Court does not possess "any right ... to substitute its discretion for that of the Security Council in determining the existence of a threat to the peace, a breach of the peace or an act of aggression, or the political steps to be taken following such a determination." ICJ Rep. (1993), at 439. See *contra*, however, Graefrath, *op. cit. supra* n.649, 242.

1174 *Prosecutor v. Joseph Kanyabashi*, Case No. ICTR-96-15-T, Decision on the Defence Motion on Jurisdiction, 18 June 1997, para. 20 at 6. For an assessment of the case see V. Morris, *Prosecutor v. Kanyabashi, Decision on Jurisdiction, Case No. ICTR-96-15-T: International Criminal Tribunal for Rwanda, June 18, 1997*, 92 AJIL (1998) 66-70.

1175 At the summit meeting of 31 Jan. 1992, the Security Council issued the following statement which further enhances the concept of threats to international peace and security: "The absence of war and military conflicts amongst States does not in itself ensure international peace and security. The non-military sources of instability in the economic, social, humanitarian and ecological fields have become threats to peace and security. The United Nations membership as a whole, working through the appropriate bodies, needs to give the highest priority to the solution of these matters." UN Doc. S/PV. 3046 (1992), at 143. *Cf.* also, for example, S/Res. 1308 (2000), adopted on 17 July 2000. Herein the Council 'stresses' that "the HIV/AIDS pandemic, if unchecked, may pose a risk to stability and security".

1176 See M. Fraas, *Sicherheitsrat der Vereinten Nationen und Internationaler Gerichtshof: Die Rechtmäßigkeitsprüfung von Beschlüssen des Sicherheitsrat der Vereinten Nationen im Rahmen des VII. Kapitels der Charta durch den Internationalen Gerichtshof* (1998), 194-230.

therefore hypothetical – case that no one in their right senses could have come to the same conclusion as the Council."[1177]

5.3.6 Judicial Review by the Court of Security Council Decisions

As seen in chapter 4, the Council is bound to comply with certain rules of international law. The analysis above indicates that the fact that the Council is seized of a matter does not preclude the Court from exercising jurisdiction over that same matter. In other words, the plea of litispendence will not be upheld by the Court. Neither is it to be expected that the invocation of the political question doctrine will compel the Court to refrain from deciding on Security Council decisions, with the exception of determinations made under Article 39.

The issue that subsequently arises is whether the Court can review the validity of Council decisions. Such a review could take place in either contentious cases or cases in which the Court is asked to give an advisory opinion.

5.3.6.1 Judicial Review in Contentious Cases

It must first be noted that the power of review is not included anywhere in the Charter or the Statute or the Rules of Court. During the UNCIO, two Belgian amendments that would have provided the Court with an explicit power to do so were not adopted.[1178] Indeed in the *Namibia* case the Court affirmed that: "Undoubtedly, the Court does not possess powers of judicial review or appeal in respect of the decisions taken by the United Nations organs concerned."[1179]

The lack of an express power of judicial review does not mean, however, that the Court does not possess any residual or implied power. As observed by Akande, "lack of an express power of review is not ... determinative. What is more important is a lack of an express prohibition from engaging in judicial review."[1180]

Skubiszewski seems to disagree with the latter statement when he states that "in analogy to municipal law, for such powers to exist there must be an express norm of

---

1177 Kooijmans, *op. cit. supra* n.1172, at 416.

1178 For a discussion hereon see Watson, *op. cit. supra* n.7, 8-14.

1179 *Legal Consequences for States of the Continued Presence of South Africa in Namibia (South-West Africa) Notwithstanding Security Council Resolution 276 (1970)*, ICJ Rep. (1971), para. 89 at 45.

1180 Akande, *op. cit. supra* n.104, at 326. At 327, furthermore, he submits that: "The lack of an express grant of judicial review does not ... bar the International Court from engaging in judicial review." See to the same effect Fassbender, *op. cit. supra* n.46, 312.

authorizing judicial review. These powers cannot be implied."[1181] Notwithstanding this remark, Skubiszewski concludes that:

> The Court is not, and it is submitted *de lege ferenda* that it should not become, a tribunal of judicial review with power to declare null and void those acts of the Security Council that it finds contrary to law. But the Court, in view of its function, cannot and in fact did not shy away from pronouncing on the conformity of Security Council acts with law in both contentious and advisory opinions.[1182]

Indeed, after the Court noted in the *Namibia* case that it "undoubtedly" does not "possess powers of judicial review", it stated that:

> The question of the validity or conformity with the Charter of General Assembly resolution 2145 (XXI) or of related Security Council resolutions does not form the subject of the request for advisory opinion. However, *in the exercise of its judicial function and since objections have been advanced the Court,* in the course of its reasoning, will consider these objections before determining any legal consequences arising from those resolutions.[1183]

An analysis of the *Lockerbie case (Provisional Measures and Preliminary Objections)*, moreover, suggests that the Court might be willing to review the validity of the underlying Security Council decisions. In the provisional measures stage the bench exhibited near consensus regarding the *prima facie* validity of resolution 748 (1992). Except for El-Kosheri, the presumption of validity, developed by the Court in the *Certain Expenses* case,[1184] was adopted by both the majority and the dissenting minority. This notwithstanding, there was disagreement on the ultimate validity of resolution 748 (1992) and several arguments addressed its possible invalidity.[1185] Judge Oda, on the one hand, stated that:

> under the positive law of the United Nations Charter a resolution of the Security Council may have binding force, irrespective whether it is consonant with international law derived from other sources. There is certainly nothing to oblige the Security Council, acting within its terms of reference, to carry out a full evaluation of the possibly relevant rules and circumstances before proceeding to the decisions it deems necessary.[1186]

Judge Lachs, on the other hand, adopted a more cautious approach. He submitted

---

1181 K. Skubiszewski, *The International Court of Justice and the Security Council*. In: V. Lowe, M. Fitzmaurice (eds.), Fifty Years of the International Court of Justice (1996) 606-629, at 623.

1182 *Ibid.*, at 628.

1183 *Legal Consequences for States of the Continued Presence of South Africa in Namibia (South-West Africa) Notwithstanding Security Council Resolution 276 (1970)*, ICJ Rep. (1971), para. 89 at 45 (emphasis added).

1184 On which see *infra*, page 274.

1185 Thus Judge Ajibola stated that "certain intrinsic defects" may invalidate resolutions 731 (1992) and 748 (1992), such as the non-recognition by the Security Council of the principle of *nemo iudex in sua causa* or Article 27(3) of the Charter." Diss. Op. Ajibola, *Lockerbie (Prov. Measures)*, 193.

1186 Declaration Oda, *Lockerbie (Prov. Measures)*, at 129.

that: "While the Court has the vocation of applying international law as a universal law, operating both within and outside the United Nations, it is bound to respect, as a part of that law, the binding decisions of the Security Council."[1187]

Later on, however, he observed that:

it is important for the purposes and principles of the United Nations that the two main organs with specific powers of binding decision act in harmony – though not, of course, in concert – and that each should perform its functions with respect to a situation or dispute, different aspects of which appear on the agenda of each, *without prejudicing the exercise of the other's powers.*[1188]

Judge Lachs was not the only judge to express his doubts on the course of action followed by the Security Council. According to Shahabuddeen:

The question now raised by Libya's challenge to the validity of resolution 748 (1992) is whether a decision of the Security Council may override the legal rights of States, and, if so, whether there are any limitations on the power of the Council to characterize a situation as one justifying the making of a decision entailing such consequences. Are there any limits to the Council's power of appreciation? In the equilibrium of forces underpinning the structure of the United Nations within the evolving international order, is there any conceivable point beyond which a legal issue may properly arise as to the competence of the Security Council to produce such overriding results? If there are any limits, what are those limits and what body, if other than the Security Council, is competent to say what those limits are?[1189]

This critical approach recurs in the dissenting opinions. Although the majority conceded as to the validity of resolution 748 (1992), emphasis was laid on the *prima facie* character of this presumption.[1190] This is exemplified by Bedjaoui, who in his thorough exposé, affirmed that resolution 748 (1992) "benefits from a presumption of validity and must be considered prima facie as both lawful and binding."[1191] In a footnote accompanying this text, however, he subjected this to a condition:

Unless one supposes that resolution 748 (1992) has as its object, or effect, not to withdraw a right from an Applicant State, but to prevent the exercise, by the Court itself, of the judicial function with which it has been invested by the Charter, in which case one might be led to ponder seriously over the lawfulness of that resolution, even at this stage of provisional measures. It would, indeed, be manifestly incompatible with the

---

1187 Sep. Op. Lachs, *ibid.*, at 138.

1188 *Ibid.*, at 139 (emphasis added). He concluded by expressing his hopes that "the two principal organs concerned will be able to operate with due consideration for their mutual involvement in the preservation of the rule of law." On this Kooijmans remarks that "one can barely imagine a more subtly formulated reproach of *excès de pouvoir*." P.H. Kooijmans, *Zwijgt het Recht als de Veiligheidsraad spreekt?*, 27 NJB (1992) 847-851, at 850.

1189 Sep. Op. Shahabuddeen, *Lockerbie (Prov. Measures)*, at 142.

1190 See, *e.g.*, Diss. Op. Weeramantry, *Lockerbie (Prov. Measures)*, at 177: "Without expressing views on the matter *at this stage of the proceedings*, I take the view that resolution 748 (1992) must be treated as binding". (Emphasis added).

1191 Diss. Op. Bedjaoui, *ibid.*, at 156.

Charter for an organ of the United Nations to prevent the Court from accomplishing its mission, or for it actually to place the Court in a state of subordination which would be contrary to the principle of separation and independence of the judicial from the executive power, within the United Nations.[1192]

In contrast to the other judges, El-Kosheri directly involved himself in examining the validity of resolution 748 (1992),[1193] and in doing so he concluded that:

it is possible to consider that the Security Council, when adopting paragraph 1 of resolution 748 (1992), impeded the Court's jurisdiction freely to exercise its inherent judicial function with regard to issues on which the argument had been heard just a few days before, and that by doing so the Security Council committed an act of *excès de pouvoir* which amounts to a violation of Article 92 of the Charter.[1194]

Indeed, he availed himself of this possibility by characterizing paragraph 1 of resolution 748 (1992) as being *ultra vires*.[1195]

In the judgment on preliminary objections, moreover, the Court joined the question of the admissibility of Libya's claim to the merits. This implies that the Court will further examine the arguments by the parties related to the validity and reviewability of Security Council resolutions 748 (1992) and 883 (1993).

It is submitted here that the Court does have a limited power of review. In contentious cases the Court has to settle disputes brought before it on the basis of international law. Binding decisions of the Council undoubtedly form part of this law. In the exercise of its judicial function, the Court will have to consider for each case whether the particular rule of international law relied upon by one or both of the parties is applicable and valid in the specific circumstances of the case. The Court will have to satisfy itself, for example, as to whether a treaty invoked by a party has entered into force and whether it applies to the relations between the parties. The same holds for the decisions of the Council. If one of the parties relies on or contests the applicability of a Council decision, the Court, in the exercise of its judicial function, should determine whether the decision is indeed *intra vires*. In other words, whether the decision does in fact form part and parcel of international law. In the *East Timor* case, Judge Skubiszewski formulated this as follows:

The Court is competent, and this is shown by several judgments and advisory opinions, to interpret and apply the resolutions of the Organization. The Court is competent to make findings on their lawfulness, in particular

---

1192 *Ibid.*, n.1 at 156.

1193 Referring, amongst other things, to the Advisory Opinion concerning the *Legal Consequences for States of the Continued Presence of South Africa in Namibia (South West Africa) Notwithstanding Security Council Resolution 276 (1970)* in order to establish the Court's power to review the validity of a decision made by a co-organ.

1194 Diss. Op. El-Kosheri, *Lockerbie (Prov. Measures)*, at 210.

1195 *Ibid.*

whether they were *intra vires*. This competence follows from its function as the principal judicial organ of the United Nations. The decisions of the Organization (in the broad sense which this notion has under the Charter provisions on voting) are subject to scrutiny by the Court with regard to their legality, validity and effect.[1196]

This competence is a form of incidental review and is to be distinguished from a general power of judicial review.[1197] As seen above, such a general power does not reside with the Court, although in exercising its advisory jurisdiction the Court could possibly function as a review body. The issue of judicial review in advisory proceedings will now be addressed.

5.3.6.2 Judicial Review in Advisory Opinions

As seen above, the General Assembly or the Security Council can request the Court to give an advisory opinion on "any legal question" under Article 96(1) of the Charter.[1198] Such questions must relate to the scope of activities of both organs under the Charter, but these are formulated very broadly in the Charter. Therefore Mosler, for example, submits that "legal questions not covered by such activities scarcely exist."[1199] In addition to the General Assembly and the Security Council, specialized agencies so authorized by the General Assembly may also request opinions on legal questions "arising within the scope of their activities" under Article 96(2). As the 1998 Advisory Opinions on Nuclear Weapons demonstrate, the latter phrase can be a hurdle for the Court to exercise its jurisdiction. In the *Legality of the Threat or Use Of Nuclear Weapons* case, the Court found the General Assembly competent to request the Court to answer the following question: "Is the threat or use of nuclear weapons in any circumstance permitted under international law?"[1200]

However, the same did not hold for the request of the World Health Organization. The organization had asked the Court to answer the question: "In view of the health and environmental effects, would the use of nuclear weapons by a State in war or other armed conflict be a breach of its obligations under international law including the

1196 *Case Concerning East Timor*, Portugal v. Australia, Diss. Op. Skubiszewski, ICJ Rep. (1995), para. 86 at 251.

1197 See King, *op. cit. supra* n.725, 532. See also the Appeals Chamber Decision on the Tadić Jurisdictional Motion, *Prosecutor v. Dusko Tadić a/k/a "Dule"*, Case No. IT-94-1-AR72, 2 Oct. 1995, para. 21, in which the Chamber refers to the "examination of the legality of the decisions of other organs as a matter of "incidental" jurisdiction, in order to ascertain and be able to exercise its "primary" jurisdiction over the matter before it".

1198 See *supra*, paragraph 5.3.1.2.

1199 Mosler, *op. cit. supra* n.948, at 1010.

1200 See *Legality of the Threat or Use Of Nuclear Weapons*, Adv. Op., 8 July 1996, paras. 11-12.

WHO Constitution?" The Court found that it was not able to give the opinion requested since the request did not relate to a question which arises "within the scope of [the] activities" of the organization.[1201]

In its practice the Court has broadly defined 'legal questions' as questions "susceptible of a reply based on law."[1202] This is in line with the Court's reluctance to adhere to the political question doctrine.[1203] The questions may furthermore "be abstract or otherwise".[1204] The conclusion is thus that the Court can give an opinion on a broad category of questions and that it will not easily shy away from giving the opinion because of the political nature and implications of the request. The case law of the International Court of Justice in which it (in)directly addressed its powers to review the acts of co-organs of the United Nations will be considered below.

5.3.6.2.1 Competence of the GA for the Admission of a State

In the Advisory Opinion on the *Competence of the General Assembly for the Admission of a State to the United Nations* the Court was faced with the following question:

Can the admission of a State to membership of the United Nations, pursuant to Article 4, paragraph 2, of the Charter, be effected by a decision of the General Assembly when the Security Council has made no recommendation for admission by reason of the candidate failing to obtain the requisite majority or of the negative vote of a permanent Member upon a resolution so to recommend?[1205]

In deciding on this question the Court held that:

It is not the object of the Request to determine how the Security Council should apply the rules governing its voting procedure in regard to admissions or, in particular, that the Court should examine whether the negative vote of a permanent Member is effective to defeat a recommendation which has obtained seven or more votes. The question, *as it is formulated*, assumes in such a case the non-existence of a recommendation.

The Court is, therefore, called upon to determine solely whether the General Assembly can make a decision to admit a State when the Security Council has transmitted no recommendation to it.[1206]

The Court indicated in this passage that if the question had been whether a negative

---

1201 See *Legality of The Use by a State of Nuclear Weapons in Armed Conflict*, Adv. Op., 8 July 1996, para. 21-32. For a critique of this decision see, *e.g.*, D. Akande, *The Competence of International Organizations and the Advisory Jurisdiction of the International Court of Justice*, 9 EJIL (1998) 437-467.

1202 *Western Sahara*, Adv. Op., 16 Oct. 1975, para. 15.

1203 See *supra*, paragraph 5.3.5.

1204 *Conditions of Admission of a State to Membership in the United Nations (Article 4 of the Charter)*, Adv. Op., ICJ Rep. (1948), at 61.

1205 ICJ Rep. (1950), at 7.

1206 ICJ Rep. (1950), at 7 (emphasis added).

vote of a permanent Member can preclude the adoption of a recommendation under Article 4(2) under the Charter, it would have examined that question. It seems that the Court did not want to venture on to this road. One could read this as an application of the presumption of validity, a principle that the Court would later fully develop in the *Certain Expenses* case. For although the Court seemed to assume that the negative vote of a permanent member is indeed effective to defeat a recommendation of the Security Council on the admission of a State under Article 4(2) of the Charter, it nevertheless decided not to pronounce itself on whether the Council had respected this voting procedure. In two later cases, the Court took a less cautious approach with regard to reviewing the procedural and substantive validity of Security Council and General Assembly resolutions.

5.3.6.2.2 Certain Expenses of the United Nations

In the *Certain Expenses* case, the Court was asked to give an opinion on the question whether the expenses incurred for the operations in the Congo could be apportioned according to the scale which the General Assembly applied under Article 17(2) of the Charter. The question was formulated as follows:

> Do the expenditures authorized in General Assembly resolutions ... relating to United Nations operations in the Congo [and] to the operations of the United Nations Emergency Force ... constitute 'expenses of the Organization' within the meaning of Article 17, paragraph 2, of the Charter of the United Nations?[1207]

Before deciding on this question, the Court noted that an amendment proposed by France had been defeated in the General Assembly. If the French amendment would have been adopted, the Court would have been asked to consider whether the resolutions authorizing the expenditures had been decided on in conformity with the Charter. The Court then stated that:

> The rejection of the French amendment does not constitute a directive to the Court to exclude from its consideration the question whether certain expenditures were "decided on in conformity with the Charter", if the Court finds such consideration appropriate. It is not to be assumed that the General Assembly would thus seek to fetter or hamper the Court in the discharge of its functions; the Court must have full liberty to consider all relevant data available to it in forming an opinion on a question posed to it for an advisory opinion.[1208]

Indeed the Court held that the resolutions authorizing the expenditures had to be

1207 *Certain Expenses of the United Nations (Article 17, Paragraph 2, of the Charter)*, Adv. Op., ICJ Rep. (1962), at 152.

1208 *Ibid.*, at 157.

reviewed in order to answer the question put to it:

In determining whether the actual expenditures authorized constitute "expenses of the Organization within the meaning of Article 17, paragraph 2, of the Charter of the United Nations", the Court agrees that such expenditures must be tested by their relationship to the purposes of the United Nations in the sense that if an expenditure were made for a purpose which is not one of the purposes of the United Nations, it could not be considered an "expense of the Organization."[1209]

In analyzing the Organization's actions with regard to the Congo the Court *inter alia* held that the "operations were undertaken to fulfil a prime purpose of the United Nations, that is, to promote and to maintain peaceful settlement of the situation." Therefore the Court concluded that the expenditures relating to the Congo which had been authorized by the Assembly did constitute "expenses of the Organization within the meaning of Article 17, paragraph 2, of the Charter of the United Nations."

In passing, the Court developed its presumption of validity by stating:

[The United Nations'] purposes are broad indeed, but neither they nor the powers conferred to effectuate them are unlimited. Save as they have entrusted the Organization with the attainment of these common ends, the Member States retain their freedom of action. But when the Organization takes action which warrants the assertion that it was appropriate for the fulfilment of one of the stated purposes of the United Nations, the presumption is that such action is not ultra vires.[1210]

5.3.6.2.3 Legal Consequences (South-West Africa)

A similar line of reasoning was employed by the Court in its *Namibia* Advisory Opinion. Herein the Court had to decide on the objections that it was not competent to render the decision. On this the Court held:

The Government of South Africa has contended that for several reasons resolution 284 (1970) of the Security Council, which requested the advisory opinion of the Court, is invalid, and that, therefore, the Court is not competent to deliver the opinion. A resolution of a properly constituted organ of the United Nations which is passed in accordance with that organ's rules of procedure, and is declared by its President to have been so passed, must be presumed to have been validly adopted. However, since in this instance the objections made concern the competence of the Court, the Court will proceed to examine them.[1211]

In the following paragraphs the Court rejected the objections that resolution 284 (1970) had not been validly adopted. The first objection related to the abstention of two permanent members in the vote, which according to South Africa meant that the resolution had not acquired the nine affirmative votes required by Article 27(3) of the

---

1209 *Ibid.*, at 167.

1210 *Ibid.*, at 168. See also *infra*, the text accompanying note 1211.

1211 *Legal Consequences for States of the Continued Presence of South Africa in Namibia (South-West Africa) Notwithstanding Security Council Resolution 276 (1970)*, Adv. Op. of 21 June 1971, para. 20.

Charter. To this the Court replied that the "members of the Council ... have consistently and uniformly interpreted the practice of voluntary abstention as not constituting a bar to the adoption of resolutions."[1212] The second objection held that the question contained in resolution 284 (1970) related to a dispute pending between South Africa and other members of the United Nations, necessitating abstention from voting by those members on the Council in accordance with Article 27(3) of the Charter; and that South Africa should have been present and voting in accordance with Article 32. The Court dismissed these arguments by noting that the Council had consistently referred to the question of Namibia as a "situation" and not a "dispute."[1213]

After deciding that it was competent to hear the case, the Court considered the contention of France and South Africa that the General Assembly, when adopting resolution 2145 (XXI) which terminated South Africa's mandate in South-West Africa, had "acted *ultra vires.*"

In a notable passage the Court held that:

> Before considering this objection, it is necessary for the Court to examine the observations made and the contentions advanced as to whether the Court should go into this question. It was suggested that though the request was not directed to the question of the General Assembly resolution and of the related Security Council resolutions, this did not preclude the Court from making such an enquiry. On the other hand it was contented that the Court was not authorized by the terms of the request, in the light of the discussions preceding it, to go into the validity of these resolutions. It was argued that the Court should not assume powers of judicial review of the action taken by the other principal organs of the United Nations without specific request to that effect, nor act as a court of appeal from their decisions.
>
> Undoubtedly, the Court does not possess powers of judicial review or appeal in respect of the decisions taken by the United Nations organs concerned. The question of the validity or conformity with the Charter of General Assembly resolution 2145 (XXI) or of related Security Council resolutions does not form the subject of the request for advisory opinion. However, in the exercise of its judicial function and since objections have been advanced the Court, in the course of its reasoning, will consider these objections before determining any legal consequences arising from those resolutions.[1214]

Subsequently the Court examined these objections, after which it reached the conclusion that the decisions made by the Security Council had been adopted in conformity with the purposes and principles of the Charter and in accordance with its Articles 24 and 25.

These three advisory opinions indicate that the Court has gone through a quite

---

1212 *Ibid.*, para. 22.

1213 *Ibid.*, paras. 25-26. The Court also rejected South Africa's contention that even if the Court was competent to deliver the opinion, it should not exercise it as a matter of judicial propriety. These objections related to the political pressure put on the Court and to the fact that the question related to a "legal dispute actually pending between two or more States." See *ibid.*, paras. 27-41.

1214 *Ibid.*, paras. 88-89.

remarkable development. In the *Competence of the General Assembly for the Admission of a State* opinion, rendered in 1950, it hinted that it could have reviewed the procedural validity of the Council's acts with regard to a recommendation under Article 4(2) of the Charter. In a quite formalistic manner it declined to do so, however, stating that the question as posed to the Court did not necessitate the Court to review this procedure. This reluctance to venture into the procedural and substantive validity of acts of the Organization was overturned in the *Certain Expenses* and the *Legal Consequences* cases. In the *Certain Expenses* case the Court decided to test the expenditures authorized by the Assembly by their relationship to the purposes of the Charter, even though a French amendment that would have asked the Court to examine the conformity of the expenditures with the Charter had been defeated. This decision was based on the consideration that "the Court must have full liberty to consider all relevant data available to it in forming an opinion on a question posed to it for an advisory opinion." In the *Legal Consequences* case the Court went even further. Therein it first noted that it did not possess a general power of judicial review. At the same time, however, it reviewed the procedural validity of resolution 284 (1970) since the objections raised against the validity of this resolution "concern the competence of the Court." It then tested the decisions of the Council by their conformity with the purposes and principles of the Charter "in the exercise of its judicial function and since objections have been advanced."

5.3.7 *De lege lata* Conditions and Consequences of Judicial Review

On the face of it the decisions of the Court in the *Certain Expenses, Legal Consequences* and *Lockerbie* cases resemble the *Marbury v. Madison* case, often referred to in the context of judicial review by the Court of Security Council decisions.[1215] In that case the US Supreme Court, although determining that the act in question was constitutional, asserted a power to review the constitutionality of actions taken by Congress, a power not mentioned in the US constitution. One has to be careful, however, with domestic analogies in this respect. For one thing, the trias politica, as developed by

---

1215 See, *e.g.*, Franck, *op. cit. supra* n.7; Watson, *op. cit. supra* n.7, 19; M. David, *Passport to Justice: Internationalizing the Political Question Doctrine for Application in the World Court*, 40 HJIL (1999) 81-150, 90-91; Alvarez, *op. cit. supra* n.5, 4-8; Gunn, *op. cit. supra* n.725, 225; L. Caflisch, *Is the International Court Entitled to Review Security Council Resolutions Adopted Under Chapter VII of the United Nations Charter?*. In: N. Al-Nauimi, R. Meese (eds.), International Legal Issues Arising Under the United Nations Decade of International Law (1995) 633-662, 635. See also, in the context of the *Nicaragua* case, M.J. Glennon, *Protecting the Court's Institutional Interests: Why not the Marbury Approach?*, 81 AJIL (1987) 121-129.

Montesquieu in his *Spirit of Laws* which was originally published in 1748, is (as yet) not applicable in the international sphere. In other words, there is no distinction between the executive, the legislative and the judicial powers known to national systems.[1216] This has been confirmed by the Court in the *Nicaragua* case, in which the Court dealt with the US contention that the Nicaraguan application was inadmissible because it related to a political issue within the Council's competence, which the Court was not qualified to address. On this contention the Court held that:

> The argument of the United States as to the powers of the Security Council and of the Court is an attempt to transfer municipal-law concepts of separation of powers to the international plane, whereas these concepts are not applicable to the relations among international institutions for the settlement of disputes.[1217]

Analogies from municipal law are also difficult to draw because the legal regimes vary considerably from country to country.[1218] Some countries explicitly mention a power of judicial review in the constitution (Germany, and to mention an international organization, the European Union). Some countries have an explicit prohibition thereof (the Netherlands) and leave it to the executive to pass judgment on the constitutionality of legislation. Others are silent on the question (the US).

5.3.7.1 Advisory Proceedings

The *Certain Expenses* and *Namibia* decisions do, however, indicate that the Court possesses a power of incidental judicial review. This means that if the questions posed relate to the interpretation and application of a Security Council decision, the Court can decide on the validity of that resolution. Indeed, as the principal judicial organ

---

1216 Rosenne, for example, observes that: "there is no analogous distribution of executive, legislative and judicial power in the international sphere. While it is frequently possible in the Charter of the United Nations and other similar constituent instruments of international organizations to differentiate between these functions, it is quite another matter when it comes to differentiating between either the organs, or the applicable techniques." Rosenne, *op. cit. supra* n.939, at 5. *Cf.* Schermers, Blokker, *op. cit. supra* n.51, §1336; Herbst, *op. cit. supra* n.947, 389-391; Shaw, *op. cit. supra* n.771, 256; Herdegen, *op. cit. supra* n.5, 150; Fassbender, *op. cit. supra* n.46, 310. For the view that the Court "has acknowledged that separation of powers is fundamental to any functioning organization" see, *e.g.*, Bortz, *op. cit. supra* n.7, 377-378.

1217 *Case Concerning Military and Paramilitary Activities in and against Nicaragua* (Jur.), Nic. v. US, 26 Nov. 1984, para. 92.

1218 See, *e.g.*, K.H. Kaikobad, *The International Court of Justice and Judicial Review: A Study of the Court's Powers with Respect to Judgements of the ILO and UN Administrative Tribunals* (2000), Part Two ('Judicial Review in Municipal and International Law'); Alvarez, *op. cit. supra* n.5, 24-28; E. de Wet, *Judicial Review as an Emerging General Principle of Law and Its Implications for the International Court of Justice*, 47 NILR (2000) 181-210, 199-202.

of the United Nations, the Court does seem an appropriate organ to ensure the legality of actions taken by the organization, including those of the Council taken under Chapter VII of the Charter. The advisory jurisdiction is, at first sight, the most appropriate mode for the Court to do so, for this jurisdiction provides for a specific institutional role of the Court. There is a formal argument against such a role that has to be considered first. According to this argument, the Court cannot effectively review the Council's decisions under its advisory jurisdiction because advisory opinions are legally non-binding.[1219] This argument is not convincing, however. It ignores the fact that the Council and the membership of the United Nations could not pursue a course of action in the knowledge that this action is illegal.[1220] It is the Court's function to apply and state the law. To maintain that the Council could ignore a declaration by the Court, that a particular Council decision is procedurally invalid or *ultra vires*, would lead to an absurd result. Member states would then be obliged to act upon an illegal decision and pursue a course of action which is illegal under international law, for example by enforcing sanctions against a member of the United Nations ordered for by an illegal resolution of the Council.

It must be noted that the situation is different in the case of obligations of the Organization towards third parties.[1221] If the Council enters into an obligation outside its competence, the obligation does not necessarily become void *vis-à-vis* the other parties because of the Council's incompetence. Thus the Court held in the *Certain Expenses* case that:

> If the action was taken by the wrong organ, it was irregular as a matter of that internal structure, but this would not necessarily mean that the expense incurred was not an expense of the Organization. Both national and international law contemplate cases in which the body corporate or politic may be bound, as to third parties, by an ultra vires act of an agent.[1222]

From the 1986 Vienna Convention on the Law of Treaties Between States and International Organizations or Between International Organizations,[1223] it can be

---

1219 See Alvarez, *op. cit. supra* n.5, 5; E. de Wet, *Judicial Review of the United Nations Security Council and General Assembly Through Advisory Opinions of the International Court of Justice*, 10 SZIER (2000) 237-277, 261-262.

1220 *Cf.* de Wet, *op. cit. supra* n.1219, at 263-264: "advisory opinions still provide authoritative statements of those points of law to which they are addressed and consequently may be in effect dispositive of the issue submitted."

1221 See M. Hirsch, *The Responsibility of International Organizations Toward Third Parties: Some Basic Principles* (1995), 88-97.

1222 *Certain Expenses of the United Nations (Article 17, Paragraph 2, of the Charter)*, Adv. Op., 20 July 1962. ICJ Rep. (1962), at 168.

1223 Adopted on 21 March 1986, reproduced in 25 ILM (1986) 543 ff.

inferred that the Council's incompetence must have been 'obvious and concerning an important rule'. Article 46 of the Convention, dealing with "Provisions of internal law of a State and rules of an international organization regarding competence to conclude treaties", holds that:

2. An international organization may not invoke the fact that its consent to be bound by a treaty has been expressed in violation of the rules of the organization regarding competence to conclude treaties as invalidating its consent unless that violation was manifest and concerned a rule of fundamental importance.
3. A violation is manifest if it would be objectively evident to any State or any international organization conducting itself in the matter in accordance with the normal practice of States and, where appropriate, of international organizations and in good faith.

The *Certain Expenses* dictum and the 1986 Convention demonstrate that not every invalid decision is non-enforceable. This is to ensure that third parties will "not be penalized as a result of an *ultra vires* act performed by an organ of an international organization."[1224]

In order to obtain legal guidance, the Security Council itself could conceivably request the Court for an advisory opinion on the validity of a proposed course of action or a decision already taken by it under Chapter VII. In the former case, the Council would await the Court's opinion before adopting a decision, in the latter the Council could suspend the operation of the decision until the Court decides on the validity of the measures taken. The likelihood of such a request is to be considered quite small, however. In its practice the United Nations organs have been reluctant to utilize the Court's advisory jurisdiction.[1225] Indeed, the Council only once requested the Court for an opinion, in the *Namibia* case, and this did not relate to the validity of its actions but rather to the legal consequences thereof. This reluctance on the part of the Council has several reasons. In the first place, the Council's need to act "swiftly and promptly".[1226] Acquiring political consensus over a course of action to be followed is difficult enough as it is and examining the legal implications of a decision would make it even more difficult to reach such a consensus. Related to this is the fact that the Council is not eager to give up its freedom of action.

It does not seem a realistic option that the Council itself will request an advisory opinion on the validity of its own decisions. The other option would be that the Assembly, or any duly authorized specialized organization under Article 96(2) of the Charter, requests such an opinion. The General Assembly could, for example, request an opinion on the congruency of a sanctions regime established by the Council with

1224 Hirsch, *op. cit. supra* n.1221, at 90.

1225 See Bowett, *op. cit. supra* n.947; de Wet, *op. cit. supra* n.1219, 270-272.

1226 See Roberts, *op. cit. supra* n.1168, 317; Fassbender, *op. cit. supra* n.46, 311.

the corpus of existing human rights law.[1227] It may be noted that Article 12(1) does not preclude the Assembly from submitting such a request to the Court, as the request is to be seen as an internal decision of the Assembly rather than a recommendation under the terms of Article 12(1).[1228] Alternatively, the World Health Organization, for example, could request an opinion on the health effects of such a sanctions regime.

These options are more viable than the Council itself requesting an opinion from the Court. It must be noted that the request for an opinion will probably not squarely relate to the validity of a Security Council decision. That could be embarrassing *vis-à-vis* the Council and could be a cause for the Court to determine that it is not competent to render an opinion in light of the absence of general "powers of judicial review or appeal" in respect of organs of the United Nations. A means of avoiding direct confrontation with the Security Council would be to couch the question in general and abstract terms. Another way of preventing a head-on course of action towards the Council would be to pose the question in terms of the legal obligations and consequences that flow from a particular resolution. In these cases the Court has "to take into account the whole law relevant to the situation",[1229] which includes the interpretation of a resolution. Before it is able to do so, the Court would have to elaborate on the legal basis of the resolution. That is, it has to be satisfied that the resolution is both procedurally and substantively valid. Thus Bedjaoui submits that "within the framework of its advisory jurisdiction the Court could give an opinion not only on interpretation of the Charter but also on any question with bearing upon the assessment of the validity of the acts of political organs."[1230]

This practice has been followed by the Court in the *Namibia* and *Certain Expenses* cases. Although the Court upheld the validity of the organization's actions in both cases, it necessarily follows from these cases that the Court could also decide that a Council action is illegal. In the light of the presumption of validity, however,[1231] a *prima facie* case for the invalidity of a decision must have been established. In deciding on the *vires* of a Security Council action the Court will impose "a heavy burden of

[1227] See Alvarez, *op. cit. supra* n.5, n.49 at 9.

[1228] Herbst, *op. cit. supra* n.947, 403-406.

[1229] Akande, *op. cit. supra* n.104, at 330.

[1230] Bedjaoui, *op. cit. supra* n.745, at 85. See also Shaw, *op. cit. supra* n.771. In the context of advisory opinions, Shaw concludes, at 257, that: "Where the Court considers that it flows from the proper exercise of its judicial function, the Court may assert the competence to examine thoroughly particular resolutions."

[1231] See *supra*, page 274.

proof on the party seeking to persuade the Court to overturn the political judgment of the Council on legal grounds."[1232]

5.3.7.2 Contentious Proceedings

A formal argument against judicial review by the Court in contentious proceedings is that judgments are only binding between parties.[1233] It is true that whenever the Court would decide that a particular decision contained in a Council resolution is invalid, it would probably hold that the decision is not applicable or enforceable in the relations between the parties. But *mutatis mutandis* the same applies as mentioned in advisory opinions. If the Court were to decide that a decision taken by the Council under Chapter VII of the Charter is invalid, member states would generally no longer be obliged to enforce the decision, for members cannot be held to abide by illegal decisions.[1234]

As seen above, there do not appear to be any a priori obstacles to the Court reviewing the legality and hence the validity of Security Council decisions. The instances in which such review can be exercised are limited, however.[1235] In contentious proceedings the instruments conferring jurisdiction on the Court must include the Court's reviewing of Council decisions. This is exemplified by the *Genocide* case, in which Bosnia asked the Court to adjudge and declare that Security Council resolution 713 (1991) must be interpreted in such a way that it did not impair Bosnia's inherent right to self-defence. The Court found that this question falls outside the scope of the instrument relied upon by Bosnia, the Genocide Convention, and that it therefore could not deal with this question.[1236]

This shows that the possibility of review by the Court in contentious procedures is directly linked with the instrument conferring jurisdiction. As the *Lockerbie* case indicates, an obligation under the Charter will prevail over a conflicting treaty

---

1232 T. Franck, *The Political and the Judicial Empires: Must there be Conflict over Conflict-Resolution?*. In: N. Al-Nauimi and R. Meese (eds.), International Legal Issues Arising Under the United Nations Decade of International Law (1995) 621-632, at 629. On the burden of proof generally see M. Kazazi, *Burden of Proof and Related Issues* (1996).

1233 Article 59 of the Court's Statute states that: "The decision of the Court has no binding force except between the parties and in respect of that particular case."

1234 An exception could be provided by obligations incurred by the Council *vis-à-vis* third parties, on which see *supra*, page 278.

1235 Indeed, de Wet observes that "this avenue for judicial review [is] the exception rather than the rule." De Wet, *op. cit. supra* n.1218, at 183.

1236 On the *Genocide* case see *supra*, paragraph 5.3.4.2.4.

obligation by virtue of Article 103 of the Charter. The matter would be different if the applicant were to base its claim on a declaration under the optional clause. Indeed, in the *Lockerbie* case Judge Oda observed that: "The claim on the ground of the violation of sovereign rights would have instituted a totally different litigation, and whether or not the Court has jurisdiction to deal with that issue is certainly a different matter."[1237]

5.3.8 The Court's Determinations of Illegality

As regards a possible determination of invalidity, it is not to be assumed that the Court would squarely declare a resolution invalid.[1238] In this context, one might refer to the possible solution mentioned by Judge ad hoc Lauterpacht in the *Genocide* case. In his separate opinion Lauterpacht considered the relationship between Security Council resolution 713 (1991), which imposed a weapons embargo on the territory of former Yugoslavia, and the prohibition on genocide, which falls under *jus cogens*. He first observed that:

> it is not to be contemplated that the Security Council would even deliberately adopt a resolution clearly and deliberately flouting a rule of *jus cogens* or requiring a violation of human rights. But the possibility that a Security Council resolution might inadvertently or in an unforseen manner lead to such a situation cannot be excluded.[1239]

Indeed, he submitted:

> And that, it appears, is what has happened here. ... the Security Council resolution can be seen as having in effect called on Members of the United Nations, albeit unknowingly and assured unwillingly, to become in some degree supporters of the genocidal activity of the Serbs and in this manner and to that extent to act contrary to *jus cogens*.[1240]

As for the 'legal consequences that may flow from this analysis', Lauterpacht suggests that the Court should refer the case back to the Council in order to remedy the defect decision:

[1237] *Lockerbie (Prov. Measures)*, at 131.

[1238] Thus Shaw notes that the Court, when engaged in judicial review "will approach this task with care and with the respect due to other principal organs. It will do this in a spirit of co-operation and in the light of the subjection of all organs to the Charter." Shaw, *op. cit. supra* n.771, at 257. Similarly, Alvarez submits that: "Over the near term, the Court will likely attempt to avoid decisions that directly question the Council's actions or their effects." Alvarez, *op. cit. supra* n.5, at 28.

[1239] *Application of the Convention on the Prevention and Punishment of the Crime of Genocide (Bosnia and Herzegovina v. Yugoslavia)*, Prov. Measures, Order of 13 Sept. 1993, Sep. Op. Lauterpacht, ICJ Rep. (1993), para. 102 at 119-120.

[1240] *Ibid.*, para. 102 at 120.

it would seem sufficient that the relevance here of *jus cogens* should be drawn to the attention of the Security Council, as it will be by the required communication to it of the Court's Order, so that the Security Council may give due weight to it in future reconsideration of the embargo.[1241]

Indeed, it is a delicate matter for the Court to engage in the judicial review of Council decisions. It is, therefore, to be expected that the Court, when pronouncing itself on a possible illegality of a Council decision, will couch this determination in careful terms. Referral back to the Council, which could then remedy the defective resolution, would avoid a collision between both organs.[1242]

5.3.9 Legal Consequences of the Court's Determination of Illegality

Notwithstanding the fact that the Court will probably exercise great caution in finding a resolution of the Council to be illegal, a possible determination of illegality by the Court leads to the question of the consequences attached to that determination. In other words, is the decision in question null and void *ab initio* (that is without legal effects from the date it was issued) or 'merely' voidable?[1243]

Generally speaking, an act is void *ab initio* when there is no procedural remedy available against the act.[1244] In the words of Zemanek:

According to the general theory of law, the absence of a procedural remedy against an alleged illegal act, *i.e.* a procedure in which the act could be declared void (relative nullity), makes the act *ipso facto* null and void (absolute nullity).[1245]

1241 *Ibid.*, para. 104 at 120.

1242 *Cf.* the Sep. Op. of Judge Sidhwa in the *Tadić* case: "Were it to find a serious flaw in its establishment, what steps the tribunal would take, I would not like to determine now. Whether it would make a simple declaration to that effect and leave it to the Security Council of the United Nations to correct the situation, or having made such a declaration, continue as an ad-hoc tribunal till the said body or Organisation comes to its aid, are some of the lines of action that may be debated". Appeals Chamber Decision on the Tadic Jurisdictional Motion, *Prosecutor V. Dusko Tadić a/k/a "Dule"*, Case No. IT-94-1-AR72, 2 Oct. 1995, Sep. Op. Sidhwa, para. 36.

1243 Voidability is described by de Wet as follows: "A voidable act is an act that produces all its effect in spite of the defects by which it is vitiated, as long as it is not annulled by the competent organ. It is only as a result of being annulled that the act loses, retroactively, its effectiveness." De Wet, *op. cit. supra* n.1219, at 268. On nullity see J.A. Frowein, *Nullity in International Law*, III EPIL (1997) 743-747; R.Y. Jennings, *Nullity and Effectiveness in International Law*. In: D.W. Bowett, *et. al.*, Cambridge Essays in International Law: Essays in Honour of Lord McNair (1965) 64-87.

1244 As observed by Verdross: "In principle, legally defective decisions are absolutely null, if no means of redress exist." A. Verdross, 44 Annuaire de l'Institut de Droit International, at 293. Quoted by Lauterpacht, *op. cit. supra* n.921, at 93.

1245 Zemanek, *op. cit. supra* n.701, at 642.

The answer to the question whether an illegal Security Council decision is voidable or null and void *ab initio* therefore depends on the availability of a procedural remedy.[1246] If one denies that the Court is competent to review Council decisions, the conclusion must be that the decision is null and void *ab initio*.[1247] If one assumes that the Court can review the Council's decisions, this implies that those decisions are voidable.[1248] It is argued above that the Court is indeed competent to review Council resolutions. At the same time, it has been submitted that the instances in which this could happen are very limited. In contentious cases the instrument conferring jurisdiction on the Court has to overlap with the substance of the Council resolutions. As the *Lockerbie* and *Bosnia* cases indicate, it is difficult to meet this requirement. In advisory proceedings, moreover, it would mean that the General Assembly or a duly authorized organ would have to take a head-on course towards the Council, a situation that is not likely to occur.

Therefore, although illegal decisions by the Council are voidable, in practice they will be considered null and void *ab initio*. This relates to the fact that the instances in which the Court can function as a procedural remedy against such decisions are limited, certainly more limited than the instances in which protests can be lodged against decisions. This absence of an effective procedural remedy can lead to difficult and uncertain situations. As observed by Lauterpacht:

1246 Thus Lauterpacht submits that "the whole question of the effect of illegal acts is closely linked with that of the existence of suitable machinery for determining whether the act is in fact illegal." Lauterpacht, *op. cit. supra* n.921, at 115.

1247 This was argued by Judge Morelli in his Separate Opinion in the *Certain Expenses* case. He wrote that: "In the case of acts of international organizations, and in particular acts of the United Nations, there is nothing comparable to the remedies existing in domestic law in connection with administrative acts. The consequence of this is that there is no possibility of applying the concept of voidability to the acts of the United Nations. If an act of an organ of the United Nations had to be considered as an invalid act, such invalidity could constitute only the absolute nullity of the act. In other words, there are only two alternatives for the acts of the Organization: either the act is fully valid, or it is an absolute nullity, because absolute nullity is the only form in which invalidity of an act of the Organization can occur. An act of the Organization considered as invalid would be an act which had no legal effects, precisely because it would be an absolute nullity. The lack of effect of such an act could be alleged and a finding in that sense obtained at any time." *Certain Expenses* case, ICJ Rep. (1962), at 222. *Cf.* Herdegen, *op. cit. supra* n.5, 149.

1248 Works endorsing this view include de Wet, *op. cit. supra* n.1219; Watson, *op. cit. supra* n.7. *Cf.* Alvarez, *op. cit. supra* n.903, at 286: "If one accepts the presumptions of the *Expenses Case* and the premise that the Advisory Jurisdiction of the ICJ can provide a remedy, under institutional international law allegedly *ultra vires* acts are neither void *ab initio* nor invariably valid but potentially voidable if the member State challenging the act (1) establishes a prima facie case for invalidity and (2) seeks judicial resolution of the question."

> We are faced here by a fundamental conflict between the principle that an illegal act is null *ab initio* and the principle that the mere assertion by an interested party that the act is unlawful should not be conclusively determinative of that question. There is no legal principle which can, by itself, resolve this conflict.[1249]

The assertion that an act of the Council is illegal implies that the (multitude of) protesting state(s) could collide with the Security Council.[1250] The Council would have to determine whether the protest is valid or not, and whether it should review its decision. Theoretically, it could refer the question to the Court for an advisory opinion. If the Council decides not to change the decision or simply ignore the protests, the members will have to decide whether to refuse to comply with the Council decisions, with the risk of additional sanctions being taken against them, or in extreme cases, whether to withdraw from the Organization.

A distinction should be made between the illegality of a Council decision and the measures taken by members of the United Nations in pursuance of that decision. Members cannot be held accountable for their compliance with obligations under law, *i.e.* their obligation to carry out decisions of the Council as stipulated by Article 25 of the Charter.[1251] Therefore, if the Court would, for example, determine that a specific sanctions regime imposed by a decision of the Council were illegal, the members that acted pursuant to the decision by the Council would not be under an obligation to make reparation for the damage inflicted upon the state targeted by the sanctions.

1249 Lauterpacht, *op. cit. supra* n.921, at 115.

1250 *Cf. supra*, paragraph 5.2.

1251 *Cf.* Weller: "The International Court has already found ... that there is a presumption of lawfulness as far as decisions of the UN organs are concerned. Therefore, States would remain under an obligation provisionally to comply with decisions of the Security Council even if they consider them *ultra vires*." Weller, *op. cit. supra* n.7, at 324.

6.

Enhancing the Council's Legitimacy

6.1 Introduction

When the United Nations was established, the then would be permanent members of the Security Council promised to use their veto only "in situations having the most serious impact on their basic interests."[1252] Notwithstanding these promises, the veto of the permanent members of the Council provided a strong check on the Council's decision-making until 1990. Prior to that date, the world was roughly divided into two camps[1253] and virtually every international conflict or situation was perceived to affect the interests of one or both of the camps. This prompted an extensive use of the veto which in most cases precluded the Council from acting at all. This indicates that the veto can be seen as the foremost political limitation on the Council's powers. Thus Reisman has submitted that:

> Although the Charter does not incorporate a constitutional theory of checks and balances between separate branches, the reciprocal operation of the veto during the Cold War and the resultant paralysis of the Security Council created a system that was its functional equivalent.[1254]

With the end of the Cold War in the late 1980s these antagonistic conditions

---

1252 T.M. Franck, *The Power of Legitimacy among Nations* (1990), at 177.

1253 Countries representing respectively a capitalist (the West) and a communist (the East) social and economic structure. This dichotomy does not include the Non-Aligned Movement (NAM), the group of developing states (currently consisting of 113 members, predominantly from the South) that was formed in order to promote the agenda of the developing countries independent from the Cold War rivalries.

1254 Reisman, *op. cit. supra* n.7, at 83-84.

disappeared, freeing the way for a more active role of the Council.[1255] During the Gulf War, which was aimed at the liberation of Kuwait, the Council for the first time in its history functioned as the instrument of collective security that it was intended to be. After that the Council was seized of numerous conflicts and situations,[1256] and has taken various innovative measures under Chapter VII of the Charter. With this increased activism, however, the conception arose that the Council only served the interests of the West, and those of the US in particular.[1257] This has led to concerns regarding the Council's 'legitimacy',[1258] which persist to the present day.

Legitimacy is a somewhat ill-defined concept that can refer to many different things.[1259] A general distinction can be made between a legal and a political dimension of legitimacy. From a legal standpoint legitimacy would refer to the question of whether the Council has acted in accordance with its powers and rules of procedure under the Charter,[1260] an issue already dealt with in chapter 4. Politically speaking, the concept refers to both the 'fairness' or 'justness' of the Council's decisions, and the procedure through which these decisions have been taken. These political aspects of legitimacy will be taken up in the remainder of this chapter.

6.2 Reform and Effectiveness of the Security Council

When one speaks of, or doubts, the legitimacy of the Security Council in the political sense of the term, this usually refers to the Council's composition and the power of veto of the permanent members. Within the Council, a small group of state enjoy certain privileges: as seen in chapter 2 these five states have a permanent seat on the Council, with which comes the right of veto. When the United Nations was founded this dissimilarity or inequality between states led to concerns among the smaller states

---

1255 See, *e.g.*, P. Wallensteen, *The United Nations in Armed Conflicts: An Overview*. In: J.R. Dupuy (ed.), The Development of the Role of the Security Council (1993) 303-316.

1256 See *supra*, note 647.

1257 See Weston, *op. cit. supra* n.371, 525; Caron, *op. cit. supra* n.4, 562-565.

1258 On the legitimacy of the Security Council see, *e.g.*, Caron, *op. cit. supra* n.4; Murphy, *op. cit. supra* n.3; Fassbender, *op. cit. supra* n.46, 315-318; Franck, *op. cit. supra* n.1252, 176-178; B. Simma, *op. cit. supra* n.372, 144-146; Dupuy, *op. cit. supra* n.46, 28-30; Conforti, *op. cit. supra* n.357, 112-113; F.B. Bankie, *Towards a Democratic World Order – The Security Council of the United Nations*, ASICL, 5th Annual Congress (1993) 75-83.

1259 See D. Bodansky, *The Legitimacy of International Governance: A Coming Challenge for International Environmental Law?*, 93 AJIL (1999) 596-627, 600; Murphy, *op. cit. supra* n.3, 248; Fassbender, *op. cit. supra* n.46, 315; Caron, *op. cit. supra* n.4, 556-562.

1260 Murphy, *op. cit. supra* n.3, 248; Fassbender, *op. cit. supra* n.46, 316.

but the 'Great Powers' of the time made it quite clear that this inequality was a *conditio sine qua non* for them to join the organization. Since the effective functioning of the collective security system depended on the participation of these powers, the smaller states somewhat reluctantly agreed to their special prerogatives under the Charter.[1261] It was thus acknowledged that greater responsibilities or duties entitled the major powers to greater powers or rights.[1262]

Since 1945, the global power constellation has changed drastically.[1263] With decolonization the number of states has risen significantly. The end of the Cold War, moreover, meant an end to the struggle between capitalism and communism and left the world with only one remaining superpower. The five permanent members of the Council, moreover, can no longer be said to constitute those powers 'able and willing to maintain international peace and security.'[1264] The UK and France, in particular, may be said to have changed from great to middle powers, to the advantage of, for example, Germany and Japan, in economic terms at least. These changes have led to increasing pressure to alter the Council's composition and procedure. Within the United Nations these issues were taken up by the General Assembly, which established an 'Open-ended Working Group on the Question of Equitable Representation on and Increase in the Membership of the Security Council and Other matters related to the Security Council' (hereinafter 'Working Group') in 1993.[1265] The general course of the debate within this group will be examined below.

6.3 Composition

In his monograph on the reform of the Security Council B. Fassbender notes that the ratio of total UN membership and seats on the Security Council changed from 5:1 in 1946, to 10:1 in 1963. With the change in composition in 1963 this ratio decreased to 7:1, and it had risen to 12:1 in 1993. The ratio of total UN membership compared

1261 See, *e.g.*, Fassbender, *op. cit. supra* n.46, 163-170; L.B. Sohn, *Modernizing the Structure and Procedure of the Security Council*. In: J.R. Dupuy (ed.), The Development of the Role of the Security Council (1993) 385-397, 385-386; Murphy, *op. cit. supra* n.3, 255-256.

1262 Franck, *op. cit. supra* n.1252, 177.

1263 On which see, *e.g.*, Fassbender, *op. cit. supra* n.46, 170-176; Murphy, *op. cit. supra* n.3, 251.

1264 In the words of Fassbender: "It has become doubtful that the five states who were chosen, or established themselves, as permanent members of the Security Council in 1945 still represent that group of states whose action alone can maintain world peace." Fassbender, *op. cit. supra* n.46, at 171.

1265 GA Res. 48/26, 3 Dec. 1993. The Working Group is composed of all members of the United Nations. For a short history of its establishment see, *e.g.*, Fassbender, *op. cit. supra* n.46, 221-225; Bailey, Daws, *op. cit. supra* n.51, 382-385.

to the permanent 5 members rose from 11:1 in 1947, to 23:1 in 1963 and 37:1 in 1993.[1266] These figures are indicative of the Council's diminishing representativeness[1267] of the total UN membership. Indeed, that the Council should be enlarged is, in view of the changed number of states and the aforementioned shifts in the distribution of power within the international environment, not controversial within the UN membership.[1268] The controversy primarily extends to the question of what category of new members should be included and whether new members should be accorded a right of veto.

The relevant provision in the Charter relating to the composition of the Council is Article 23, paragraph 1 of which reads:

> The Security Council shall consist of fifteen Members of the United Nations. The Republic of China, France, the Union of Soviet Socialist Republics, the United Kingdom of Great Britain and Northern Ireland, and the United States of America shall be permanent members of the Security Council. The General Assembly shall elect ten other Members of the United Nations to be non-permanent members of the Security Council, due regard being specially paid, in the first instance to the contribution of Members of the United Nations to the maintenance of international peace and security and to the other purposes of the Organization, and also to equitable geographical distribution.[1269]

Within the Working Group a general division exists between the (industrialized) North and the (developing) South, although positions sometimes vary considerably within these groups.[1270] In view of its current privileged position on the Council, the North

---

1266 See Fassbender, *op. cit. supra* n.46, 197-207.

1267 Fassbender uses the term 'representativeness' to denote that the – permanent – membership of the Council should reflect or incorporate the inequalities existing within the international community of states. See *ibid.*, 296-301. The term representativeness employed below, however, follows the usage within the Working Group. Representativeness in this sense means the extent to which the composition reflects the composition of (total) UN membership.

1268 See, for example, the 'Report of the Open-ended Working Group on the Question of Equitable Representation on and Increase in the Membership of the Security Council and Other Matters related to the Security Council', A/50/47, 13 Sept. 1996, para. 5, in which it is noted that in the discussions within the Working Group "there was a convergence of views that the membership of the Security Council should be enlarged."

1269 The People's Republic of China replaced the Republic of China in 1971, and the Russian Federation replaced the Soviet Union in 1992. The Council originally consisted of six non-permanent members, a number that was changed by an amendment of the Charter in 1963. By GA resolution 1991 A (XVIII), 17 Dec. 1963 (which entered into force on 31 Aug. 1965), the Assembly agreed to raise the non-permanent members to ten. According to the same resolution these members "shall be elected according to the following pattern: (a) five from African and Asian States; (b) one from Eastern Europe; (c) two from Latin American States; (d) two from Western European and Other States."

1270 See I. Winkelmann, *Bringing the Security Council into a New Era: Recent Developments in the Discussion on the Reform of the Security Council*, 1 Max Planck Yearbook of United Nations Law (1997)

is resistant towards major modifications of its composition and accordingly emphasizes the need for an efficient and effective Council. The South, on the other hand, emphasizes a more equitable and democratic geographic distribution and proposes an increase in the number of permanent members. Both groups refer to Article 23(1) to support their case for increasing the Council, but with different emphases. The North stresses the importance of contributions to the maintenance of international peace and security, whilst the South emphasizes an equitable geographic distribution. There is consensus that the expanded Council should consist of approximately 20-25 members.[1271]

The primary candidates of the North are Japan and Germany, the second and third largest contributors to the UN regular budget.[1272] Given that the current permanent members will almost certainly veto any attempts to alter their status, an enlargement with those two states will only increase the privileged position of the North, and Europe in particular, on the Council. Fassbender, for example, has shown that Europe is already over-represented on the Security Council. Whilst Eastern European States constitute 12% of the United Nations membership, they are awarded 13% of the seats on the Security Council. Western European states comprise 14% of the membership and have 33% of the seats. Africa and Asia combined account for 55% of the membership and 40% of Security Council seats, and finally Latin America makes up 18% of the United Nations membership and 13% of the seats on the Council.[1273] Although measuring representativeness solely in terms of states may not be the only viable method,[1274] these figures are indicative of an imbalance in representation between different regions and supply the South with ammunition to call for additional

35-90, 58-75.

1271 See the 'Report of the Open-ended Working Group on the Question of Equitable Representation on and Increase in the Membership of the Security Council and Other Matters related to the Security Council', A/52/47, 24 Aug. 1998, 55-57; and the 'Suggested general observations and recommendations for inclusion in the 2000 report of the Working Group', Conference room paper submitted by the Bureau of the Working Group, A/AC.247/2000/CRP.6, annexed to the 2000 Report of the Working Group (A/54/47, 25 July 2000). Para. 6(f) of that paper holds that: "In the discussion of the size of an enlarged Security Council, there has been some increased flexibility, but there is still a span in views between 20 to 26 members."

1272 However, the candidacy of Germany is opposed by Italy as it fears a loss of status whilst both Russia and China are not overly enthusiastic about Japan's aspirations. See Fassbender, *op. cit. supra* n.46, 235-245.

1273 See *ibid.*, 197-207.

1274 Indeed, the size of the population, the size of the country, the GNP, or the military capabilities can all be used as criteria for determining a state's strength, and assuming the Council should reflect the realities in terms of political power these criteria can also be used for determining 'representativeness'. See also Fassbender's use of the term, *supra* note 1267.

seats. The foremost candidates mentioned are Nigeria on behalf of Africa,[1275] India for Asia, and Brazil on behalf of Latin America. These candidacies, however, are met with opposition by other major regional players, notably South Africa and Egypt, Pakistan, and Argentina. Together with Italy these regional competitors prefer a category of semi-permanent seats, to be occupied by states elected periodically. Proposals aimed at introducing a third category of members on the Council have, however, met with criticism.[1276] It is felt that such a category would only aggravate "the present situation in which the prerogatives of the permanent members compromise the equality of states."[1277]

The consensus is that the Council should be expanded with approximately 10 seats. Leaving aside the question of what category of new members would be included (permanent, semi-permanent or merely non-permanent), and how the new seats would be apportioned, the possibility of an expanded Council has led to concerns that the Council might turn into too large a body, incapable of taking decisive action. Thus Reisman submits that "a further expansion of the Council ... would make the Council more unwieldy and less efficient in the performance of its primary task."[1278] An easy solution for maintaining a manageable size of the Council would perhaps be to provide the members of the European Union with one permanent seat, as has sometimes been suggested.[1279] France and the UK are strongly opposed to this, however.[1280]

On the other hand, as applies to all Security Council decisions, the political will of the members of the United Nations determines to what extent the decisions of the Council will be implemented. The greater the number of states that have contributed

---

1275 Officially the OAU claims two seats with a right of veto for Africa, to be filled on a rotational basis. The states occupying the seats would be elected for a certain period of time by the African Heads of State. See AHG/Dec.6 (XXXIV), 1998, reproduced in the 'Report of the Open-ended Working Group on the Question of Equitable Representation on and Increase in the Membership of the Security Council and Other Matters related to the Security Council', A/52/47, 24 Aug. 1998, 63.

1276 For a discussion of the proposals on the creation of a third category of members see Fassbender, *op. cit. supra* n.46, 255-263.

1277 *Ibid.*, at 260.

1278 Reisman, *op. cit. supra* n.7, at 96.

1279 See para. II.B(3) of the conference room paper submitted by the Bureau of the Working Group, entitled 'Decision-making in the Security Council, including the veto; expansion of the Security Council; periodic review of the enlarged Security Council', A/AC.247/2000/CRP.2/Rev.3. Reproduced as annex 11 to the 2000 Report of the Working Group, A/54/47, 25 July 2000.

1280 See, *e.g.*, B. Crossette, 'U.S. Ready for Much Larger Security Council', NY Times, 4 April 2000. Accessed at http://www.nytimes.com on 10 July 2000.

to the decisions will *prima facie* enhance their and others' willingness to comply with, and enforce, those decisions.[1281]

The above indicates that although there is consensus that the Council's composition should be altered, the exact modalities of such a change give rise to a heated debate.[1282] The same is true for the corresponding right of veto for the new members.

6.4 The Right of Veto

From the inception of the United Nations onwards, many states have been uncomfortable with the right of veto accorded to the permanent members of the Council. A consequence of the veto is, *inter alia*, that the permanent members are effectively immune from enforcement action by the Council.[1283] Given the unease of the general membership of the United Nations with the existing veto arrangements, it should come as no surprise that within the Working Group the question whether new (semi-)permanent members of the Council should be granted such a right is controversial.[1284] Indeed, some states call for the abolition of the veto altogether.[1285]

1281 *Cf.* Bailey, Daws, *op. cit. supra* n.51, 388.

1282 *Cf.* the 'Report of the Open-ended Working Group on the Question of Equitable Representation on and Increase in the Membership of the Security Council and Other Matters Related to the Security Council', A/53/47, 5 Aug. 1999, para. 26. In this paragraph, included under the heading 'General Observations', it is observed that: "Owing to the importance of the subjects being debated in the Working Group, which affect vital interests of States, and the great sensitivity and caution with which all matters — whether procedural or substantive — are approached by delegations, progress towards a general agreement on the main issues has been very slow. Differences of opinion continue to exist with regard to, among other issues, the category or categories of the new members in an enlarged Security Council." Significantly, para. 30 of the 2000 Report of the Working Group (A/54/47, 25 July 2000) reads: "There was no agreement this year on any general observations."

1283 See Caron, *op. cit. supra* n.4, 565; Murphy, *op. cit. supra* n.3, 247; L.B. Sohn, *Important Improvements in the Functioning of the Principal Organs of the United Nations that can be Made Without Charter Revision*, 91 AJIL (1997) 652-662, 652.

1284 Generally see Fassbender, *op. cit. supra* n.46, 263-275. For a summary of the arguments involved see, *e.g.*, the 'Conference room paper submitted by the Bureau of the Open-ended Working Group: summary of the proposals made on the issue of the extension of the veto to the new permanent members, dated 6 July 1998', A/AC.247/1998/CRP.12/Rev.1/Add.1. Reproduced in the annual 'Report of the Open-ended Working Group on the Question of Equitable Representation on and Increase in the Membership of the Security Council and Other Matters related to the Security Council', A/52/47, 24 Aug. 1998, 59. See also the conference room paper submitted by the Bureau of the Working Group, entitled 'Decision-making in the Security Council, including the veto; expansion of the Security Council; periodic review of the enlarged Security Council', A/AC.247/2000/CRP.2/Rev.3. Reproduced as Annex XI to the 2000 Report of the Working Group,

Others object to the extension of this right to the new permanent members. The OAU has adopted a position somewhere in between. It strives for abolition of the veto on the Council, but maintains that as long as the right exists, new (semi-)permanent members are equally entitled to it. In this view, the possible paralyzing effects of a proliferation of the veto could be countered by increasing the number of vetoes required to block any action.[1286] Alongside these positions, various states[1287] propose that the use of the veto should be limited to decisions taken under Chapter VII of the Charter.[1288] To mention one aspect, this would mean that a permanent member could no longer by itself block an amendment of the Charter. Whether the current permanent members will give up this prerogative, however, is very doubtful.

In conclusion, the positions taken in the Working Group on the reform of the Council in terms of its composition and the associated right of veto, vary considerably. States aspiring for permanent membership are met with opposition from regional competitors, which justifiably invoke the argument that the regional superpower of today may only be a marginal player in fifty years from now, necessitating a new reshuffle of the Council's composition. Arguments to the effect that new members should therefore be elected on a semi-permanent or rotational basis, however, lead to allegations of second-class 'permanent' citizenship on the Council. The same holds true for the veto. A majority of the membership of the United Nations is uncomfortable with the existence of the veto. Extension of this right to new members is therefore controversial. But adding new (semi-)permanent members to the Council without a corresponding right of veto also meets with objections that this will create an unwarranted inequality between the members of the Council. These objections are put forth by the OAU, which represents a large number of states, the support of which is

---

A/54/47, 25 July 2000.

1285 For example Colombia, Cuba, Guatemala, Libya, Malaysia, New Zealand, Sudan, and Yemen.

1286 See 'African Common Position on Security Council Reform', OAU document, 29 Sept. 1994, para. 33(e). Reproduced as A/AC.247/1996/CRP.6 in 'Report of the Open-ended Working Group on the Question of Equitable Representation on and Increase in the Membership of the Security Council and Other Matters related to the Security Council', A/50/47, 13 Sept. 1996.

1287 The Movement of Non-Aligned Countries, and Costa Rica, Ghana, Jamaica, Mexico, Peru, Singapore and Spain.

1288 See 'Conference room paper submitted by the Bureau of the Open-ended Working Group: summary of proposals made by delegations of the Open-ended Working Group dated 12 May 1998', A/AC.247/1998/CRP.10/Rev.1. Reproduced in the annual 'Report of the Open-ended Working Group on the Question of Equitable Representation on and Increase in the Membership of the Security Council and Other Matters related to the Security Council', A/52/47, 24 Aug. 1998, 59. For an overview of the matters that are currently subject to a veto in the Council see Fassbender, *op. cit. supra* n.46, 333-334.

necessary for any amendment of the Council to take place. Indeed the conclusion must be that due to the strongly divergent views held by the members of the United Nations, discussions on reform "seem to have reached a deadlock."[1289]

6.5 Transparency

Another aspect of the issue of legitimacy is the transparency of the Council's decision-making. With the aforementioned fear of dominance by the permanent members or subgroups therein, notably the US, the UK and France, discomfort has been expressed as to the lack of openness in the way in which decisions are reached.[1290] It is felt that the major powers conclude agreements behind closed doors and that those agreements are consequently beyond the reach of public scrutiny.[1291] In addition, the Council's practice of holding 'consultations of the whole' has led to concern on the part of non-members of the Council. These consultations are "private gatherings of all 15 Council members", while "no official records of consultations of the whole are kept, and ... non-members of the Council cannot attend."[1292] Decisions by the Council are taken during these closed consultations rather than in public meetings.[1293] Indeed it has been observed that at present "everyone knows that when the Council goes into public meeting everything has been decided in advance."[1294] Unease with this secrecy induced states to make proposals in the Working Group in order to enhance the transparency of the Security Council's work. The suggested improvements were, *inter alia*, that "the

---

1289 *Ibid.*, at 275. Fassbender observes that the US will have to take the lead if this deadlock is to be overcome. See *ibid.*, 341-347.

1290 For a discussion of the role of the so-called P-3 (the US, UK and France) among the permanent members (sometimes referred to as the P-5) see, *e.g.*, Caron, *op. cit. supra* n.4, 562-565.

1291 See, *e.g.*, N. Woods, *Good Governance in International Organizations*, 5 Global Governance (1999) 39-61, 50. Murphy, however, downplays this fear by stating that: "Most major initiatives of the Security Council emerge from informal consultation among the permanent members, but these consultations must then widen to take account of the views of non-permanent members, and ultimately must take account of the intense scrutiny given by non-members, the media, and the public to the final decision rendered by the Security Council, and the associated public statements made by its members." Murphy, *op. cit. supra* n.3, at 252.

1292 Bailey, Daws, *op. cit. supra* n.51, at 61.

1293 Thus Wood observes that: "Much of the real work of Council members takes place away from the glare of publicity in so-called 'informal consultations of the whole'." M.C. Wood, *Security Council Working Methods and Procedure: Recent Developments*, 45 ICLQ (1996) 151-161, at 155. *Cf.* A. Aust, *The Procedure and Practice of the Security Council Today*. In: J.R. Dupuy (ed.), The Development of the Role of the Security Council (1993) 365-374, 366-367.

1294 Statement by the French Permanent Representative during the 3,483rd meeting held on 16 December 1994, S/PV.3483.

Security Council should, as a rule, conduct its business in public" and that "the Security Council should hold open and substantive orientation debates at the beginning of the consideration by the Council of any substantive matter."[1295] Indeed the Council did respond to the criticism by placing the issue of "Security Council working methods and procedure" on its agenda for its meeting held on 16 December 1994. After the meeting the President issued a statement which read:

> The Security Council has heard the views of members of the Council and many other United Nations Member States on the item under discussion. These have revealed widespread support for greater recourse to open meetings of the Council and a clear will on the part of the members of the Council to respond to this. It is therefore the intention of the Council, as part of its efforts to improve the flow of information and the exchange of ideas between members of the Council and other United Nations Member States, that there should be an increased recourse to open meetings, in particular at an early stage in its consideration of a subject. The Council will decide on a case-by-case basis when to schedule public meetings of this sort. The Security Council's working group on documentation and procedure will examine further this question in the light of the views expressed and submit a report without delay.[1296]

Other measures taken by the Council include the Council making the tentative forecast of work as well as the draft programme of work for consultations of the whole available to all members as of 1993. Since 1994, moreover, draft resolutions have been made available to non-members of the Council and the President of the Council holds briefings after the consultations.[1297]

Measures to enhance the transparency of the Council will have to strike a balance between the openness and the effectiveness of the Council.[1298] As observed by Bailey and Daws, the danger of opening up of 'consultations of the whole' for example is that the "discussion of confidential matters would be driven into more secretive and informal fora."[1299] Improving the working methods of the Council does not require a formal amendment of the Charter or even of the Council's Rules of Procedure and is,

---

1295 'Conference room paper submitted by the Bureau of the Open-ended Working Group: working methods of the Security Council, transparency of its work, as well as its decision-making process', A/AC.247/1998/CRP4, Section II(A), 2 (a) and (b). The paper is reproduced in the annual 'Report of the Open-ended Working Group on the Question of Equitable Representation on and Increase in the Membership of the Security Council and Other Matters related to the Security Council', A/52/47, 24 Aug. 1998, 10-17.

1296 S/PRST/1994/81, 16 Dec. 1994. The statement concluded that "The Security Council will consider further this question." In practice, however, the Council has not decreased its use of non-public meetings.

1297 See Bailey, Daws, *op. cit. supra* n.51, 66-68. For an overview of the Council's measures towards greater transparency see Wood, *op. cit. supra* n.1293, 156-159.

1298 Bailey, Daws, *op. cit. supra* n.51, 291; Wood, *op. cit. supra* n.1293, 156.

1299 Bailey, Daws, *op. cit. supra* n.51, at 291. See also Reisman, *op. cit. supra* n.7, 98.

given the current lack of consensus on the reform of the Council, more viable. In the words of Wood:

> What matters is what happens in practice, and it is unlikely that more progress will be made through formal steps than through the kind of gradual and informal development described above. Informal and incremental change is more likely to be effective, and has been more effective, than changes through the Rules of Procedure or the formal establishment of new machinery.[1300]

6.6 Conclusions

The debate within the UN on an enlargement of the Security Council and corresponding changes to the right of veto seems to have reached a deadlock. Although consensus exists that the sharp increase of total UN membership warrants a parallel increase in members on the Council, the exact ramifications and modalities of such an increase are a matter of considerable controversy.

The Council has displayed an awareness of the perceptions of illegitimacy surrounding its work. It has discussed and adopted ways to improve the transparency of its working methods, but in practice its decisions remain to be taken outside the scrutiny or participation of non-members of the Council. This notwithstanding, for the time being changes in the working procedure of the Council seem to be the most viable option for improving the Council's transparency.

1300 Wood, *op. cit. supra* n.1293, at 161. *Cf.* Sohn, *op. cit. supra* n.1261, 387-388.

Conclusions

The Charter of the United Nations is the constituent treaty of the Organization and was adopted in 1945. As seen in chapter 1, the drastic changes in the membership of the United Nations, together with the constitutional quality of the Charter, favour an interpretation of its provisions based not so much on the original will and intentions of the founding states, but rather on the intentions of the present members, as evidenced by the practice of the organs of the United Nations. Furthermore, an interpretation based on the effectiveness of the Organization in achieving its object and purpose is to be favoured over an interpretation that focuses on the intentions of the parties at the time the United Nations was founded.

Chapter 2, which provides an overview of the Security Council's powers under the Charter, indicates that its authority is considerable. First of all, the members of the United Nations confer primary responsibility for the maintenance of international peace and security on the Security Council under Article 24(1). Moreover, when the Council acts in pursuance of that responsibility member states are obliged to carry out the decisions of the Council by virtue of Article 25.

The specific powers of the Council with regard to the maintenance of international peace and security are laid down in Chapter VII of the Charter. Chapter VII is introduced by Article 39, which holds that the Council shall determine whether a situation poses a threat to, or breach of, international peace and security, or constitutes an act of aggression. Once the Council has made such a determination, it can take measures necessary to restore the peace. In the first place this entails measures not involving the use of force, to be taken under Article 41. This article lists examples of possible measures, but from its wording ("may include") it follows that the list is not exhaustive. Should the Council consider that measures under Article 41 have not been, or would not be, effective to restore international peace and security, it may take action including the use of force under Article 42. Article 43 provides for special agreements between members states and the Council, by which the member states make armed forces available to the Council. Such agreements, however, have not been concluded and in their absence actions taken under Article 42 of the Charter can only be carried out by forces supplied on an *ad hoc* basis. According to Article 53, moreover, the Council can utilize regional "arrangements or agencies" when taking enforcement measures under Article 42.

The composition and voting procedures of the Council are governed by Articles 23 and 27 of the Charter. The Council presently consists of five permanent and ten non-permanent members. Decisions on non-procedural matters are taken by a simple majority, including the concurring votes of the permanent members. As seen in chapter 3, this right of veto has effectively precluded the Council from maintaining international peace and security between 1945 and 1990, the era commonly referred to as the Cold War. The survey of cases in which the Council took measures under Chapter VII of the Charter shows that during that era the Council was able to take measures under Article 41 and/or Article 42 in two cases only, *i.e.* South Africa (1977) and Rhodesia (1966). With the collapse of the Soviet Union in 1991, the antagonistic relations within the Security Council, and in particular between the permanent members, eased, which enabled the Council to assert a more active role in international relations. Thus in the 1990s the Council took measures under Chapter VII of the Charter against both state and non-state entities in twelve cases: Libya, Iraq, Liberia, former Yugoslavia, Angola, Somalia, Rwanda, Haiti, Sudan, Sierra Leone, Afghanistan, and Ethiopia-Eritrea. The unprecedented scope and form of the Council's measures in these twelve cases led to – at times severe – criticism by states and international legal scholars.

The specific objections to the Council's handling of these cases can be categorized as follows. The first category relates to the competence of the Council to deal with the situation at hand, which is intimately connected to the legitimacy of the Council's determination under Article 39 of the Charter. Such objections have been forwarded in the cases of South Africa, Rhodesia, Libya, Iraq, Somalia and Rwanda. They took the form of objections to the way the Council handled matters under Chapter VII of the Charter because these matters allegedly fell within the domestic jurisdiction of the targeted states, in which the Council was therefore not qualified to intervene (South Africa, Rhodesia); or of arguments related to the fact that the situations dealt with by the Council did not have any repercussions on a – restrictively defined concept of – international peace and security (Libya, Iraq, Somalia, Rwanda).

The second category of objections to the Council's actions relate to the form and consequences of the measures taken by the Council. It has been asserted on several occasions that measures taken by the Council under Articles 41 and 42 were illegal under international law. When the Council decided to establish the UNCC and UNIKOM in the Iraqi case, or the ICTY and ICTR in the Yugoslavia and Rwanda cases, it was argued that the Council had acted *ultra vires*. These allegations assume that the powers of the Council under Chapter VII of the Charter do not extend to a power to establish judicial or quasi-judicial bodies, and, subsidiarily, that even if the Council were to possess such powers, they would have to be exercised in strict conformity with the relevant pre-existent law. In sum, it has been argued that in exercising its functions and powers under Chapter VII the Council can only apply the law, it cannot make it.

Moreover, in the cases of Libya and the former Yugoslavia, it was contended that the Council's decisions violated both Charter law and general international law, contentions that were eventually taken to the International Court of Justice. In the *Lockerbie* case Libya argued that the Council should have respected the 1971 Montreal Convention for the Suppression of Unlawful Acts Against the Safety of Civil Aviation, and consequently that it should not have interfered with the Court's competence to indicate provisional measures of protection by adopting resolution 748 (1992) under Chapter VII of the Charter. In the Bosnia *Case Concerning Application of the Convention on the Prevention and Punishment of the Crime of Genocide* it was argued that the Council's decision to impose a weapons embargo on the region should be interpreted in a way that would not impair Bosnia's inherent right of self-defence, and that the embargo in effect contributed to the ongoing genocide against its population. Furthermore, in the context of the continued sanctions against Iraq, concerns have been expressed as to the compatibility of those sanctions with international human rights law.

These objections have led to a debate on the legal limits, if any, on the Council's authority to take measures under Chapter VII of the Charter. Chapter 4 of this volume identified two possible sources for such limits. The first are the legal limits imposed by the constituent instrument of the United Nations and hence the Security Council: the Charter. The second are the limits imposed by extra-Charter sources, *i.e.* general international law.

As an organ established by the Charter, the Council has to act in conformity with the purposes and principles of the Charter. This is not only a principle common to all international organs, but is also expressly stipulated in Article 24(2) of the Charter. Although the purposes and principles of the Charter are formulated in broad terms, a closer examination reveals that they do provide for limits to the Council's discretion to take enforcement measures. Specifically the Council, when acting under Chapter VII, should respect the right of self-determination, basic human rights, the principle of good faith and the core principles of international humanitarian law. Consequently it should weigh, in good faith, the consequences of its measures on these norms, and in particular ensure that its actions are proportionate to the aim it is pursuing, that is, the restoration or maintenance of international peace and security. Another Charter-based limit on the Council's powers under Chapter VII is provided by Article 51, which indicates that the measures taken by the Council should be effective in maintaining or restoring international peace and security. In the absence of effective measures of protection, member states retain their right to self-defence, notwithstanding decisions by the Council that may curtail that right.

To a certain extent Article 103 of the Charter disposes of the question whether or not the Council should respect general international law when acting under Chapter VII of the Charter. This article provides for the primacy of member states' obligations under the Charter over obligations under treaty law. From this it follows that a Council decision that runs contrary to existing treaty relations is not rendered illegal because of that contravention.

Analogous to the impact of Article 103 on the compatibility of the Council's decisions with pre-existing rights and duties under treaty law, the Council is not *a priori* required to act in accordance with customary international law. A special category of customary international law, *jus cogens* or the peremptory norms of international law, provides for an exception to this general rule. When recognized as such by the international community of states as a whole, these norms may not be violated in any circumstance by any actor. Although the exact content of these norms is controversial, they include the outlawing of aggression and its corresponding right of self-defence; the prohibition on genocide; basic human rights such as the prohibition of apartheid, slavery and torture; and the core principles of international humanitarian law. This means that the Security Council cannot violate these norms. Another exception to the primacy of the Charter over customary international law is the requirement that the Council, when exercising its quasi-judicial powers thereunder, should limit itself to applying, and not changing, customary international law.

The above indicates that there exist several legal limits to the Council's authority under Chapter VII of the Charter. This requires some qualifications, however. In the first place the Charter aims at an effective Council capable of maintaining international peace and security, and various of its provisions accordingly emphasize the obligations of the members towards the Organization. Article 103, moreover, already contemplates conflicts between Security Council enforcement action and international treaty law. And in the *Certain Expenses* and *Lockerbie* cases the International Court of Justice developed and applied the presumption of validity principle, which assumes an act of the United Nations to be legal unless determined otherwise. This implies that the burden of proof shall lie with the state(s) which claim(s) that the Security Council has acted illegally. Furthermore, the requirements of proof must and will be strict. Any incompatibility of a Council decision with basic human rights, for example, will not by itself constitute a ground for illegality. The claimant would, in addition, have to establish that the decision in question was not effective or necessary in order for the

Council to restore the peace; or that it constituted a disproportionate response to a threat of the peace; or a *mala fide* or manifestly absurd act.

Having established, in chapter 4 of this volume, that legal limits to the Council's authority under Chapter VII of the Charter do exist, the question that follows is who is entitled to pass judgment on the legality of decisions taken by the Council under that chapter. The first category identified in chapter 5 are the member states themselves. They can protest against a decision during and after the decision-making process on the ground that the decision would be, or was, illegal. When the Security Council rejects, or simply ignores, those objections, however, member states remain obliged to comply with the decision, with the exception of cases in which the Council has taken measures that are ineffective in safeguarding the survival of a state under attack. Generally however, states cannot unilaterally disregard Council decisions, for that would undermine the United Nations' capacity to maintain international peace and security. A measure of last resort would be to withdraw from the organization, or not to comply with the decision. In the latter case the Organization could penalize the non-complying state. In this context it is to be assumed that the political weight and number of the protesting state(s), will influence the Council's response to such non-compliance.

An alternative to these actions would be either to initiate contentious proceedings at the International Court of Justice, or to mobilize the General Assembly or specialized agencies duly authorized in order to obtain a request for an advisory opinion on the decision alleged to be illegal. A possible preliminary objection to the exercise of jurisdiction in contentious proceedings is provided by the plea of litispendence. It could be, and has been, argued that the Court and Council cannot simultaneously exercise jurisdiction over the same matter. However, the analysis of the case law of the World Court undertaken in chapter 5, an analysis dating back to the Permanent Court of International Justice, indicates that the Court does not consider the fact that a case was or is pending before the League or Security Council to be an obstacle to a simultaneous exercise of jurisdiction. A different conclusion could possibly arise from the *Lockerbie* case. In this case the Court, in its decision on interim measures of protection, was obliged to defer to the Council by virtue of resolution 748 (1992), adopted by the Council under Chapter VII. In the jurisdictional phase of the case, however, the Court decided that it was competent to entertain the merits of the case, rendering the deferral somewhat ambiguous. The further developments in the case are to be awaited in order to make any definitive conclusions.

Another objection to the exercise of jurisdiction by the Court in cases also covered by Security Council decisions is the 'political question' doctrine. According to this doctrine the judiciary cannot adjudicate questions of an essentially political nature, such as a decision by the Council taken pursuant to its responsibility for the maintenance of international peace and security. International law as it stands today, however, does not support this contention. Both the ICTY and the International Court of Justice, moreover, have explicitly rejected such claims. An exception must nonetheless be made for determinations made by the Council under Article 39. Such determinations are generally not suitable for judicial scrutiny, unless an act of bad faith can be established, or that the invocation of Article 39 by the Security Council was manifestly absurd.

The plea of litispendence and the political question doctrine therefore do not *a priori* preclude the International Court of Justice from exercising jurisdiction alongside the Council. An analysis of the Court's Statute and case law, moreover, indicates that it is competent to incidentally review the legality of Security Council decisions, even though a general power of judicial review was deliberately not included in the Charter or the Statute of the Court. The Court is expected to state and apply the law, and decisions of the Council are part and parcel of that law. Before ruling on the interpretation and applicability of Council decisions, the Court has to satisfy itself that they are valid from a procedural and a substantive point, just as it would do with any other rule of international law allegedly governing the legal relations between the parties involved in the dispute. A difference with other rules of international law would be that the Court would start with the presumption that the act of the Organization, *i.e* the Council, is valid, a presumption it first applied in the *Certain Expenses* case.

The Court can only exercise its power of incidental judicial review in contentious proceedings to the extent that the instrument conferring jurisdiction overlaps with the Security Council decision. As the Bosnia *Case Concerning Application of the Convention on the Prevention and Punishment of the Crime of Genocide* demonstrates, this requirement can be difficult to overcome. The General Assembly can request an advisory opinion by the Court on "any legal question", whilst an opinion requested by a specialized agency must relate to its scope of activities. As the *Nuclear Weapons* advisory opinions indicate, the latter hurdle can be difficult to overcome.

As regards a possible determination of illegality by the Court in either proceedings, it is not to be expected that the Court will squarely declare a Council decision to be illegal. In order to avoid direct conflict with the Council and to prevent embarrassment for the Council, the Court will probably refer the decision back to the Council for a remedy. Moreover, in its case law the Court has indicated that when the illegal decision relates to obligations towards third parties incurred upon the Organization by the Council, the illegality will not automatically discharge the responsibility of the Council towards those parties.

The question as to the legal limits to the Council's authority is related to the larger issue of the perceived illegitimacy of the Council. Chapter 6 of this book shows that discussions and proposals within the United Nations to enhance the Council's legitimacy by changing its composition and the distribution and invocability of the veto have reached a deadlock. Improvements in the transparency of the Council's decision-making, therefore, seem to provide for the most viable option to enhance the Council's legitimacy, modest as that may be.

This work started with two operative questions. The first was: *What are the legal limits to the Council's authority under Chapter VII of the Charter of the United Nations?* From the above, and subject to the qualifications mentioned there, it follows that these limits are primarily to be found in the purposes and principles of the Charter, and the peremptory norms of international law. The second question was: *To what extent can the International Court of Justice determine the legal limits of the Security Council's authority under Chapter VII of the Charter of the United Nations, and judicially review decisions taken under that Chapter?* To this it must be answered that the Court can exercise a power of incidental judicial review in both advisory and contentious proceedings. The occasions on which the Court can review will be limited in number, however. In contentious proceedings the instrument on which the Court bases its jurisdiction must overlap with the subject matter of the Council's decisions. An advisory opinion, moreover, will have to be requested by a General Assembly or a specialized agency that demonstrates the political will to 'take on' the Council. This notwithstanding, from a legal standpoint a clarification by the Court of the limits to the Council's authority would benefit the Organization as a whole.

List of References

In the footnotes the following format has been applied: Author, Title of the Article, Source and Page Numbers (and if applicable, Specific Pages Referred to). *E.g.* M. Akehurst, The Hierarchy of the Sources of International Law, 47 BYIL (1974-1975) 273-285, 275-278.

Articles and Books

Abi-Saab, G., *et. al.*, *Symposium on State Responsibility*, 10 EJIL (1999) 339-460.

Abi-Saab, G., *International Criminal Tribunals and the Development of International Humanitarian and Human Rights Law*. In: Yakpo, E., Boumedra, T. (eds.), Liber Amicorum Mohammed Bedjaoui (1999) 649-658.

Addi, L., *Algeria's Tragic Contradictions*, 7 Journal of Democracy (1996) 94-107.

Adibe, C.E., *The Liberian Conflict and the ECOWAS-UN Partnership*. In: Weiss, T.G. (ed.), Beyond UN Subcontracting: Task-Sharing with Regional Security Arrangements and Service-Providing NGOs (1998) 67-90.

Affaki, B.G., *The United Nations Compensation Commission: A New Era in Claims Settlements?*, 10 Journal of International Arbitration (1993) 21-57.

Akande, D., *The Role of the International Court of Justice in the Maintenance of International Peace*, 8 AJICL (1996) 592-616.

Akande, D., *The International Court of Justice and the Security Council: Is there Room for Judicial Control of Decisions of the Political Organs of the United Nations?*, 46 ICLQ (1997) 309-343.

Akande, D., *The Competence of International Organizations and the Advisory Jurisdiction of the International Court of Justice*, 9 EJIL (1998) 437-467.

Akehurst, M., *The Hierarchy of the Sources of International Law*, 47 BYIL (1974-1975) 273-285.

Akehurst, M., *A Modern Introduction to International Law*, London, Unwin Hyman, 6th ed. (1987).

Akhavan, P., *Lessons from Iraqi Kurdistan: Self-Determination and Humanitarian Intervention Against Genocide*, 11 Netherlands Quarterly of Human Rights (1993) 41-62.

Akhavan, P., *The International Criminal Tribunal for Rwanda: The Politics and Pragmatics of Punishment*, 90 AJIL (1996) 501-510.

Akkerman, R.J., Krieken, P.J. van, Pannenborg, C.O. (eds.), *Declarations on Principles: A Quest for Universal Peace*, Leiden, Sijthoff (1977).

Al-Nauimi, N., Meese, R. (eds.), *International Legal Issues Arising Under the United Nations Decade of International Law*, The Hague, M. Nijhoff (1995).

Alexander, K.W., *NATO's Intervention in Kosovo: The Legal Case for Violating Yugoslavia's National Sovereignty in the Absence of Security Council Approval*, 22 Houston JIL (2000) 403-449.

Alston (ed.), P., *The United Nations and Human Rights: A Critical Appraisal*, Oxford, Oxford University Press (1995).

Alvarez, J.E., *Legal Remedies and the United Nations' à la Carte Problem*, 12 MJIL (1991) 229-311.

Alvarez, J.E., *Judging the Security Council*, 90 AJIL (1996) 1-39.

Alvarez, J.E., *Financial Responsibility*. In: Joyner, C.C. (ed.), The United Nations and International Law (1997) 409-431.

Alzamora, C., *Reflections on the UN Compensation Commission*, 9 Arbitration International (1993) 349-358.

Amerasinghe, C.F., *Interpretation of Texts in Open International Organizations*, 65 BYIL (1994) 175-209.

Amerasinghe, C.F., *Principles of the Institutional Law of International Organizations*, Cambridge, Cambridge University Press (1996).

Angelet, N., *Protest Against Security Council Decisions*. In: Wellens, K. (ed.), International Law: Theory and Practice (1998) 277-285.

Anghie, A., Sturgess, G. (eds.), *Legal Visions of the 21st Century: Essays in Honour of Judge Christopher Weeramantry*, The Hague, Kluwer Law International (1998).

Arangio-Ruiz, G., *The 'Federal Analogy' and UN Charter Interpretation: A Crucial Issue*, 8 EJIL (1997) 1-28.

Aristodemou, M., *Choice and Evasion in Judicial Recognition of Governments: Lessons from Somalia*, 5 EJIL (1994) 532-555.

Ascensio, H., *The Rules of Procedure and Evidence of the ICTY*, 9 LJIL (1996) 467-478.

Aust, A., *The Procedure and Practice of the Security Council Today*. In: Dupuy, J.R. (ed.), The Development of the Role of the Security Council (1993) 365-374.

Bailey, S.D., *The Security Council*. In: Alston, P. (ed.), The United Nations and Human Rights: A Critical Appraisal (1995) 304-336.

Bailey, S.D., Daws, S. *The Procedure of the Security Council*, Oxford, Clarendon Press, 3rd ed. (1998).

Baldus, C., *Regelhafte Vertragsauslegung nach Parteirollen im klassischen römischen Recht und in der modernen Völkerrechtswissenschaft*, Frankfurt, Peter Lang (1998).

Bankie, F.B., *Towards a Democratic World Order – The Security Council of the United Nations*, ASICL, 5th Annual Congress (1993) 75-83.

Barkin, J.S., Cronin, B., *The State and the Nation: Changing Norms and the Rules of Sovereignty in International Relations*, 48 International Organization (1994) 107-130.

Bederman, D.J., *The United Nations Compensation Commission and the Tradition of International Claims Settlement*, 27 NYUJILP (1994) 1-42.

Bedjaoui, M., *The New World Order and the Security Council: Testing the Legality of its Acts*, Dordrecht, M. Nijhoff (1994).

Bennet, T.W., *A Linguistic Perspective of the Definition of Aggression*, 31 GYIL (1988) 48-69.

Bermejo Perez, M.P., *International Justice and the United Nations Security Council: Towards Meaningful Reform*, 16 Thesaurus Acroasium (1997) 859-882.

Bernhardt, R., *et. al.* (eds.), *Völkerrecht als Rechtsordnung, International Gerichtsbarkeit, Menschenrechte, Festschrift für Hermann Mosler*, Berlin, Springer-Verlag (1983).

Bernhardt, R., *Interpretation in International Law*, 2 EPIL (1995) 1416-1426.

Bernhardt, R., *Ultra Vires Activities of International Organizations*. In: Makarczyk, K. (ed.), Theory of International Law at the Threshold of the 21st Century (1996) 599-609.

Bernhardt, R., *Encyclopedia of Public International Law*, Amsterdam, North Holland.

Bettauer, R.J., *The United Nations Compensation Commission-Developments since October 1992*, 89 AJIL (1995) 416-423.

Beveridge, F., *The Lockerbie Affair*, 41 ICLQ (1992) 907-920.

Beyerlin, U., *Sanctions*. In: Wolfrum, R. (ed.), United Nations: Law, Policies and Practice (1995) 1111-1128.

Beyerlin, U., *et. al.* (eds.), *Recht zwischen Umbruch und Bewahrung*, Berlin, Springer (1995).

Bix, B., *Law, Language, and Legal Determinacy*, Oxford, Clarendon Press (1993).

Blokker, N.M., *Is the Authorization Authorized? Powers and Practice of the UN Security Council to Authorize the Use of Force by 'Coalitions of the Able and Willing'*, 11 EJIL (2000), 541-568.

Blokker, N.M., Kleiboer, M. *The Internalization of Domestic Conflict: The Role of the UN Security Council*, 9 LJIL (1996) 7-35.

Blomeyer-Bartenstein, H., *Conference of Ambassadors*, 7 EPIL (1984) 48-49.

Bloom, E.T., *Protecting Peacekeepers: The Convention on the Safety of United Nations and Associated Personnel*, 89 AJIL (1995) 621-631.

Blum, Y.Z., *Russia Takes Over the Soviet Union's Seat at the United Nations*, 3 EJIL (1992) 345-361.

Blum, Y.Z., *UN Membership of the 'New' Yugoslavia: Continuity or Break*, 86 AJIL (1992) 831 833.

Blum, Y.Z., *Eroding the United Nations Charter*, Dordrecht, M. Nijhoff (1993).

Blumenwitz, D., *Maintenance of International Peace and Security*. In: Wolfrum, R. (ed.), United Nations: Law, Policies and Practice (1995) 865-870.

Böckstiegel, K.H., *Perspectives of Air Law, Space Law, and International Business Law for the Next Century*, Köln, Heymann (1996).

Bodansky, D., *The Legitimacy of International Governance: A Coming Challenge for International Environmental Law?*, 93 AJIL (1999) 596-627.

Bodley, A., *Weakening the Principle of Sovereignty in International Law: The International Criminal Tribunal for the Former, Yugoslavia*, 31 NYUJIL (1999) 417-471.

Boelaert-Suominen, S., *Iraqi War Reparations and the Laws of War: A Discussion of the Current Work of the United Nations, Compensation Commission with Specific Reference to Environmental Damage During Warfare*, 50 Zeitschrift für öffentliches Recht (1996) 225-316.

Bortz, S.I., *Avoiding a Collision of Competence: The Relationship between the Security Council and the International Court of, Justice in Light of Libya v. United States*, 2 Florida State University Journal of Transnational Law & Policy (1993) 353-378.

Bothe, M., *The Legitimacy of the Use of Force to Protect Peoples and Minorities*. In: Brölmann, C. *et. al.* (eds.), Peoples and Minorities in International law (1993) 289-299.

Bothe, M., *Les Limites des Pouvoirs du Conseil de Sécurité*. In: Dupuy, J.R. (ed.), The Development of the Role of the Security Council (1993) 67-81.

Bothe, M., *Peace-Keeping*. In: Simma, B., *et. al.* (eds.), The Charter of the United Nations: A Commentary (1994) 565- 603.

Bourantonis, D., Evriviades, M. (eds.), *A United Nations for the Twenty-First Century: Peace, Security and Development*, The Hague, Kluwer Law International (1996).

Bowett, D.W., *et. al.*, *Cambridge Essays in International Law: Essays in Honour of Lord McNair*, London, Stevens & Sons (1965).

Bowett, D.W., *The Law of International Institutions*, London, Stevens & Sons, 4th ed. (1982).

Bowett, D.W., *The Impact of the Security Council Decisions on Dispute Settlement Procedures*, 5 EJIL (1994) 89-101.

Bowett, D.W., *The Court's Role in Relation to International Organizations*. In: Lowe, V., Fitzmaurice, M. (eds.), Fifty Years of the International Court of Justice (1996) 181-192.

Bowett, D.W., *Judicial and Political Functions of the Security Council and the International Court of Justice*. In: Fox, H. (ed.), The Changing Constitution of the United Nations (1997) 73-88.

Bowett, D.W., *Crimes of State and the 1996 Report of the International Law Commission on State Responsibility*, 9 EJIL (1998) 163-173.

Brölmann, C., *et. al.* (eds.), *Peoples and Minorities in International law*, Dordrecht, M. Nijhoff (1993).

Brower, C.N., *The Lessons of the Iran-U.S. Claims Tribunal Applied to Claims Against Iraq*. In: Lillich, R.B. (ed.), The United Nations Compensation Commission (1995) 15-27.

Brownlie, I., *Principles of Public International Law*, Oxford, Clarendon Press, 4th ed. (1990).

Brownlie, I., *The Decisions of Political Organs of the United Nations and the Rule of Law*. In: MacDonald, R.St.J. (ed.), Essays in Honour of Wang Tieya (1994) 91-102.

Bruha, T., *Die Definition der Aggression*, Berlin, Duncker & Humblot (1980).

Bruha, T., *Security Council*. In: Wolfrum, R. (ed.), United Nations: Law, Policies and Practice (1995) 1147-1161.

Burley, A.M., *Commentary on Intervention Against Illegitimate Regimes*. In: Damrosch, L.F., Scheffer, D.J. (eds.), Law and Force in the New International Order (1991) 177-180.

Caflisch, L., *Is the International Court Entitled to Review Security Council Resolutions Adopted Under Chapter VII of the United Nations Charter?*. In: N. Al-Nauimi, R. Meese (eds.), International Legal Issues Arising Under the United Nations Decade of International Law (1995) 633-662.

Campbell, L.M., *Defending Against Terrorism: A Legal Analysis of the Decision to Strike Sudan and Afghanistan*, 74 Tulane Law Review (2000) 1067-1096.

Caron, D.D., *The Legitimacy of the Collective Authority of the Security Council*, 87 AJIL (1993) 552-588.

Caron, D.D., *The UNCC and the Search for Practical Justice*. In: Lillich, R.B. (ed.), The United Nations Compensation Commission (1995) 367-377.

Carver, J., Hulsmann, J., *The Role of Article 50 of the UN Charter in the Search for International Peace and Security*, 49 ICLQ (2000) 528-577.

Cassese, A. (ed.), *United Nations Peace-Keeping*, Alphen ad Rijn, Sijthoff (1978).

Cassese, A. (ed.), *The Current Legal Regulation of the Use of Force*, Dordrecht, M. Nijhoff (1986).

Cassese, A., *Ex iniuria ius oritu: Are We Moving Towards International Legitimation of*

Humanitarian Countermeasures in the World Community?, 10 EJIL (1999) 23-30.

Charney, J.I., *Universal International Law*, 87 AJIL (1993) 529-551.

Charney, J.I., *Anticipatory Humanitarian Intervention in Kosovo*, 93 AJIL (1999) 834-841.

Cheng, B., *General Principles of Law as Applied by International Courts and Tribunals*, Cambridge, Grotius Publications (1987).

Cherif Bassiouni, M., *Former Yugoslavia: Investigating Violations of International Humanitarian Law and Establishing an International Criminal Tribunal*, 18 Fordham ILJ (1995) 1191-1211.

Chinkin, C.M., *Kosovo: A 'Good' or 'Bad' War?*, 93 AJIL (1999) 841-847.

Ciobanu, D., *Preliminary Objections Related to the Jurisdiction of the United Nations Political Organs*, Cambridge, M. Nijhoff (1975).

Ciobanu, D., *Litispendence between the International Court of Justice and the Political Organs of the United Nations*. In: Gross, L. (ed.), The Future of the International Court of Justice (1976) 209-275.

Ciobanu, D., *The Power of the Security Council to Organize Peace-Keeping Operations*. In: Cassese, A. (ed.), United Nations Peace-Keeping (1978) 15-53.

Combacau, J., *The Exception of Self Defence in U.N. Practice*. In: Cassese, A. (ed.), The Current Legal Regulation of the Use of Force (1986) 9-38.

Condorelli, L., *A Propos de L'attaque Américaine Contre L'irak du 26 Juin 1993: Lettre D'un Professeur Désemparé aux Lecteurs du Jedi*, 5 EJIL 5 (1994) 134-144.

Condron, S.M., *Justification for Unilateral Action in Response to the Iraqi Threat: A Critical Analysis of Operation Desert Fox*, 161 Military Law Review (1999) 115-180.

Conetta, C. Knight, C., *Vital Force: A Proposal for the Overhaul of the UN Peace Operations System and for the Creation of a UN Legion*, Cambridge, Massachusetts, Commonwealth Institute (1995).

Conforti, B., *Non-Coercive Sanctions in the United Nations Charter: Some Lessons from the Gulf War*, 2 EJIL (1991) 110-113.

Conforti, B., *Le Pouvoir Discrétionnaire du Conseil de Sécurité en Matière de Constatation d'une Menace Contre la Paix, d'une Rupture de la Paix ou d'un Acte d'Agression*. In: Dupuy, J.R. (ed.), The Development of the Role of the Security Council (1993) 51-60.

Conlon, P., *Legal Problems at the Centre of United Nations Sanctions*, 65 NJIL (1996) 73-90.

Corten, O., *La Résolution 940 du Conseil De Sécurité Autorisant une Intervention Militaire en Haïti: L'émergence d'un Principe de Légitimité Démocratique en Droit, International?*, 6 EJIL (1995) 116-133.

Cot, J.P., A. Pellet, *La Charte des Nations Unies*, Paris, Economica (1985).

Crawford, J., *The Charter of the United Nations as a Constitution*. In: Fox, H. (ed.), The Changing Constitution of the United Nations (1997) 3-16.

Crook, J.R., *The UNCC and its Critics: Is Iraq Entitled to Due Process?*. In: Lillich, R.B. (ed.), The United Nations Compensation Commission (1995) 77-101.

Cryer, R., *The Security Council and Article 39: A Threat to Coherence?*, 1 Journal of Armed Conflict (1996) 161-195.

Currie, J., *NATO's Humanitarian Intervention in Kosovo: Making or Breaking International Law?*, 36 CYIL (1998) 303-331.

D'Amato, A., *Good Faith*, 7 EPIL (1984) 107-109.

Damrosch, L.F., *The International Court of Justice at a Crossroads*, New York, Transnational Publishers (1987).

Damrosch, L.F., Scheffer, D.J. (eds.), *Law and Force in the New International Order*, Boulder, Westview Press (1991).

Damrosch, L.F., *et. al.*, *Agora: The 1994 U.S. Action in Haiti*, 89 AJIL (1995) 58-87.

David, M., *Passport to Justice: Internationalizing the Political Question Doctrine for Application in the World Court*, 40 HJIL (1999) 81-150.

Deen-Racsmány, Z., *A Redistribution of Authority Between the UN and Regional Organizations in the Field of the Maintenance of Peace and Security*, 13 LJIL (2000) 297-331.

Degan, V.D., Bring, O.E., Malone, M.K., *Correspondents' Agora: UN Membership of the former Yugoslavia*, 87 AJIL (1993) 240-248.

Delbrück, J., *Peacekeeping by the United Nations and the Rule of Law*. In: Akkerman, R.J, Krieken, P.J. van, Pannenborg, C.O. (eds.), Declarations on Principles: A Quest for Universal Peace (1977) 73-99.

Delbrück, J., *Proportionality*, 7 EPIL (1984) 396-400.

Delbrück, J. (ed.), *The Future of International Law Enforcement: New Scenarios – New Law?*, Berlin, Duncker & Humblot (1993).

Delbrück, J., *Apartheid*. In: Wolfrum, R. (ed.), United Nations: Law, Policies and Practice (1995) 27-38.

Delbrück, J., *Allocation of Law Enforcement Authority in the International System*, Berlin, Duncker & Humblot (1995).

Delbrück, J., *New trends in International Lawmaking - International 'Legislation' in the Public Interest*, Berlin, Duncker & Humblot (1997).

Denters, E, Schrijver, N. (eds.), *Reflections on International Law from the Low Countries: In Honour of Paul de Waart*, The Hague, M. Nijhoff (1998).

Dicke, K., *National Interest vs. the Interest of the International Community – A Critical Review of Recent UN Security Council Practice*. In: Delbrück, J., New trends in International Lawmaking - International 'Legislation' in the Public Interest (1997) 145-169.

Dinstein, Y., Tabori, M. (eds.), *War Crimes in International Law*, The Hague, M. Nijhoff (1996).

Dixon, M., *Textbook on International Law*, Glasgow, Blackstone, 3rd ed. (1996).

Dixon, R., *New Developments in the International Criminal Tribunal for the Former Yugoslavia: Prominent Leaders Indicted and Jurisdiction Established*, 8 LJIL(1995) 449-462.

Doehring, K., *Self-Determination*. In: Simma, B., *et. al.* (eds.), The Charter of the United Nations: A Commentary (1994) 56-72.

Doehring, K., *Unlawful Resolutions of the Security Council and their Legal Consequences*, 1 Max Planck Yearbook of United Nations Law (1997) 91-109.

Doyle, M.W., Suzuki, M.W., *Transitional Authority in Cambodia*. In: Weiss, T.G. (ed.), The United Nations and Civil Wars (1995) 127-149.

Dupuy, J.R. (ed.), *The Development of the Role of the Security Council: Colloque de Academie de Droit International de la Haye 1992*, Alphen ad Rijn, M. Nijhoff (1993).

Dupuy, P.M., *Sécurité Collective de la Paix dans la pratique contemporaine du Conseil de*

Sécurité. In: Beyerlin, U., *et. al.* (eds.), Recht zwischen Umbruch und Bewahrung (1995) 41-56.

Dupuy, P.M., *The Constitutional Dimension of the Charter of the United Nations Revisited*, 1 Max Planck Yearbook of United Nations Law (1997) 1-33.

Eagleton, C., *The Jurisdiction of the Security Council over Disputes*, 40 AJIL (1946) 513-533.

Eitel, T., *The Escape and Parole of the Imprisoned God of War: An Overview of the Second Gulf War from the Perspective of International Law*, 35 GYIL (1992) 170-189.

Elsen, T.J.H., *Litispendence between the International Court of Justice and the Security Council*, The Hague, T.M.C. Asser Institute (1986).

Emerson, R., *Self-Determination*, 65 AJIL (1971) 459-475.

Engel, S., *'Living' International Constitutions and the World Court (The Subsequent Practice of International Organs Under their Constituent Instruments*), 16 ICLQ (1967) 865-910.

Ezejiofor, G., Quashigah, G., *The United Nations and Humanitarian Intervention in the Contemporary World Situation*, ASICL, 5th Annual Congress (1993) 36-63.

Ezetah, R.C., *Legitimate Governance and Statehood in Africa: Beyond the Failed State and Colonial Self-Determination*. In: Quashigah, E.K., Okafor, O.C. (eds.), Legitimate Governance in Africa: International and Domestic Legal Perspectives (1999) 419-459.

Falk, R.A., *Kosovo, World Order, and the Future of International Law*, 93 AJIL (1999) 847-857.

Farer, T., *The Future of International Law Enforcement under Chapter VII: Is There Room for 'New Scenarios'?*. In: Delbrück, J. (ed), The Future of International Law Enforcement: New Scenarios – New Law? (1993) 39-56.

Fassbender, B., *UN Security Council Reform and the Right of Veto: A Constitutional Perspective*, The Hague, Kluwer Law International (1998).

Fassbender, B., *Quis judicabit? The Security Council, Its Powers and Its Legal Control*, 11 EJIL (2000) 219-231.

Fawcett, J.E.S., *Security Council Resolutions on Rhodesia*, 41 BYIL (1965-1966) 103-121.

Ferencz, B.B., *Defining Aggression: Where it Stands and Where it's Going*, 66 AJIL (1972) 491-508.

Fielding, L.E., *Taking a Closer Look at Threats to the Peace: The Power of the Security Council to Address Humanitarian Crises*, 73 University of Detroit Mercy Law Review (1996) 551-568.

Fitzmaurice, G., *The Law and Procedure of the International Court of Justice*, Cambridge, Grotius Publications (1986).

Fox, H. (ed.), *The Changing Constitution of the United Nations*, The British Institute of International and Comparative Law, London (1997).

Fraas, M., *Sicherheitsrat der Vereinten Nationen und Internationaler Gerichtshof: Die Rechtmäßigkeitsprüfung von Beschlüssen des Sicherheitsrat der Vereinten Nationen im Rahmen des VII. Kapitels der Charta durch den Internationalen Gerichtshof*, Frankfurt, Peter Lang (1998).

Franck, T.M., *The Power of Legitimacy among Nations*, Oxford, Oxford University Press (1990).

Franck, T.M., *Intervention Against Illegitimate Regimes*. In: Damrosch, L.F., Scheffer, D.J. (eds.), Law and Force in the New International Order (1991) 159-176.

Franck, T.M., Patel, F., *UN Police Action in Lieu of War: The Old Order Changeth*, 85 AJIL (1991) 63-74.

Franck, T.M., *The 'Powers of Appreciation': Who is the Ultimate Guardian of UN Legality?*, 86 AJIL (1992) 519-523.

Franck, T.M., *The Emerging Right to Democratic Governance*, 86 AJIL (1992) 46-91.

Franck, T.M., *The Security Council and 'Threats to the Peace': Some Remarks on Remarkable Recent Developments*. In: Dupuy, J.R. (ed.), The Development of the Role of the Security Council (1993) 83-110.

Franck, T.M., *The United Nations as Guarantor of International Peace and Security: Past, Present and Future*. In: Tomuschat, C. (ed.), The United Nations at Age Fifty: A Legal Perspective (1995) 25-38.

Franck, T.M., *The Political and the Judicial Empires: Must there be Conflict over Conflict-Resolution?*. In: Al-Nauimi, N., Meese, R. (eds.), International Legal Issues Arising Under the United Nations Decade of International Law (1995) 621-632.

Franck, T.M., *Fairness in International Law and Institutions*, Oxford, Clarendon Press (1995).

Franck, T.M., *Lessons of Kosovo*, 93 AJIL (1999) 857-860.

Freudenschuß, H., *Between Unilateralism and Collective Security: Authorizations of the Use of Force by the UN Security Council*, 5 EJIL (1994) 492-531.

Frowein, J.A., *Collective Enforcement of International Obligations*, 47 ZaöRV (1987) 67-79.

Frowein, J.A., *Legal Consequences for International Law Enforcement in Case of Security Council Inaction*. In: Delbrück, J. (ed), The Future of International Law Enforcement: New Scenarios – New Law? (1993) 111-124.

Frowein, J.A., *Nullity in International Law*, 3 EPIL (1997) 743-747.

Gaeta, P., *Is NATO Authorized or Obliged to Arrest Persons Indicted by the International Criminal Tribunal for the Former Yugoslavia?*, 9 EJIL (1998) 174-181.

Gardam, J.G., *Proportionality and Force in International Law*, 87 AJIL (1993) 391-413.

Gardam, J.G., *Legal Restraints on Security Council Military Enforcement Action*, 17 MJIL (1996) 285-322.

Garris, C.J., *Bosnia and the Limitations of International Law*, 34 Santa Clara Law Review (1994) 1039-1087.

Gill, T.D., *Litigation Strategy at the International Court*, Oxford, M. Nijhoff (1989).

Gill, T.D., *Legal and Some Political Limitations on the Power of the U.N. Security Council to Exercise its Enforcement Powers under Chapter VII of the Charter*, 26 NYIL (1995) 33-138.

Gilman, D., *The Gulf War and the United Nations Charter: Did the Security Council Fulfill its Original Mission?*, 24 Connecticut Law Review (1992) 1131-1157.

Glennon, M.J., *Protecting the Court's Institutional Interests: Why not the Marbury Approach?*, 81 AJIL (1987) 121-129.

Glennon, M.J., *Sovereignty and Community after Haiti: Rethinking the Collective Use of Force*, 89 AJIL (1995) 70-74.

Goodrich, L.M., Hambro, E., *Charter of the United Nations*, Boston, World Peace Foundation (1949).

Goodrich, L.M., Hambro, E., Simons, A.S., *Charter of the United Nations*, New York, Columbia University Press, 3rd ed. (1969).

Gordon, E., *The World Court and the Interpretation of Constitutive Treaties: Some Observations on the Development of an International Constitutional Law*, 59 AJIL (1965) 794-833.

Gordon, R., *United Nations Intervention in Internal Conflicts: Iraq, Somalia, and Beyond*, 15 MJIL (1994) 519-589.

Gowlland-Debbas, V., *Collective Responses to Illegal Acts in International Law: United Nations Action in the Question of Southern Rhodesia*, Dordrecht, M. Nijhoff (1990).

Gowlland-Debbas, V., *Security Council Enforcement Action and Issues of State Responsibility*, 43 ICLQ (1994) 55-98.

Gowlland-Debbas, V., *The Relationship between the International Court of Justice and the Security Council in the light of the Lockerbie Case*, 88 AJIL (1994) 643-677.

Graefrath, B., Mohr, M., *Legal Consequences of an Act of Aggression: The Case of the Iraqi Invasion and Occupation of Kuwait*, 43 Österreichische Zeitschrift für öffentliches Recht und Völkerrecht (1992) 109-138.

Graefrath, B., *Leave to the Court What Belongs to the Court: The Libyan Case*, 4 EJIL (1993) 184-205.

Graefrath, B., *Iraqi Reparations and the Security Council*, 54 ZaöRV (1994) 1-68.

Graefrath, B., *International Crimes and Collective Security*. In: Wellens, K. (ed.), International Law: Theory and Practice (1998) 237-252.

Gray, C., *After the Ceasefire: Iraq, the Security Council and the Use of Force*, 65 BYIL (1994) 135-174.

Gray, C., *Regional Arrangements and the United Nations Collective Security System*. In: Fox, H. (ed.), The Changing Constitution of the United Nations (1997) 91-116.

Greenwood, C., *The International Court of Justice and the Use of Force*. In: Lowe, V., Fitzmaurice, M. (eds.), Fifty Years of the International Court of Justice (1996) 373-385.

Greenwood, C., *International Humanitarian Law and United Nations Military Operations*, 1 Yearbook of International Humanitarian Law (1998) 3-34.

Greenwood, C., *The Impact of Decisions of the Security Council on the International Court of Justice*. In: W.P. Heere (ed.), International Law and The Hague's 750th Anniversary (1999) 81-86.

Greig, D.W., *Self-defence and the Security Council: What does Article 51 Require?*, 40 ICLQ (1991) 366-403.

Grewe, W.G., *History*. In: Simma, B., *et. al.* (eds.), The Charter of the United Nations: A Commentary (1994) 1-23.

Groom, A.J.R., Newman, E., Taylor, P., *Burdensome Victory: The United Nations and Iraq*. In: Bourantonis, D., Evriviades, M. (eds.), A United Nations for the Twenty-First Century: Peace, Security and Development (1996) 149-167.

Gross, L., *Voting in the Security Council: Abstention from Voting and Absence from Meetings*, 60 Yale Law Journal (1951) 209-257.

Gross, L., *The Question of Laos and the Double Veto in the Security Council*, 54 AJIL (1960) 118-131.

Gross, L., *Voting in the Security Council: Abstention in the Post-1965 Amendment Phase and Its Impact on Article 25 of the Charter*, 62 AJIL (1968) 315-334.

Gross, L. (ed.), *The Future of the International Court of Justice*, New York, Oceana Publications (1976).

Gunn, A.M., *Council and Court: Prospects in Lockerbie for an International Rule of Law*, 52 University of Toronto Faculty of Law Review (1994) 206-258.

Halberstam, M., *The Right to Self-defense once the Security Council takes Action*, 17 MJIL (1996) 229-248.

Halderman, J.W., *Legal Basis for United Nations Armed Forces*, 56 AJIL (1962) 971-996.

Hannum, H., *Rethinking Self-Determination*, 34 Virginia JIL (1993) 1-69.

Hargreaves, J.D., *Decolonization in Africa*, London, Longman (1988).

Harper, K., *Does the United Nations Security Council have the Competence to Act as Court and Legislature?*, 27 NYUJILP (1994) 103-157.

Harris, D.J., *Cases and Materials on International Law*, London, Sweet & Maxwell, 4th. ed. (1991).

Helman, G.B., Ratner, S.R., *Saving Failed States*, 89 Foreign Policy (1992-1993) 3-20.

Henkin, L., *Kosovo and the Law of 'Humanitarian Intervention'*, 93 AJIL (1999) 824-828.

Herbst, J., *Rechtskontrolle des UN–Sicherheitsrates*, Frankfurt, Peter Lang (1999).

Herdegen, M., *The 'Constitutionalization' of the UN Security System*, 27 Vanderbilt Journal of Transnational Law (1994) 135-159.

Herdegen, M., *Der Sicherheitsrat und die autoritative Konkretisierung des VII. Kapitels der UN-Charter*. In: Beyerlin, U., *et. al.* (eds), Recht zwischen Umbruch und Bewahrung (1995) 103-109.

Herdegen, M., *Die Befugnisse des UN-Sicherheitsrates: Aufgeklärter Absolutismus im Völkerrecht?*, Heidelberg, C.F. Müller (1998).

Herndl, K., *Reflections on the Role, Functions and Procedures of the Security Council of the United Nations*, 206 Recueil des Cours (1987) 289-395.

Higgins, R., *Policy Considerations and the International Judicial Process*, 17 ICLQ (1968) 58-84.

Higgins, R., *The Development of International Law through the Political Organs of the United Nations*, Oxford, Oxford University Press (1969).

Higgins, R., *The Place of International Law in the Settlement of Disputes by the Security Council*, 64 AJIL (1970) 1-18.

Higgins, R., *The Advisory Opinion on Namibia: Which UN Resolutions are Binding Under Article 25 of the Charter?*, 32 ICLQ (1972) 269-286.

Higgins, R., *Peace and Security: Achievements and Failures*, 6 EJIL (1995) 445-460.

Higgins, R., *The UN Security Council and the Individual State*. In: Fox, H. (ed.), The Changing Constitution of the United Nations (1997) 43-51.

Hilderbrand, R.C., *Dumbarton Oaks: The Origins of the United Nations and the Search for Postwar Security*, Chapel Hill, University of North Carolina Press (1990).

Hingorani, R.C., *Modern International Law*, Dobbs Ferry, Oceana Publications (1984).

Hirsch, M., *The Responsibility of International Organizations Toward Third Parties: Some Basic Principles*, Dordrecht, M. Nijhoff (1995).

Houck, J.W., *The Commander in Chief and United Nations Charter Article 43: A Case of Irreconcilable Differences?*, 12 Dickinson JIL (1993) 1-28.

Howland, T., Calathes, W., *The UN's International Criminal Tribunal, Is It Justice or Jingoism for Rwanda? A Call for Transformation*, 39 Virginia JIL (1998) 135-168.

James, A., *Peacekeeping in International Politics*, New York, St. Martins Press (1990).

Jennings, R.Y., *Nullity and Effectiveness in International Law*. In: Bowett, D.W., *et. al.*, Cambridge Essays in International Law: Essays in Honour of Lord McNair (1965) 64-87.

Jennings, R.Y., *What is International Law and How do we Tell It when we see It?*, 37 SJIR (1981) 59-88.

Jennings, R.Y., *Broader Perspectives in International Law*. In: Anghie, A., Sturgess, G. (eds.), Legal Visions of the 21st Century: Essays in Honour of Judge Christopher Weeramantry (1998) 497-507.

Jennings, R.Y., Watts, A., *Oppenheim's International Law*, New York, Longman, 9th ed. (1996).

Johnson, L.D., *The International Tribunal for Rwanda*, 67 Revue Internationale de Droit Pénal (1996) 211-232.

Jones, J.R.W.D., *The Implications of the Peace Agreement for the International Criminal Tribunal for the former Yugoslavia*, 7 EJIL (1996) 226-244.

Joyner, C.C., Rothbaum, W.P., *Libya and the Aerial Incident at Lockerbie: What Lessons for International Extradition Law?*, 14 MJIL (1993) 222-261.

Joyner, C.C., *Enforcing Human Rights Standards in the Former Yugoslavia: The Case for an International War Crimes Tribunal*, 22 Denver JIL and Policy (1994) 235-274.

Joyner, C.C. (ed.), *The United Nations and International Law*, Cambridge, Cambridge University Press (1997).

Kahng, T.J., *Law, Politics, and the Security Council*, The Hague, M. Nijhoff (1969).

Kaikobad, K.H., *Self-defence, Enforcement Action and the Gulf Wars, 1980-88 and 1990-91*, 63 BYIL (1992) 299-366.

Kaikobad, K.H., *The International Court of Justice and Judicial Review: A Study of the Court's Powers with Respect to Judgements of the ILO and UN Administrative Tribunals*, The Hague, Kluwer Law International (2000).

Kapinga, W.B.L., *The United Nations System and Collective Uses of Force under the New World Order*, ASICL, 5th Annual Congress (1993) 6-20.

Karagiannakis, M., *The Definition of Rape and its Characterization as an Act of Genocide - A Review of the Jurisprudence of the International Criminal Tribunals for Rwanda, and the Former Yugoslavia*, 12 LJIL (1999) 479-490.

Karhilo, J., *The Establishment of the International Tribunal for Rwanda*, 64 NJIL (1995) 683- 713.

Karl, W., *Vertrag und spätere Praxis im Völkerrecht*, Berlin, Springer (1983).

Kazazi, M., *Burden of Proof and Related Issues*, The Hague, Kluwer Law International (1996).

Kearny, R.D., Dalton, R.E., *The Treaty on Treaties*, 64 AJIL (1970) 495-561.

Keller, E.J., Rothschild, D. (eds.), *Africa in the New International Order: Rethinking State Sovereignty and Regional Security*, Boulder, Lynne Rienner (1996).

Kelsen, H., *Collective Security and Collective Self-Defense under the Charter of the United Nations*, 42 AJIL (1948) 783-796.

Kelsen, H., *The Law of the United Nations*, London, Stevens & Sons (1964).

Kenny, K.C., *Self-Defence*. In: Wolfrum, R. (ed.), United Nations: Law, Policies and Practice (1995) 1162-1170.

Kirgis, F.L., *The Degrees of Self-Determination in the United Nations Era*, 88 AJIL (1994) 304-310.

Kirgis, F.L., *The Security Council's First Fifty Years*, 89 AJIL (1995) 506-539.

Kirgis, F.L., *Claims Settlement and the United Nations Legal Structure*. In: Lillich, R.B. (ed.), The United Nations Compensation Commission (1995) 103-116.

King, F.P., *Sensible Scrutiny: The Yugoslavia Tribunal's Development of Limits on the Security Council's Powers under Chapter VII of the Charter*, 10 Emory ILR (1996) 509-591.

Kiss, A.C., *Abuse of Rights*, 7 EPIL (1984) 1-5.

Klabbers, J., *No More Shifting Lines?: The Report of the Iraq-Kuwait Boundary Demarcation Commission*, 43 ICLQ (1994) 904-913.

Klein, E., *Paralleles Tätigwerden von Sicherheitsrat und Internationalem Gerichtshof bei friedensbedrohenden Streitigkeiten*, 43 ZaöRV (1983) 467-491.

Kooijmans, P.H., *Zwijgt het Recht als de Veiligheidsraad Spreekt?*, 27 NJB (1992) 847-851.

Kooijmans, P.H., *The Enlargement of the Concept 'Threat to the Peace'*. In: J.R. Dupuy (ed.), The Development of the Role of the Security Council (1993) 111-121.

Kooijmans, P.H., *The International Court of Justice: Where does It Stand?*. In: Muller, A.S., Raič, D., Thuránszky, J.M. (eds.), The International Court of Justice: Its Future Role after Fifty Years (1997) 407-418.

Kooijmans, P.H., *The Security Council and Non-state Entities as Parties to Conflicts*. In: Wellens, K. (ed.), International Law: Theory and Practice (1998) 333-346.

Koskenniemi, M., *From Apology to Utopia: The Structure of International Legal Argument*, Helsinki, Finnish Lawyers' Publishing Company (1989).

Koskenniemi, M., *The Police in the Temple Order, Justice and the UN: A Dialectical View*, 6 EJIL (1995) 325-348.

Koskenniemi, M., *The Place of Law in Collective Security*, 17 MJIL (1996) 455-490.

Kritsiotis, D., *The Legality of the 1993 US Missile Strike on Iraq and the Right of Self-Defence in International Law*, 45 ICLQ (1996) 162-177.

Kritsiotis, D., *The Kosovo Crisis and NATO's Application of Armed Force Against the Federal Republic of Yugoslavia*, 49 ICLQ (2000) 330-359.

Kunz, J.L., *Legality of the Security Council Resolutions of June 25 and 27, 1950*, 45 AJIL (1951) 137-142.

Kuyper, P.J., *The Limits of Supervision: The Security Council Watchdog Committee on Rhodesian Sanctions*, 25 NILR (1978) 159-194.

Lachs, M., *Pacta Sunt Servanda*, 7 EPIL (1984) 364-371.

Lagoni, R., *Resolution, Declaration, Decision*. In: Wolfrum, R. (ed.), United Nations: Law, Policies and Practice (1995) 1081-1091.

Lange, R. de, *Publieke Rechtsvinding*, Zwolle, T. Willink (1991).

Lapidoth, R., *Some Reflections on the Law and Practice Concerning the Imposition of Sanctions by the Security Council*, 30 Archiv des Völkerrechts (1992) 114-127.

Lauterpacht, E., *The Legal Effect of Illegal Acts of International Organizations*. In: Bowett, D.W., *et. al.*, Cambridge Essays in International Law: Essays in Honour of Lord McNair (1965) 88-121.

Lauterpacht, H., *Restrictive Interpretation and the Principle of Effectiveness in the Interpretation of Treaties*, 16 BYIL (1949) 48-85.

Lauterpacht, H., *The Development of International Law by the International Court*, London, Stevens & Sons (1958).

Lauterpacht, H., *International Law*, Cambridge, Cambridge University Press (1970).

Lavalle, R., *The Law of the United Nations and the Use of Force, under the Relevant Security Council Resolutions of 1990 and 1991, to Resolve the Persian Gulf Crisis*, 23 NYIL (1992) 3-65.

Lee, D.E., *The Genesis of the Veto*, 1 International Organization (1947) 33-42.

Lee, R.S., *The Rwanda Tribunal*, 9 LJIL (1996) 37-61.

Lefebvre, J.A., *Moscow's Cold War and Post-Cold War Policies in Africa*. In: Keller, E.J., Rothschild, D. (eds.), Africa in the New International Order: Rethinking State Sovereignty and Regional Security (1996) 206-226.

Leporatti, A., *Some Aspects of the Relationship between the International Court of Justice and the Security Council in the Light of Recent Cases: In Particular, are there Limitations to the Security Council's Powers?*, 16 Thesaurus Acroasium (1997) 725-732.

Lerner, N., *Ethnic Cleansing*. In: Dinstein, Y., Tabori, M. (eds.), War Crimes in International Law (1996) 107-122.

Leurdijk, D.A., *The United Nations and NATO in Former Yugoslavia, 1991-1996: Limits to Diplomacy and Force*, Nijmegen, Clingendael (1996).

Leurdijk, D.A., *Before and After Dayton: the UN and NATO in the Former Yugoslavia*. In: Weiss, T.G. (ed.), Beyond UN Subcontracting: Task-Sharing with Regional Security Arrangements and Service-Providing NGOs, York (1998) 49-66.

Leurdijk, D.A., *Rapid Deployment: A Capacity Gap*. In: Denters, E, Schrijver, N. (eds.), Reflections on International Law from the Low Countries (1998) 301-314.

Liang, Y.L., *Abstention and Absence of a Permanent Member in Relation to Voting Procedure in the Security Council*, 44 AJIL (1950) 694-708.

Lillich, R.B. (ed.), *Humanitarian Intervention and the United Nations*, Charlottesville, University Press of Virginia (1973).

Lillich, R.B. (ed.), *The United Nations Compensation Commission*, Irvington, Transnational Publishers (1995).

Lobel, J., *Colloquy – The Use of Force to Respond to Terrorist Attacks: The Bombing of*

Sudan and Afghanistan, 24 Yale JIL (1999) 537-557.

Lobel, J., Ratner, M., *Bypassing the Security Council: Ambiguous Authorizations to Use Force, Cease-fires and the Iraqi Inspection Regime*, 93 AJIL (1999) 124-154.

Lowe, V., Fitzmaurice, M. (eds.), *Fifty Years of the International Court of Justice*, Cambridge, Cambridge University Press (1996).

Lukashuk, I.I., *The United Nations and Illegitimate Regimes: When to Intervene to Protect Human Rights*. In: Damrosch, L.F.,Scheffer, D.J. (eds.), Law and Force in the New International Order (1991) 143-158.

MacDonald, R.St.J., *The United Nations Charter: Constitution or Contract?*. In: MacDonald, R.St.J., Johnston, D.M. (eds), The Structure and Process of International Law (1991) 63-86.

MacDonald, R.St.J., Johnston, D.M. (eds.), *The Structure and Process of International Law*, The Hague, Nijhoff (1991).

MacDonald, R.St.J., *Changing Relations between the International Court of Justice and the Security Council of the United Nations*, 31 CYIL (1993) 3-32.

Macdonald, R.St.J. (ed.), *Essays in Honour of Wang Tieya*, Dordrecht, M. Nijhoff (1994).

Maier, H.G. (ed.), *Appraisals of the ICJ's Decision: Nicaragua v. United States (Merits)*, 81 AJIL (1987) 77-183.

Makarczyk, J. (ed.), *Theory of International Law at the Threshold of the 21st Century*, The Hague, Kluwer Law International (1996).

Makinda, S.M., *Sovereignty and International Security: Challenges for the United Nations*, 2 Global Governance (1996) 149-168.

Malanczuk, P., *The Kurdish Crisis and Allied Intervention in the Aftermath of the Second Gulf War*, 2 EJIL (1991) 114-132.

Malanczuk, P., *Humanitarian Intervention and the Legitimacy of the Use of Force*, Amsterdam, Het Spinhuis (1993).

Malanczuk, P., *International Business and New Rules of State Responsibility?: The Law Applied by the United Nations (Security Council) Compensation Commission for Claims Against Iraq*. In: Böckstiegel, K.H., Perspectives of Air Law, Space Law, and International Business Law for the Next Century (1996) 117-145.

Malanczuk, P., *Akehurst's Modern Introduction to International Law*, New York, Routledge, 7th ed. (1997).

Malanczuk, P., *Reconsidering the Relationship between the ICJ and the Security Council*. In: Heere, W.P. (ed.), International Law and The Hague's 750th Anniversary (1999) 87-99.

Marauhn, T., *The Implementation of Disarmament and Arms Control Obligations Imposed upon Iraq by the Security Council*, 52 ZäöRV (1992) 781-803.

Martenczuk, B., *The Security Council, the International Court and Judicial Review: What Lessons from Lockerbie?*, 10 EJIL (1999) 517-547.

McDougal, M.S., Gardner, N., *The Veto and the Charter: An Interpretation for Survival*, 60 Yale Law Journal (1951) 258-292.

McDougal, M.S., Lasswell, H.D., Miller, J.C., *The Interpretation of Agreements and World Public Order: Principles of Content and Procedure*, New Haven, Yale University Press (1967).

McDougal, M.S., Reisman, W.M., *Rhodesia and the United Nations: The Lawfulness of International Concern*, 62 AJIL (1968) 1-19.

McGovern, F.E., *The Intellectual Heritage of Claims Processing at the United Nations Compensation Commission*. In: Lillich, R.B. (ed.), The United Nations Compensation Commission (1995) 187-203.

McWhinney, E., *The International Court as Emerging Constitutional Court and the Co-ordinate UN Institutions (especially the Security Council): Implications of the Aerial Incident at Lockerbie*, 30 CYIL (1992) 261-272.

Meindersma, C., *Violations of Common Article 3 of the Geneva Conventions as Violations of the Laws or Customs of War under Article 3 of the Statute of the International, Criminal Tribunal for the Former Yugoslavia*, 42 LJIL (1995) 375-398.

Meledje Djedjro, F., *La Guerre Civile du Libéria et la Question de L'ingérence dans les Affaires Intérieures des États*, 26 Revue Belge de Droit International (1993) 393-436.

Mendelson, M.H., Hulton, S.C., *The Iraq-Kuwait Boundary*, 64 BYIL (1993) 135-195.

Menon, P.K., *The Law of Treaties Between States and International Organizations*, Lampeter, Edwin Mellen Press (1992).

Meron, T., *Extraterritoriality of Human Rights Treaties*, 89 AJIL (1995) 78-82.

Metzl, J.F., *Rwandan Genocide and the International Law of Radio Jamming*, 91 AJIL (1997) 628-651.

Mohr, M., *Der Lockerbie-Fall vor UN-Sicherheitsrat und Internationalen Gerichtshof*, 20 D&R (1992) 305-314.

Morgenstern, F., *Legality in International Organizations*, 48 BYIL (1976-1977) 241-257.

Morris, V., Scharf, M.P., *An Insider's Guide to the International Criminal Tribunal for the Former Yugoslavia*, New York, Transnational Publishers (1995).

Morris, V., *Prosecutor v. Kanyabashi, Decision on Jurisdiction, Case No. ICTR-96-15-T: International Criminal Tribunal for Rwanda, June 18, 1997*, 92 AJIL (1998) 66-70.

Mortimer, R.A., *ECOMOG, Liberia, and Regional Security in West Africa*. In: Keller, E.J., Rothschild, D. (eds.), Africa in the New International Order: Rethinking State Sovereignty and Regional Security (1996) 149-164.

Mosler, H., *General Principles of Law*, 2 EPIL (1995) 511-527.

Muller, A.S., Raič, D., Thuránszky, J.M. (eds.), *The International Court of Justice: Its Future Role after Fifty Years*, The Hague, M. Nijhoff (1997).

Murphy, J.F., *Force and Arms*. In: Joyner, C.C. (ed.), The United Nations and International Law (1997) 97-130.

Murphy, S.D., *The Security Council, Legitimacy, and the Concept of Collective Security After the Cold War*, 32 CJTL (1994) 201-288.

Murphy, S.D., *Humanitarian Intervention: The United Nations in an Evolving World Order*, Philadelphia, University of Pennsylvania Press (1996).

Murphy, S.D., *Progress and Jurisprudence of the International Criminal Tribunal for the Former Yugoslavia*, 93 AJIL (1999) 57-97

Mwagiru, M., *International Law, Politics, and the Re-invention of the Humanitarian Intervention: The Lesson of Somalia*, 34 Indian JIL (1994) 33-44.

Nanda, V.P., *Self-Determination Under International Law: Validity of Claims to Secede*, 13 Case W. Res. JIL (1981) 257-280.

Nanda, V.P., *Commentary on International Intervention to Promote the Legitimacy of Regimes*. In: Damrosch, L.F., Scheffer, D.J. (eds.), Law and Force in the New International Order (1991) 181-184.

Natsios, A.S., *Humanitarian Relief Interventions in Somalia: The Economics of Chaos*, 3 International Peacekeeping (1996) 68-91.

Neuhold, H., *Threat to the Peace*, 3 EPIL (1997) 935-938.

Nkala, J., *The United Nations, International Law, and the Rhodesian Crisis*, Oxford, Clarendon Press (1985).

Nolte, B., *Uniting for Peace*. In: Wolfrum, R. (ed.), United Nations: Law, Policies and Practice (1995) 1341-1348.

Nolte, G., *Restoring Peace by Regional Action: International Legal Aspects of the Liberian Conflict*, 53 ZaöRV (1993) 601-637.

O'Brien, J.C., *The International Tribunal for Violations of International Humanitarian Law in the Former Yugoslavia*, 87 AJIL (1993) 639-658.

Osieke, E., *The Legal Validity of 'Ultra Vires' Decisions of International Organizations*, 77 AJIL (1983) 239-256.

Österdahl, I., *By All Means Intervene! The Security Council and the Use of Force under Chapter VII of the UN Charter in Iraq (to Protect the Kurds), in Bosnia, Somalia, Rwanda, and Haiti*, 66 NJIL (1997) 241-271.

Partsch, K.J., *Self-Determination*. In: Wolfrum, R. (ed.), United Nations: Law, Policies and Practice (1995) 1171-1179.

Patel, B.N., *Do the Rules of Evidence and Procedure of the International Criminal Tribunal for ex-Yugoslavia ensure a Fair Trial?*, 39 Indian JIL (1999) 464-469.

Patil, A.V., *The UN Veto in World Affairs, 1946-1990: A Complete Record and Case Histories of the Security Council's Veto*, London, Mansell (1992).

Paul, V., *The Abuse of Rights and Bona Fides in International Law*, 28 Österreichische Zeitschrift für öffentliches Recht und Völkerrecht (1977) 107-130.

Paust, J.J., *Peace-making and Security Council Powers: Bosnia-Herzegovina Raises International and Constitutional Questions*, 19 Southern Illinois University Law Journal (1994) 131-151.

Petrovic, D., *Ethnic Cleansing – An Attempt at Methodology*, 5 EJIL (1994) 342-359.

Pollux, *The Interpretation of the Charter*, 23 BYIL (1946) 54-82.

Post, H.H.G. (ed.), *International Economic Law and Armed Conflict*, Dordrecht, M. Nijhoff (1994).

Post, H.H.G., *Adjudication as a Mode of Acquisition of Territory?: Some Observations on the Iraq-Kuwait Boundary Demarcation in Light of the Jurisprudence of the International Court of Justice*. In: Lowe, V., Fitzmaurice, M. (eds.), Fifty Years of the International Court of Justice (1996) 237-263.

Pruitt, R.C., *Guilt by Majority in the International Criminal Tribunal for the Former Yugoslavia: Does This Meet the Standard of Proof 'Beyond Reasonable Doubt'?*, 10 LJIL (1997) 557-578.

Quashigah, E.K., Okafor , O.C. (eds.), *Legitimate Governance in Africa: International and Domestic Legal Perspectives*, The Hague, Kluwer Law International (1999).

Quigley, J., *The 'Privatization' of Security Council Enforcement Action: A Threat to Multilateralism*, 17 MJIL (1996) 249-283.

Ragazzi, M., *The Concept of International Obligations Erga Omnes*, Oxford, Clarendon Press (1997).

Raič, D., *The Gulf Crisis and the United Nations*, 4 LJIL (1991) 119-134.

Randelzhofer, A., *Great Powers*, 9 EPIL (1986) 142-166.

Reichert, D.R., *Problems with Parallel and Duplicate Proceedings: The Litispendence Principle and International Arbitration*, 8 Arbitration International (1992) 237-255.

Reisman, W.M., *Sovereignty and Human Rights in Contemporary International Law*, 84 AJIL (1990) 866-876.

Reisman, W.M., *The Constitutional Crisis in the United Nations*, 87 AJIL (1993) 83-100.

Reisman, W.M., *Peacemaking*, 18 Yale JIL (1993) 415-423.

Reisman, W.M., *The Raid on Baghdad: Some Reflections on its Lawfulness and Implications*, 5 EJIL (1994) 120-133.

Reisman, W.M., *Haiti and the Validity of International Action*, 89 AJIL (1995) 82-84.

Reisman, W.M., *Humanitarian Intervention and Fledgling Democracies*, 18 Fordham JIL (1995) 794-805.

Reisman, W.M., Stevick, D.L., *The Applicability of International Law Standards to United Nations Economic Sanctions Programmes*, 9 EJIL (1998) 86-141.

Reisman, W.M., *Kosovo's Antinomies*, 93 AJIL (1999) 860-862.

Ress, G., *The Interpretation of the Charter*. In: Simma, B. (ed.), The Charter of the United Nations: A Commentary (1994), 25-44.

Reuter, P., *Introduction to the Law of Treaties*, New York, Pinter Publishers (1989).

Roberts, K., *Second-guessing the Security Council: The International Court of Justice and its Powers of Judicial Review*, 7 Pace International Law Review (1995) 281-327.

Rosenne, S., *The Election of Five Members of the International Court of Justice in 1981*, 76 AJIL (1982) 364-370.

Rosenne, S., *The Law of Treaties: A Guide to the Legislative History of the Vienna Convention*, Leiden, Sijthoff (1970).

Rosenne, S., *Developments in the Law of Treaties 1945-1986*, Cambridge, Cambridge University Press (1989).

Rosenne, S., *The Law and Practice of International Court: 1920-1996*, The Hague, M. Nijhoff, 3rd ed. (1997).

Rossanet, B. de, *Peacemaking and Peacekeeping in Yugoslavia*, The Hague, Kluwer Law International (1996).

Rostow, E.V., *Until What? Enforcement Action or Collective Self-Defense?*, 85 AJIL (1991) 506-516.

Rostow, N., *The International Use of Force after the Cold War*, 32 HILJ (1991) 411-421.

Rudolph, K., *Peace-Keeping Forces*. In: Wolfrum, R. (ed.), United Nations: Law, Policies and Practice (1995) 957-969.

Sapru, T., *Into the Heart of Darkness: A Case Against the Foray of the Security Council Tribunal into the Rwandan Crisis*, 32 Texas ILJ (1997) 329-354.

Sarooshi, D., *The United Nations and the Development of Collective Security: The Delegation by the UN Security Council of its Chapter VII Powers*, Oxford, Clarendon Press (1999).

Sato, T., *Evolving Constitutions of International Organizations*, The Hague, Kluwer Law International (1996).

Schachter, O., *The Quasi-Judicial Role of the Security Council and the General Assembly*, 58 AJIL (1964) 960-965.

Schachter, O., *Disputes Involving the Use of Force*. In: Damrosch, L.F. (ed.), The International Court of Justice at a Crossroads (1987) 223-241.

Schachter, O., *Self-Defense and the Rule of Law*, 83 AJIL (1989) 259-277.

Schachter, O., *Authorized Uses of Force by the United Nations and Regional Organizations*. In: Damrosch, L.F., Scheffer, D.J. (eds.), Law and Force in the New International Order (1991) 65-93.

Schachter, O., *United Nations Law in the Gulf Conflict*, 85 AJIL (1991) 452-473.

Schachter, O., *United Nations Law*, 88 AJIL (1994) 1-23.

Schachter, O., Joyner, C.C. (eds.), *United Nations Legal Order*, Cambridge, Cambridge University Press (1995).

Scharf, M., Epps, V., *The International Trial of the Century? A 'Cross-Fire' Exchange on the First Case Before the Yugoslavia War Crimes Tribunal*, 29 Cornell ILJ (1996) 635-664.

Schermers, G., Blokker, N.M., *International Institutional Law: Unity within Diversity*, The Hague, M. Nijhoff (1995).

Schrijver, N., *The Use of Economic Sanctions by the UN Security Council: An International Law Perspective*. In: Post, H.H.G. (ed.), International Economic Law and Armed Conflict (1994) 123-161.

Schröder, M., *International Court of Justice*. In: Wolfrum, R. (ed.), United Nations: Law, Policies and Practice (1995) 673-685.

Schwelb, E., *Some Aspects of International Jus Cogens as Formulated by the International Law Commission*, 61 AJIL (1967) 946-975.

Scott, C., Chang, F., Querehi, A., Mitchell, P., Kalajdzic, J., Copeland, P., *A Memorial for Bosnia: Framework of Legal Arguments Concerning the Lawfulness of the Maintenance of the United Nations Security Council's Arms Embargo on Bosnia and Herzegovina*, 16 MJIL (1994) 1-140.

Seidl-Hohenveldern, I., *German Interests in Polish Upper Silesia Cases*, 2 EPIL (1981) 111-114.

Seyersted, F., *United Nations Forces in the Law of Peace and War*, Leiden, Sijthoff (1966).

Shaw, M.N., *International Law*, Cambridge, Cambridge University Press, 3rd ed. (1995).

Shaw, M.N., *International Law*, Cambridge, Cambridge University Press, 4th ed. (1997).

Shaw, M.N., *The Security Council and the International Court of Justice: Judicial Drift and Judicial Function*. In: Muller, A.S., Raič, D., Thuránszky, J.M. (eds.), The International Court of Justice: Its Future Role after Fifty Years (1997) 219-259.

Shihata, I.F.I., *The Power of the International Court to Determine its Own Jurisdiction: Compétence de la Compétence*, The Hague, M. Nijhoff (1965).

Shraga, D., Zacklin, R., *The International Criminal Tribunal for the Former Yugoslavia*, 5 EJIL (1994) 360-380.

Shraga, D., Zacklin, R., *The International Criminal Tribunal for Rwanda*, 7 EJIL (1996) 501-518.

Siekmann, R.C.R., *Basic Documents on United Nations and Related Peace-Keeping Forces*, The Hague, T.M.C. Asser Instituut, 2nd ed. (1989).

Simma, B., *Does the UN Charter provide an Adequate Legal Basis for Individual or Collective Responses to Violations of Obligations Erga Omnes?*. In: Delbrück, J. (ed), The Future of International Law Enforcement: New Scenarios – New Law? (1993) 125-146.

Simma, B., *et. al.* (eds.), *The Charter of the United Nations: A Commentary*, Oxford, Oxford University Press (1994).

Simma, B., *NATO, the UN and the Use of Force: Legal Aspects*, 10 EJIL (1999) 1-22.

Simons, A., *Somalia: A Regional Security Dilemma*. In: Keller, E.J., Rothschild, D. (eds.), Africa in the New International Order: Rethinking State Sovereignty and Regional Security (1996) 71-84.

Sinclair, I., *The Vienna Convention on the Law of Treaties*, Manchester, Manchester University Press, 2nd ed. (1984).

Singh, N., *The Role and Record of the International Court of Justice*, Dordrecht, M. Nijhoff (1989).

Skubiszewski, K., *Peace and War*, 4 EPIL (1982) 74-78.

Skubiszewski, K., *Remarks on the Interpretation of the United Nations Charter*. In: Bernhardt, R., *et. al.* (eds.), Völkerrecht als Rechtsordnung, International Gerichtsbarkeit, Menschenrechte, Festschrift für Hermann Mosler (1983) 891-902.

Skubiszewski, K., *The International Court of Justice and the Security Council*. In: Lowe, V., Fitzmaurice, M. (eds.), Fifty Years of the International Court of Justice (1996) 606-629.

Sohn, L.B., *Modernizing the Structure and Procedure of the Security Council*. In: Dupuy, J.R. (ed.), The Development of the Role of the Security Council (1993) 385-397.

Sohn, L.B., *The UN System as Authoritative Interpreter of its Law*. In: Schachter, O., Joyner, C.C. (eds.), United Nations Legal Order (1995) 169-229.

Sohn, L.B., *Important Improvements in the Functioning of the Principal Organs of the United Nations that can be Made Without Charter Revision*, 91 AJIL (1997) 652-662.

Sonnenfeld, R., *The Obligation of UN Member-States 'to Accept and Carry out the Decisions of the Security Council'*, 8 PYIL (1976) 129-154.

Sonnenfeld, R., *Resolutions of the United Nations Security Council*, Dordrecht, M. Nijhoff (1988).

Stavropoulos, C.A., *The Practice of Voluntary Abstentions by Permanent Members of the Security Council under Article 27, Paragraph 3, of the Charter of the United Nations*, 61 AJIL (1967) 737-752.

Stein, T., *Das Attentat von Lockerbie vor dem Sicherheitsrat der Vereinten Nation und dem Internationalen Gerichtshof*, 31 Archiv des Völkerrechts (1993) 206-229.

Stoll, P.T., *Conflicts, South Africa*. In: Wolfrum, R. (ed.), United Nations: Law, Policies and Practice (1995) 317-329.

Stoll, P.T., *Conflicts, Rhodesia/Zimbabwe*. In: Wolfrum, R. (ed.), United Nations: Law, Policies and Practice (1995) 311-316.

Stoll, P.T., *Namibia*. In: Wolfrum, R. (ed.), United Nations: Law, Policies and Practice (1995) 904-912.

Stone, J., *Hopes and Loopholes in the 1974 Definition of Aggression*, 71 AJIL (1977) 224-246.

Subedi, S.P., *The Doctrine of Objective Regimes in International Law and the Competence of the United Nations to Impose Territorial or Peace Settlements on States*, 37 GYIL (1994) 162-205.

Sucharitkul, S., *The Process of Peace-Making following Operation 'Desert Storm'*, 43 AJPIL (1992) 1-30.

Sugihara, T., *The Judicial Function of the International Court of Justice with Respect to Disputes Involving Highly Political Issues*. In: Muller, A.S., Raič, D., Thuránszky, J.M.

(eds.), The International Court of Justice: Its Future Role after Fifty Years (1997) 117-138.

Suy, E., *International Organization*, 43 NILR (1996) 237-244.

Swaak-Goldman, O.Q., *The ICTY and the Right to a Fair Trial: A Critique of the Critics*, 10 LJIL (1997) 215-222.

Szasz, P.C., *Centralized and Decentralized Law Enforcement: The Security Council and the General Assembly Acting under Chapters VII and VIII*. In: Delbrück, J. (ed.), Allocation of Law Enforcement Authority in the International System (1995) 17-38.

Tanzi, A., *Problems of Enforcement of Decisions of the International Court of Justice and the Law of the United Nations*, 6 EJIL (1995) 539-572.

Taylor, G.D.S., *The Content of the Rule Against Abuse of Rights in International Law*, 46 BYIL (1972-1973) 323-352.

Ténékidès, G., *L' Exception de Litispendance devant les Organismes Internationaux*, 26 RGDIP (1929) 502-527.

Tesón, F.R., *Humanitarian Intervention: An Inquiry into Law and Morality*, Irvington-on-Hudson, NY, Transnational Publishers, 2nd ed. (1997).

Thürer, D., *The 'Failed State' and International Law*, 81 International Review of the Red Cross (1999) 731-761.

Tomuschat, C., *The Lockerbie Case Before the International Court of Justice*, 48 RICJ (1992) 38-48.

Tomuschat, C., *The United Nations at Age Fifty: A Legal Perspective*, The Hague, Kluwer Law International (1995).

Tzartzouras, M.E., *The Law of Humanitarian Intervention after Somalia*, 46 Revue hellénique de Droit International (1993) 197-224.

Ullman, R.H. (ed.), *The World and Yugoslavia's Wars*, New York, Council on Foreign Relations (1996).

Ullman, R.H., *Introduction: The World and Yugoslavia's Wars*. In: Ullman, R.H. (ed.), The World and Yugoslavia's Wars (1996) 1-8.

Ullman, R.H., *The Wars in Yugoslavia and the International System after the Cold War*. In: Ullman, R.H. (ed.), World and Yugoslavia's Wars (1996) 16-20.

United Nations Department of Public Information, *Blue Books Series, The United Nations and Apartheid, 1948-1994*, New York, UNDPI (1994).

United Nations Department of Public Information, *Blue Books Series: The United Nations and Somalia, 1992-1996*, New York, UNDPI (1996).

United Nations Department of Public Information, *The Blue Helmets: A Review of United Nations Peace-keeping*, New York, UNDPI, 3rd ed. (1996).

Verdross, A., *Jus Dispositivum and Jus Cogens in International Law*, 60 AJIL (1966) 55-63.

Verdross, A. von, *Forbidden Treaties in International Law: Comments on Professor Garner's Report on the 'Law of Treaties'*, 31 AJIL (1937) 571-577.

Verzijl, J.H.W., *The Jurisprudence of the World Court*, Leiden, Sijthoff (1965).

Virally, M., *Review Essay: Good Faith in Public International Law*, 77 AJIL (1983) 130-134.

Vogt, M.A., *The Involvement of ECOWAS in Liberia's Peacekeeping*. In: Keller, E.J., Rothschild, D. (eds.), Africa in the New International Order: Rethinking State Sovereignty and Regional Security (1996) 165-183.

Vu, N.T., *The Holding of Free and Fair Elections in Cambodia: The Achievement of the United Nations' Impossible Mission*, 16 MJIL (1995) 1177-1241.

Waldock, H., *General Course on Public International Law*, 106 Recueil des Cours (1962).

Wallensteen, P., *The United Nations in Armed Conflicts: An Overview*. In: Dupuy, J.R. (ed.), The Development of the Role of the Security Council (1993) 303-316.

Walter, C., *Security Council Control over Regional Action*, 1 Max Planck Yearbook of United Nations Law (1997) 129-193.

Walters, F.P., *A History of the League of Nations*, London, Oxford University Press (1965).

Warbrick, C., *The Invasion of Kuwait by Iraq – Part I*, 40 ICLQ (1991) 482-492.

Wassgren, H., *The UN Compensation Commission: Lessons of Legitimacy, State Responsibility, and War Reparations*, 11 LJIL (1998) 473-492.

Watson, G., *Constitutionalism, Judicial Review, and the World Court*, 34 HILJ (1993) 1-45.

Watson, J.S., *Autointerpretation, Competence, and the Continuing Validity of Article 2(7) of the UN Charter*, 71 AJIL (1977) 60-83.

Wedgwood, R., *War Crimes in the Former Yugoslavia: Comments on the International War Crimes Tribunal*, 34 Virginia JIL (1994) 267-276.

Wehberg, H., *Pacta Sunt Servanda*, 53 AJIL (1959) 775-786.

Weiss, T.G. (ed.), *The United Nations and Civil Wars*, Boulder, Lynne Rienner (1995).

Weiss, T.G., *Collective Spinelessness: U.N. Actions in the Former Yugoslavia*. In: Ullman, R.H. (ed.), The World and Yugoslavia's Wars (1996) 59-96.

Weiss, T.G. (ed.), *Beyond UN Subcontracting: Task-Sharing with Regional Security Arrangements and Service-Providing NGOs*, New York, St. Martin's Press (1998).

Wellens, K.C. (ed.), *International Law: Theory and Practice: Essays in Honour of Eric Suy*, The Hague, M. Nijhoff (1998).

Wellens, K.C. (ed.), *Resolutions and Statements of the United Nations Security Council (1946-1992): A Thematic Guide*, Dordrecht, M. Nijhoff & T.M.C. Asser Instituut (1993).

Weller, M., *Premature End to the 'New World Order'?*, 4 AJICL (1992) 303-324.

Weller, M., *The International Response to the Dissolution of the Socialist Federal Republic of Yugoslavia*, 86 AJIL (1992) 569-607.

Weston, B.H., *Security Council Resolution 678 and Persian Gulf Decision Making: Precarious Legitimacy*, 85 AJIL (1991) 516-535.

Wet, E. de, *Judicial Review as an Emerging General Principle of Law and Its Implications for the International Court of Justice*, 47 NILR (2000) 181-210.

Wet, E. de, *Judicial Review of the United Nations Security Council and General Assembly Through Advisory Opinions of the International Court of Justice*, 10 SZIER (2000) 237-277.

White, N.D., *The United Nations and the Maintenance of International Peace and Security*, Manchester, Manchester University Press (1990).

White, N.D., McCoubrey, H., *International Law and the Use of Force in the Gulf*, 10 International Relations (1991) 347-373.

White, N.D., Ülgen, Ö., *The Security Council and the Decentralized Military Option: Constitutionality and Function*, 44 NILR (1997) 378-413.

Winkelmann, I., *Bringing the Security Council into a New Era: Recent Developments in the Discussion on the Reform of the Security Council*, 1 Max Planck Yearbook of United Nations Law (1997) 35-90.

Wolf, J., *Regional Arrangements and the UN Charter*, 6 EPIL (1983) 289-295.

Wolfrum, R., *Der Beitrag regionaler Abmachungen zur Friedenssicherung: Möglichkeiten und Grenzen*, 53 ZäöRV (1993) 576-602.

Wolfrum, R. (ed.), *United Nations: Law, Policies and Practice*, Dordrecht, M. Nijhoff (1995).

Wood, M.C., *Security Council Working Methods and Procedure: Recent Developments*, 45 ICLQ (1996) 151-161.

Wood, M.C., *The Interpretation of Security Council Resolutions*, 2 Max Planck Yearbook of United Nations Law (1998) 73-95.

Woods, N., *Good Governance in International Organizations*, 5 Global Governance (1999) 39-61.

Woodward, S.L., *Failed States: Warlordism and 'Tribal' Warfare*, LII Naval War College Review (1999) 55-68.

Wright, H.G.A., *Sovereignty of the People – the New Constitutional Grundnorm*, 26 Federal Law Review (1998).

Wühler, N., *Causation and Directness of Loss as Elements of Compensability before the United Nations Compensation Commission*. In: Lillich, R.B. (ed.), The United Nations Compensation Commission (1995) 207-234.

Yakpo, E., Boumedra, T. (eds.), *Liber Amicorum Mohammed Bedjaoui*, The Hague, Kluwer Law International (1999).

Zemanek, K., *Is the Security Council the Sole Judge of Its Own Legality?*. In: Yakpo, E., Boumedra, T. (eds.), Liber Amicorum Mohammed Bedjaoui (1999) 629-645.

Zoller, E., *The 'Corporate Will' of the United Nations and the Rights of the Minority*, 81 AJIL (1987) 610-634.

Reports and Documents: General

Bruderlein, C. (Special Advisor to the Office for the Coordination of Humanitarian Affairs (OCHA)), *Coping with Humanitarian Impact of Sanctions: An OCHA Perspective*, Dec. 1998.

Garfield, R., *The Impact of Economic Sanctions on Health and Well-being*, Relief and Rehabilitation Network Paper No. 31, Nov. 1999.

Harvard Law School, *Research in International Law: Draft Convention on the Law of Treaties*, 29 AJIL (1935), Supplement.

ILA, *Second Report of the ILA Committee on Accountability of International Organisations*, March 2000.

ILA, *First Report of the ILA Study Group on the Law of State Responsibility*, 8 June 2000.

Security Council Official Records (SCOR).

Stremlau, J., *Sharpening International Sanctions*, Report of the Carnegie Commission on Preventing Deadly Conflict (1996).

United Nations Conference on International Organization (UNCIO) Official Documents.

Waldock, H., *Third Report on the Law of Treaties*, 2 YBILC (1964) 5-65.

Waldock, H., *Sixth Report on the Law of Treaties*, 2 YBILC (1966) 51-103.

Wirick, G., *The Prospects for a United Nations Rapid Reaction Capability*, March 1996.

Reports and Documents: United Nations

(listed alphabetically)

An Agenda for Peace, Preventive Diplomacy, Peacemaking and Peace-keeping, A/47/277-S/24111, 17 June 1992.

Annual Report of the Secretary-General on the Work of the Organization, A/54/1, 31 Aug. 1999.

Annual Report of the Secretary-General on the Work of the Organization, A/53/1, 27 Aug. 1998.

Fifth report of the Secretary-General on the United Nations Mission in Sierra Leone, S/2000/751, 31 July 2000.

Final report of the International Commission of Inquiry (Rwanda), annexed to 'Letter Dated 18 November 1998 from the Secretary-General Addressed to the President of the Security Council', S/1998/1096, 18 Nov. 1998.

Final Report of the Secretary-General on The United Nations Observer Mission in Liberia, S/1997/712, 12 Sept. 1997.

Final Report of the United Nations Iraq-Kuwait Boundary Demarcation Commission, annexed to 'Letter dated 21 May 1993 from the Secretary-General addressed to the President of the Security Council', S/25811.

Final Report to the Prosecutor by the Committee Established to Review the NATO Bombing Campaign Against the Federal Republic of Yugoslavia, June 2000.

Fourth report of the Secretary-General on the United Nations Mission in Sierra Leone, S/2000/455, 19 May 2000.

Preliminary Report of the Independent Commission of Experts Established in Accordance with Security Council Resolution 935 (1994), annexed to 'Letter Dated 1 October 1994 from the Secretary-General Addressed to the President of the Security Council', S/1994/1125, 4 Oct. 1994.

Progress Report of the Secretary-General on the United Nations Observer Mission in Angola (MONUA), S/1997/640, 13 Aug. 1997.

Progress Report of the Secretary-General on the United Nations Assistance Mission for Rwanda, S/1994/1133, 6 Oct. 1994.

Report of the Secretary-General on the situation in Somalia, proposing to dispatch a technical team to prepare an operational plan for the monitoring of the cease fire in Mogadishu and to explore ways of ensuring the unimpeded delivery of humanitarian assistance, S/23693, 11 March 1992.

Report of the Panel of Experts on Violations of Security Council Sanctions Against UNITA, annexed to 'Letter Dated 10 March 2000 from the Chairman of the Security Council

Committee Established Pursuant to Resolution 864 (1993) Concerning the Situation in Angola Addressed to the President of the Security Council', S/2000/203, 10 March 2000.

Report of the Secretary-General on the Situation in Rwanda, S/1994/565, 13 May 1994.

Report of the Panel on United Nations Peace Operations, annexed to 'Identical letters dated 21 August 2000 from the Secretary-General to the President of the General Assembly and the President of the Security Council', A/55/305-S/2000/809, 21 Aug. 2000.

Report of the Secretary-General on the Situation in Rwanda, S/1994/640, 31 May 1994.

Report of the Expert Committee established in pursuance of Security Council resolution 191 (1964), S/6210, 2 March 1965.

Report of the Independent Inquiry into the Actions of the United Nations During the 1994 Genocide in Rwanda, 15 Dec. 1999.

Report of the Secretary-General on the situation in Somalia, recommending the establishment of the United Nations Operation in Somalia (UNOSOM), S/23829, 21 April 1992.

Report of the Secretary-General on the United Nations Observer Mission in Angola (MONUA), S/1997/959, 4 Dec. 1997.

Report of the Secretary-General on Ethiopia and Eritrea, S/2000/643, 30 June 2000.

Report of the Secretary-General submitted in pursuance of paragraphs 18 and 19 of resolution 794 (1992), S/25354, 3 March 1993.

Report by the Working Group on a Multinational United Stand-by Forces High Readiness Brigade, annexed to 'Letter dated 29 February 1996 from the Permanent Representative of Denmark to the United Nations addressed to the Secretary-General', A/51/75-S/1996/166, 5 March 1996.

Report of the Open-ended Working Group on the Question of Equitable Representation on and Increase in the Membership of the Security Council and Other Matters related to the Security Council, A/52/47, 24 Aug. 1998.

Report of the Secretary-General on Implementation of provisions of the Charter related to assistance to third States affected by the application of sanctions, A/53/312, 27 Aug. 1998.

Report of the Secretary-General Pursuant to Paragraph 19 of Security Council Resolution 687, S/22559.

Report of the Open-ended Working Group on the Question of Equitable Representation on and Increase in the Membership of the Security Council and Other Matters related to the Security Council, A/50/47, 13 Sept. 1996.

Report of the Panel Appointed by the Secretary-General of the United Nations to Gather Information on the Situation in Algeria in Order to Provide the International Community with Greater Clarity on That Situation, submitted to the Secretary-General on 10 Sept. 1998.

Report of the Open-ended Working Group on the Question of Equitable Representation on and Increase in the Membership of the Security Council and Other Matters related to the Security Council, A/54/47, 25 July 2000.

Report of the Secretary-General submitted pursuant to resolution 721 (1991), S/23280, 11 Dec. 1991.

Report of the Secretary-General submitted pursuant to paragraph 2 of resolution 808 (1993), S/25704, 1993.

Secretary-General's Bulletin on Observance by United Nations Forces of International Humanitarian Law, ST/SGB/1999/13, 6 Aug. 1999.

Special Report of the Secretary-General on the United Nations Assistance Mission for Rwanda, S/1994/470, 20 April 1994.

Third Report of the International Commission of Inquiry (Rwanda), annexed to 'Letter Dated 1 November 1996 from the Secretary-General Addressed to the President of the Security Council', S/1997/1010.

Table of Cases

International Court of Justice

Permanent Court of International Justice

Others

Index